Feb 10 c1
Room A36

THIS BOOK IS THE PROPERTY OF
THE UNITED STATES GOVERNMENT

It is placed in your custody by your employing agency.
You may retain it for reference as the needs of the
agency may require. When it has served this purpose,
or when you leave your agency, it should be returned
to an appropriate official of your agency.

UNITED STATES
GOVERNMENT
PROPERTY

MODERN DATA PROCESSING

MODERN DATA PROCESSING

ROBERT R. ARNOLD

Dean of Vocational Education
San Diego Mesa College

HAROLD C. HILL

Professor of Data Processing
San Diego City College

AYLMER V. NICHOLS

Manager, Electronic Data Processing Services
County of San Diego

JOHN WILEY & SONS, INC.,

NEW YORK | LONDON | SYDNEY | TORONTO

Copyright © 1969 by John Wiley & Sons, Inc.

All rights reserved. No part of this book may
be reproduced by any means, nor transmitted,
nor translated into a machine language without
the written permission of the publisher.

10 9 8 7 6 5 4 3

Library of Congress Catalog Card Number: 69-16121
SBN 471 03348 0
Printed in the United States of America

PREFACE

The primary objectives of this book are:

1. To provide a broad insight into the many techniques and applications of modern data processing for those desiring a general knowledge of this important and dynamic field.

2. To provide a good foundation for those planning further study in specific areas of data processing.

The book is designed for use as a text in basic data processing classes or for independent study.

Modern Data Processing incorporates the format and basic content of the authors' previous book, *Introduction to Data Processing.* However, this book has been reorganized and expanded to reflect the increasing scope and complexity of data processing activities. Specifically, a more extensive treatment of the various facets of electronic data processing has been included.

Technical topics are presented in a manner that will make them understandable to readers with little or no background in the subjects discussed. Pertinent illustrations are used liberally as a further aid to comprehension. However, no attempt has been made to omit or oversimplify challenging topics, as it is our conviction that this would deprive readers of a full appreciation of the technological accomplishments of modern data processing. Nevertheless, any reader wishing to skip some of the more technical material, such as the analyses of computer programs, can do so without affecting the continuity or usefulness of the remaining text.

Another objective of this book is to create an awareness of the great variety of data processing methods and devices that are now in use, their relative significance, advantages, and limitations. Thus, manual and mechanical data processing techniques are covered along with punched card machines and electronic computers. This approach reflects our opinion that the well-informed reader should be cognizant of all types of data processing, not just the most sophisticated. Nevertheless, major emphasis is placed on electronic data processing, related data collection techniques, and data communications. In addition, a chapter dealing with industrial uses of computers has been included in recognition of the growing interest in this important field.

The text is organized as follows. Chapter 1 presents an overview of data processing that serves as a general introduction and frame of reference for comprehending and relating the topics in succeeding chapters. Chapter 2 is devoted to the history of data processing from ancient recording and computing techniques to modern mechanical and electronic devices. Chapter 3 presents a brief survey of types of business, legal forms of business, internal organization of business, basic operations including accounting procedures, and sources of data. Chapter 4 surveys manual and mechanical data processing methods and devices—some conventional and others newly developed.

The material in Chapters 5 to 9 covers punched card data processing. The punched card unit record is discussed in Chapter 5 with the succeeding three chapters devoted to punched card recording functions, manipulation of punched card data, and punched card summarizing and reporting. Chapter 9 includes procedure development, flow charting, and a comprehensive punched card application.

Chapter 10 outlines the codes, media, and devices used to collect machine-sensible data. Chapters 11 to 17 are concerned with electronic data processing, including a survey of computer characteristics, physical elements and functions of a computer system, numbering systems, basic programming techniques, coding, programming systems, problem-oriented languages, and electronic data processing operations. Data communications is discussed in Chapter 18. The uses of computers in industrial automation are outlined in Chapter 19. Chapter 20 is devoted to systems study and design.

End-of-chapter questions are furnished to help the student review the text material and as a basis for discussion. The glossary contains definitions of terms that appear in this book, or that the reader is likely to encounter in supplementary reading.

We express appreciation to the many individuals and companies who provided information and illustrations for this book, or who otherwise assisted in its preparation. Specific credit is included with illustrations wherever appropriate.

Robert R. Arnold
Harold C. Hill
Aylmer V. Nichols

CONTENTS

CHAPTER 14   EDP PROGRAM DEVELOPMENT   226

CHAPTER 15   PROGRAMMING SYSTEMS   250

CHAPTER 16   PROBLEM-ORIENTED PROGRAMMING LANGUAGES   261

MODERN DATA PROCESSING

SCOPE AND
SIGNIFICANCE OF
DATA PROCESSING

Although the term "data processing" is of relatively recent origin, this does not mean that the activity itself is new. On the contrary, there is evidence that the need to process data originated as far back as the beginning of recorded history when man's activities first exceeded his ability to remember the details of his actions. Throughout history, commercial and governmental activities have created the need for record keeping of one sort or another.

In its broadest sense, data processing refers to the recording and handling that are necessary to convert data into a more refined or useful form. In the past these tasks were referred to as record keeping or paperwork. They were accepted as a routine clerical activity. With the advent of more sophisticated electromechanical and electronic business machines in recent times, the terms "paperwork" and "record keeping" have been replaced by the phrase "data processing." In addition, the proc-

essing of data has grown to such an extent that the activity itself has become a center of interest. This interest is justifiable, but it should not lead to the conclusion that data processing is an end in itself. It is rather a means of achieving objectives that are almost as varied as the nature of data.

DEFINITION OF DATA

Because of the widespread application of new data processing techniques to banking operations, billing, and other financial situations, there is a tendency to assume that the term "data" refers primarily to accounting functions. Actually, data can include any facts, figures, letters, words, charts, or symbols that represent an idea, object, condition, or situation. Thus data can include such diverse things as completed election ballots, inventory figures, gas meter readings, school attendance records, medical statistics, engineering performance reports, and production figures. In fact, this list could continue for pages because examples of data can be found in every field of activity.

There is, of course, a difference in the type of data being handled in various fields. In science, for example, chemists, physicists, and mathematicians find it necessary to perform vast calculations on relatively limited amounts of data. This is also true of the many fields of engineering where extremely complex design and performance calculations must be made.

In business and government operations the situation is usually quite different. Here the data being handled is voluminous and repetitive, but processing requirements, although varied, are less complex. Attention in this book will be focused on this type of data processing, although the techniques to be discussed will be found to some extent in virtually every field.

DATA VERSUS INFORMATION

A distinction is often made between data and information; namely, that data is the raw material from which information is derived. According to this concept, the significant characteristic that separates data from information is usefulness. Thus a compilation of data may, in itself, be of little value unless it provides knowledge leading to the achievement of some objective. Although any collection of data may have potential informational value, what constitutes information for one individual in a specific instance may lack significance for another or even for the same individual at a different time or for a different problem. Specifically, information consists of *selected data*—data selected and organized with respect to user, problem, time, place, and function. The conversion of data to information is a primary function of data processing.

THE NEED FOR DATA PROCESSING

Although the needs for gathering and processing data have many specific origins, in general, they may be classified as *external* or *internal*. In business organizations external requirements may be regarded as mandatory since they are imposed by various government agencies, unions, or stockholders. The federal government, for example, requires quarterly reports on the income taxes and social security taxes withheld from the pay of employees, and state and local agencies require reports of sales taxes collected.

In addition to the financial and statistical data required by governmental agencies, business enterprises must furnish annual reports to stockholders, and various data to customers, creditors, and the general public. Some external data needs have their counterparts within the organization. Payroll records, for example, provide necessary internal data and also form the basis for financial and personnel reports to the government and to unions.

Internal needs fall broadly into two classes: *operations* and *control*. First, a tremendous amount and variety of routine operating documents are necessary as evidence of (1) primary transactions with customers and vendors; and (2) subsequent activities involving production, personnel, materials, equipment, and accounting. For example, the issuance of a purchase requisition indicating a departmental need for materials may start a chain of events requiring the completion of many additional forms and records. These might include a request for quotation, purchase order, receiving record, inspection report, inventory record, and voucher check in addition to necessary accounting entries.

The second internal need is for data to be compiled in informative reports for use in analyzing progress, determining policy, solving problems, and planning actions of the future. The much-discussed "information revolution" of recent years has created a whole new dimension in data processing. The objectives of data processing now extend far beyond the routine handling of transaction documents and records of other types. Providing management with timely information to facilitate greater control and improved decisions has become increasingly important.

The demands and opportunities of the new information technology are tremendous. There is a growing awareness that information is a vital resource of any organization and that improved data processing is a means of providing the needed information. Thus, as never before, central management is now in touch with its entire organization; as never before it is conscious of the effects of various influences on its goals; and as never before it is in a position to take prompt and appropriate action in time to produce desired results.

THE NEED FOR IMPROVED DATA PROCESSING TECHNIQUES

Throughout the centuries the changing nature and volume of data, combined with technological progress, resulted in a gradual evolution in data processing methods. In this century, especially in the last two decades, the evolution has been accelerated by the urgent need for better ways of handling data. Let us consider some of the factors that created the need for more efficient data processing techniques.

Volume of Data

Business organizations have grown in size and complexity during the past century, particularly since World War II. This growth has resulted in an enormous amount of paperwork generated, among other contributing factors, by a large volume of transactions. For example, one large insurance company with approximately three million accounts sends out over ten million premium notices each year and processes an equal number of payments. It is apparent that if this mass of data had to be processed manually, the results would be chaotic. The number of people who would have to participate in such a clerical operation would cause confusion, delay, and an excessive amount of errors.

The growth of business has been matched by an increase in government agencies that demand extensive data of many types. Until the 1930's, for example, payroll accounting was a fairly simple matter in most companies, consisting mainly of employee identification, hourly rate, number of hours worked, and total wage for the week. Payroll accounting has since become complex because of the large number of payroll deductions that must be made and the records that must be kept pertaining to unemployment insurance, disability compensation, social security, and income tax. The heavier work load placed upon business has, of course, been duplicated in government offices, thus adding to the need for better methods of processing data.

Clerical Costs

The rapid increase in the number of clerical workers during the past fifty years is a clear indication of the mounting paperwork burden. In 1910, only one in twenty employed persons was engaged in clerical work. By 1940, the proportion of clerical workers had risen to one in ten. Today, about one in seven employed persons is in a clerical occupation. This influx of clerical employees has been accompanied by rising wage rates and fringe benefits which have greatly increased clerical costs.

The awareness of rising personnel costs in business and government has stimulated interest in the use of mechanical and electronic devices as a more efficient and economical means of processing data. Although more and more mechanical and electronic equipment will be used to replace human effort, it is expected that new clerical jobs created by growth of business and government will outnumber the jobs eliminated by automation.

Accuracy Requirements

In large organizations, clerical jobs are usually specialized to facilitate the orderly division of work. As a result, clerical work is likely to consist of the routine and repetitive handling of large quantities of similar data. Human beings tend to become bored with repetitious work, and boredom leads to carelessness which, in turn, increases the chance of error. In this respect, machines have a distinct advantage over humans. A human cannot be depended upon to react in

exactly the same way time after time to a given set of conditions. Neither can two humans be depended on to react in the same way to the same set of conditions. Machines, on the other hand, are not subject to boredom, are consistent in their reactions, and are more accurate than humans. Thus, the search for improved techniques has been spurred by the realization that the more the human element can be eliminated from the processing of data, the more accurate the results will be.

The Need for More Timely Information

The fast pace of modern business activity places new demands on management for accurate and rapid responses to changing conditions. The effective control of large organizations requires that executives make daily or even hourly decisions about many matters. An executive who is deprived of up-to-the-minute information by inefficient processing methods is therefore seriously handicapped.

Success in business today is based not only on a good product. A company's competitive survival may depend on the way it manages information—on its ability to maintain control over costs, and on the speed and flexibility with which it responds to new market conditions, actions of competitors, and technological advancements. The development of information systems capable of providing the complete and prompt information needed for today's management decision-making requires improved data processing techniques.

THE DATA PROCESSING CYCLE

Aside from the sheer volume of data, we might ask what there is about processing data that consumes so much time and effort and creates such a need for mechanical and electronic devices. Actually, from the time of origin to the time of arrival in a final, more useful form, data may go through a number of operational steps referred to as the *data processing cycle*. This cycle may be roughly divided into the following steps: origination of data, data recording, data manipulation, report or document preparation, data communication, and data storage. These steps are illustrated in Figure 1-1.

Origination of Data

The raw material for data processing originates on various business forms, often referred to as *source documents*. This original data might be handwritten, typewritten, or prepared in a variety of other ways. For example, payroll time data might be handwritten by the worker or a timekeeper, stamped in numerals by a time clock, or punched into a card. Other examples of source documents include sales orders, purchase orders, checks, invoices, and material requisitions. These original documents are especially important for two reasons: (1) they provide verification of all transactions, and (2) they are the basis for all further actions.

Recording Data

The basic function of this step is the recording of data in some form that permits its convenient handling in whatever system is being used. This might involve making a manual entry in a journal or register of some type; punching holes in a card; punching holes in paper tape; recording magnetized spots on magnetic tape; writing or printing data in

magnetic ink; or using some other medium acceptable to the system as a means of entering and later transferring the data from one step to another.

In some cases recording may be combined with the preparation of original documents through a technique called *source data automation*. For example, by using a typewriter equipped with a paper tape punching device, it is possible

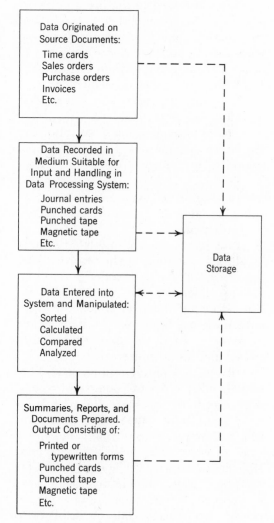

Figure 1-1. Steps in the data processing cycle.

to prepare simultaneously a typewritten document, such as a sales invoice, and a punched tape containing the same or selected data. Thus, the original data is automatically recorded in a form that can be processed by machines capable of reading punched paper tape.

In other cases data may be recorded and transmitted directly into a data processing system without the need for document preparation. As an example, the time reporting discussed in the preceding section could be accomplished by inserting the worker's coded badge or identification card into a data collection device capable of reading and transmitting directly to a remote computer the data about the employee and his time of arrival or departure.

The following steps can also be considered as important parts of the data recording function.

Editing. This is the process of selecting significant data and eliminating that which does not need to be recorded for further processing.

Coding. As a means of further reducing the amount of data to be recorded and processed, abbreviated codes are often used to condense the data being expressed. The technique of converting data to symbolic form has been used in many fields as a means of saving time, effort, and space, and as a convenient device for identifying and distinguishing data. The most familiar types of codes used to express words or ideas are the *alphabetic,* which consists of letters; the *numeric,* in which numbers are used; and the *alphanumeric,* which uses both numbers and alphabetic characters. The designation of units in a large organization as departments A, B, C, etc., is an example of the use of an alphabetic code. A well-known example of the use of numerical codes is

the Dewey decimal system of classifying library books by subject.

When recording data for processing by machine, coding is generally a necessity. Of the three types of codes, numeric codes are the most prevalent because they are the simplest to use in machine data processing. For example, the digits 1 to 12 can be used to designate months, customers can be given numbers, and so on.

Classifying. Classifying is the process of identifying one or more common characteristics to be used as a means of systematically grouping data into classes. Categories might include type of product, location, department, price range, etc. Classifying may occur as a separate step. However, since the need is usually anticipated at the time data is recorded, classifications are generally determined and entered as part of the recording process.

As defined here, classification is an initial step that precedes the actual sorting of data. For example, classifications such as department number, age group, sex, etc., may be entered on personnel records even though they are to be filed alphabetically. The presence of such classification data makes it easy to rearrange records at any time for statistical or other purposes.

Codes are used extensively as a means of identifying different classes of data. Numbers or letters of the alphabet, or a combination of both, can be assigned to previously planned classifications to provide quick recognition and ease of writing.

Conversion. Conversion is a means of transforming data from one recorded form to another. For example, data recorded in punched cards may be converted to punched paper tape, or vice versa, by the use of special equipment designed for this purpose. Such conversion changes the recorded form of data but not the nature of the data. Conversion, as well as re-recording in the same form, may occur at various times during the processing cycle.

Copying and Duplicating. These are processes by which facsimiles of data can be prepared for distribution to more than one user or for use in different steps in the processing cycle.

Verifying. This essential function assures that all parts of the recording process have been accomplished without error, and that accurate data is entered into the processing system.

Manipulation of Data

If the original form of data were suitable for all purposes, less processing would be necessary. Seldom, however, can the real objective of a transaction or situation be attained without converting data into a more useful form. This conversion is accomplished by means of one or more of the following procedures.

Sorting. Sorting is the process of arranging or selecting data according to (1) order or rank or (2) common characteristic. Sorting according to order or rank, known as sorting in *sequence,* takes place when data is arranged in numeric or alphabetic sequence. Sales invoice data, for example, might be arranged according to sequence of invoice numbers or customers' names. Sorting according to common characteristic, known as sorting by *classification,* takes place when data is arranged in similar groups. For example, customers could be classified by geographic area, by salesman, or by type of business. Like other steps in the processing cycle, sorting is simplified by expressing data in codes.

Comparing and Analyzing. By these processes we determine such factors as the nature, proportion, relationship, order, similarity, or relative value of data.

Calculating. Calculating refers to the arithmetical processes of multiplication, division, addition, or subtraction which are necessary to convert data into a more significant form. For example, an employee's weekly hours of work and his hourly rate of pay become much more significant when they are multiplied together to determine his weekly earnings.

Summarizing and Report Preparation

Summarizing. Summarizing is the process of condensing data so that the main points are emphasized. Summarizing generally involves listing or tabulating data and totaling each list. The running of a list on an adding machine is one form of summarization.

Summarizing is related to sorting since the arrangement of data into categories is usually part of the summary process. The sorting operation in itself may be meaningless, however, unless the results of the separation are known. Summarizing carries the process one step further by providing totals to indicate the individual or comparative values of various classes of data. As an illustration, the daily sales of a store may be listed by departments. This operation achieves a distribution of sales data. However, the relative performance of each department cannot be ascertained at the end of a weekly or monthly period until the data is summarized by totaling each list. Thus the detailed lists are condensed into totals that provide useful information.

Report Preparation. The processed information that results from the data processing cycle is known as *output*. This could include documents such as payroll checks or statements of account; or finished reports such as a sales analysis, expense distribution, inventory, or weekly payroll. The means by which the processed information is finally recorded is known as the *output medium*. Depending on the type of processing system being used, output media could consist of typewritten documents or reports, printed forms, punched cards, punched paper tape, magnetic tape, or other special forms.

Data Communications

Communication is the process of transferring data from one point to another during the processing cycle or of delivering the final results to the user. Many methods may be used ranging from the very simple to the highly complex. Data in written, punched card, or other form may be transported internally by hand or by a conveyor mechanism of some type. Externally, data is often transported by mail.

Almost any process of transmitting information may be considered a form of data communications. However, in this period of advanced technology the term *data communications* generally refers to the electrical transmission of data that has been transformed into a special code. It is now possible to transmit data between a wide variety of devices, internally or externally, by direct connection or by means of telephone circuits, telegraph circuits, or microwave. Teletypewriter service is probably the most familiar example of wire communication. This method enables data in typewritten or punched tape form to be transmitted between units in the same building or city, or thousands of miles apart.

Data Storage

Upon completion of the processing cycle, or possibly at a point of intermediate results during the cycle, data must be stored so that it is readily retrievable. The storage of data is a matter of monumental proportions in some organizations. This is especially true of certain governmental agencies, libraries, and business firms that have a large number of documented transactions. Storage techniques depend, of course, on the type and volume of data involved.

In conclusion, let us emphasize that the steps of the data processing cycle outlined above are the basic elements into which all data processing problems subdivide. All or part of these functions have to be performed whether they are done manually, by mechanical means, by punched card machines, or by electronic computer. In spite of the vast differences in these methods, however, the procedures and objectives of data processing remain basically the same.

METHODS OF PROCESSING DATA

Detailed discussions of the methods of processing data will appear in later chapters. However, to provide the reader with a frame of reference for use in relating these methods, the following summary of manual, mechanical, punched card, and electronic data processing is offered.

Manual

Manual data processing techniques are used to a certain extent in every organization and they are still the predominant method of processing data in countless small organizations. It is possible to complete by hand all the operations in the data processing cycle, from the preparation of original documents to final reports, by using the tools and materials that have been standard for hundreds of years and which are still the most universal forms of data processing: pens, pencils, journals, ledgers, worksheets, folders, trays, files, and various other manual devices. However, few organizations today can tolerate time-consuming methods. Consequently, organizations that still find a manual system to be the most practical employ at least some of the modern devices that have been developed to improve efficiency.

Such devices as accounting boards, or pegboards, document control registers, and edge-notched card systems provide a means of eliminating the tedious recopying and resorting of data. These and other devices, which will be discussed in detail in Chapter 4, have done much to improve the speed and accuracy of manual data processing.

Mechanical

A wide variety of mechanical equipment is in use today not only in small offices but also as part of the most complex data processing systems. Included are typewriters, still the most used office machine; adding, calculating, and accounting machines; and cash registers.

Although mechanical devices generally require manual aid, recent advancements have made them much more automatic. In addition, the versatility of these machines has been increased by the attachment of mechanisms that enable them to simultaneously produce punched paper tape, magnetic tape, or punched cards while performing a primary function. These by-products then serve as input to computers and other machines. For example, sales transactions that are recorded on

a cash register may be simultaneously recorded on punched paper tape by means of a special attachment. The paper tape may then be used as a means of entering and processing the sales transactions in an electronic computer. It is also possible for data to be transmitted directly into a computer system while being recorded on an adapted mechanical device.

Punched Card Machines

Although the origin of punched card data processing dates back to 1887, the use of punched card equipment developed very slowly until the 1940's. Since that time the growth of this method has been phenomenal.

Because punched card equipment is very automatic, it eliminates much of the human effort that is required in the processing of data by manual or other mechanical methods. Punched card machines perform six data processing operations automatically: recording, sorting, comparing, calculating, summarizing, and reporting.

Although many models, sizes, and types of punched card machines are available, there are eight basic classes of machines. These are:

1. *Card Punch.* Records source data in punched cards. By means of a keyboard similar to that of a standard typewriter, the operator punches holes in cards in the form of a code representing the original data. These holes make it possible for other machines to process the data automatically by sensing and interpreting the meaning of the punched holes.

2. *Verifier.* Verifies the accuracy of the card punch operation. This is a machine similar to the card punch, except that punching is replaced by electrical impulses that compare the data punched in the card

with the key stroked. A discrepancy between the verifying operation and the data already punched in a card will cause the machine to stop and to signal a discrepancy.

3. *Sorter.* Arranges punched cards in alphabetical and/or numerical sequence, or groups cards according to any classification punched in them.

4. *Interpreter.* Prints on cards the data punched in them.

5. *Collator.* Merges two sets of cards in similar sequence into a single set, or matches two comparable sets of cards to see if they are in agreement.

6. *Reproducer.* Prepares duplicate copies or sets of cards, or punches data from one master card into a group of following cards.

7. *Calculator.* Performs fairly complex calculations from data in punched cards and punches the results.

8. *Accounting Machine* (tabulator). Reads, summarizes, and prints information from data recorded in punched cards.

A number of advantages of the punched card method have given rise to its widespread use:

1. All machines except the card punch and verifier are highly automatic. Therefore, in a punched card system the tedious handling and summarizing of data are taken over by machines. Manual activity is reduced to classifying data before it is entered in the punched cards that are to be used in the system, operating the machines, transferring decks of cards from one machine to another, and inserting performance instructions into the machines.

2. The punched card is compact, uniform in size, easily transferred and stored, and easily duplicated.

3. Each card is an independent rec-

ord that can be added to or removed from a stack of cards without difficulty.

4. Once data has been accurately recorded in a punched card, it can be processed by machine repeatedly to obtain various results. There is seldom any need for further reference to the source document from which the data was originally copied.

5. The punched card is an especially convenient device for high-volume operations such as billing: it can be automatically produced, easily interpreted by the recipient, and re-entered into the system for further processing, provided it has not been folded, stapled, or mutilated.

Punched card machines do have certain limitations, however. Since they are predominantly mechanical, the speed of processing is limited by the movement of mechanical parts and devices. Moreover, since each machine in the system performs a special function, the processing steps are not continuous. Cards must be transferred from one machine to another for the performance of various operations.

Electronic Data Processing

The most recent development in data processing is the electronic computer, which has attracted great interest because of its vastly superior capacity to perform computations and other functions at incredible speeds. This results from the fact that processing in a computer is accomplished by the movement of electrical impulses through the computer's circuitry rather than by the movement of mechanical parts. Through instructions programmed into the computer by means of magnetic tapes, punched paper tapes, or punched cards, thousands of complex operations can be completed in a second.

Computers are generally able to perform all the manipulative steps in the data processing cycle automatically. However, in spite of the impressive speed with which computers operate, processing is less dramatic than in other systems because there is no visible evidence of what is taking place: the manipulation of data occurs entirely within the computer. Computer operations are usually classified under three headings: input, processing, and output.

Input. Before data from source documents can be entered into the system, the data must be converted to code symbols recorded in one of several ways: as punched holes in cards; as punched holes in paper tape; as minute magnetized spots on magnetic tape; or as actual characters, readable by man as well as machine, which have been printed by hand or by machine. Some source documents may be entered directly into the system. Included are prepunched bills, or checks on which information has been preprinted in magnetic ink. Data also may be read directly into a computer by means of optical character recognition equipment which can interpret printed copy and handwritten numbers.

Processing. After the data has been recorded in one of the forms mentioned, it is read by an input component of the computer system and transferred electronically to a storage unit within the computer. The *storage unit*, or *memory*, is the mechanism that retains information for recall or use in further processing.

Classifying, sorting, comparing, analyzing, calculating, and summarizing are performed automatically within the components of the system in accordance with a series of instructions called a *program*, which is stored in the computer. The computer is also able to make logical decisions according to the instructions it has been given. It is the completely automatic execution of these functions at fantastic speeds that makes the electronic computer unique and gives it the greatest advantage over other systems.

Output. The results of the processing that has taken place within the computer may be recorded on magnetic tape, punched paper tape, or punched cards; or may be recorded by direct connection between the processing unit and a printing device.

Electronic data processing has a number of advantages over other methods. The principal ones are as follows:

1. The speed of processing is many times faster than that attainable in punched card or other mechanical systems.

2. Once data is entered into the system, the processing is continuous. There is no need to handle or transport data between each operation.

3. More compact equipment and storage results in a saving of space.

4. Accuracy is generally greater than in other systems.

5. The superior speed, capacity, and versatility of the electronic computer make possible the completion of tasks never attempted under other systems because of the impossibility of completing them in time for the results to be useful.

DATA PROCESSING APPLICATIONS

Business

The importance of data processing to the successful operation of every business today has already been stressed. Data processing requirements do vary, however, depending on the size and nature of business organizations. Certain types of business stand out as having been most aggressive in adopting punched card systems and more recently electronic computer systems as a means of solving their paperwork problems. A nationwide survey revealed the following relative positions of business groups according to the number of computers in use: *

1. Manufacturing
2. Insurance
3. Distribution (wholesale-retail)
4. Banking—finance
5. Data processing service bureaus
6. Public utilities (electric, gas, water, telephone)
7. Transportation
8. Petroleum
9. Publishing
10. Construction

A high volume of essential data handling and need for control are major characteristics of the organizations that rank high on the preceding list. For example, manufacturing concerns use electronic data processing equipment for such activities as sales forecasting, material requirements determination, inventory management, production scheduling and control, and many other functions. In addition, they process vast amounts of accounting and payroll data, often involving thousands of employees. Computers, usually highly specialized, are also used to position machine tools and to control other manufacturing processes. These functions are part of industrial automation which is discussed in Chapter 19.

In large insurance operations, machines may be used to prepare notices of

* Edith H. Goodman, "Computer Use and Personnel Survey," *Data Processing Yearbook 1962–1963,* p. 9.

premiums due, compute dividends, calculate agents' commissions, make the millions of computations used in actuarial departments, and prepare statistical tables.

An increasing number of banks throughout the country are converting to electronic data processing as a means of handling the estimated 20 billion checks that circulate annually in the United States. In 1956 the American Bankers Association adopted magnetic ink character recognition (MICR) which permits characters printed in magnetic ink on checks and deposit slips to be read directly by both man and machine. After the essential data has been printed on documents in magnetic ink, the documents can be entered into an electronic system and processed automatically.

Electric, gas, and telephone companies find high-speed computers useful in preparing monthly bills for thousands of customers. Data obtained by reading meters is entered into the system by punched cards or possibly magnetic tape. Adjustments are then made automatically on customers' records, and the computer completes the task of printing names and addresses on bills, listing consumption figures, calculating costs, adding taxes, and totaling bills.

In organizations of all types, both punched card machines and computers have been used extensively for personnel record keeping, billing, payroll, and other accounting. Inventory control is another area where these techniques have been applied with very satisfactory results.

Electronic computers have proved to be especially valuable for management purposes. Because of their great capacity and speed, they offer an efficient means of solving difficult one-time problems. They can also be used to simulate complex events to assist management in making decisions concerning production, marketing, finance, facilities, and other strategic questions. The technique known as *management by projection* requires that a situation to be simulated be well defined. Its desired and actual characteristics are recorded in as much detail as possible. Variables are then introduced and altered as required to bring about a result that closely approximates or exactly matches a predetermined objective. This rapid form of trial and error enables management to try solutions and test results before making a decision. As an example, a firm considering the opening of a new branch may use the simulation technique to test many different locations as a means of choosing the one most likely to be successful. This approach may require consideration of anticipated rather than actual conditions. Nevertheless, it provides management with a more scientific method of planning actions than would otherwise be possible.

The use of punched card machines and electronic computers has resulted in another new management approach known as *management by exception*. This is a means of cutting down the amount of detail usually brought to the attention of managers by selecting only those items that require action. For example, in an inventory control situation minimum and maximum quantities can be established for each item. As inventory balances are reviewed automatically, only those items that are overstocked or understocked are called to management's attention. The items that meet satisfactory standards are passed over. The extension of this principle to many facets of business control and planning relieves management of much tedious analysis of data, promptly focuses attention on matters requiring decision, and allows management to concentrate on more productive tasks.

Government

Because of population increase, the data processing work load at all levels of government has grown tremendously. Consequently, punched card and electronic data processing systems are being used today in virtually every area of government. Applications cover a very wide range from standard accounting to extremely complex systems for the processing of special kinds of data. For example, the Internal Revenue Service, faced with the probability of having to process 114 million yearly tax returns of all classes in the early 1970's, has established a National Computer Center in Martinsburg, West Virginia. This large-capacity electronic computer complex assembles and records on magnetic tapes a continuously updated account for each business and individual taxpayer. Seven regional service centers receive tax returns from Internal Revenue Service district offices and carry out the preliminary processing and verification. The tax data is then converted to magnetic tapes that are transmitted to the center in Martinsburg for entry on the consolidated master files. Thus, the Internal Revenue Service maintains a complete record at a central location of all taxpayers who file or should file federal tax returns.

The Veterans Administration has converted 4.5 million compensation and pension accounts to electronic data processing. Under the current system, the Department of Veterans Benefits processes claims for payments and provides check-payment data on magnetic tape to the Treasury Department for the automatic preparation of checks, and for the sorting of checks by destination code to facilitate delivery by the Post Office Department.

Electronic data processing equipment is also used at the Social Security Administration in Baltimore to maintain the records for 172,000,000 accounts. This agency is probably the largest record-keeping organization in the world.

Because of the large volume of data it must handle, the Bureau of the Census has necessarily pioneered the use of new data processing techniques. A summary of the methods employed by the Bureau of the Census during the past century provides a clear indication of the degree of progress that has been made in data processing. In the first century of census taking, the pencil was the principal tool used. With it, a clerk could record about two items a minute. The first punched card tabulator used in the 1890 census could tabulate 200 items a minute. By 1950 the speed of punched card tabulation had been increased to 6,800 items a minute. The UNIVAC I computer, installed in 1951, raised the tabulating speed to 30,000 items a minute. In 1963 the UNIVAC I was replaced by a new UNIVAC computer that can handle about 3,000,000 items a minute.

Applications of the magnitude of these examples are a good indication of why the federal government has become the largest single user of electronic computers. Computers have been adopted for many operations on the state, county, and local levels also.

In addition to business and government applications of the types mentioned above, modern data processing techniques play a vital role in many other fields including science, engineering, education,

and medicine. Examples of specific applications in these and other fields will appear throughout the book.

CONCLUSION

Inevitably, the electronic computer tends to dominate any discussion of data processing methodology today. This is understandable because computers are the most versatile and spectacular performers in the field of data processing. They have not, however, caused the extinction of other methods nor is it likely that they will do so in the foreseeable future. On the contrary, sales of other data processing and general office machines are rising annually. However, these machines are increasingly oriented to the requirements of new electronic data processing systems.

In all probability, because of differences in volume and nature of data, some organizations will always find it practical to use punched card machines, other mechanical devices, or even manual methods to process data. It should also be pointed out that when electronic computers are used, they do not operate in isolation. Their performance usually is supplemented by other operations involving a variety of manual and mechanical methods. It is not uncommon to find manual, mechanical, punched card, and computer methods used side-by-side in organizations because each one is the most suitable for a certain type of operation.

For these reasons, in the succeeding chapters of this book, computers will be treated as the most significant method of processing data, but nevertheless as one of many methods currently in use. Attention will also be given to the other techniques that form the basis of manual and mechanical data processing systems and that perform auxiliary functions in electronic data processing systems.

We hope that this approach to data processing will develop an appreciation of the full range of data processing methods and devices now available and of the basic operations that they perform.

Review Questions

1. Define "data."
2. What is the basic difference in the processing requirements of business data and scientific or engineering data?
3. Distinguish between data and information.
4. Discuss the nature of external and internal needs for processing data.
5. What main factors have created the need for more efficient data processing techniques?
6. What are the steps in the data processing cycle?
7. What is the basic purpose of the data recording step?
8. Define coding, classifying, and converting.
9. Explain the ways in which data may be manipulated in order to change its form or arrangement.
10. What are the four main methods of processing data? Describe each.
11. What are the principal advantages of electronic data processing over other methods?
12. Define "management by projection" and "management by exception."

2

HISTORY OF
DATA PROCESSING

The history of data processing consists primarily of man's search for more efficient ways of gathering, recording, and handling data in order to keep pace with the increasing volume and complexity of governmental and commercial activity.

The techniques that appeared in response to changing needs throughout the centuries were at times a clearer indication of the facilities then available than of the true need. Thus the history of data processing also reflects the technological progress of civilization.

Technological advancements have been readily adapted for data processing purposes. The discovery of better ways of processing data has not always resulted in the abandonment of older methods, however. Instead, many of the older techniques have been adopted as part of later developments. In many cases it has been found expedient to continue using the older methods in their original or somewhat modified form. For this reason, the events to be related in this chapter will

not be presented in a single chronological sequence. Instead, special techniques will be grouped so that the various steps in their evolution may be more easily related. The history of data processing will be considered under four headings: recording techniques, computing devices, punched card machines, and electronic computers.

HISTORY OF RECORDING TECHNIQUES

Today's data processing requirements and the incredibly technical devices that are used to fulfill them present a dramatic contrast to man's earliest record-keeping activities. The greatest contrast, of course, is found in prerecorded history. In the day-by-day struggle for existence in the Stone Age, the exchange of goods by force rather than by trade created no need for a record of transactions. However, as families joined to form tribal groups, and as the tribes grew into nations, trade became the means of exchange. Because business transactions date back further than recorded history, it is conceivable that some situations arose in which there was a need for record keeping. As an aid to his memory, the early businessman probably used scratches on rocks, notches on trees, or marks on the mud wall of his house.

As trading activity grew, transactions increased in complexity and a solution was found to the need for some kind of written record. The oldest surviving written records are in the form of pictographic writing on clay tablets made by the ancient Sumerians, the predecessors of the Babylonians, during the period 3700 to 3000 B.C. Other archeological findings dating from 3000 to 2600 B.C. include clay tablets with cuneiform characters in the Sumerian language. These tablets were prepared by marking wet clay with the cut end of a reed. Since this method produced wedge-shaped marks, such writing was called cuneiform, from the Latin *cuneus*, meaning wedge. To make the records permanent, tablets were placed in the sun or baked in an oven.

Clay tablets were also used by later Near Eastern and Mediterranean cultures, including the Assyrian and the Babylonian (Figure 2-1). The first records of actual business transactions date from around 2600 B.C. in Babylon, which was a well-developed civilization and commercial center even before that time. The merchants of Babylon had scribes prepare records of receipts, disbursements, contracts of barter, sales, money-lending, and many other business transactions by scratching the necessary information on slabs of wet clay with a stylus. These scribes played an important role in the commercial and governmental affairs of the Babylonian Empire.

Figure 2-1. Babylonian clay tablets. (*Courtesy Yale University.*)

It is interesting to note that the later Babylonians seemed to anticipate our modern ledgers and filing cabinets by storing their tablets in jars and arranging them in approximately the same way that we now arrange card systems and loose-leaf books.

The clay tablets used by the Babylonians were cumbersome and difficult to handle. (One is tempted to speculate on the amount of excessive record keeping that might have been discouraged in more recent times by the continued use of this technique.) Therefore, the need for a more practical recording medium became apparent.

This need was met in Egypt by the use of papyrus and the calmus. The papyrus was a tall water plant formerly abundant on the delta and banks of the Nile. Its stems were used to make the writing material, also called papyrus, which was the predecessor of paper. This was accomplished by soaking, pressing together, and drying thin sheets of the bark laid crosswise to form a fairly substantial writing surface. The calmus was a sharp-pointed pen also made from the reed plant. The exact origin of these writing materials is not known, but it is placed in the third millennium B.C., possibly even before the clay tablets of the Babylonians.

Government bookkeeping grew to enormous proportions under the Pharaohs who could be regarded as the leaders of a large business concern. In effect, the entire state was one establishment with thousands of employees. The Egyptian scribes kept exacting records of practically everything, including slaves; harvesting operations; accounts and lists of wages for day-workers; and receipts and payments of jewels, gold, grain, or livestock from warehouses which constituted the Egyptian treasury. The multitude of documents necessary to record the many transactions were maintained by a large staff of scribes and assistants who reported to the prime minister, who, in turn, reported regularly to the king on the status of the treasury.

It is not definitely known whether the Babylonians learned bookkeeping from the Egyptians or vice versa, or if their bookkeeping systems developed independently. In any event, the same kinds of primary entries, the same classification of accounts, and the same control methods are found on Egyptian papyrus rolls and on Babylonian clay tablets.

Papyrus, which originated with the Egyptians, was used later by the Greeks and Romans. In fact, it was the most widely used ancient writing material until it was gradually replaced during the third and fourth centuries A.D. by parchment made from the skins of animals. Single sheets of papyrus were usually about two feet long. For more lengthy documents, however, a number of sheets were stuck together to form rolls of 10 to 50 feet. It is interesting to note that after almost two thousand years the roll has reappeared in such forms as adding machine tapes and magnetic or paper tapes used as input or output media for computers.

Another recording device of ancient times was the tablet book consisting of two to ten sheets of wood coated with wax and tied together with thongs. Records were scratched on the waxed surfaces with a pointed bone or metal stylus. By obliterating the writing, the tablets could be used again and again. This device was used extensively by the Greeks and Romans for record keeping. In Cicero's time, around the second quarter of the last century B.C., it appears that most of the public and private accounts at Rome were written on waxed tablets. This is presumed to have been true of most of the Graeco-Roman world at that time.

These tablet books, or codices, had several disadvantages, however. They were clumsy, there were limitations on the size of leaves and the number of leaves that could be conveniently bound together, and the records were not permanent since the wax was soft and could be rubbed off. These disadvantages were overcome by some Romans by using a codex made up of leaves of parchment instead of wood. At first scribes used these for everyday purposes, making entries with split-reed pens. In the latter part of the first century A.D. they were used occasionally for literature in place of the papyrus roll.

In spite of the fact that the parchment codex seemed to be a forward step, it did not develop greatly in the first two centuries A.D. and the use of wooden tablets remained much more common. This technique was still in use in England at the end of the fourteenth century A.D.

Orderly bookkeeping procedures were a characteristic of both the Greeks and Romans, although their techniques were far from reaching the double-entry stage of accounting. Their accounting consisted mainly of individual records of debts, receipts, expenditures, and miscellaneous inventories, rather than accounts in the modern sense with debit and credit entries. Nevertheless, they were aware of the importance of efficient record keeping. The Athenians were first to employ the technique of auditing records to get accurate unbiased facts, discover shortages, and prevent losses. They took inventories regularly, and enacted laws requiring the publication of financial statements. The Romans designated officials known as *quaestors* to examine the accounts of provincial governors. Julius Caesar insisted on proper accounting of receipts and disbursements, and thus maintained the treasury of the Roman Empire at its highest level. The emperor Augustus is said to have established the first government budget in the year A.D. 5 in order to control the spending in the Empire.

During the Dark Ages there were few record-keeping developments of any significance. The next interesting event in the story of business records was the development of wooden tallies in England. Although the notching or scoring of sticks as a means of recording numbers may be traced back to neolithic and even paleolithic times, this technique was probably used most widely in England after the invasion of William the Conqueror in 1066. During his reign a survey was made showing all the crown property and the tributes, or taxes, due on the property. The details of the survey were included in a record called the Doomsday Book, which was used to determine the revenue to be collected from each taxpayer.

The sheriff of each county had the responsibility of collecting for the king all the rents, taxes, fines and penalties, and other revenues. It was customary for the sheriff to travel to Westminster each year at Easter to pay into the Exchequer approximately one-half of the total amount for which his region was liable. For this he received a receipt in the form of a tally, a narrow shaft of wood, usually hazel wood, on which notches were cut to represent the total value. A notch as thick as a man's palm represented £1,000; the thickness of a thumb, £100; and of a little finger, £20. The thickness of a grain of barley corn was worth £1, and scratches took care of the shillings and pence.

After being cut and inscribed, the tally was split in two, one part being retained by the sheriff for a receipt and the other being kept by the department of the Exchequer. Later in the year, at Michaelmas, when the time came for final settlement, the sheriff submitted his halves of the tallies as evidence of payments already made. If they matched the halves held by the Exchequer, he was given credit for them. However, if the sheriff's portion of any tally had been altered, he was subject to imprisonment.

In spite of the crudeness of tallies, they were used extensively, mainly because this carefully scored wooden object was a comprehensible record to the men of that era, most of whom were illiterate. Although tallies were used mainly for the settlement of government revenues, this system of recording transactions was later extended for commercial use. It continued in use even after better writing methods were available and the people were more literate. In fact, it was not until 1826 that the use of tallies was abolished by an act of parliament. In 1834 they were condemned to be destroyed by a statute of William IV and, consequently, were thrown into the heating stoves of the House of Commons. Apparently the stokers lacked restraint because the resulting blaze not only destroyed the tallies but also the parliament buildings, which were set on fire by the overheated stoves and burned to the ground.

Developments in commercial accounting that led to our modern methods were an outgrowth of Italian commerce during the thirteenth century. The initial departure from simple bookkeeping methods is credited to a Florentine banker who devised the first complete bookkeeping system in 1211. The earliest known system of complete double-entry bookkeeping is one that originated in Genoa in 1340. The first printed text on double-entry bookkeeping was written by Luca Pacioli, a monk of the order of St. Francis, at Venice in 1494. Pacioli's *Summa de Arithmetica, Geometria, Proporcioni et Proporcionalita* includes a detailed description of the double-entry system then practiced which extended the knowledge of double entry well beyond the boundaries of Italy. The name "Venetian method" or "Italian method" was given to the method he outlined, which formed the basis of double entry as we know it today.

During the four hundred years following Pacioli's treatise, there was a further refinement and development of bookkeeping systems. However, relatively little change occurred in the techniques of recording business transactions except for an improvement in writing materials. Of particular significance was the increased use of paper. Although paper can be traced back to the second century B.C. in China, it did not become available to the rest of the world until the eighth century A.D. when it was discovered by the Arabs. The manufacture of paper in Europe was originated by the Moors in Spain about the middle of the twelfth century. The first large-scale manufacture of paper in Italy occurred in 1276. Mills were subsequently set up in France, Germany, and England, and by the second half of the fourteenth century the use of paper had become well established in all of Western Europe.

The introduction of paper brought the quill pen into use. Metal pens were known to the Romans and were produced in small quantities in Europe in the eighteenth century. However, they did not come into common use until 1828 when large-scale production of pens with efficient slip-in points began in Birmingham, England. The first significant production of fountain pens occurred in the 1880's.

Another noteworthy development was the widespread use of graphite lead pencils. Earlier, the Egyptians used metallic lead to rule lines, as did medieval monks, but it was not until the sixteenth century that graphite became a standard writing material. In the beginning stages metal clips were used to hold the graphite rods, or the rods were held with twine that was unwound as the graphite wore down. About 1686 the lead pencil took on its present form when a method was found for casing the graphite in wood. Starting in the late eighteenth century, pulverized graphite was mixed with clay to bind it and to provide varying degrees of hardness—the more clay, the harder the pencil.

As the twentieth century approached, there was a most significant occurrence in the history of recording techniques: the development of the typewriter. Although many attempts were made to invent typewriters, starting as early as 1714, the first practical machine was patented in 1868 by Christopher Latham Sholes, Carlos Glidden, and Samuel W. Soulé of Milwaukee, Wisconsin. It was crude and lacked the keyboard arrangement that was adopted later. However, after many improvements, on March 1, 1873, E. Remington and Sons, the famous Mohawk Valley, New York manufacturers, contracted to make the machine. The first commercial typewriter, the Remington No. 1 (Figure 2-2), was made in September, 1873. The early Remington had many of the features of a modern typewriter except for the shift key, which was not invented and added until 1878.

This typewriter marked the beginning of a series of advancements that were to be of tremendous significance in the field of data processing. Many of the most important devices used today in data processing and related fields were made possible by the development of the electric typewriter by James Smathers in 1920. This led to the design of many special purpose machines, including composing machines to set up copy for offset printing; bookkeeping machines which combine a typewriter with a computing mechanism to facilitate the preparation of accounting records; Graphotype machines used to make impressions on printing plates for addressing machines; Teletypewriters which activate distant units by means of telegraph or telephone lines; automatic typewriters that produce perforated paper tape which, in turn, can be used to activate the originating machine or others like it; and input or output devices for electronic computers. This list could be much more extensive but these examples provide ample evidence of the value of the typewriter in addition to its basic usefulness for routine office work.

With the dawn of the twentieth century came the invention and perfection of many other business machines that were to relieve the manual drudgery that had been inherent in the handling of data for centuries. Most of these machines are classified as adding, calculating, or bookkeeping machines, which will be discussed in the following section.

Figure 2-2. Remington No. 1 typewriter with foot-pedal carriage return, 1873. (*Courtesy Remington Rand, Division of Sperry Rand Corporation.*)

EVOLUTION OF COMPUTING DEVICES

Throughout history man has experienced an ever-increasing need for numerical calculations and has continually sought ways to meet this need with a minimum of mental and manual effort.

Primitive man, like his successors, was blessed with an inherent means of counting in the form of fingers and toes. There were, of course, limitations on how far one person could go with these facilities. Eventually these limitations were overcome by the discovery that pebbles, grains of corn, and other small objects could be used for counting.

The problem of how to handle pebbles conveniently was solved in the Tigres-Euphrates Valley about five thousand years ago by the design of a clay board with a number of grooves into which the pebbles were placed. This device enabled the pebbles to be moved from one side of the board to the other to facilitate counting operations. This technique, which was the predecessor of the abacus, became known in Asia where it was adopted and modified by the Chinese and Japanese. The *abacus* in its present form is believed to have been invented in China about 2600 B.C. The Japanese had a similar device called the *soroban*. The abacus apparently did not reach Europe until the beginning of the Christian era because the *abax,* as it was called by the Romans, was first described by Greek authors about A.D. 300. It is of exactly the same design as the Chinese and Japanese devices.

The abacus consists of several rows of beads which slide on sticks or wires mounted in a rectangular frame. The frame is divided by a cross member so that each row of beads has a sector with one, or on some abacuses, two beads, and another sector with four or sometimes five beads. Figure 2-3 shows a typical abacus.

Figure 2-3. Abacus. (*Courtesy International Business Machines Corporation.*)

Although simple in appearance, the abacus, in skilled hands, is an amazingly versatile and efficient computing device. It is still used extensively in certain parts of the world.

After this first milestone, around four thousand years elapsed before the next significant developments in computational aids. One obstacle to the invention of mechanical computing devices was the use of Roman numerals throughout Europe. Roman numerals may add dignity to monuments, but the multiplication of MCMXIX by XVIII presents quite a challenge. The gradual acceptance of the Arabic numeral system, starting around A.D. 1200, provided a simpler means of calculating.

However, in spite of the improved numeral system, no mechanical aid to calculation of any merit appeared until the seventeenth century, the great century of mathematical progress. Then, in 1617, a Scot by the name of John Napier developed logarithms, a tabular system of numbers by which many arithmetical calculations are simplified. By using tables of logarithms the operations of multiplication and division may be more easily performed through addition and subtraction, respectively.

This development stimulated the invention of various devices that substituted the addition of logarithms for multiplication. Included was a device invented by John Napier in 1617 which later became known as "Napier's bones." It was a mechanical arrangement of strips of bone on which numbers were printed. When brought into combination, these strips could perform direct multiplication.

Another outgrowth of logarithms was the slide rule, conceived by William Oughtred in 1621. The slide rule, which was perhaps the first analog computer, performs multiplication and division by adding and subtracting. "Log tables," and their embodiment in slide rules, were immensely helpful in certain fields. The engineer, for example, needs to multiply more often than to add, and is often content with the degree of accuracy obtained from the highly portable slide rule, which is approximate rather than absolute. The businessman, however, needs to add, and even a fractional error can be costly if applied to a large sum of money or if repeated in a large volume of transactions. To add figures exactly, measuring an analogy of the quantities as the slide rule does is of no use; it is necessary to count actual digits as the abacus does. Thus the slide rule proved to be most useful in activities that required fast relational computations.

Success in the development of a digital counter was first achieved by Blaise Pascal. In 1642, at the age of 19, he invented a device to assist in adding long columns of figures at his father's tax office in Rouen, France. His gear-driven machine, the size of a shoe box, consisted of a row of wheels with teeth numbered from 0 to 9 (Figure 2-4). The first wheel represented units; the second, tens; and so on. On turning the first wheel five spaces, 5 would show in a window at the top of the machine. Turning it two more spaces produced a total of 7. The addition of seven more caused the indicator to proceed through 0 to 4. Meanwhile, a lever on the units dial had moved the tens dial one-tenth of a revolution so that the machine had "carried one," showing a total of 14.

It was a simple device, more like a mileage gauge or revolution counter than a modern computer. However, it pointed out three principles that were utilized in later developments: that "carry over" should be automatic, that subtraction could be accomplished by turning dials

Figure 2-4. Pascal's adding machine invented in 1642. (*Courtesy International Business Machines Corporation.*)

in reverse, and that multiplication could be performed by repeated addition.

The German philosopher and mathematician, Gottfried Leibniz, conceived a calculating machine in 1671 which employed the principle of multiplication by repeated addition. The most important component of this device, completed in 1674, was the stepped wheel, a cylindrical drum with nine teeth of increasing length along its surface. When the drum was rotated, a gear sliding on an axis parallel to that of the drum engaged some of the teeth, thus being rotated an equivalent number of steps. This feature of the Leibniz machine is still found in some present-day calculators.

Numerous attempts were made throughout the next century to produce a satisfactory machine. Unfortunately, although the ideas were good the results were not. The first commercially successful calculating machine was that of the Alsatian inventor, Charles Xavier Thomas, who in 1820 further improved on the Leibniz cylinder idea by adding a crank. This machine is often considered the predecessor of all present-day desk calculators because it was widely copied in Europe and was brought to the United States where it led to further developments.

In 1850 D. D. Parmalee obtained a United States patent for the first key-driven machine. It was a considerable stride toward today's office machines, although the machine could add only a single column of digits at a time. The first key-driven four-process calculator was developed in the United States in 1857 by Hill.

Frank Stephen Baldwin invented the first practical reversible four-process calculator in the United States in 1872 (Figure 2-5). Somewhat later, in 1878 in Russia, W. T. Odhner designed a similar machine using a new type of wheel that made possible the more compact machines of today.

The first machine to perform multiplication successfully by a direct method instead of repeated addition was invented in 1887 by Leòn Bollée of France. The mechanism had a multiplying piece consisting of a series of tongued plates repre-

Figure 2-6. The first practical adding-printing machine designed by William S. Burroughs in 1884. (*Courtesy Burroughs Corporation.*)

senting in relief the ordinary multiplication table up to "nine times."

In 1887 Dorr Eugene Felt patented a key-driven adding machine known then as the "Macaroni Box," and now as the Comptometer. The machine has, of course, undergone considerable refinement since Felt's day. About the same time, William S. Burroughs, a bank clerk who was suffering from poor health, decided to invent a machine that would alleviate the drudgery of bookkeeping. In 1884 he succeeded in developing a key-set adding-printing machine with a crank (Figure 2-6). The machine was patented in 1888 and was successfully marketed in 1891. This was a significant advance for the machine had the ability to record and summarize as well as calculate.

In 1899 Egli marketed the "Millionaire" machine patented by Otto Steiger in 1893 (Figure 2-7). It embodied the mechanical multiplication table invented by Bollée. The machine required only one turn of the handle for each figure of the multiplier and provided for automatic shift to the next position.

Figure 2-5. Original Baldwin calculator invented in 1872. (*Courtesy Monroe International, Inc.*)

Figure 2-7. "The Millionaire," the first successful direct multiplying machine, 1899. (*Courtesy International Business Machines Corporation.*)

The Monroe calculator, incorporating previous designs by Frank S. Baldwin, was introduced in 1911 by Jay R. Monroe and Baldwin (Figure 2-8). It was the first keyboard rotary machine to attain commercial success. This was the culmination of forty years of work for Baldwin, who invented his first calculator in 1872.

In 1914 Oscar and David Sundstrand invented the ten-key adding machine, thus increasing the speed of operation.

The first accounting machine, a teller machine for certifying passbooks, was developed for the National Cash Register Company in 1909 by Charles F. Kettering. However, the large-scale development of the accounting machine did not occur until after the close of World War I. By means of a tabulating carriage, this machine made it possible to sort data into a number of columns in addition to performing the functions of recording, calculating, and summarizing.

Another device that is now used for computing as well as for recording and controlling purposes is the cash register. The cash register was invented in 1879 by James Ritty of Dayton, Ohio (Figure 2-9). It was made commercially successful by John H. Patterson, who founded the National Cash Register Company in 1884. Since the advent of these machines, they have provided invaluable service in stores throughout the world.

Electromechanical machines came into general use about 1920. Electric activation provided greater speed and facility in the use of adding, calculating, and bookkeeping machines. However, all these machines, while quite efficient, were limited in two ways. First, they were a manual rather than automatic type of equipment, since they required some form of action by an operator, such as depressing a key, bar, or lever, to perform each processing step. Second, the machines functioned independently of other units of equipment, although each machine was capable of performing one or more of four processing steps: recording, summarizing, calculating, and, to a limited extent, sorting.

The second limitation was overcome by the use of punched tape which made possible the compatibility of a wide range

Figure 2-8. An early model rotary calculator, about 1914. (*Courtesy Monroe International, Inc.*)

Figure 2-9. Original cash register invented in 1879. (*Courtesy National Cash Register Company.*)

of equipment. Accounting machines, typewriters, adding machines, calculators, and other mechanical equipment can now be used in combination with each other and with punched card or electronic computer equipment. Punched paper tape provides the common language that permits communication between the various types of equipment.

Both of the limitations mentioned above were overcome by the punched card system which first introduced compatibility of machines. In addition, these machines provided a means of performing a greater number of operations automatically. For the first time, a series of machines was able to perform a variety of functions through the use of a single medium—the punched card.

HISTORY OF PUNCHED CARD MACHINES

Although the punched card medium was new to the field of data processing,

it had been used earlier for other purposes. As far back as 1725, perforated paper was employed in the operation of a loom designed by Basile Bouchon. In 1728, M. Falcon, a French engineer, invented a loom that operated through the medium of perforated cards. This technique was later adopted for use in the first successful machine to operate from punched cards—a textile loom conceived in 1801 by another Frenchman named Joseph Marie Jacquard. In his automatic loom, which revolutionized the weaving industry, weaving was directed by a card in which punched holes supplied instructions that controlled the selection of threads and application of designs.

The first attempt to use the punched card principle in a mathematical application was made by the English mathematician, Charles Babbage. In 1812 he began work on what harsh critics called his "folly." It was a "difference engine" designed to calculate and print mathematical tables. After almost a decade of work on the "difference engine," Babbage turned his attention to a more ambitious project, the "analytical engine," a device with many far-reaching innovations. Included was a memory unit that would store data in the form of holes punched in cards. In addition, the device had a mill or arithmetic unit where the mathematical computations would be made, and a control unit for directing operations. Unfortunately, Babbage's engine seemed to be capable of everything except functioning. It was too far ahead of its time; many of the problems of constructing a mechanism such as Babbage had in mind were not solved for a full century.

Surprisingly, Jacquard's success in the use of punched cards failed to inspire another successful application of this technique until 1887 when Dr. Herman Hollerith, a statistician with the Census Bureau, developed a mechanical system of recording, computing, and tabulating census data. Hollerith, who had been engaged by the Census Bureau in 1880, was motivated by the obvious need for a more practical method of handling census data. The 1880 census data was written on large cards which had to be hand sorted into desired classifications, such as age, sex, occupation, and location, and counted manually. They were resorted and counted again and again to provide all the required information.

The magnitude of the task made it apparent that the 1890 census, involving millions of additional people, might not be completed by the end of the decade. This would have prevented the reallocation of Congressional seats as required every ten years by the Constitution.

By 1887, when the 1880 census report was finally completed, Dr. Hollerith had finished his plans for a new system which utilized punched holes in a long strip of paper tape as a means of recording facts. However, this was found to be impractical, so the 1890 census data was placed on cards by means of holes cut with a hand-operated punch. The cards were individually positioned over mercury-filled cups. Rows of telescoping pins descending on the card's surface dropped through the holes into the mercury, thus completing electrical circuits and causing pointers on appropriate counting dials to move one position (Figure 2-10). By the use of this device, which could tabulate cards at the rate of 50 to 75 a minute, it was possible to complete the 1890 census of 62 million people in one-third the time needed for the 1880 census of 50 million.

In 1896 Dr. Hollerith organized the Tabulating Machine Company to promote the commercial use of his machines. Among the first users were railroads, insurance companies, department stores,

Figure 2-10. Hollerith tabulating machine, 1890. (*Courtesy International Business Machines Corporation.*)

and a steel company. Other early users of punched cards were the city of Baltimore, the Bureau of Vital Statistics of New Jersey, and the Board of Health of New York City.

Meanwhile, James Powers, a statistical engineer employed by the Census Bureau, was asked to develop improved methods for handling the 1910 census. In 1908, Powers patented his first punching machine, which contained several innovations. The success of this machine and related sorters and tabulators in the 1910

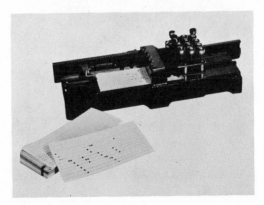

Figure 2-11. Mechanical key punch, 1901. (*Courtesy International Business Machines Corporation.*)

census encouraged Powers to start the Powers Accounting Machine Company in 1911. Through a series of mergers, the Powers line later became part of the Remington Rand Company and more recently the UNIVAC Division of Sperry Rand Corporation.

In the same year, 1911, the company that had been formed by Dr. Hollerith to develop his equipment merged with two other companies and became the Computing-Tabulating-Recording Company. In 1924 the C.T.R. Company's name was changed to International Business Machines Corporation.

The use of punched card machines developed gradually from 1900 to 1915, during which time about three hundred companies adopted the equipment, then

Figure 2-12. Vertical punched card sorter, 1908. (*Courtesy International Business Machines Corporation.*)

with increasing speed in the 1920's. Several significant advancements occurred in the late 1920's and early 1930's. Punched cards with a greatly increased capacity of 80 and 90 columns of information were introduced. Machines were developed that could not only add and subtract figures but also multiply. This gave them the ability to perform full-scale record-keeping and accounting functions. The introduction of machines that could handle alphabetic information made it possible to use the punched card method for name-and-number jobs such as payrolls and inventories.

These innovations and many others increased the speed, versatility, and usefulness of punched card machines. This resulted in the constantly increasing use of these devices for business data processing as well as for scientific computations and statistical studies. However, since standard punched card machines are electromechanical, they have several limitations. First, the speed of the machines is limited by their basic design and by the physical or mechanical manipulation of cards. Second, since each machine is designed to perform a special function, the transfer of cards from one piece of equipment to another for various operations not only takes time but also creates the possibility of error.

The first successful attempt to overcome these limitations by combining the various operations in a single device was made by Professor Howard Aiken of Harvard University, who worked from 1939 to 1944 in conjunction with engineers from International Business Machines Corporation. This joint effort resulted in the completion in 1944 of the Automatic Sequence Controlled Calculator, known as Mark I. This was an electromechanical machine, consisting mostly of parts from standard IBM equipment or modifications

Figure 2-13. Lever set gang punch, 1914. (*Courtesy International Business Machines Corporation.*)

of them. It made use of relays and was controlled by punched paper tape. Thus, Babbage's dream of a hundred years earlier was fulfilled.

Several other large-scale digital machines using electromechanical techniques followed the one at Harvard. Aiken designed the so-called Mark II for the U.S. Naval Proving Ground at Dahlgren, Virginia; and several relay calculators were designed and built in the Bell Telephone Laboratories during the World War II period.

In spite of the fact that these computers were a great improvement over devices previously available, they failed to meet the vast data requirements of science and engineering that developed swiftly during World War II. Since these machines were electromechanical devices employing electrical relays or counter wheels, their effectiveness was restricted by slowness and mechanical operating difficulties. These problems were overcome by the next major development in data processing history, the advent of the electronic computer.

DEVELOPMENT OF ELECTRONIC COMPUTERS

The first machine to use electronic tubes for calculating was the ENIAC, Electronic Numerical Integrator and Computer, developed between 1942 and 1946 at the University of Pennsylvania by Dr. John W. Mauchly, J. Presper Eckert, and their associates. ENIAC occupied the entire basement of the university's Moore School of Electrical Engineering (Figure 2-15). The computer weighed almost 30 tons, contained more than 18,000 vacuum tubes, and required more than 1,500 square feet of floor space.

It was designed mainly for solving problems in ballistics at the Aberdeen Proving Ground but it contained advancements that were adopted for use in other computers designed for business applications. In this machine the switching and control functions, once performed by re-

Figure 2-14. Punched card sorter, 1925. (*Courtesy International Business Machines Corporation.*)

Figure 2-15. ENIAC, the first all-electronic digital computer, 1946. (*Courtesy* UNIVAC, *Division of Sperry Rand Corporation.*)

lays, were handled by vacuum tubes. Thus the relatively slow movements of switches in electromechanical computers were replaced by the rapid motion of electrons. This innovation made it possible to perform computations one thousand times as fast as before. However, although ENIAC represented a great advancement and was adaptable to a variety of applications, its limited storage facilities and the difficulty of presenting instructions were serious restrictions.

In the early stages of computer development, machine instructions were programmed on interchangeable control panels, cards, or paper tapes. It was necessary to wire or read detailed instructions into the machine as work progressed. Since the computer processed data according to predetermined instructions, its operations were very inflexible.

To increase the computer's capacity to work problems without the assistance of an operator, it was necessary to have its program stored in a high-speed internal storage unit or memory. This would give the computer access to instructions as rapidly as they were needed. With an internal stor-

age system, the computer could process a program in a manner similar to that in which it processed data. It could also modify its own instructions as required by progressive stages of work.

These characteristics were incorporated in the stored program-type digital computers that marked the next great milestone in the development of electronic computers. The first to be completed was the EDSAC (Electronic Delayed Storage Automatic Computer), which came from the laboratories of Cambridge University in England and was placed in operation in May 1949. This machine utilized mercury acoustic delay lines as storage. These devices consist of thin tubes of mercury with crystals at both ends. When an electrical impulse is entered on the input crystal, it causes the crystal to vibrate mechanically, thus sending an acoustic signal through the fluid to the output crystal. When this sound wave hits, it causes a mechanical vibration in the second crystal. This vibration becomes an electrical signal: the image of the one originally transmitted. The reformed and amplified electrical impulse is fed back to the input crystal and the process is repeated. Through this loop process data represented by a set of impulses spaced periodically can be kept circulating through the mercury until needed.

The EDVAC (Electronic Discrete Variable Automatic Computer), which was comparable to the EDSAC, was completed in the early 1950's. This machine was designed at the University of Pennsylvania for the United States Army. It also used the sonic delay properties of mercury for storage. The EDVAC was maintained at Aberdeen Proving Ground until March 1963 when it was discarded.

Another project for a high-speed electronic computer using delay line storage was started in 1945 and completed in 1950 at the National Physical Laboratory, London. This well-designed machine called the ACE (Automatic Calculating Engine) was compact and highly reliable in operation. It used standard punched card equipment for input and output. Whereas both the EDVAC and the EDSAC operated in the mode in which instructions are placed in consecutive positions in storage, the ACE adopted the so-called two-address code whereby each instruction contains not only the location of the number to be acted upon, but also the location of the next instruction. This procedure reduced the waiting time inherent in delay line storage devices by allowing the use of better programming techniques.

Several other machines were constructed using the principle of acoustic delay line storage. Notable among these was SEAC (Standards Eastern Automatic Computer), developed by the Bureau of Standards in Washington, D.C., for government use. Another computer in this group was UNIVAC (Universal Automatic Computer), developed by Eckert and Mauchly, builders of the ENIAC. The first UNIVAC was delivered to the Bureau of the Census in 1951. This computer was used almost continuously 24 hours a day, 7 days a week for over 12 years. In 1963 it was judged of sufficient historical interest to be placed on exhibition at the Smithsonian Institution after having been replaced at the Bureau of the Census by new computers.

UNIVAC was one of the first machines to use magnetic tape as an input-output medium. It featured speed, reliability, memory capacity, and the ability to handle both numbers and descriptive material equally well. These features made computers economically attractive for commercial use. As a result, the first UNIVAC computer was delivered to a business concern in 1954.

UNIVAC I was the first of a line of computers produced by Remington Rand, which in 1949 acquired the Eckert-Mauchly Computer Corporation, originally formed as a partnership in 1946. The Remington Rand organization later became the UNIVAC Division of Sperry Rand Corporation.

During the early 1950's many new computers were developed by universities, industrial laboratories, and machine manufacturers. A family of machines typical of this period employed an entirely different type of internal storage comprised of a cathode ray tube system. Many of these machines derived their logical inspiration from a series of now classical reports by Dr. John von Neumann. Dr. Herman Goldstine, and Dr. Arthur Burks dating back to 1946. The prototype for an extensive group of machines sponsored by the United States Government was the computer built at the Institute for Advanced Study in Princeton by a group including von Neumann and Goldstine. This computer was completed in March 1952.

Dr. Jay W. Forrester at the Massachusetts Institute of Technology directed the production of Whirlwind I. This machine used a special cathode ray tube of a type devised by Forrester. Another type of cathode ray storage machine was developed at the University of Manchester in England.

An additional form of storage introduced in the early 1950's to enlarge the memory capacity of computers was the magnetic drum. The first fully electronic computer constructed with this type of storage was the prototype SEC (Simple Electronic Computer), developed at the Electronic Computation Laboratory of

Birkbeck College, University of London. A very large class of machines using the magnetic drum as the principal form of memory was prevalent later in the 1950's. Particularly notable was the IBM 650 which was used extensively for business calculations as well as scientific purposes.

The mid 1950's constituted a period of transition in the history of computers. Many of the computers developed were designed expressly for business use. Although basically similar to previous computers in the way they processed data, the new business systems were adapted to handle the vast quantities of data typical of business operations. Instead of the punched cards or punched tape used for input of data in early computers, magnetic tape was used for externally storing data. The new technique increased input speed from 50 to 75 times that of cards and also improved output and storage.

As far as internal storage was concerned, the cathode ray tube was abandoned and the acoustic delay line diminished in use. The magnetic drum remained but was relegated to a secondary position in favor of magnetic cores, a more rapid technique that was destined to become the most widely used form of internal storage. Magnetic cores are small rings of ferromagnetic material. When strung on a complex of wires, these cores constitute a high-speed internal storage system in which items of information can be located and made available for processing in a few millionths of a second.

Technological advancements in electronics and solid-state physics resulted in the so-called second generation of computers in the mid-1950's. The first generation used vacuum tubes in their circuits. They were bulky, demanded considerable power, and produced heat which created air conditioning problems. The second generation used solid-state devices, such as transistors, which generate less heat and are generally smaller and more reliable. As a result, the physical size of computer systems was reduced significantly.

Modular or "building block" concepts were applied to the design of internal circuitry and to the design of other major pieces of hardware in computer systems. This allowed the systems to be easily expanded instead of being replaced as users required more speed or more storage capacity. Improvements in peripheral devices, such as increasing the printing speed of output units, allowed them to be directly interconnected with the computer and used on-line, without unduly reducing the overall speed of the system. Other advancements included built-in error detection and correction devices and improved programming techniques, which reduced the need for operator intervention. Also, teleprocessing equipment was developed to expedite the flow of information to and from computers over long distances.

Along with these improvements came the development of disk storage, which provided a new means of storing information in a unit resembling a coin-operated record player. Before its development, in both electromechanical and electronic data processing systems, information was batched, or sorted into sequence before processing. With the introduction of disk storage, the processing of individual transactions in random sequence became practical as it was possible to locate and update any one record in a stack of rotating disks in a fraction of a second.

The next major advancement occurred in 1964 with the introduction of what has been described as the third generation of computer equipment. This equipment features microminiaturized components such as integrated circuits and thin-film memory, and other significant innovations resulting from continued progress in electronic technology. Techniques include etching or printing instead of wiring circuits and the use of tiny crystal structures rather than tubes or relatively large transistors. These features have made possible the development of computer systems that are smaller in size, greater in capacity, and faster, with operating speeds measured in billionths of a second. Another important characteristic of the newer equipment is greater compatibility of components, which affords flexibility in modifying or expanding computer systems without altering the basic systems. Of particular significance is the fact that most third-generation computers are truly general purpose and thus can handle both business and scientific applications with equal facility (Figure 2-16).

Along with improvements in the basic design of computers, the following developments have occurred. Many data re-cording devices have been devised to capture data at the point and time of origin in a form the computer can process. Optical scanners and magnetic ink character recognition devices provide more effective methods of collecting data. Increased use of random access storage devices, such as magnetic disks, has facilitated the storage and rapid retrieval of greater amounts of data. Data communications equipment is increasingly being used to transmit data directly to computer storage, to connect computers with other computers, and to permit interrogation of a computer system from remote terminals. In addition to these advancements, the sophistication of programming techniques has increased tremendously.

Rather than to speculate about future possibilities, let it suffice to say that continuing changes are inevitable as designers strive to develop more versatile and useful computers that will perform at even faster speeds, store more information, require fewer instructions, need less power, occupy less space, and reduce the ratio of cash to performance.

Figure 2-16. Third-generation electronic data processing system, 1964. (*Courtesy Radio Corporation of America.*)

In view of the progress that has been made in the relatively short history of electronic computers, it seems safe to conclude that even the most fantastic predictions of today may in time prove to have been conservative.

Review Questions

1. Describe the two oldest surviving records of actual business transactions.
2. What was the purpose of wooden tallies? What was the main reason for their extensive use?
3. Where and in what period did the double-entry system of accounting originate?
4. Where and by whom was the first successful digital counter developed?
5. Who was the inventor of the first punched card data processing system? Under what circumstances was the system developed?
6. When and where did the first electronic computer originate? What was its abbreviated name?
7. What principal characteristic distinguishes each of the three generations of electronic computers?
8. What were the significant contributions of the following men to the development of data processing equipment? (a) Dorr Eugene Felt, (b) William S. Burroughs, (c) Jay Monroe and Frank Baldwin, (d) Charles Babbage, (e) Professor Howard Aiken, (f) John W. Mauchly and J. Presper Eckert.

3

BUSINESS ORGANIZATION
AND SOURCES OF DATA

This book is primarily concerned with methods of processing data regardless of its specific origin or nature. Nevertheless, it must be recognized that the majority of data processing takes place in a business environment. For this reason some knowledge of the structure and function of business organizations is essential as a means of understanding the major sources of data and the important role of data processing.

This chapter presents a brief survey of the types of business, legal forms of business, internal organization of business, basic operations, and sources of data. Also included is a brief review of the basic accounting cycle.

TYPES OF BUSINESS

Basically there are three major types of business firms: (1) those that produce goods, (2) those that distribute goods, and (3) those that render services. These classi-

fications, although comprehensive, do not reflect the variety of business activity. This may be indicated more clearly by the type of division employed in Table 3-1. Although the outline of business activity in Table 3-1 is by no means complete, it does give some idea of the diversity and scope of business today.

LEGAL FORMS OF BUSINESS

Sole Proprietorship

The sole proprietorship is the simplest form of business enterprise. It has only one owner who maintains complete control. He makes all decisions, assumes all risks, and receives all profits. On the other hand, he has no one with whom to share his problems, and he must bear all the losses.

Although there are more sole proprietorships than any other form of business, they rank below corporations in volume of

TABLE 3-1   TYPES OF BUSINESS

Manufacturing	Transportation
Processing	Railroads
Food products	Air lines
Metals	Ship lines
Petroleum	Express companies
Chemicals	Truck lines
Mining	Professional services
Agriculture	Hospitals
Textile and clothing industries	Schools
Distribution	Accounting firms
Wholesale	Law firms
High-volume bulk goods	Personal services
Retail merchandising	Hotels, motels, and
Public utilities	restaurants
Electricity	Moving and hauling
Gas	Laundries and dry cleaners
Water	Appliance repair, etc.
Telephone	Banking and Finance
Publications and printing	Banks
Entertainment	Savings and loan companies
Radio and television	Brokerage firms
Movies	Insurance companies
Sports	Advertising
Clubs	Construction
Resorts	

sales. The sole proprietorship form of organization is generally used when a limited amount of capital is required, the volume is small, and labor or supervision can be performed by one person.

Partnership

A partnership is an association of two or more persons who carry on a business as co-owners and who share the profits or losses. This form of organization provides an enterprise with the capital resources, experience, judgment, and responsibility of more than one person. There is, however, the possibility of disagreement and the risk of sudden termi-

nation if a partner withdraws or is unable to continue because of illness or death. In addition, each partner may be individually liable for all debts of the firm and may be bound by acts of other partners.

Corporation

A corporation is an association of individuals legally authorized by the state or federal government to carry on certain activities. A corporation is an artificial entity separate and distinct from the individuals who operate it. Ownership is in the form of shares of stock generally divided among many shareholders. One of the advantages of the corporate form of organization is that stockholders are liable only to the extent of their investment. Another advantage is that the life of the organization is not affected by the death or disability of individual stockholders, or by the transfer of stock to other investors.

The corporation has tremendous growth possibilities through the sale of securities to the general public. This accounts for the fact that most large organizations in the United States are corporations. Large corporations have the resources to hire the most skilled personnel, to build good facilities, and to save money by large-scale purchases.

Corporations have certain disadvantages, however. They are subject to legal restrictions and high taxes. Further, the

difficulty of managing a large corporation may lead to inefficiency and red tape.

INTERNAL ORGANIZATION OF BUSINESS

Line Organization (Figure 3-1)

This type of organization is one in which lines of authority flow in a direct line from the top to the bottom of the organization. It is a simple and rigid form of organization based upon military procedures. A line organization is easy to understand for lines of supervision, promotion, and communication are clearly defined. Each person knows exactly to whom and for whom

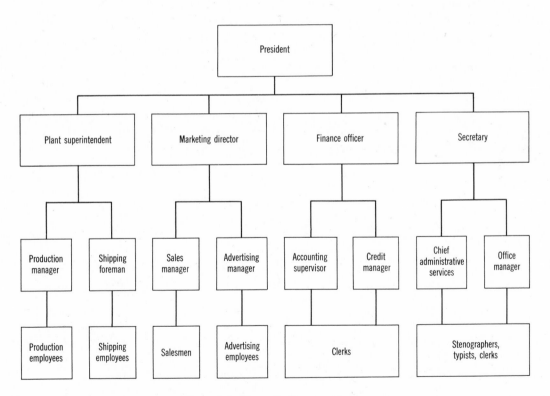

Figure 3-1. Chart of a line organization.

he is responsible. Each division, department, or section is under a supervisor who is completely responsible for the work of his unit. There is little relationship between different departments.

Although this plan functions smoothly and quickly on a limited basis, it can become unwieldy and inefficient in a large organization. For this reason it is seldom used in its pure form except in small companies.

Functional Organization

This form of organization employs a group of specialists at the top level. Each specialist has direct supervision over the operating employees in any department who perform activities related to his field. Figure 3-2 illustrates an organization in which the employees in each of four departments are responsible to three managers who are specialists in different fields.

This plan has the advantage of utilizing experts to whom workers can turn for competent advice. However, since each subordinate may have several bosses, the system may result in confusion, overlapping authority, and inability to determine responsibility for errors and oversights.

Line-and-Staff Organization

The disadvantages of the line and the functional types of organization have led to the adoption and widespread use of the line-and-staff type of organization. This type combines the best features of the other systems. Control and stability in the operating divisions are maintained by line organization methods. Expert planning, research, and analysis are provided by staff personnel. In this case the staff function is strictly advisory and carries no authority to put its advice into operation. The staff personnel submit ideas to top management. If top management adopts an idea, orders are issued down the line.

In the organization illustrated by Figure 3-3, production and sales appear as line functions which classifies them as primary activities. The other departments appear as staff functions which classifies them as supporting activities needed to keep the primary functions in operation.

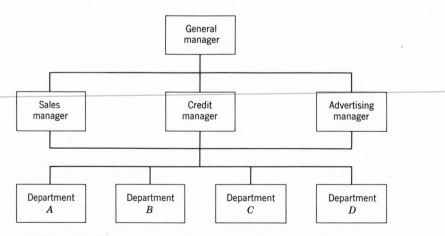

Figure 3-2. Chart of a functional organization in a department store.

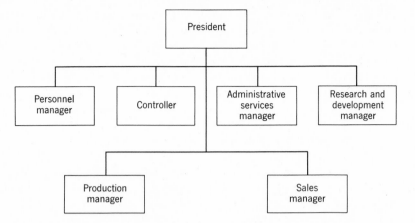

Figure 3-3. Chart of a line-and-staff organization.

DATA PROCESSING IN THE ORGANIZATIONAL STRUCTURE

Data processing is generally regarded as a service function for other operations in the organization. This is especially true in organizations that have electronic computers or large punched card machine installations, or a combination of both.

When computers first began to appear in large organizations, they were almost always placed in the controller's department. This was a natural decision since so many of the clerical functions of that department could be performed by the computer. However, the range of computer applications soon extended far beyond accounting operations. Computer services to the entire organization increased and the computer was recognized as a vast source of management information.

In some companies separate computer departments have been established in the controller's organization. This has often led to the creation of a key position near the top of the financial organization structure. In other cases, data processing has been established as a separate staff function outside the controller's organization.

This means that the department can make a more direct contribution to management planning and control, and can serve all functional departments since it is not subordinate to any one department (Figure 3-4). The data processing department may be headed by a top-ranking staff executive with a title such as "Vice-President, Management Services," or "Vice-President, Management Information."

The emergence of electronic data processing as a separate function was documented in a survey of 108 manufacturing firms in which Booz, Allen and Hamilton, international management consultants, identified a "top computer executive" in 97 of the firms.* According to the survey, in nearly all cases the executive is found at the corporate level where he coordinates the activities of other computer managers and is responsible for overall quality, performance, and future planning of the company's computer activities. The top computer executive was also reported to be responsible for working with noncomputer executives in deter-

* "EDP's New Management Man," *Business Automation,* February 1968, p. 44.

mining what the computer is to do for them. Another part of his job is working with the chief executive officer in planning the overall use of the computer in current as well as future operations. The study also revealed use of the computer in functional areas other than finance and administration. Included are marketing, manufacturing, distribution, research, development and engineering, and management planning.

It should be noted that the prominent status and position of data processing within the organizational structure occurs primarily when a computer is involved. Punched card machine installations also provide service to many departments.

However, punched card machines generally have a more limited range of applications and their use in management activities has been less extensive. In organizations utilizing manual and mechanical methods, the processing of data usually takes place within the various departments.

BASIC BUSINESS OPERATIONS AND SOURCES OF DATA

In business, most data results from the need to record transactions as they occur. Thus data reflects the routine day-by-day activities of the various operating areas.

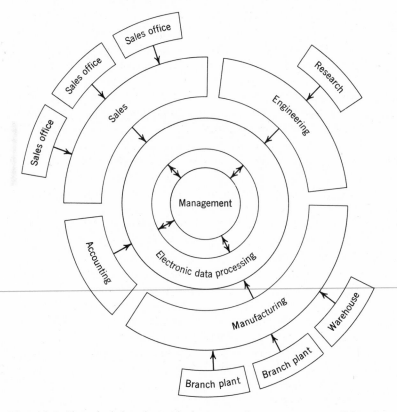

Figure 3-4. Chart depicting electronic data processing as a separate staff function.

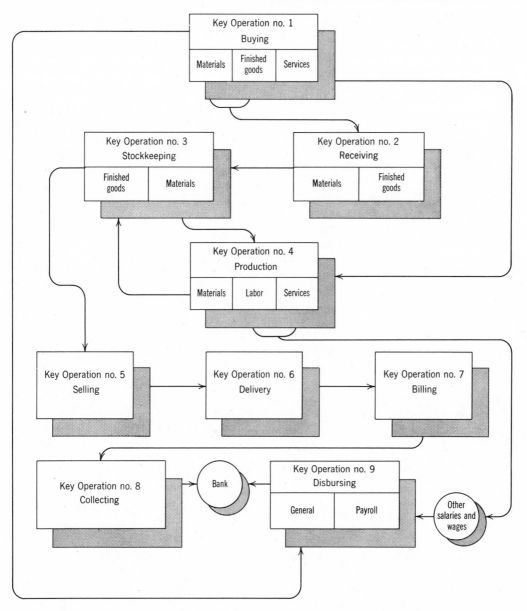

Figure 3-5. Interrelationship of basic business operations. (*Courtesy Moore Business Forms, Inc.*)

According to the organization concept illustrated in Figure 3-5, there are nine basic operations, most of which exist to some degree in every concern. The fact that these operations are interrelated and must exchange information results in a flow of paperwork throughout an organization. In a large organization literally hundreds of different forms may be used. Many of these operating records serve as source documents for accounting functions, and the combined operating and accounting records form the basis of the reports that are so important to management.

The chart in Figure 3-5 is not a conventional organization chart. It is designed to illustrate the flow of goods through a business and their conversion to cash by a series of related operations. It is apparent that the designated operations are regarded as primary activities. This implies that other functions not mentioned, including accounting and data processing, are supporting activities in accordance with the line-and-staff concept described earlier. As indicated in the preceding section, it is reasonable to assume that a central data processing department might provide service to each of the nine operations.

The outline presented in Figure 3-5 will be used as a basis for describing briefly the basic business operations and the principal types of records and reports that originate with each operation. Although the outline reflects the operations of a manufacturing organization, most of these operations, except production, are typical of other firms that distribute goods and render services.

Purchasing

Purchasing involves the procurement of merchandise, materials, equipment, supplies, and services necessary to equip, maintain, and operate a business. Purchases generally comprise goods and services such as the following:

1. Merchandise bought for resale.
2. Materials used in manufacturing operations.
3. Equipment, furniture, and other fixed assets required to operate various departments.

4. Supplies needed for maintenance, operating, and office activities.
5. Utilities and other services required from outside sources.

In small organizations each department may be responsible for its own purchases. A large organization ordinarily has a centralized purchasing department that is responsible for the procurement of all goods and services.

The procurement process in a large organization usually begins with the completion of a *purchase requisition*. This document is a request that the purchasing department secure certain goods or services. It may be prepared in the department where the goods or services are required or in the stockkeeping department. Purchase requisitions are usually made in two copies, one of which is retained by the originator.

Purchasing departments generally have available information about sources of supply, prices, specifications, terms, and shipping conditions. In the absence of such information, the purchasing department may send a *request for quotation* to prospective suppliers. This document requests prices for goods or services in the quantities specified.

When the source of supply has been determined, the next step is to issue a *purchase order*. This is the basic procurement document which authorizes the vendor to deliver specified goods or services at the prices indicated. The original and one copy are usually sent to the vendor with one copy to be returned as an acknowledgment. Additional copies may be distributed as follows:

1. To the purchasing department files.
2. To the receiving department so that the shipment may be checked when received.

3. To the accounting or accounts payable department.

4. To the stockkeeping department.

5. To the department originating the request.

Additional responsibilities of the purchasing department may include (1) following up to assure delivery at the proper time, (2) checking and approving invoices for payment, and (3) securing adjustments for shortages, poor quality, and other problems.

Receiving

The primary work of the receiving department consists of receiving, unloading, and unpacking materials. The goods are then inspected and compared to the description on the purchase order, with any discrepancies being noted. After checking has been completed, a *receiving report* is prepared. This is the basic document of the receiving department. It is designed to record in detail what materials were received and from whom. The report also may include an *inspection record*. Copies may be distributed to some or all of the following departments:

1. To the receiving department files.

2. To the purchasing department so that the receipt of the goods may be audited.

3. To the accounting or accounts payable department.

4. To the stockkeeping department or other department originating the request.

5. To the inspection department if it is separate from the receiving department.

6. To the production department if raw materials were received.

After the checking of goods and preparation of reports have been completed, the goods are delivered to the stockkeeping department or other department requesting them. The department that takes possession of the goods generally acknowledges receipt by signing a copy of the receiving report.

Stockkeeping

The stores (stockkeeping) department is responsible for the storage and protection of all materials and supplies received by or made by a company that are not required for immediate use. The transfer of materials from an outside source to the stores department is documented by the *receiving report* discussed in the preceding section. The transfer of goods from the production department is documented by a *production order*.

In industrial organizations the storeroom serves as a source of materials that are issued whenever needed. Materials are issued in response to a *material requisition*. This form generally consists of at least four copies distributed as follows:

1. To the files of the requisitioning department.

2. To the accounting or cost department.

3. To the stockroom. (Two copies, one of which is attached to the goods being transferred.)

Goods that are being held for sale are released for delivery upon receipt of a *sales order* originating in the sales department.

An important responsibility of the stockroom is the maintenance of *stock records*. A stock record is kept for each item of inventory and shows quantities received, quantities issued, and quantities on hand. Depending upon the methods of the particular business, the stock record may be a loose leaf ledger, ledger card, visible card or record, punched card, or a form of computer storage.

Stockkeeping also encompasses the replenishment of supplies that reach a specified minimum level called an *order point*. When the quantity of any item reaches the order point, the stock clerk prepares a *purchase requisition* for a new supply and sends it to the purchasing department.

Production

The production of goods involves many problems. First, suitable products must be designed and developed. Then facilities, equipment, and tools must be provided to manufacture the products. Personnel must be recruited and trained to use the equipment and tools. Raw materials and parts must be selected and made available as needed. Work must be planned, routed, scheduled, and followed up. The quality of the products must be controlled. Finally, the facilities and equipment must be kept in good condition.

Goods may be manufactured and stored in anticipation of demand, or they may be manufactured to fill an order. If the goods are being manufactured to order, a copy of a sales order may serve as the production order. However, it is more likely that production will be initiated by a *production order* originating in the production planning or production control department. Copies of the production order may be distributed as follows:

1. To the production department files.
2. To the cost accounting and general accounting departments.
3. To the stores department if production is for stock.
4. To the traffic or shipping depart-

ment if the production is to fill an order.
5. To the inspection department.

Materials needed for the manufacturing process may be obtained by preparing a *purchase requisition* if they are to be procured from an outside source, or by preparing a *stockroom requisition* if they are to be provided by the stores department.

Other records and reports that may be involved in the manufacturing process are *time records, daily production reports, material usage reports, inspection reports, cost analysis reports, tool orders* and *receipts,* and *progress reports.*

Sales

Retail sales other than routine cash transactions are generally recorded on a *sales slip.* It is prepared by the sales person at the time of a sale or when an order is received by telephone or by mail. One copy is given to the customer and another copy is used for accounting purposes. Additional copies may be distributed to the delivery or shipping department and to the stockkeeping department.

Sales transactions in wholesale and manufacturing firms are recorded on a *sales order.* The sales order is originated by a salesman or by the order department as the result of a mail order, telephone call, or personal contact with the customer. Copies may be distributed as follows:

1. To the files of the sales or order department.
2. To the customer to acknowledge the order.
3. To the stockkeeping department.
4. To the production department if manufacturing is involved.
5. To the shipping department.
6. To the salesman.
7. To the billing department for prep-

aration of a sales invoice, or to the accounting department if the sales order also serves as a sales invoice.

The selling process may require the preparation of other forms and reports including *contracts, estimates* and *bids, order confirmations, back orders, change orders,* and *sales analysis reports.*

Delivery

Delivery encompasses the packing, labeling, and transportation of goods to a customer. The basic document for this operation is the *shipping order* which authorizes delivery of merchandise sold. This may be a special form or a copy of the sales order. One copy is delivered to the customer along with or in advance of the goods. If direct delivery is made, the customer is usually asked to acknowledge receipt of goods by signing a copy of the shipping order which is then filed in the delivery office.

Firms that ship by public carrier prepare a *bill of lading* which contains the contract between the consignor and the carrier. Two copies accompany the shipment. One is for the customer and the other is retained by the carrier as a delivery receipt. A third copy is retained in the files of the shipping department.

Billing

The purposes of the billing operation are to prepare customers' *invoices* and to provide the accounting department with a record of charges to be made against customers' accounts. Invoices are the basis on which the seller claims payment for goods furnished or services rendered. Billing may be done manually, by a combination of manual and machine methods, or by punched card or electronic computer equipment. The method is determined mainly by the volume of work.

Regardless of the method employed, the billing procedure generally involves the following steps:

1. Coding descriptions for classification purposes and to reduce them to more concise form.
2. Inserting unit prices from catalogs or price lists.
3. Making extensions by multiplying the quantity of each item by the unit price.
4. Totaling extended prices.
5. Adding taxes, shipping costs, or other charges and entering the total amount of the invoice.
6. Writing or typing invoices in the required number of copies.

In a large organization with heavy volume, each of the preceding steps might be handled separately by one or more clerks. In a small business, all billing might be handled by one or two clerks.

One copy of the sales invoice is sent to the customer. Other copies are usually distributed to the department responsible for posting accounts receivable, to the salesman or sales department, and to the files of the billing department.

Collecting

The collecting operation includes the maintenance of accounts receivable, the sending of statements or collection notices, and the receipt of payments for goods sold or services rendered.

The basic document in this operation is the *statement of account.* It is customary to provide customers with statements at regular intervals to inform them of the status of their accounts. The usual time for mailing statements is at the end of each month. However, when the volume of accounts is very large, a *cycle billing* plan may be used as a means of spreading the work load over the entire month. Cycle billing is accomplished by dividing customers into groups and mailing predetermined batches of statements daily, weekly, or at other convenient intervals.

Statements may be prepared (1) by copying data from the customer's ledger account, (2) by posting to the statement and to the customer's ledger account simultaneously during the month, or (3) by using a combination statement-ledger form whereby a copy of the statement is used as the ledger.

Another important document used in the collecting process is the *cash receipt.* This is used to record payments to be credited to customers' accounts. One copy is sent to the accounting department for posting to accounts receivable, and one copy is retained in the treasurer's department or other department where cash is received. A copy may be sent to the customer but this is generally considered unnecessary if the payment is in the form of a check. In some cases a voucher stub attached to the statement may be returned by the customer with his payment. If so, this voucher serves as the record of cash received.

Disbursing

There are two major types of disbursements: (1) payroll, which represents payments for the services of personnel; and (2) payments of invoices for purchases of materials, supplies, equipment, and outside services.

The payroll function involves the preparation of many types of forms and reports. *Time cards* originating in production or other departments generally provide the data from which payrolls are prepared. A time card is ordinarily made out for each employee showing the time worked during a pay period. Time cards also may be used for making labor distribution charges to expense accounts.

The *payroll* generally consists of a list of employees, hours worked, rates of pay, gross earnings, deductions, and net pay. *Payroll checks* and *earnings statements* are prepared from the payroll. The earnings statement is a statement showing the computation of gross earnings, various deductions, and net earnings. The payroll check and the payroll may be prepared simultaneously using methods that will be discussed in later chapters.

The *earnings record* is a permanent document showing the cumulative earnings and deductions for each employee. This record provides a basis for preparing reports of social security, unemployment insurance, and income tax withheld. It also serves to indicate when the employee has reached the maximum earnings subject to social security or unemployment insurance.

Accounts payable disbursement procedures include checking invoices and verifying liability by means of purchase orders and receiving reports. Upon receiving approval for payment, the disbursing office issues an ordinary *check* or a *voucher-check*. A voucher-check is a check with an attached voucher containing spaces for date, description, gross amount, discount, and net payment. Copies of the voucher are usually distributed to the payee, to the accounting department for accounts payable posting, and to the files of the disbursing office.

GOVERNMENT OPERATIONS

Although government agencies exist for different reasons than business organizations, they process comparable types of data. In fact, a large quantity of the data handled by some government agencies originates in business offices. Examples of such data are income tax reports, reports of unemployment insurance and social security withheld, and sales taxes collected.

An analysis of the basic operations of business reveals that most of these operations also exist in government, the exceptions being production, selling, and delivery for profit. There are, however, additional types of data that are unique to federal, state, and local governmental agencies. Examples include census data; election results; records pertaining to veterans' benefits, unemployment benefits, and social security; motor vehicle registration; law enforcement data; and licensing activities. Government agencies also handle tremendous amounts of statistical data of all kinds which are compiled into elaborate reports. In the final analysis, however, government and business data differ more in volume than in nature.

BASIC ACCOUNTING CYCLE

It was stated earlier that financial data is only one of the many kinds of data with which this book is concerned. Neverthe-less, many of the data processing methods discussed throughout the book are used for accounting operations. For this reason, a brief review of accounting fundamentals and of the basic accounting cycle might aid in relating new methods to traditional procedures.

As indicated in Chapter 2, the principles of double-entry accounting as we know them today were outlined in 1494 by Luca Pacioli. He decided that everything owned by a business should be called "property." Thus, the original accounting equation was: Property = Ownership.

Property includes such items as cash, equipment, merchandise, buildings, and land. The term "property" is not comprehensive, however. Customers often purchase goods and promise orally to pay for them at a future time. This type of transaction produces, instead of cash, an item known as an *account receivable*. If the promise were made in the form of a written note, it would be known as a *note receivable*. Consequently, modern accounting refers to property and amounts due the business as *assets*. Obligations incurred by a firm are known as *liabilities*. Ownership is more commonly known today as *proprietorship* or *net worth*.

A firm's proprietorship is determined by the amount of its assets, less the amount of its liabilities. This is illustrated by the basic accounting format that is shown in Figure 3-6.

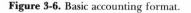

ASSETS	−	LIABILITIES	=	PROPRIETORSHIP
Cash		Accounts payable		
Accounts receivable		Notes payable		
Notes receivable				
Equipment				
Merchandise				

Figure 3-6. Basic accounting format.

Another way of stating the equation illustrated in Figure 3-6 is:

Assets = Liabilities + Proprietorship

This equation can be illustrated by the brief example of one of the standard business reports called a *balance sheet* which is shown in Figure 3-7.

The basic accounting cycle consists of the following steps:

Recording Source Data

Sales invoices, credit memorandums, purchase invoices, cash receipts vouchers, disbursement vouchers, and other records of business transactions are the initial sources of data from which journal entries are made.

Journalizing Transactions

(Classifying and sorting.) The first step in the accounting process is the recording of transactions in a book of original entry called the *journal*. Common types of journals include the cash receipts jour-nal, cash payments journal, purchases journal, sales journal, and general journal. The most common transactions are classified in special journals and miscellaneous transactions are entered in the general journal. The number and kinds of journals used are determined by the size and requirements of the business.

The journal serves three basic purposes:

1. It shows in chronological sequence the pertinent facts about all transactions.
2. It shows and explains the offsetting debit and credit entries for each transaction, thus providing in one place a complete record of all transactions.
3. It decreases the chance of error by clearly indicating what debit and credit entries are to be made in ledger accounts.

As an example of journal entries, let us assume that the company whose balance sheet is illustrated in Figure 3-7 paid $500 cash for merchandise, $1,000 cash for equipment, and purchased $2,000 worth of equipment on account. These transactions would appear in the general journal as indicated in Figure 3-8.

John Alden Company

Balance Sheet

December 31, 19—

Assets		*Liabilities*	
Cash	$ 3,500	Accounts payable	$ 2,500
Accounts receivable	1,500	Notes payable	4,000
Notes receivable	1,000	Total liabilities	$ 6,500
Equipment	2,000		
Merchandise	3,000	*Proprietorship*	
Total assets	$11,000	John Alden, owner	$ 4,500
		Total liabilities and proprietorship	$11,000

Figure 3-7. Balance sheet.

Posting to Ledgers

(Sorting and summarizing.) The next step in the cycle is the posting of data in journals to the book of final entry called the *ledger*. All of the accounts of a business are contained in the general ledger. Subsidiary ledgers are also used in many businesses. The *accounts receivable ledger* and the *accounts payable ledger* are the most common subsidiary ledgers. The accounts receivable ledger contains an account for each customer which reflects the balance he owes to the company. The accounts payable ledger contains an account for each creditor and indicates the amount payable to the creditor.

The left side of an account is known as the *debit* side and the right side is known as the *credit* side. Increases in asset accounts are entered on the left or debit side, and all decreases are entered on the right or credit side. Just the opposite is true with liability and proprietorship accounts. Increases in liability and proprietorship accounts are entered on the right or credit side and decreases are entered on the left or debit side. This can be illustrated as follows:

ASSETS		LIABILITIES AND PROPRIETORSHIP	
Increase	Decrease	Decrease	Increase

The balances shown on the balance sheet in Figure 3-7 would appear on ledger accounts as shown in the simplified "T account" format in Figure 3-9.

After posting of the journal entries illustrated in Figure 3-8, the ledger accounts would appear as shown in Figure 3-10.

Asset accounts usually have debit balances, and liability and proprietorship accounts usually have credit balances. The

General Journal

Date	Description	Ref.	Debit	Credit
7/1	Merchandise		500	
	Cash			500
7/1	Equipment		1,000	
	Cash			1,000
7/1	Equipment		2,000	
	Accounts payable			2,000

Figure 3-8. Journal entries.

sum of the balances in asset accounts should equal the sum of the balances in liability and proprietorship accounts. Thus the amount of net worth or proprietorship is determined by subtracting the liabilities from the assets.

Completing a Trial Balance

A *trial balance* consists of a list of the accounts in the ledger and their debit and credit balances. The trial balance is prepared to assure that the debits and credits in the ledger are equal before using the figures for other steps in the cycle.

Preparing the Financial Reports

There are two standard accounting reports, the balance sheet and the profit and loss statement. The *balance sheet* (Figure 3-7) is a cumulative report showing the assets, liabilities, and proprietorship of a business on a certain date. This report may be prepared monthly, quarterly, or annually.

The *profit and loss statement,* or *income statement,* is a noncumulative report showing the results of operations for a certain period. The statement shows the income for the period, the cost of operations, and

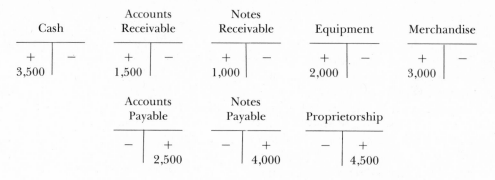

Figure 3-9. Ledger accounts representing source of entries for balance sheet shown in Figure 3-7.

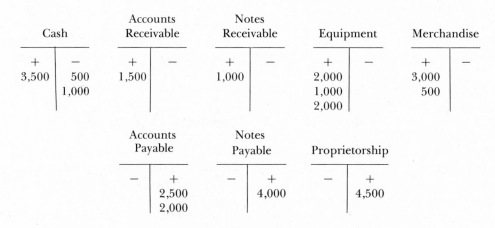

Figure 3-10. Ledger accounts after posting of journal entries shown in Figure 3-8.

the net profit or loss for the period. This report also may be prepared monthly, quarterly, or annually.

Making Closing Entries

At the end of each accounting period, it is customary to journalize and post adjusting entries and to make entries closing the current income and expense accounts.

The final steps in the cycle are the balancing and ruling of ledger accounts and the preparation of a post-closing trial balance.

Review Questions

1. What are the three major types of business firms?
2. What are the advantages and disadvantages of the proprietorship, the partnership, and the corporate forms of business?

3. What is the major weakness of the line type of organization?
4. How does a line-and-staff type of organization operate?
5. What is the outstanding characteristic of a functional plan of organization?
6. Discuss the role of the data processing department in a large organization.
7. Identify and describe briefly the nine basic operations of business.
8. Describe the purpose and origin of each of the following basic documents: (a) purchase order, (b) receiving report, (c) material requisition, (d) production order, (e) sales order, (f) shipping order, (g) invoice, (h) statement of account, (i) voucher-check.
9. What is the modern accounting equation, as reflected by a balance sheet?
10. What are the steps in the basic accounting cycle?

4

MANUAL AND MECHANICAL DATA PROCESSING

In addition to the modern developments in punched card and electronic data processing, a number of techniques and devices have also been developed to simplify the processing of data by traditional manual methods. Likewise, a great many new and improved devices have been developed to increase the efficiency of mechanical data processing.

At times the standard mechanical business machines have been all but written off in favor of the more sophisticated electronic data processing systems. Mechanical devices have not become obsolete, however. Instead, machine manufacturers have been stimulated to make advancements in traditional equipment, to develop new manual and electrical units with added features, and to produce new types of equipment and devices that speed individual operations and make them more automatic and accurate.

As a result, improved mechanical devices are filling a constantly growing demand for easy-to-use equipment that is practical for organizations with moderate data processing requirements. Such equipment also plays an important role in organizations with computers. It may be used independently to perform special functions in any part of an organization, or it may be used in a decentralized location—branch office, warehouse, etc.—as an adjunct to a centralized computer system. Many machines become an integral part of more sophisticated systems by preparing original documents and simultaneously producing by-products such as punched cards or tapes for processing by punched card machines or by electronic computers.

Technological advances in data processing equipment and related office machines are now progressing with amazing speed. For this reason, it would be futile to try to discuss specific features and models of equipment. A detailed discussion would soon be outdated by rapid developments. Instead, this chapter will present a survey of the general characteristics of the major manual and mechanical data processing techniques and equipment. To the extent possible, equipment will be grouped according to steps in the data processing cycle.

RECORDING TECHNIQUES

The traditional method of completing accounting and other record-keeping procedures is by means of pen-and-ink entries in standard journals, ledgers, and other record books. This manual approach to record keeping generally involves rewriting the same data several times, which consumes much time and creates a chance of error.

Thus as the volume of record-keeping activities increases, the need for more rapid and economical methods becomes evident. As a result, transaction documents and, in the case of accounting, subsequent entries in journals, subsidiary ledgers, and general ledgers are not always prepared in the conventional step-by-step manner. Instead, more than one document or record may be prepared simultaneously by means of special forms and devices. Original data also may be recorded in such a way that it may be used repeatedly without having to be rewritten.

There are various ways of eliminating the need to rewrite data. Later chapters will include such methods as recording data on punched cards, punched tapes, or magnetic tapes. In manual data processing this objective may be achieved by the use of carbon paper in handwritten or type-

written documents. Variations of this technique and some of the other methods that can be used to decrease manual effort are outlined in the following sections.

Special Forms

Most manual and mechanical recording operations are greatly facilitated by the use of special forms. Printed forms serve a number of important purposes including the following:

1. They identify the specific data that must be recorded for various uses.

2. They standardize the arrangement of data on source documents. This makes it easy to locate specific items of data and to process the documents.

3. They make records easy to recognize and to file.

4. They eliminate the need for recopying repetitive data that must appear on all transactions of a similar type.

5. They facilitate the use of multiple copies.

The last purpose is important in any type of operation. The use of multicopy forms is especially valuable in a manual operation, however, since it greatly reduces clerical costs by eliminating the need to recopy data. In addition, specially prepared sets of forms can eliminate many handling steps such as aligning separate forms and inserting and removing carbons.

Multicopy forms are generally constructed in two ways. *Unit sets* are groups of forms containing an original and a number of copies assembled as a unit. Each unit is self-contained, instead of being part of a large pad, and may be completed by hand or by typewriter. *Continuous forms* are similar to unit sets in basic construction except that individual sets are joined in a continuous arrangement of accordion-pleated folds (Figure 4-1). The folds are perforated to facilitate separation of individual sets. Continuous forms may be processed on a variety of equipment including typewriters, punched card accounting machines, and computer print-out units.

The carbon handling problem is often solved by the use of one-time carbon paper. In this method, sheets of inexpensive carbon paper are interleaved between the various pages of multicopy forms. After a form has been completed, the carbon paper is separated and discarded. Carbon handling can be eliminated entirely by the use of carbonless paper. The preparation of copies without carbon is accomplished by chemically treating the reverse side of each form in a set, except the last, and the face of each form, except the original. When someone writes or types on the first sheet, the sensitized surfaces are pressed together. The reaction between the surfaces causes the writing on the original form to be instantly reproduced on all

Figure 4-1. Fanfold continuous forms with disposable carbon. (*Courtesy Moore Business Forms, Inc.*)

other forms in the set. Another type of paper will react to pressure and produce images without the need for contact with another specially treated surface.

Accounting Board (Figure 4-2)

The *accounting board,* or *pegboard,* makes it possible to record the various steps of a transaction simultaneously. The accounting board is a flat writing surface generally equipped with pegs along the edge of the board. The pegs are used to hold in place different forms that are especially designed with corresponding holes along the edges. Forms are planned so that moving a form one step in either direction changes its position one writing line in relation to the other forms on the board.

Boards vary in design. Some have a series of stationary pegs. Others are equipped with stationary pegs combined with pegs on a sliding holder used to place forms in proper writing position. One type of board uses clamps rather than pegs. In this system forms are held firmly by two clamps: a stationary rubber face clamp and a sliding clamp that is used to align the forms.

When a series of related forms are aligned with carbons between them, it is possible to record data on all of the forms at once by writing with pencil or ball-point pen. This method requires that the various forms be designed so that identical data appears in the same location on each form. Thus, data written on the top form also appears by means of carbons in appropriate spaces on the forms beneath. For example, in a payroll application a check can be prepared and the necessary entries can be made on the employee's earnings record and on the pay-

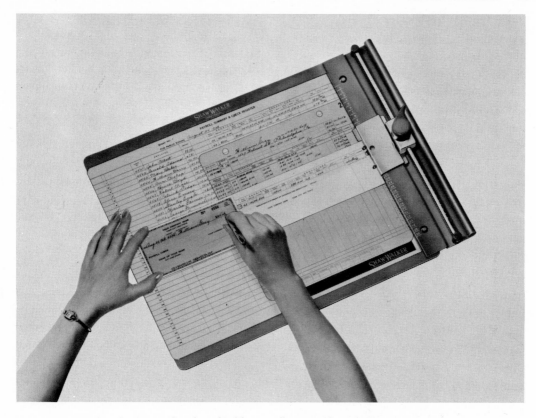

Figure 4-2. Accounting board with payroll setup. (*Courtesy Shaw-Walker Company.*)

roll journal all in one writing. A payroll journal page is first placed on the board where it remains. Next, a pay check and the proper employee's earnings record are positioned on the board. They are arranged so that as the check is completed and as the detailed earnings data is entered on a stub attached to the check, the entries are simultaneously recorded on the next vacant line of the employee's earnings record and on the payroll journal (Figure 4-2). This procedure is repeated until all pay checks are written. Thus as pay checks are prepared manually, two additional records are prepared automatically.

This principle is useful for other accounting work such as recording accounts receivable. In this case, a customer's statement and entries to the customer's ledger account and the sales journal can be completed at the same time. Additional applications include simultaneous preparation of checks and check registers, and checks and accounts payable records.

Accounting boards are an effective and yet relatively inexpensive method of handling accounting data. They eliminate a great deal of recopying that would otherwise be necessary in a manual system, and provide an efficient means of recording and summarizing data.

Document Control Register
(Figure 4-3)

Another method of handling accounting forms is the *document control register.* This is a metal box designed to hold and feed continuous multicopy forms. By means of a hand crank or electric drive, forms are automatically fed and positioned on a writing surface so that all copies can be completed simultaneously by hand. Carbon copies result from the insertion of roll carbon between the various copies. Forms feed across the sheets of roll carbon that are held in a fixed position from within the register. Carbonless forms may also be used.

Registers are manufactured in various models including manual and electric desk units and portable units used by outside salesmen. Some models contain a cash drawer that opens only when a form is issued or a key is used. As completed forms are ejected from the desk units or cash-drawer models, one of the copies is automatically retained in the register with the remaining supply of blank prenumbered forms. Thus, control is maintained over both forms and documents since the con-

tents of the locked register are accessible only to authorized persons with keys.

These devices can be used to record on the same type of form such transactions as cash sales, charge sales, cash received on account, credits and allowances on charge sales, and cash paid out. Document control registers improve manual operations by (1) reducing the time spent on paperwork, (2) increasing the accuracy of accounting work, and (3) facilitating the control of documents.

Typewriters

Although standard manual and electric typewriters are the most widely used methods of recording business data, automatic typewriters are of greater significance to data processing. Automatic typewriters can type complete letters, contracts, and documents of many types without human intervention. These machines may be operated singly or as a battery of machines automatically controlled from one source with an operator changing paper and inserting variable data as required.

Automatic typewriters are important to data processing not only because they can be activated by tapes or other media but also because of their ability to produce by-products such as paper tape. These by-products serve as input to computers and other machines.

Most automatic typewriters are controlled in one of three ways:

1. Punched Tape. Correspondence or data of any type may be punched into tape by the tape punch on the typewriter. When this master copy is fed through the typewriter's reader unit, the tape, in turn, mechanically activates the keys and controls the other machine operations necessary to type a document or letter (Fig-

Figure 4-3. Document control register. (*Courtesy Standard Register Company.*)

Figure 4-4. Automatic typewriter with tape reader at left and tape punch at right. (*Courtesy Dura Business Machines, Inc.*)

ure 4-4). The tape even stops the typewriter at predetermined places for the manual insertion of variable data such as names and addresses, prices, quantities, or parts specifications. Tapes can be filed for future use.

2. Magnetic Tape. This method is utilized in a machine developed by IBM which combines the company's Selectric typewriter with an electronic unit (Figure 4-5). As a typist operates the machine's conventional keyboard, the typed information is recorded and stored on half-inch wide tape mounted on a changeable cartridge. Each tape is 100 feet long and can hold 24,000 characters. The machine automatically locates stored typing by scanning tapes at the rate of 900 characters a second. Errors can be corrected or text can be revised by backspacing or repositioning the tape and typing over the unwanted information. The new information is automatically stored in place of the old.

Completed tapes can be used for the automatic production of documents at speeds up to 180 words a minute. As in the case of punched tape, magnetic tape can be coded to instruct the machine to stop typing at certain points so that variable information may be inserted manually. The machine will then continue to type the stored sections of the document, auto-

matically adjusting word spacing and line endings to the manual insertions.

3. Punched Cards. Automatic typewriters read edge-punched or standard punched cards mechanically or pneumatically depending upon the model. Individual cards may be prepared for standard paragraphs, lines of copy, or nonvariable data of any type. For example, a card containing product number and description might be punched for each stock item for use in the automatic preparation of purchase orders.

Automatic typewriters are especially useful in high-volume applications containing a great deal of repetitive data that can be typed automatically. For example, sales orders can be handled automatically by preparing the following input material:

1. A master tape or card for each customer, containing name, address, code, delivery instructions, and terms.

2. A master tape or card for each product sold by the firm, including description and code.

Figure 4-5. Magnetic tape "Selectric" typewriter. (*Courtesy International Business Machines Corporation.*)

Using these master inputs, an operator can easily prepare a sales order as follows:

1. The master input for the customer placing the order is first selected.

2. Inputs for each item being sold are then assembled.

3. These inputs are fed into the machine which automatically types the standard data on a sales order form and automatically stops at predetermined places for the manual insertion of variable data.

4. The operator manually types the variable data such as date, quantities, prices, totals, and discount. (Some automatic typewriters can be coupled with computing devices that automatically extend prices and compute totals.)

5. While typing the sales order, the machine can make a master input to be used in preparing production orders, bills of lading, and invoices.

Purchase orders can be handled in a similar manner. In fact, any procedure that involves the repetitive typing of standard data may be performed efficiently on an automatic typewriter at speeds up to 180 words a minute.

By using continuous forms or stationery combined with a special platen and automatic forms-feeding device, it is possible for an automatic typewriter to type a series of documents or form letters without the help of an operator.

Addressing Machines

Addressing machines provide another means of mechanizing the writing of repetitive data. The master form in this case may be an embossed metal plate, a paper stencil in a pressboard frame, or a card imprinted with chemical dye. Data is embossed in metal plates by a Grapho-

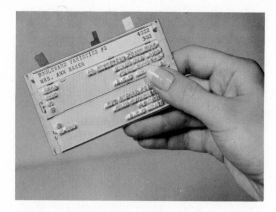

Figure 4-6. Embossed metal plate for addressing machine. (*Courtesy Addressograph Multigraph Corporation.*)

type machine. The embossed plates (Figure 4-6) are fed into the addressing machine together with the documents upon which the data is to be reproduced. The impression is made through an inked ribbon that is automatically inserted between the plate and the document as they are pressed together.

Stencil plates (Figure 4-7) may be pre-

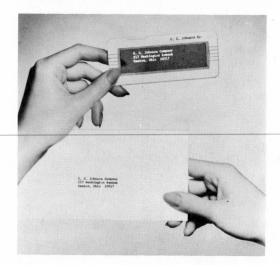

Figure 4-7. Addressing stencil. (*Courtesy Elliott Business Machines, Inc.*)

pared on a regular typewriter with the aid of a small attachment designed for this purpose. An inked impression is created by contact of a printing pad with the stencil. When this occurs, ink passes through the perforations in the stencil and is deposited on the document to be printed.

Master cards using the spirit duplicating principle are prepared by typing on a

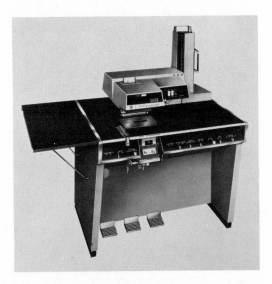

Figure 4-8. Addressing machine. (*Courtesy Addressograph Multigraph Corporation.*)

card with a backing strip containing a chemically treated surface facing the card. This produces a readable impression on the front of the card and a reversed dye image on the back. As the master passes through the addressing machine, the negative image contacts a moistened area on the mailing label and transfers a portion of the dye to form the address.

Addressing machine models range from portable hand-operated machines to large, high-speed automatic machines that can produce over a hundred impressions a minute (Figure 4-8).

The original purpose of these machines was to address envelopes, postcards, shipping labels or tags, and other mailing pieces. However, their use has been expanded to include many other procedures where the same names, addresses, descriptions, instructions, or other data must be written repeatedly on records, forms, or on lists. Records and reports that may be partially prepared by this method include: time cards, labor tickets, payroll checks, payroll registers and other payroll records, purchase orders, and routing slips.

Reproducing Processes

Organizations often require more copies of a document than can be provided by the use of carbon paper. In other cases it may be discovered sometime after the initial preparation of a document that additional copies are needed but are not available. A wide variety of duplicating and copying machines are produced today to meet both of these requirements.

Duplicating. *Duplicating* is a high-volume process that generally involves the preparation of master copies such as stencils and plates. These are used to reproduce copies by means of ink or the transfer of dye. Included in this category are the well-known stencil, spirit, and offset processes.

Stencil duplicating requires the preparation of a master consisting of a wax-coated fibrous sheet. Material to be reproduced is generally recorded on a stencil by means of a typewriter. Impressions are made by pushing aside the wax coating, thus exposing the porous fibers through which the ink can pass as the stencil is rotated on the drum of the duplicating machine.

The *spirit* process, often referred to

as the *hectograph* process, is one of the most widely used duplicating methods. This results from the fact that masters can be prepared easily by typewriter, handwriting, and punched card or computer printing devices. Masters can also be prepared through special processes by copying machines and microfilm reader-printers. The master used in this method is a sheet of smooth paper. To prepare a master, a sheet of special carbon paper containing aniline dye is placed under the master with the carbon side up. The pressure of typing or writing on the master sheet causes dye to be transferred from the carbon sheet to the back of the master, thus creating a reversed image.

The master is then placed on the rotating drum of a duplicator. As the drum rotates, copy sheets are fed into the machine and are moistened by a special liquid solvent as they enter. As a moistened copy sheet comes into direct contact with the negative impression on the master sheet, a small portion of the dye is transferred, thus producing a positive copy.

Offset duplicating is a versatile method producing a high quality of work. Offset is the process used most often in data processing for the reproduction of documents, reports, and other materials where quantity and appearance are important factors. Continuous form offset masters can be used with computer print out devices and other business machines to prepare data for reproduction.

There are two main types of offset duplicating: direct image and photo-offset. *Direct image* masters can be prepared by typing, printing, drawing, or tracing directly on a master sheet or plate with a grease-base ribbon, ink, or carbon paper. *Photo-offset* copy also may be typed, printed, drawn, or traced as in the direct method. However, the material is prepared on a layout sheet. Photographs, detailed charts, diagrams, or any other printed material may be added to the layout sheet. When the layout is completed, it is photographed and reproduced on an offset plate or master.

The completed master is placed around the master cylinder of the duplicator. As the cylinder rotates, the master contacts water and ink rollers which apply a thin film of water and grease-based ink to the master. The water adheres only to the nongreasy blank areas of the master. Since the greasy ink used will not adhere to a wet surface, it is picked up only by the grease-based letters and lines on the master. The inked image is then transferred from the master to another cylinder wrapped with a rubber blanket. In turn, the blanket transfers the image to copy paper that is fed into the machine and pressed against the blanket by an impression cylinder. Although this may seem to be a complicated process, the entire cycle takes place in a split second.

Copying. *Copying* is a process by which reproductions are made directly from the original by chemical reaction or photography. Because of the relative slowness and greater expense of the copying process, it has been used mainly for single-copy or low-volume reproduction of 12 to 15 copies. However, copying machines can also be used as a basis for high-volume duplication since most machines are capable of making masters for at least one of the duplicating processes. Consequently, by means of a two-step process: (1) a copying machine may be used to prepare a master from an original document, and (2) the master can then be used to produce multiple copies. This could occur immediately after the preparation of the original document or at some later time when the need arises.

The functions of copying and duplicating have been associated even more closely by the introduction of copier/duplicators. These are devices that combine the functions of copying and duplicating in a single system operating in an automatic cycle. Examples of such systems include electrostatic copying combined with offset, and heat-transfer copying combined with spirit duplicating. Depending upon the methods employed, high-speed copier/duplicators are able to produce up to 5,000 copies an hour.

There are many different kinds of machines and methods that can be used to produce exact copies of documents. However, the four principal categories of processes are: diazo, heat, wet, and electrostatic.

Diazo produces positive prints from originals that are transparent or translucent by passing light through the master onto paper coated with light-sensitive chemicals.

In the heat process, also called *thermography,* a sheet of special copy paper is placed on top of the document to be copied. Both sheets are then exposed to infra-red or heat rays which burn an image of the original document on the copy paper.

The wet process includes dye transfer, diffusion transfer, and stabilization. *Dye transfer* is a two-step process requiring the preparation of a matrix on which the original document appears as an image in dyelike substance. The image is then transferred to a copy sheet. *Diffusion transfer* requires a negative and a positive paper for each copy. *Stabilization* is similar to a photographic process but is much simpler and faster.

Electrostatic copying is an electrical dry process that uses fused powder or charged microstatic particles instead of ink to produce a permanent print. This is also referred to as the *xerographic* process. Two methods are used: transfer and direct. Transfer employs ordinary bond paper, and the direct process requires specially coated paper.

Although the office copier field has rapidly grown into a major industry, the regular use of copiers for data processing applications has been fairly limited. However, it appears that the need to copy continuous-form computer print out, already a copier application, will bring about a significant increase in the use of this technique for data processing purposes. Computer systems that print at the rate of over 2,000 lines a minute will produce only one copy. Consequently, as these systems become more prevalent copiers will have to be used to reproduce additional copies.

Microfilming is generally regarded as a technique for storing and retrieving data rather than as a copying method. However, paper copies of original documents can now be prepared conveniently by the use of microfilm. This was made possible by the development of reader-printers that not only project a filmed image on a screen but also produce a full-sized paper print of the projected document when a button is pressed (see Figure 4-27). Microfilm equipment can also be used to prepare offset and spirit masters from microfilm negatives for multiple reproduction of documents.

The following examples illustrate the value of microfilming not only as a storage technique, but also as a means of reproducing filmed documents for reference purposes.

At the end of each monthly accounting period, banks furnish customers with statements and the canceled checks that have been charged against their accounts.

Before returning the checks, however, many banks make microfilm copies of the front and back of each check. This provides a filmed record of each transaction which can be filed and retrieved later if needed. Claims of error can be settled by viewing microfilmed records or, if necessary, by producing a full-sized print of any check in question.

Many department stores follow a similar procedure in handling monthly charge accounts. In this case the problem of filing and retaining the original sales slips prepared by clerks is avoided by microfilming each sales slip. The original copies of sales slips can then be mailed to customers along with their monthly statements. This enables the customers to check the original slips against their statements. Again, if any question about the accuracy of an account arises, transaction records can be viewed or prints of sales slips can be prepared on a microfilm reader-printer.

MANIPULATION OF DATA

Sorting

One of the most common sorting operations in data processing is the arrangement of numerically coded data into proper sequence. In some cases it may be necessary to sort the same documents several times according to different classifications. For example, sales documents might be arranged by codes representing products, salesmen, or customers for various reporting or recording purposes. The following methods may be used to sort numerically.

Reverse-Digit Sorting. A fast method of sorting a large volume of data is the *reverse-digit method.* In this method, the digits are sorted from right to left. The

arrangement of a group of coded documents into numeric sequence would proceed as indicated in Figure 4-9. It should be noted that in the second and succeeding sorts the order of sorting must be from the bottom of the right-hand stack to the top of the left-hand stack. This is necessary to keep the digits in proper sequence. One of the main advantages of this method of numerical sorting is that data is never sorted into more than ten groups at one time regardless of the number of documents or number of digits.

Block Sorting. When the volume of documents is so great that it is inconvenient to complete all sorting in one operation, the documents may be separated into smaller groups by means of *block sorting.* To accomplish this the left-hand digits of the codes are sorted first. Sorting operations can then be performed on individual groups using the reverse-digit method. For example, in the preceding illustration of reverse-digit sorting, the codes beginning with "0" would be sorted first. This method allows the documents in the first group to be released for other processing while the remainder of the sorting is being completed.

Similar techniques can be used to facilitate the handling of alphabetic data. In this case, the first step might be to sort the documents into groups such as A–D, E–H, I–M, N–S, and T–Z. Each of these groups may then be sorted into single alphabetic units. The first group, for example, would be sorted into separate stacks for A, B, C, and D. Finally, papers in each alphabetic stack may be sorted into proper order. The first two steps of this procedure are known as *rough sorting*, and the last step is known as *fine sorting.*

Manual sorting is used extensively and can be performed quite efficiently with the aid of various devices. Some of

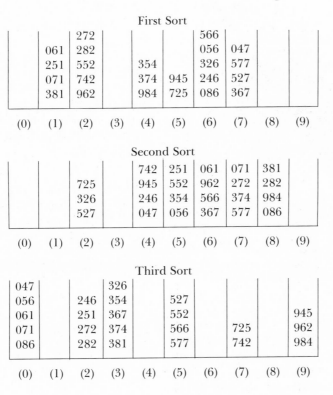

Original Random Sequence

725	071	251	945	326	061
984	086	527	246	282	566
381	367	742	552	354	272
374	962	577	047	056	

First Sort

(0)	(1)	(2)	(3)	(4)	(5)	(6)	(7)	(8)	(9)
		272				566			
	061	282				056	047		
	251	552		354		326	577		
	071	742		374	945	246	527		
	381	962		984	725	086	367		

Second Sort

(0)	(1)	(2)	(3)	(4)	(5)	(6)	(7)	(8)	(9)
				742	251	061	071	381	
		725		945	552	962	272	282	
		326		246	354	566	374	984	
		527		047	056	367	577	086	

Third Sort

(0)	(1)	(2)	(3)	(4)	(5)	(6)	(7)	(8)	(9)
047			326						
056		246	354		527				
061		251	367		552				945
071		272	374		566		725		962
086		282	381		577		742		984

Figure 4-9. Reverse-digit sorting.

the most commonly used techniques and devices are as follows:

Box Sort or Pigeonhole Sort. A sorting rack with tiers of boxes or pigeonholes is a simple yet effective method of sorting. The boxes can be labeled according to the number of alphabetical or numerical breakdowns required. Sorting racks may be placed along a wall or on the top of a table.

Leaf Sort. *Leaf sorters* or *sorting straps* consist of hinged leaves or dividers fastened to a long, narrow base that rests on a desk or table (Figure 4-10). Each leaf is labeled with a classification group. These devices are made in different sizes to handle any number of breakdowns and different sizes of documents. More elaborate models consist of complete units containing a work table and hinged leaves mounted on a horizontal rail. A person using a leaf sorter locates the proper leaf, lifts it with the left hand, and inserts the document under the leaf with the right hand.

Edge-Notched Cards. This sorting

Figure 4-10. Leaf sorter. (*Reprinted with permission by Remington Office Systems, Division of Sperry Rand Corporation.*)

system involves the use of specially designed cards with holes prepunched around the four edges. Cards are available in various sizes and shapes. Data can be transferred to these cards from other documents or entered directly by means of typewriter or handwriting. Thus, the cards can be used both as recording documents and as a sorting system.

The holes spaced along the edges of the card are used to code data. Numerical coding is accomplished by using a group of four holes for each digit in the code. These holes are assigned values of 7, 4, 2, and 1. Data is coded by notching appropriate holes with a hand notcher or electric key-operated notcher so that the holes become slots. By notching one hole or a combination of two holes in each group, it is possible to record all numbers from 1 to 9.

Zeros are not notched. Figure 4-11 shows the pattern of notched holes used to represent each digit.

Sorting of edge-notched cards is accomplished by running a needle through one of the holes in a group of cards. When the needle is lifted, the cards with the holes notched out fall free and the cards without notched holes remain on the needle (Figure 4-12). In this way the unnotched cards are easily sorted into a separate group. The following description shows how a group of cards can be arranged in sequence according to a single digit in four sorts:

1. Assume that the values notched and the order of ten cards before sorting are as follows: 7, 3, 4, 8, 6, 9, 5, 2, 1, 0.

2. The 1 position is sorted first which causes the 3, 8, 5, and 1 cards to fall. This results, of course, from the fact that all of these values are notched on the 1 position. These cards are placed in back of the cards remaining on the needle. The cards are now in this order: 7, 4, 6, 9, 2, 0, 3, 8, 5, 1.

3. The 2 position is sorted next which separates the 6, 9, 2, and 3 cards. Upon placing these at the back, the order is 7, 4, 0, 8, 5, 1, 6, 9, 2, 3.

4. Next the 4 position is sorted and the 4, 5, and 6 cards drop down and are

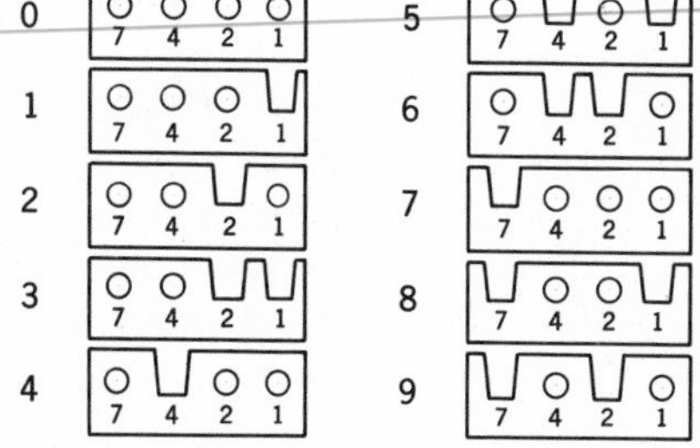

Figure 4-11. Coding system used to express digits on edge-notched cards.

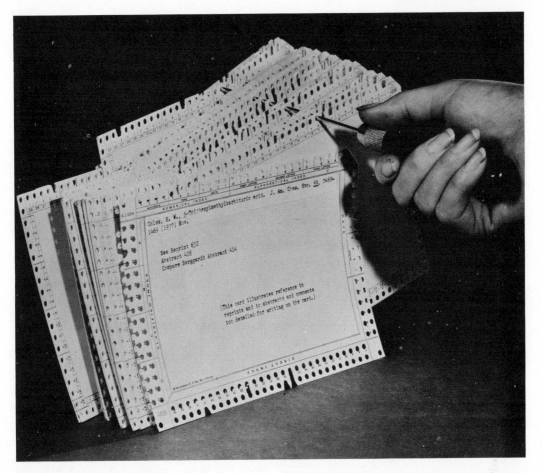

Figure 4-12. Sorting edge-notched cards with a needle. (*Courtesy McBee Systems, A Division of Litton Industries.*)

placed at the back. The order is now 7, 0, 8, 1, 9, 2, 3, 4, 5, 6.

5. Finally, the 7 position is sorted which separates the 7, 8, and 9 cards. These are placed at the back of the deck and the cards are now in numerical sequence.

This process is repeated for each digit in the code number. For example, to place code numbers ranging from 1 to 999 in sequence, the operation described above would be performed three times. The cards would be sorted through the four positions of the units field, the four positions of the tens field, and finally through the four positions of the hundreds field. When the quantity of cards to be sorted is relatively small, the sorting is done from units to hundreds. However, when the quantity is large, the cards may be block sorted into hundreds first in order to produce manageable batches. Sorting would then continue through the units and tens positions.

Coding methods other than the one described here may be used. Included is an alphabetical system in which letters can be expressed by a combination of the four numeral positions and a special NZ code position. Another method is direct coding in which a certain condition or identification can be expressed by notching a special hole designated for this purpose.

The edge-notched card system has been found useful for a number of applications including sales analysis, payroll, expense distribution, property records, inventory, billing operations, and bibliographic data. The system can be used by small, medium-sized, or large organizations. The basic units necessary to use the system are a hand punch, a sorting needle, and an alignment block. However, other equipment is available for larger operations. Included are hand-operated groovers for multiple notching; electric key punch devices (Figure 4-13); a device for selective multiple sorting; and a tabulating punch for automatic punching, tabulating, and printing on tape. The tabulating punch also calculates and punches eight-channel tape for further processing. Also available are converters that translate the notches along the perimeter of a standard edge-notched card into any five- to eight-

Figure 4-13. Key punch used to notch entire side of a card at a time. (*Courtesy McBee Systems, A Division of Litton Industries.*)

channel punched tape code or 80-column punched card code.

Calculating and Summarizing

Next to the typewriter, machines that perform arithmetic operations are probably the most widely used business machines. Included in this category are adding, calculating, and accounting machines. These machines have been used for many decades to assist in compiling statistics, figuring payrolls, preparing statements, and performing hundreds of other arithmetical functions.

Even with the increased use of more powerful electronic computers, these standard machines are likely to remain prevalent. One reason for this is that in large automated systems it is often more practical to perform minor tasks on standard machines. These machines may even be used to provide input for computers. Also, there will continue to be many offices that will be unable to justify the use of more expensive electronic computing devices.

These devices will be discussed under the following classifications: adding machines and printing calculators, key-driven calculators, rotary calculators, electronic desk calculators, and accounting machines.

Adding Machines and Printing Calculators (Figure 4-14). These devices will be considered together because of their similarity in construction and function. Both adding machines and printing calculators are made in ten-key models. The ten-key machine is designed for one-hand touch operation. Full numbers are entered by depressing the key corresponding to the left-most digit, then proceeding with all succeeding digits, including zeros, to the right. Adding machines are also made in full-keyboard models. The full-key-

Figure 4-14. Ten-key printing calculator. (*Courtesy Monroe International, Inc., A Division of Litton Industries.*)

board type has keys arranged in vertical columns with each column containing keys from one to nine. The capacity of a machine depends on the number of columns of nine keys.

Both adding machines and printing calculators print results on paper tape. Both add, subtract, divide, and multiply. There is a difference in the way multiplication and division are performed, however. The adding machine multiplies by repeated addition and divides by repeated subtraction, which are cumbersome and time-consuming procedures. Printing calculators multiply and divide automatically. In addition, some models carry and print credit balances, carry a constant, print decimals in answers to division calculations, do automatic squaring, and perform negative multiplication.

Since these machines can be used to record or list a series of figures, they also qualify as summarizing devices.

Key-Driven Calculators (Figure 4-15). These are full-keyboard machines

with columns of keys numbered from one to nine, similar to full-keyboard adding machines. The principal advantage of these machines is that figures are entered immediately as the keys are depressed. It is not necessary to depress a motor bar or wait for the machine to cycle. The cumulative results of operations are visible in a dial, generally below the keyboard. Some models have two answer dials. The front dial is for individual calculations. The rear dial is for automatic grand totals and net results. This eliminates writing intermediate results. Manual or electric models are available.

Although these machines are capable of performing all four arithmetic functions, they are especially suitable for rapid addition and multiplication which is accomplished by repeated addition. For this reason they are used extensively for checking, pricing, and extension work.

Rotary Calculators (Figure 4-16). Although these machines can perform all four arithmetic operations, they are used mainly for the rapid solution of complex multiplication and division problems. In a fully automatic machine, difficult prob-

Figure 4-15. Key-driven calculator. (*Courtesy Burroughs Corporation.*)

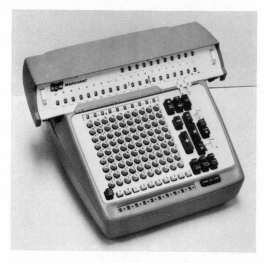

Figure 4-16. Fully automatic rotary calculator. (*Courtesy SCM Corporation.*)

lems can be solved by simply entering the factors and depressing the multiply or divide key. The machine does the rest. Semiautomatic machines have automatic division only.

Although most rotary calculators are nonlisting and indicate answers in dials, machines can be obtained with the tape feature. Rotary calculators are available with ten-key or full keyboards. They are easily activated by depressing various bars and keys. Manual models are activated by turning a crank. Calculators vary as to complexity, especially in the number of registers. A register is a device used to store a number that is usually displayed on a dial. Some machines have only one register, while others have as many as five. Each register holds a figure which can be applied to other registers for calculations. Some machines have split registers that enable the operator to clear one half and not the other, thus showing individual totals in one half of the register while accumulating them in the other half. Other special features include automatic squar-

ing, decimal placement, and carriage alignment; and fully automatic short-cut multiplication which requires fewer machine cycles and greatly increases the speed of multiplying.

Rotary calculators are widely used for statistical work where a large number of percentages and ratios are computed, for billing and payroll work, and for other operations that require extensive multiplication and division.

Electronic Desk Calculators. The electronic calculator is the most recent development in desk calculators and is by far the most sophisticated in its capabilities and operation. Although this is not a mechanical device, it is included here since its function is closely related to that of electromechanical calculators.

Electronic calculators have a number of advantages. Since they have no moving parts, they operate silently at speeds measured in milliseconds. As control keys are released, answers appear almost instantaneously above the keyboard on a cathode ray tube (Figure 4-17) or an illuminated window accommodating one row of figures. A main feature of this type of calculator is the automatic storage of intermediate answers so that they can be used as a basis for further calculations. In addition, constant figures such as constant divisors or multipliers may be stored. This enables the operator to retrieve constant or repeat factors for use in current computations by pressing a "recall" key, thus, eliminating manual re-entry.

Electronic calculators may have as many as ten registers, making possible the completion of a wide range of mathematical operations. Most electronic machines have automatic or "floating" decimal placement, and some have a key to select the number of decimal places desired and another to control rounding

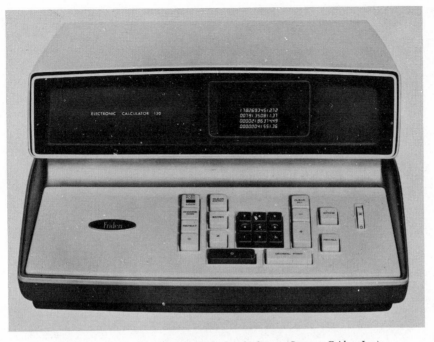

Figure 4-17. Ten-key electronic desk calculator. (*Courtesy Friden, Inc.*)

off or straight elimination of extra digits. Some models can be programmed to carry out the same mathematical routine repetitively upon manual insertion of the necessary figures for each new problem. Electronic printing calculators have all these advantages, plus the ability to record operations permanently on a paper tape. The characteristics of speed, silence, ease of operation, and versatility are certain to result in the further development and widespread use of electronic calculators.

Accounting Machines. This term covers a variety of equipment also described as bookkeeping, posting, and billing machines. In spite of the varied terminology, most of these machines belong in the same general classification. With the exception of certain special equipment that will be described later, most accounting machines are designed to prepare a number of basic accounting records such as journals, ledg-

ers, statements, and other records and reports. Although different models have characteristics that make them especially useful for certain applications, this does not mean that they cannot be used for other purposes.

The major classifications into which accounting machines may be divided are nondescriptive and descriptive.

Nondescriptive Machines (Figure 4-18). Since these machines are equipped with a numerical keyboard only, they cannot record descriptive alphabetical data. However, they do have a limited number of keys with dates and abbreviated symbols used to identify various transactions. Full-keyboard and ten-key models are available.

This type of equipment is used primarily for posting to the progressive balance-type of ledger card. This is a three-column record showing charges (debits), credits,

Figure 4-18. Nondescriptive accounting machine. (*Courtesy Burroughs Corporation.*)

and current balance. There are generally four operations in posting:

1. The old balance is recorded in the machine.
2. Charges are recorded.
3. Credits are recorded.
4. A new balance is automatically recorded as a result of horizontal addition and subtraction of entries.

The new balance on a ledger card is calculated by a mechanism called the *crossfooter*. As the term implies, it crossfoots (adds or subtracts) the account as the entries are made in the various columns across the sheet. The crossfooter is nor-

mally cleared when the balance of the account is printed.

Ledger cards, monthly statements, and journal records may be prepared on these machines in one operation by the use of carbon paper or special carbonless forms. Some machines complete several original records by the use of duplicate registers and a repeat print operation. Thus items and balances entered on one record are automatically repeat-printed on an adjoining record. Other machines have dual printing devices which print two records simultaneously.

One electronic model utilizes records with magnetic ink stripes on the back. By recording and reading data on these stripes the machine is able to perform automatically such functions as picking up old balances, aligning ledger cards, verifying account numbers, and recording new balances.

Nondescriptive machines may be used for various types of bookkeeping that do not require fully itemized descriptions.

Descriptive Machines (Figure 4-19). These machines are equipped with a typewriter keyboard in addition to an adding or computing mechanism. This makes them useful for bookkeeping work such as billing that requires the typing of names, descriptions, or other pertinent data. As in the case of nondescriptive machines, ten-key and full-keyboard models are available. Since these machines can also be used for nondescriptive work, it is apparent that they have a wider range of applications.

The versatility of both descriptive and nondescriptive accounting machines varies considerably according to size, basic design, and optional features. One of the most significant factors in determining the versatility of a machine is the number of registers it contains. *Registers* are the accumulating mechanisms in which the entries in various columns are accumulated. Most accounting machines can accumulate amounts entered in the vertical columns of a record while carrying totals horizontally across a page. At the foot of each column the machine can print the total of the accumulated amounts entered in that column. In effect, a multiple-register accounting machine is like a row of adding machines with the ability to add horizontally as well as vertically.

The number of columns of figures that a machine can handle is determined by the number of registers it contains. Obviously the more columns that can be re-

Figure 4-19. Descriptive accounting machine with ten-key numerical keyboard. (*Courtesy SCM Corporation.*)

corded and added simultaneously by a machine, the more flexible and useful it will be. For example, with a multiple-register machine it is possible to distribute data into various sales analysis columns in a sales journal, or into a number of expense distribution columns in an invoice register. Machines with as many as 25 registers are available.

Another feature that adds to the versatility of accounting machines is the ability to multiply. Machines with *computing features* can be used to extend prices on invoices; compute payrolls; calculate interest, dividends, and discounts; and perform many other jobs requiring similar calculations. The standard models of accounting machines do not perform multiplication.

The capacity of accounting machines has been extended even further by the development of a new class of electronic equipment (Figure 4-20). These machines combine the features of basic accounting equipment with advanced computer techniques. They are designed mainly for organizations whose needs are beyond the capabilities of conventional accounting equipment but that cannot justify the cost of large-scale electronic data processing systems.

Figure 4-20. Accounting machine with electronic computer characteristics. (*Courtesy International Business Machines Corporation.*)

This equipment contains such characteristics as magnetic core or disk storage; solid-state logic for computation, decisions, and comparisons; and auxiliary punched tape, punched card, or magnetic stripe ledger card input and output. The punched card or punched tape output may be used for later processing by punched card machines or computers. Data on punched tape may also be transmitted by wire to other locations.

Some accounting machines print in special optical fonts that can be read by scanning devices and converted into computer language. The newest accounting machines can also feed data directly to computers and retrieve information needed for a current posting operation.

Special Purpose Machines. *Window posting machines* are especially designed for posting and controlling transactions originating at a cashier's window. They can be used, however, for any application in which it is desired to make simultaneous entries on a customer's statement or pass-

book, ledger card, and journal. The journal in this case consists of a tape on which all transactions, subtotals, and totals are listed.

These machines have a numerical keyboard only. Transactions are identified by code numbers or letter symbols in certain applications. Instead of a movable carriage, machines of the type illustrated in Figure 4-21 have a flat printing table directly in front of the operator. Ledger cards and statements or passbooks are inserted between special guides on the table for printing.

Window posting machines are used extensively in hotels for posting guests' accounts. Data from source documents showing details of charges to guests are recorded on account cards by depressing keys to enter the amount and identify the nature of each charge. While producing account cards, the machine also prepares a detailed summary of revenue classified by room rentals, food, beverages, telephone, and so on.

These machines are also used to eliminate duplication of processing in businesses that receive large numbers of col-

Figure 4-21. Window posting machine. (*Courtesy National Cash Register Company.*)

lections on account from customers or depositors appearing in person. For example, banks and savings and loan organizations may keep customers' ledger cards in tub files at the cashier's window. When a payment is received, the cashier inserts the ledger card and passbook or bill into the machine and records the transaction on these records and the master tape simultaneously.

Bank proof machines are highly specialized accounting machines used to sort checks according to the banks on which they were drawn. These multiple-register machines perform a number of operations automatically when code and amount keys are depressed by an operator who verifies deposit slips against the items deposited. Depending on the model of machine, these automatic operations may include:

1. Sorting of checks into special compartments for various banks.

2. Itemized listing and summarizing of checks by bank.

3. Imprinting of amounts and transaction codes in magnetic ink for later processing by equipment that can recognize magnetic ink characters.

4. Endorsing of checks.

The discussion of general purpose and special purpose accounting machines in this section is by no means exhaustive. Other specialized machines exist but have been omitted because they are not of general interest. In addition, the machines discussed here have been adapted in many ways to make them useful for special purposes.

The importance of accounting machines may be summarized by noting that machines with multiple registers and the ability to multiply can perform five data processing operations: they can record data, sort it into various categories, cal-culate, summarize by taking columnar totals, and prepare reports and documents.

DATA STORAGE

Filing Systems and Equipment

Filing is the process of arranging and storing records systematically so that they may be located easily and quickly when needed. Filing is an extremely important part of any business or governmental operation. It is a means of safeguarding data needed in the current operations of an organization and of preserving data that may be needed for reference in the future.

The two basic methods of arranging data in files are *alphabetical* and *numerical.* Material in an alphabetic file may be arranged by *name* of individual or organization, by *subject,* or by *geographic area.* The basic form of numeric filing is the arrangement in sequence of documents that are numbered serially, such as invoices or checks. Data may also be arranged chronologically or by code numbers. Many variations of both alphabetic and numeric methods have been devised to meet special needs. It is not uncommon to find different forms of each method being used in the same organization to handle various types of data.

Filing is largely a manual operation. This is true even in systems where other operations are highly mechanized or automated. The nature of filing activity is such that materials to be filed are usually transported manually. Cabinet drawers and doors must be opened and shut, filing locations must be identified, and documents must be inserted and removed. Thus, two of the primary objectives in designing modern filing equipment have been to reduce as much as possible the physical effort required to file and remove data, and to increase the visibility of stored materials. The conservation of space is another important factor.

A wide variety of specialized filing equipment has been developed in recent years to meet virtually every filing need. Only a brief review of the major classes of equipment will be included here.

Vertical filing cabinets are the most widely used type of equipment. In this system materials are filed on edge in a vertical position. Letter-size and legal-size cabinets are available in single-drawer to six-drawer models for use in filing correspondence, forms, catalogues, and other materials. Card cabinets are made in various sizes to accommodate checks, job tick-

ets, address cards, index cards, punched cards, and other small items.

Shelf files are increasing in popularity because of several advantages. With this type of file, illustrated in Figure 4-22, records can be kept in less space, and there is good visibility and accessibility to files. Papers are held in folders placed on open shelves in a vertical position. These folders are similar to those used in vertical cabinets except that classification guides are placed on the outside edge of shelf folders. In vertical cabinets, guides are placed horizontally across the top of folders. Shelf files may be obtained with from one to ten shelves, and with or without slide-away doors.

Visible record files are designed so that cards or other records overlap in shingle

Figure 4-22. Wall of shelf filing cabinets. (*Courtesy Tab Products Company.*)

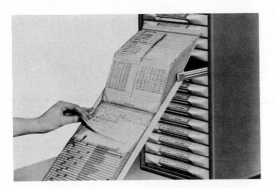

Figure 4-23. Visible record file. (*Reprinted with permission by Remington Office Systems, Division of Sperry Rand Corporation.*)

fashion. With this arrangement, part of each record containing a name, inventory description, or other index classification is always visible. This makes it possible to locate records quickly for posting or reference purposes.

Visible record files are available in a variety of forms. Most common is the horizontal-tray type, illustrated in Figure 4-23, which forms a sloping writing surface when pulled out of the cabinet. This allows entries to be made on records without removing the cards. Also available are a floor model, which holds trays in a vertical position, and a mechanized model. The latter model is equipped with an automatic electric elevator device. By depressing an appropriate key, any tray of cards can be brought into desk-height working position in a few seconds. Loose leaf binders are also used to hold cards in overlapping positions so that the index edge of each card is visible.

Rotary card files are another type of equipment stressing visibility and quick accessibility. These units consist of a series of shelves containing trays of record cards that are suspended somewhat like the seats on a Ferris wheel. By pushing a button on

the control panel of an electrically powered model, a desired tray, or set of trays, can be automatically located and positioned for use in a few seconds. Since the shelves can be revolved vertically in either direction, a selected shelf can reach the operator by the shortest route.

Rotary card files are available in a variety of models. These range from small models approximately fourteen inches wide to large models capable of storing up to half a million records in approximately 26 square feet of floor area (Figure 4-24). The degree of automatic control varies with the size and type of equipment.

Rotary shelf files operate in much the same manner as rotary card files. This system of power-driven rotating shelves may be used for any type of materials that can be stored on open shelves. This may include file folders, binders, account ledgers,

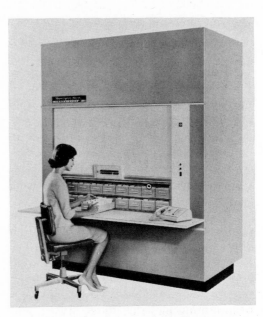

Figure 4-24. Automated card storage and retrieval unit. (*Reprinted with permission by Remington Office Systems, Division of Sperry Rand Corporation.*)

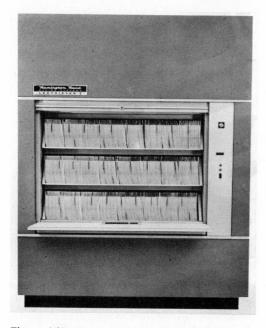

Figure 4-25. Automated rotary shelf file. (*Reprinted with permission by Remington Office Systems, Division of Sperry Rand Corporation.*)

or electronic data processing tapes. This method has the advantage of concentrating a large volume of records in one area. For example, one model has a capacity of up to 160,000 letter-size documents (Figure 4-25).

Also available is a horizontal rotary unit consisting of a large outer shell containing a series of circular shelves that revolve in the same manner as a Lazy-Susan food tray.

Other types of files are available for special needs. Included are tub files that house removable card trays of various sizes; ledger trays for machine-posting applications; mechanized random filing systems for cards; desk wheel files; and reciprocating files that slide forward and backward for an operator who works from a seated position.

Microfilming

The use of microfilm to place records in storage and to retrieve information from stored records has greatly increased in recent years. Microfilming is the process by which records are photographed at a very high rate of speed and at great reduction in size. About 98 per cent of the space normally required to store records is saved when they are microfilmed. For example, it is estimated that one microfilm storage unit will hold the photographic images of the contents of 160 standard four-drawer file cabinets. In addition to saving space, microfilming has the following advantages:

1. The cost of filing equipment needed to store materials is greatly reduced.

2. The cost of labor in maintaining files is also reduced considerably.

3. Since microfilmed records occupy so little space, they can be retained indefinitely by the department using them. This eliminates the inconvenience of having to retrieve records from a storage warehouse if they are needed for reference at a later date.

4. Filmed duplicates of important records can be prepared and stored in a separate location for protection against fire or other loss.

5. With certain types of equipment, full-sized paper prints of microfilmed documents can be made easily in less than a minute.

A basic microfilm system consists of a camera, a storage unit, and a reader for projecting images. Two types of cameras are used in microfilming: the *rotary* and the *planetary*. Rotary cameras are designed primarily for office use in recording transaction documents and business records. They are similar to office copying machines in appearance and methods of operation. Documents to be photographed are fed into a slot, either manually or automatically. They are conveyed through the machine on a revolving belt and are photographed as they pass an aperture. Documents leave the machine on the same side they entered and are stacked in a tray. Pictures are usually taken on rotary cameras with 16-millimeter or 35-millimeter film similar to that used in motion-picture cameras.

Planetary cameras are designed for filming engineering drawings, blueprints, maps, and open books. In this system a camera is mounted on a post so that it can be raised or lowered. The camera faces down on a lighted table where the material to be photographed is placed. Most planetary cameras use 35-millimeter or 70-millimeter film.

Microfilmed data is usually stored in the same form in which it was originally exposed: in long strips mounted on reels. However, the unit record concept of data processing has resulted in the increased use of cut, rather than roll film. In this approach, individual pictures called frames are clipped from the roll and mounted on specially designed cards. One type of card, the *aperture card,* contains a rectangular die-cut opening designed specifically for mounting a film image (see Figure 5-7). It is possible to obtain special camera-processors that photograph documents up to 18 by 24 inches and automatically produce developed films mounted on an aperture card in less than a minute.

Groups of closely related documents, such as pages of a report or book, may also be filmed on a single sheet of micro-film called *microfiche.* A microfiche can be any size, but is usually a standard 3×5, 4×6, or 5×8 inches, or the standard punched card size, $3\frac{1}{4} \times 7\frac{3}{8}$ inches. The number of images varies with the size of the card. For example, a 4×6 inch card holds 98 images, and a standard punched card size holds up to 90 images. The microfiche form generally has a legible heading (Figure 4-26).

Since microfilm cannot be read with the naked eye, it must be magnified in some way. Special microfilm readers are used for this purpose. Machines called *reader-printers* not only project an image on the screen but also produce a full-sized paper print of the projected document when a button is pressed (Figure 4-26).

In spite of the advantages of microfilm in records storage, the most rapid advancement in the use of this technique is in the field of *information retrieval.* Retrieval of microfilmed information may be accomplished in several ways. Microfiche forms are usually stored in card files from which they can be easily retrieved manually, although the index information is often stored in a computer. If aperture cards are used, they also may be manually indexed, coded, filed, and retrieved like cards in any other card file. However, in large installations, identifying data may be punched into the cards by a card punch machine. Cards can then be arranged and retrieved by a punched card sorter.

A system of this type has been installed at the U.S. Patent Office. To make patent records quickly and easily accessible, 3.25 million patents have been microfilmed. Microfilm images of up to eight pages of patent are contained in a single 35mm frame mounted in the aperture of a standard size punched card. More than 19 million pages of patents have

Figure 4-26. Microfiche card and microfilm reader-printer. (*Courtesy Minnesota Mining and Manufacturing Company.*)

been microfilmed and stored in this manner, thus, making it possible to fill within a few hours the more than 25,000 orders for patent copies received each day.

As copies of the patents are ordered by patent number, the film card is retrieved from the file and a facsimile of each page is photo-enlarged to letter size from the microfilm image. The aperture-card files are also used to fill orders for copies of patents in microfilm form for the patent files of industry, universities, libraries, and individuals. This system has resulted in a great saving of space and equipment as printed copies of patents previously had to be filed numerically in pigeon-holes covering nearly $2\frac{1}{2}$ acres in the basement of the Department of Commerce building.

A number of highly sophisticated systems combining microfilming with electronic equipment have been developed in recent years. They are designed to accommodate a large volume of microfilmed documents, perhaps in the millions. These systems vary in concept, but in general they provide for automatic retrieval of specified microfilms, projection of the documents, and printing of reproductions — all in less than a minute.

LIMITATIONS OF MANUAL AND MECHANICAL DEVICES

In spite of the importance of manual and mechanical methods and devices and the remarkable improvements that have increased their usefulness, they still have certain shortcomings. Some of these are:

1. Human beings participate to some extent in most of the operations of recording, copying, classifying, sorting, calculating, and summarizing which creates the possibility of error at each point in the cycle.

2. The limited communication that exists between many manual and mechanical devices prevents the smooth flow of data from one operation to the next. Again, human intervention in transcribing or otherwise handling data creates the risk of error.

3. The transfer of data from one location or step to another is sometimes cumbersome and time consuming and can result in misplacement of data.

4. Although manual and mechanical devices and methods have made impressive gains in speed and efficiency, they still fail to meet the demands of large organizations for the rapid processing of vast amounts of data.

The limitations outlined above have been overcome to a great extent by punched card and electronic data processing systems to which the remainder of this book will be devoted.

Review Questions

1. What are the advantages of printed forms?
2. Describe the manner in which the accounting board makes it possible to record the various steps in a transaction simultaneously.
3. In what ways do document control registers improve manual operations?
4. What are the three ways in which most automatic typewriters are controlled?
5. Describe the technique of preparing sales orders with an automatic typewriter.
6. Explain the difference between the duplicating and copying methods of reproducing.
7. What are the three principal methods of duplicating? Describe the unique characteristic of each.
8. Identify and describe the four principal copying processes.
9. Describe the process of combining the use of copying and duplicating machines to produce multiple exact copies of documents.

10. Describe the process of reverse-digit sorting.
11. What is the purpose of block sorting? How is it accomplished?
12. Describe the pattern of notched holes used to represent each digit from 1 to 9 on an edge-notched card.
13. How many sorts would be necessary to place in sequence a group of edge-notched cards with code numbers ranging from 1 to 99?
14. What are the main categories of adding and calculating machines?
15. Explain the difference between descriptive and nondescriptive accounting machines. What are the principal applications of each type?
16. Describe a typical application of a window posting machine.
17. What are the advantages of shelf files? How do they differ from vertical filing cabinets?
18. Describe the operation of rotary card files and rotary shelf files?
19. What are the advantages of microfilming?
20. What are the nature and function of an aperture card?
21. Describe a microfiche card.
22. What are the limitations of manual and mechanical methods and devices?

5

PUNCHED CARD
UNIT RECORDS

The ultimate in office aids would be a machine that could accept documents in their original form as input, and which would produce other documents and all necessary reports as output. For such a machine to be applied, from a practical standpoint, the following obstacles would have to be overcome:

1. Variations in the size and shape of documents to be processed.

2. Variations in methods used to enter data on documents.

3. Variations in the types of transactions included on a single document.

Much of the success of punched card data processing results from the fact that it has overcome these three obstacles.

The problem of variable sizes and shapes has been solved by using cards of standard dimension and weight. This facilitates the mechanical selection and conveyance of cards through machines one at a time.

Mechanical data processing also requires that data be recorded in a form that can be read by machines. One of these forms is the punched hole which can be read mechanically or electronically to accomplish automatically the various steps in data processing. Once data are punched (recorded) in a card, the card is a permanent record; the data can be used over and over again for different purposes.

The sorting and further processing of transactions according to classification is difficult if one record contains transactions of several different types. For example, in a sales situation, it might be desirable to summarize transactions in three ways: by salesman, by customer, and by product. Records could easily be sorted and totaled according to customer and salesman since only one customer or salesman would be identified on each record. However, the summarizing of sales by product would be difficult if each record listed sales of several different products. This problem can be solved by recording the sale of only one type of product to a customer on each record. This technique is known as *unit record* data processing.

The basic principle of unit record data processing is that only one type of transaction is recorded on a single card. Thus, a sales invoice listing three different products would require three punched cards to record all the information. Each card would contain the information pertaining to one type of product as well as other basic data such as customer name and number, salesman number, invoice number, and date.

Since each card contains information about a single type of transaction, all similar items can be easily grouped for statistical, inventory, or other purposes. Furthermore, as each card is an independent record, it can be easily added to or removed from a file of records. The unit record principle can be applied to any business situation where the isolation of individual transactions or grouping of similar transactions is desirable.

CARD STRUCTURE, MATERIAL, AND CODES

The punched card is familiar to almost everyone because of the frequency with which it appears in such forms as payroll checks, insurance premium notices, utility bills, magazine subscription notices, money orders, and cashiers' checks.

Standard cards measure $7\frac{3}{8}$ inches by $3\frac{1}{4}$ inches and are cut from durable card stock to provide strength and long life. Cards must meet rigorous specifications in dimension and quality to assure accuracy of results and the proper functioning of machines. To facilitate card handling and machine processing, cards can now be obtained with round corners.

Cards are often ruled and printed with column headings to assist in reading the information that is recorded by punched card machines (Figure 5-1). To aid in identification, cards are available in a number of solid colors or with special stripes. Cut corners at the upper right or upper left provide another visual aid in detecting cards that may be backward or upside-down in the deck. Corner cuts also provide a means of visually distinguishing two classes of data. For example, accounts receivable transactions might be recorded on cards with left-corner cuts and accounts payable transactions on cards with right-corner cuts.

All of the physical characteristics just mentioned are recognizable by humans and are designed for that purpose. With one exception, they are not detectable by machines and have no influence on the machine processing of cards. The exception consists of a special device that can be installed on certain machines to mechanically recognize corner cuts.

80-Column Card (Figure 5-2)

The standard punched card is divided into 80 vertical areas called card columns. These are numbered 1 to 80 from the left side of the card to the right. Each column is then divided into 12 punching positions called rows, which are designated from the top to the bottom of the card. Each column of the card is used to accommodate a digit, a letter, or a special character.

Digits are recorded by holes punched in the appropriate positions of the card from 0 to 9. The top three punching positions of the card (12, 11, and 0) are called the *zone* punching positions. (The 0 punch may be either a zone or a digit punch.) In order to accommodate any of the 26 letters of the alphabet in one column, a combination of a zone and a digit punch is

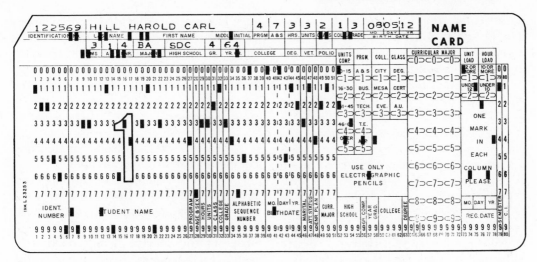

Figure 5-1. 80-column card printed to assist in reading data.

used. The various combinations of punches which represent the alphabet follow a simple pattern. The first nine letters of the alphabet, A to I, are coded by the combination of a 12 zone punch and one of the digit punches from 1 to 9. Letters J through R are coded by an 11 zone punch and one of the digit punches 1 to 9. S through Z are coded by a 0 zone punch and one of the digit punches 2 to 9. The 11 special characters are recorded by one, two, or three punches in a column.

In addition to providing one of the punches necessary to record alphabetic characters in the punched card, the zone punches also serve to provide control over special operations and machine functions. For example, an 11 zone punch in a designated column of a card field may be used to identify the figure recorded there as a

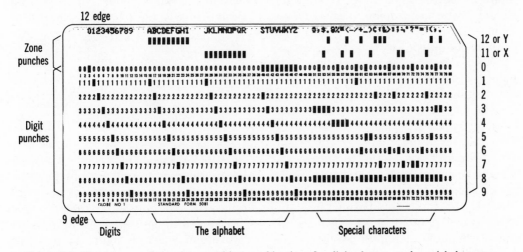

Figure 5-2. 80-column card showing punching combinations for digits, letters, and special characters.

negative item, that is, one to be subtracted. The 11 and 12 zones also provide the necessary punching to actuate special devices and machine functions. When used for purposes of machine control the 11 zone is known as an *"X"* punch and the 12 zone as a *"Y"* punch.

In accordance with the designated rows on a punched card, the top edge is known as the "12-edge," and the bottom edge is known as the "9-edge." Some processing operations require that cards be fed into the machine 12-edge first; others require that cards be fed 9-edge first. Instructions also may specify that cards are to be placed in the feed hopper "face up" or "face down" meaning that the printed side of the card faces in the direction indicated.

Codes

A code is a system of writing in which numbers or letters, or a combination of both, are used arbitrarily to condense lengthy data into a smaller space. This technique is a necessity in recording data on punched cards because of the maximum capacity of 80 columns. In addition, codes provide a convenient means of identifying and distinguishing data for classification purposes.

Although a variety of coding techniques are used, most codes are constructed by using numerals to represent original data. The use of numerals in place of state names is a clear example of the advantage of using codes. Fourteen columns would be required to record the longest state name. Five columns would be necessary even if abbreviations were used. However, by numbering the states alphabetically from 1 to 50, only two columns would be required, leaving three to twelve columns available for other data.

The use of codes to express many classifications of data not only saves space, but also increases efficiency by reducing the number of card columns to be processed for certain items of data.

Coding Methods

The following are some of the most commonly used coding methods.

Sequence Codes. In this method, numbers are assigned to a list of items in a straight sequence, starting with one, without regard to the classification or order of the subjects being coded. It is useful for any short list of names, products, or accounts where the only object is the application of simple code numbers and where arrangement of data is not important.

Group Classification Codes. In this system, major and minor classifications are coded in groups of thousands, hundreds, and tens. Various categories under each classification are represented by the assignment of succeeding digits. This method is suitable for coding all classes of products, accounts, and items in which division of groups under a major heading is the primary objective. For example,

2000	Packaging materials
2100	Paper
2110	Kraft
2111	Plain
2112	Laminated
2120	Tissue
etc.	

Block Codes. This method involves the assignment of numbers in sequence by groups of various sizes other than tens, hundreds, and thousands. Instead, a block can consist of any quantity of numbers necessary to cover the items in a particular classification. In the original design of the code, a few blank numbers may be left in each block to provide for later additions.

Significant Digit Codes. In this method, all or part of the numbers are related to some characteristic of the data such as weight, dimension, distance, capacity, or other significant factor. This type of coding reduces the work of decoding by providing a code number that can be read directly. This method is suitable for coding long lists of items where complete decoding would be laborious or impractical. The following example illustrates the application of significant digit coding to packaged products so that the last two digits represent package weights.

1000	Sugar, sacks
1005	5-pound sacks
1010	10-pound sacks
1020	20-pound sacks
1050	50-pound sacks

Mnemonic Symbols. This term is used to describe the assignment of numbers and letters in a combination that is mnemonic or memory aiding to the eye or to the ear. For example, IL-12-W-39L might be used to describe an Ivy League model suit made of 12-ounce worsted fabric in size 39 long. Mnemonic symbols are used extensively for coding whenever it is deemed an advantage to be able to memorize code designations.

CARD DESIGN

Cards are divided into segments called *fields*. Each field consists of one or more consecutive columns which are reserved for punching a specific type of data. The length of a field is determined by the maximum length of the particular type of data to be recorded in it. For example, in a field designed to accommodate prices, a five-digit field would be planned if it were known that no price would exceed $999.99. (Dollar signs, commas, and decimals are not punched in the card.) To permit the recording of prices from $1,000.00 to $9,999.99, a six-digit field would be required.

Figure 5-1 illustrates a card that contains both alphabetic and numeric data punched in fields of various sizes.

Because the amount of data that can be entered on a single card is necessarily limited, it is essential to select the most important data to be included. The data to be recorded on a card will, of course, be largely dependent on the requirements of the reports and documents that will be prepared from them. Although the specific nature of data varies greatly, they will generally be of three types.

1. *Reference data,* such as invoice number, page number, identification number, or date, which indicates the original source of the data and its relationship to other data.

2. *Classification data,* such as occupation, organizational department, or geographic area, which permits the grouping and summarizing of comparable data.

3. *Quantitative data,* such as price, hours, quantity, or weight, to be used in performing calculations.

The arrangement of data is not invariable, but it is considered desirable to place reference data on the left side of the card, classification data in the center, and quantitative data on the right.

BASIC TYPES OF CARDS

Choice of the type of card to be designed can normally be made only after completing a preliminary study of reports, procedures, and machine operations that are anticipated. This study will dictate the type of card that will be most satisfactory. Cards are usually of eight basic types:

1. *Transcript cards* are manually punched by a card punch operator from data previously recorded on other documents. The operator reads a source document and transcribes the data into punched holes by depressing keys on the card punch keyboard. Any card that is completely punched from an original source document, such as an invoice, is known as a transcript card (Figure 5-1).

2. *Dual cards* are punched by a card punch operator from data written on the card itself; thus the card serves a dual purpose as source document and punched card. Such cards are used in inventory situations where quantities may be recorded on a card in pen or pencil and later punched into the same card.

3. *Mark-sensed cards* are automatically punched from electrically conductive pencil marks recorded in designated places on the face of the card (Figure 5-3). To re-

Figure 5-3. Mark-sensed card showing electrically conductive pencil marks. (*Courtesy International Business Machines Corporation.*)

cord data on mark-sensed cards the user marks certain positions on the cards with an electrographic pencil. The cards are later fed into a punched card reproducer which senses the marks and converts them into punched holes.

4. *Stub cards* can be adapted to situa-

Atlantic Richfield Company

Statement
Please keep this stub for your record.

Terms: Net due upon receipt of statement.
A service charge will be added for past due balances.

Checks may be made payable to ARCO

| Account Number | Past Due Balance |

Service Charges

| Time Payment Installments Incl. in current charges | Current Charges |

| Date | Statement Amount |

| Check number | Date |

A gasoline tax table is on reverse side

RICHFIELD

Print any change of address

Atlantic Richfield Company
Wilshire Blvd. at Mariposa
P. O. Box 76850, Sanford Station
Los Angeles, California 90005

Please
return this portion
with payment

Please pay
this amount

Figure 5-4. Short card. (*Courtesy Atlantic Richfield Company.*)

Figure 5-5. Continuous form cards. (*Courtesy Moore Business Forms, Inc.*)

tions requiring tags, labels, or stubs. Stub cards are available with a perforated stub on either the right or left end which when torn off leaves a regular card. Stub cards

are often prepared in sets for such uses as monthly loan payments, and are bound into booklet form providing notation stubs similar to those in checking account books.

5. *Short cards* are standard-sized cards with perforations which make it possible to detach stubs. Although the cards are of less than standard size after the stubs have been removed, machines can be adapted to process them. These cards can be used in the same manner as stub cards (Figure 5-4).

6. *Continuous form cards* are attached at top and bottom so that they can be processed in standard form-feeding devices. Such cards may be prenumbered and prepunched for document control purposes (Figure 5-5).

7. *Multipurpose cards* are cards in which several related card designs are combined into one card format. For example, the card shown in Figure 5-6 serves three different functions in a home loan application. These are represented by three printed horizontal sections comprising:

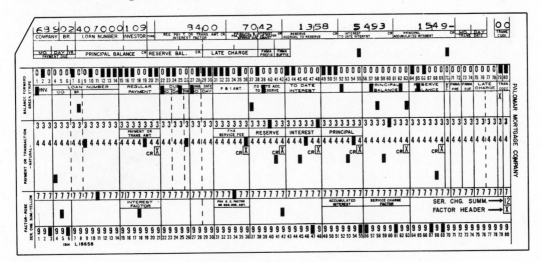

Figure 5-6. Multipurpose card.

(1) Balance forward data.
(2) Payment or transaction data.
(3) Interest factor data.

As a result of this type of design, a data field used for common identification data such as "Investor," columns 1 to 3, is applicable to all three sections.

8. *Aperture cards* are standard-sized cards with rectangular die-cut openings on the right side designed for mounting microfilm frames. The filmed images contained in the frames can be read on the screens of viewing devices and copied from one card to another. Enlarged paper copies of the images can also be made from the cards. Information identifying the images can be key punched and interpreted on the cards which can be reproduced, sorted, and collated on punched card equipment. Aperture cards are used for the storage and retrieval of a wide range of filmed documents including business records, library materials, and engineering drawings (Figure 5-7).

CLASSIFICATIONS OF PUNCHED CARD RECORDS

Unit records are generally classified in accordance with their primary function within the data processing organization. The major types may be defined as follows:

Master Records

Master records generally contain permanent data that does not change until it is affected by a transaction. Balance-forward cards that constantly reflect the status of an item in inventory are master records.

Detail Records

Detail records contain data relating to individual transactions or changes of status. Such records are used to update the master record. Transaction records reflecting an issue or receipt of material are an example of detail records.

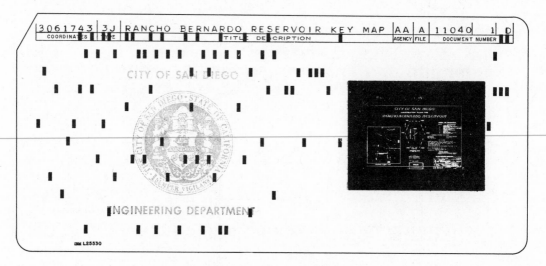

Figure 5-7. Aperture card.

Summary Records

Summary records are prepared as a result of totals accumulated by a punched card accounting machine. The totals are automatically punched into unit records by the summary punch machine. Summary records can subsequently be used to prepare other reports which do not require the detail that provided the basis for the totals.

Thus the basic unit in punched card data processing is the card which contains numerical and alphabetical data in the form of punched holes. These holes may be read electrically by machines which respond by performing automatically the various record-keeping operations such as printing, adding, subtracting, multiplying, dividing, comparing, sorting, and summarizing, all of which will be explored in detail in the following chapters. Before proceeding, however, let us consider the means by which machines are able to read and interpret punched holes.

READING THE PUNCHED HOLE

Most punched card machines contain a brush or brushes that read the holes punched in a card. As the card passes through the machine it passes between an electric contact roller and a reading brush (Figure 5-8). As long as there is no hole punched in the column the brush is reading, the card acts as an insulator to prevent the brush from making contact with the roller. When a punched hole reaches the brush, contact is made between the roller and the brush through the punched hole. An electrical impulse then flows from the roller through the brush, and can be directed by control panel wiring or by internal machine circuits to perform a specific function.

Machines ascertain which hole is punched in the card by the time at which contact is made between the contact roller and the brush. If cards are to be fed 9-edge first, and an impulse is available just after the 9-edge has passed between the

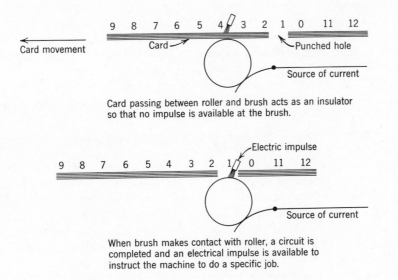

Card passing between roller and brush acts as an insulator so that no impulse is available at the brush.

When brush makes contact with roller, a circuit is completed and an electrical impulse is available to instruct the machine to do a specific job.

Figure 5-8. Schematic of brush reading numeral 1.

roller and the brush, this punch is recognized as a 9. If the impulse occurs a little later, it is recognized as an 8. This is true of all the positions that can be punched into a card. The machine recognizes which punch is being read by the amount of time that passes from the moment the leading edge of the card passes under the brush to the moment when the brush drops into a punched hole and an impulse is created. Most punched card machines contain 80 brushes, one for each column of the card, so that the entire card may be read as it passes through the machine.

THE CONTROL PANEL

Since most punched card machines can perform more than one function, there must be a way to direct each machine so that it will know what function it is to perform and how to handle the information it receives from punched holes. A control panel is provided with most IBM machines so that they may be instructed to produce the desired results. The control panel or board can be removed from, or inserted into, the machine when desired. The panel has many small holes, called *hubs,* into which wires with special tips can be inserted to control the functions of the machine. Each of these hubs has a specific function (Figure 5-9).

A control panel is comparable in principle to a telephone switchboard which produces a signal light that tells the operator which line an incoming call is on. After the operator answers the call, she plugs the cord into a hub on the board that is internally connected to the desired line. In this way the operator completes an electrical circuit to establish a telephone connection. A control panel accomplishes the same thing by enabling electrical cir-

Figure 5-9. Wired control panel for an accounting machine. (*Courtesy International Business Machines Corporation.*)

cuits to be completed through wires inserted into the panel (Figure 5-10). When a control panel is fitted into place on the machine, each inserted wire connected to a jack makes contact with one of the metal contacts on the sub-panel of the machine itself. In this way the external wiring completes the desired circuits (Figure 5-11).

Control Panel Wiring

A detailed description of the control panel for each model of equipment and of the details for wiring each panel for the great variety of jobs and functions that can be performed would be too voluminous and beyond the scope of this text. Therefore, in this chapter the discussion will be confined to the major techniques of control panel wiring.

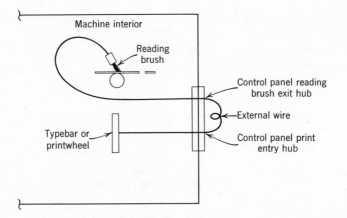

Figure 5-10. Electrical impulse directed to a typebar through a wired control panel.

There are two types of control panels in general use. Control panel wires with specially designed tips are used with both of these types. One type of panel has metal prongs that touch the stationary internal contacts when the panel is fitted into the machine (Figure 5-11). The external wires plug into these prongs in order to complete the internal circuits in the machine (Figure 5-12).

The second type of panel consists only of hubs into which the external wires can be inserted. In order to complete the circuit, the wires have longer and larger tips that pass through the control panel and

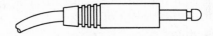

Figure 5-12. Control panel wire.

press directly against the prongs on the stationary machine panel. This is known as a *self-contacting wire* (Figure 5-13). Each of the two types of wires is available in various colors to distinguish different lengths.

Hubs representing circuits that emit impulses to wires are called *exits*. Impulses may be from reading brushes or may be generated by other conditions originating within the machine. Hubs representing circuits that accept impulses from wires are called *entries*. The impulses wired from exit hubs into entry hubs may activate such machine operations as printing, punching, comparing, adding, or subtracting.

Hubs may be single, or two or more hubs may be internally connected to each

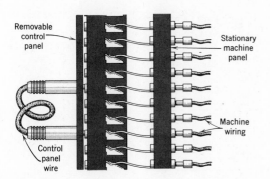

Figure 5-11. Jack contacts on a control panel.

Figure 5-13. Self-contacting control panel wire.

other. If they are internally connected they are called *common hubs*. Common hubs are identified on the face of the control panel by lines connecting them (Figure 5-14).

Figure 5-14. Common hubs.

If these hubs are exit hubs, identical impulses are available out of all hubs connected by a line. Likewise, an impulse wired externally into any one of connected entry hubs is directed into the machine and is available out of all hubs common to each other.

Figure 5-15. Bus hubs.

Bus hubs are also several hubs connected to each other; however, they are neither entry nor exit hubs. Even though they are connected to each other, bus hubs are not connected to any internal machine circuit. Bus hubs permit the distribution of impulses from one source to two or more functions (Figure 5-15).

Control Panel Diagrams

Diagrams of the hub layouts on each type of machine control panel are available (Figure 5-16). These are used to plan the actual wiring of control panels and to

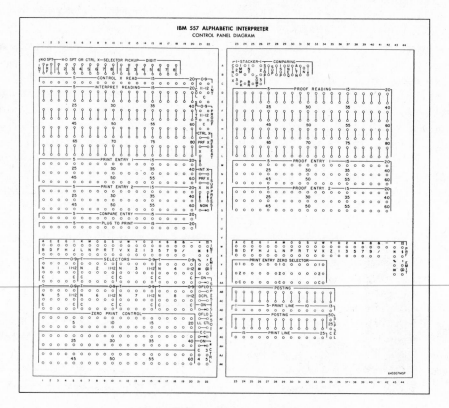

Figure 5-16. Control panel diagram.

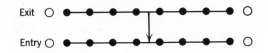

Figure 5-17. Use of single lines to represent wiring of entire fields.

keep a record of control panel setups. To make diagrams more legible and uniform, certain rules are followed in completing them. For example, different colored pencils may be used to diagram wiring that makes the machine perform different functions. Thus wiring for the printing function might be a different color on the diagram than the wiring for addition.

The hubs of an entire field are filled in and connected with a horizontal line. Actually this line may represent any number of individual wires in the control panel itself. However, a single line is used to make the diagram easy to read. Al-

though only one line is shown on the diagram, it should be understood that an eight-position field requires eight wires in the actual control panel, i.e., one wire from each exit to each entry hub (Figure 5-17).

When it is necessary to cross lines on a diagram, two techniques may be used: (1) one line may be broken, or (2) one crossing line may be drawn with a half circle or tunnel. This prevents the possibility of following the wrong line to the entry hub. Both techniques are illustrated in Figure 5-18.

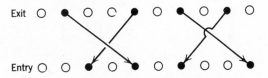

Figure 5-18. Techniques of drawing crossed lines on a wiring diagram.

Review Questions

1. What is the basic principle of unit record data processing?
2. What are the advantages of recording only one transaction on each card?
3. Explain the ways in which cards may be visually identified.
4. The standard punched card is divided into how many vertical columns? How many units of data may be recorded in one column?
5. Describe the two punching positions of a card. How are they used?
6. Which is the 9-edge of a card? Which is the 12-edge?
7. What punches would be needed to record the following letters, digits, and special characters on a card? 2, 7, C, H, L, R, S, V, &, $, %.
8. Why is it necessary to use codes in recording data on punched cards? Explain how it would be possible to identify the State of Massachusetts on a punched card by using two columns only.
9. What are the most commonly used coding methods? Describe each one briefly.
10. What three types of data are generally entered on a punched card?
11. What is a card field? How is the length of a card field determined?
12. Describe the following: (a) transcript cards, (b) mark-sensed cards, (c) aperture cards.
13. Describe the three major types of punched card records according to their primary function within the data processing organization.
14. Describe the process by which machines read the holes that are punched in cards.
15. Discuss the purpose and operation of the control panel.

6

PUNCHED CARD
RECORDING FUNCTIONS

To facilitate the presentation of punched card machine functions and applications, this chapter and Chapters 7 and 8 are based mainly on equipment manufactured by the International Business Machines Corporation, producers of the majority of the punched card equipment used in the United States. The basic functions performed by UNIVAC and other makes of equipment are comparable, however, even though the machines vary considerably in mechanical detail and methods of performing operations.

CARD PUNCHING

The first step in punched card data processing is the recording of data in a form that can be read by machines. This is accomplished by punching data into cards.

The most commonly used method of converting source data into punched cards is by the use of a manually operated machine called a *card punch,* also referred to as a *key punch.* The operator of this machine reads a source document and transcribes the information into punched holes by depressing keys on a keyboard. The machine feeds, positions, and ejects cards automatically, thus enabling the operator to concentrate on depressing the proper keys in the correct sequence.

IBM 29 Card Punch

Although many IBM 24 Card Punches are still in use, the most commonly used card punch today is the IBM 29 shown in Figure 6-1.

Two types of keyboards are available on the IBM 29 as well as on other card punch machines. One keyboard, which resembles the keyboard on a ten-key adding machine, records numeric data only (Figure 6-2). The other, which is similar to the keyboard of a typewriter in appearance and operation, will record alphabetic as well as numeric data (Figure 6-3). On

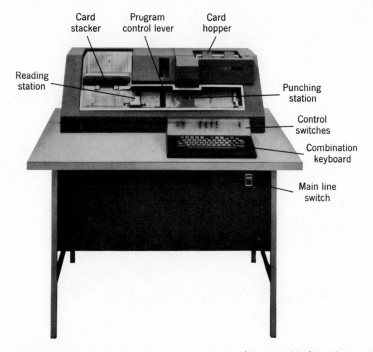

Figure 6-1. IBM 29 Card Punch. (*Courtesy International Business Machines Corporation.*)

the combination keyboard a group of keys controlled by the right hand serves for punching numbers as well as letters (Fig-

Figure 6-2. IBM 29 or 59 numerical keyboard. (*Courtesy International Business Machines Corporation.*)

ure 6-4). The shift from numbers to letters is made manually by a shift key or automatically by the program unit which will be discussed later. Since most card punching is composed of numerical data, the numerical keys on the card punch are conveniently grouped for one-hand, ten-key operation. This eliminates the more difficult two-hand motions that would be required if the numerical keys were arranged as they are on a typewriter.

Cards are fed into the card punch from the card hopper located at the upper right of the machine. The hopper has a capacity of about 500 cards which are deposited face forward with the 9-edges down. A card is fed from the front of the hopper to the card bed by depressing the feed key. The first two cards to be punched must be fed by key depression, but all other cards in the hopper can be fed au-

Figure 6-3. Close up of keyboard and switches on IBM 29 Card Punch. (*Courtesy International Business Machines Corporation.*)

tomatically by setting an automatic feed switch.

Cards are punched at the first of two stations along the card bed. Punching operations are normally started by feeding two cards into the card bed at the right of the punching station. As the second card is fed, column 1 of the first card is automatically positioned at the punching station. While the first card is being punched, the second card remains at its right. When column 80 of the first card passes the punching station, the second card moves into position at the punching station, and the next card in the hopper feeds down to the card bed. It is also possible for a single card to be inserted in the card bed by hand and then positioned at the punching station by depressing the register key.

After the punching of a card has been completed, the card proceeds from the punching station to the reading station, which performs an important function.

Some of the information in a group of cards is often repetitive. Duplicating these holes from card to card by manual punching would be time consuming. Instead, the duplication can be performed automatically by depressing a *duplicate key* which results in the automatic punching of the holes that are being sensed in the corresponding column of the preceding card at the reading station.

The cards at the punching and the reading stations can be backspaced as far as desired by holding down the backspace key located below the card bed, between the reading and punching stations. The backspace key is also used to release the keyboard when it becomes locked. This may happen if keys 1 to 18 are depressed while the keyboard is in numerical shift.

The operator is able to determine the position of cards passing the punch and read stations by means of a column indicator which identifies the next column to

Key Number	ALPHABETIC		NUMERIC	
	Card Code	Graphic	Card Code	Graphic
1	11-8	Q	12-8-6	+
2	0-6	W	0-8-5	—
3	12-5	E	11-8-5	)
4	11-9	R	12-8-2	¢
5	0-3	T	0-8-2	0-8-2
6	0-8	Y	12-8-7	|
7	12-1	A	none	none
8	0-2	S	0-8-6	>
9	12-4	D	8-2	:
10	12-6	F	11-8-6	;
11	12-7	G	11-8-7	¬
12	12-8	H	8-5	'
13	0-9	Z	none	none
14	0-7	X	0-8-7	?
15	12-3	C	8-7	"
16	0-5	V	8-6	=
17	12-2	B	11-8-2	!
18	11-5	N	12-8-5	(
19	11-7	P	12	&
20	0-1	/	0	0
21	0-4	U	1	1
22	12-9	I	2	2
23	11-6	O	3	3
24	11-1	J	4	4
25	11-2	K	5	5
26	11-3	L	6	6
27	11-4	M	7	7
28	0-8-3	,	8	8
29	12-8-3	.	9	9
33	11	-	11	-
40	8-4	@	8-3	#
41	0-8-4	%	0-8-3	,
42	11-8-4	*	11-8-3	$
43	12-8-4	<	12-8-3	.

The remaining keys, numbers 30–32, 34–39, and 44–48 control the various functions of the card punch as follows:

30. *Numeric (Numeric Shift)*
31. *Alpha (Alphabetic Shift)*
32. *Dup (Duplicate)*
34. *Rel (Release)*
35. *Feed (Card Feed)*
36. *Skip*
37. *Reg (Card Register)*
38. *Aux Dup (Auxiliary Duplicate)*
39. *Prog Two (Program Two)*
44. *Mult Pch (Multiple Punch)*
45. *Prog One (Program One)*
46. *MC (Master Card)*
47. *Error Reset*
48. *Left Zero*

Figure 6-4. IBM 29 Card Punch and 59 Verifier combination keyboard and keyboard chart.

be punched. Column numbers appear on the base of a drum which turns synchronously with the cards being punched and read. The indicator greatly facilitates the location of a particular column while spacing forward or backward.

Certain repetitive operations can be accomplished automatically by means of a device called the *program unit.* This is a simple and flexible device that permits programs for automatic card punching operations to be easily prepared and inserted (Figure 6-5). The program unit controls automatic skipping over columns not to be punched, automatic duplicating of repetitive information, and the shifting from numerical to alphabetic punching positions and vice versa. These actions are controlled by the *program card* and are determined by the manner in which the card is prepared. A separate program card must be prepared for each different series of cards being punched.

The program card is punched with code numbers that indicate to the machine what to do as each column of the card passes the punch dies. The program card is wrapped around the program drum which is inserted at the top of the machine. The holes in the program card are detected by tiny starwheels that ride along the top of the card as it rotates in unison with the card being punched. When a starwheel drops into a hole in the program card, it causes the card punch to perform a number of steps or operations as follows:

1. An 11 punch in the program card causes the machine to start skipping columns automatically. The length of the field to be skipped is indicated by consecutive 12 punches immediately following the 11 punch.

2. A punch in the 0 position of the program card starts the automatic duplication of data recorded in the same columns of the punched card located in the reading station of the card punch. Again, the length of the field to be duplicated is indicated by the number of consecutive 12 punches following the 0 punch.

3. A 1 punch in the program card causes the keyboard to shift to alphabetic position so that alphabetic rather than numeric characters will be recorded. During duplication of alphabetic information, the 1 punches permit automatic spacing over blank columns.

Whenever a 1 punch is absent from the program card, the keyboard is automatically placed in numerical shift.

Figure 6-6 illustrates a program card that provides for the following operations:

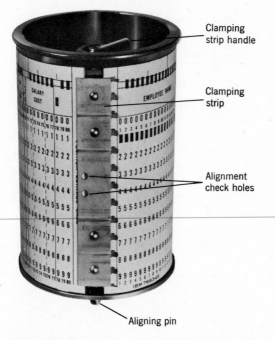

Figure 6-5. Program drum for IBM 29 Card Punch and 59 Verifier. (*Courtesy International Business Machines Corporation.*)

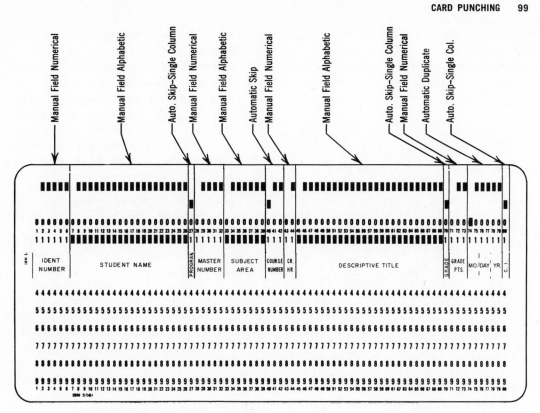

Figure 6-6. Program card showing the use of the 12, 11, 0, and 1 punches.

Columns	Operations
1–6	Numerical data is punched by the operator.
7–26	Alphabetic data is punched by the operator.
27	This column is skipped.
28–32	Numerical data is punched by the operator
33–39	Alphabetic data is punched by the operator.
40–42	These columns are skipped.
43–44	Numerical data is punched by the operator.
45–69	Alphabetic data is punched by the operator.
70	This column is skipped.

Columns	Operations
71–73	Numerical data is punched by the operator.
74–79	Numerical data from the card at the reading station is automatically punched.
80	This column is skipped.

After each card passes the reading station, it is fed into the card stacker located at the upper left of the machine. Cards are stacked 12-edges to the rear, face up. Cards are deposited in the stacker, which holds about 500 cards, in the same sequence as they were punched. The main line switch is turned off automatically when the stacker is full.

The Type 29 Card Punch illustrated in Figure 6-1 contains features that simplify and speed the task of converting source data into punched cards. Such features include:

1. Automatic left zero insertion. This function automatically inserts preceding left zeros under program control. The operator merely keys in significant digits, depresses the left zero bar, and the data is punched with the proper number of left zeros. With automatic left zero insertion the three fields of the card illustrated in Figure 6-7 can be punched with only eight keystrokes.

2. Expanded character set. This feature permits punching of any of the 64 characters with one keystroke. Characters included in the set are the letters A through Z, digits 0 through 9, and special characters as shown in Figure 6-4.

3. Two-level programming. The 29 Card Punch provides for the placement of two programs in a single program card. This feature allows the operator to select program 1 or 2 as the normal program at the start of the card. The operator may shift between program levels at any point during the punching operation.

The printing model of the 29 Card Punch prints data along the top of the card as holes are being punched.

Portable Punches

In addition to the card punch machine, a number of manual punches are available. Included is the IBM *Port-A-Punch,* a device that enables on-the-spot punching of data which later may be machine processed. The Port-A-Punch uses special cards with prescored punching positions that may be punched out with a pencil point or special instrument. The basic device includes a punching board and a clear plastic template perforated with guide holes to assure proper positioning of the punching instrument (Figure 6-8).

There are other portable punches available for capturing data at its point of origin, some of which are electrically powered. Most can be conveniently placed on a desk and others are small enough to be held in the hand.

VERIFYING

The incorrect punching of cards means that wrong information will be included in reports or that time must be spent in searching for correct data on

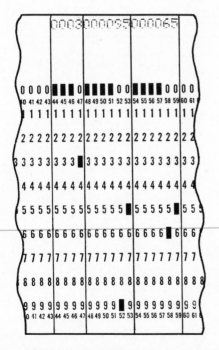

Figure 6-7. Punched card illustrating automatic insertion of zeros in selected card fields.

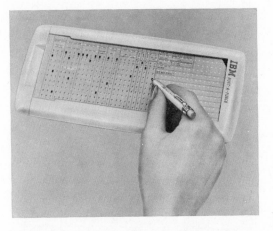

Figure 6-8. IBM Port-A-Punch. (*Courtesy International Business Machines Corporation.*)

source documents and repunching cards. It is, therefore, important to verify the accuracy of original card punching. The most commonly used method is machine verification. Machine verification involves the use of a machine similar to the card punch except that it is equipped with a sensing device to read holes rather than with a punching mechanism.

Visual verification is possible if cards are punched with a machine that prints. In this case, the printed data at the top of the cards can be visually compared with the data on source documents to assure accuracy.

IBM 59 Verifier

The features of the IBM 59 Verifier are comparable to those of the IBM 29 Card Punch and the operating techniques are almost identical.

After a group of cards have been punched by a card punch operator, they may be given to a verifier operator to be checked for accuracy. Using the same source documents in the same sequence, the verifier operator duplicates the key

strokes of the card punch operator, but in the verification process no holes are punched. Instead, a sensing mechanism consisting of 12 pins determines the location of the holes that were previously punched. If the verifier operator strikes the same key that the card punch operator used to punch a certain column, the card proceeds to the next column to be checked. If, however, the verifier operator strikes a different key, the machine locks and a signal light indicates that an error occurred either in the original or in the verifying keystroke. The verifier operator has two more chances to obtain agreement between the verifying and the original keystrokes. If there is no agreement after three attempts, the top edge of the card is notched in the column being checked (Figure 6-9). This identifies the column in which the error occurred so that the card punch operator can prepare a new card to replace the one punched in error. All cards that pass the verifier test are notched on the right edge of the card opposite the 1 row and are then ready for the next processing step (Figure 6-10).

AUTOMATIC PUNCHING

The need for repetition is a basic characteristic of record keeping. For example, identical dates are entered repeatedly on data processing records originating on the same date. Records of common origin must contain identical source location data. Information used for one purpose may need to be duplicated for other purposes. Partial changes may have to be made on entire sets of cards or original records may have to be partially changed on a continuing basis in order to keep them up to date. When records are maintained in punched card form, these repe-

Error Notch

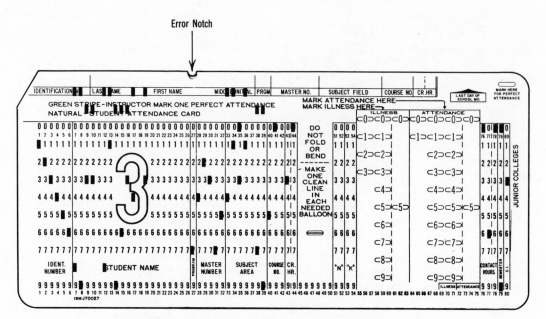

Figure 6-9. Punched card with error notch over card column 27.

Final OK Notch

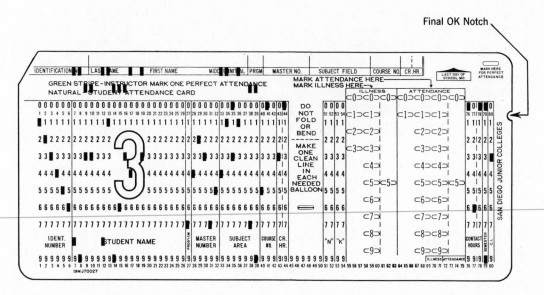

Figure 6-10. Verified card with final OK notch on the right side.

titious operations can be performed by *automatic punches* or *reproducers* (Figure 6-11).

Automatic Punching Operations

Automatic punches are capable of performing the following operations.

Reproducing. All or part of the data contained in a card may be automatically punched into another card. The data may be punched into the same location as on the original card or fields of data may be rearranged into a different sequence. The accuracy of this operation can be simultaneously verified by a comparing feature which proves agreement between originals and reproductions. Differences are automatically detected and cause the machine to stop reproducing.

Gangpunching. Data recorded on a master card can be transferred automatically to each detail card that follows it.

Emitting. By means of a special device the reproducer can be wired to automatically punch into any position of any column without the necessity of reading a comparable punch from another card.

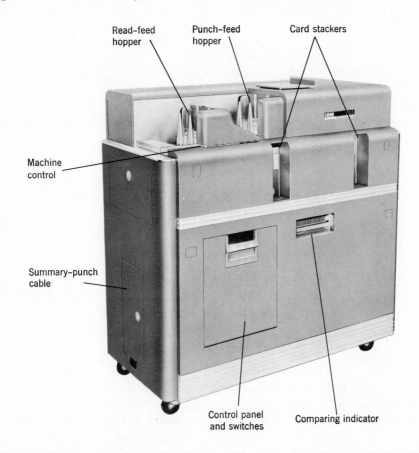

Figure 6-11. IBM 519 Document-Originating Machine. (*Courtesy International Business Machines Corporation.*)

This repetitive punching can be performed in conjunction with any other operation.

Summary Punching. When the automatic punch and punched card accounting machine are connected by a cable, totals that have been accumulated in the accounting machine from detail cards can be punched into a total card. These total or summary cards can then be used for various purposes without the need for repeated processing of the detail cards.

Mark Sensing. Data recorded on a card by electrically conductive pencil marks can be detected by the machine and automatically converted into punched holes.

Double-Punch and Blank-Column Detection. A special device makes it possible for the machine to detect blank columns which should be punched, or columns with two punches where there should be only one, as with numerical data.

End Printing. Reproducers also may be equipped to interpret some of the data punched in a card and print it across the end of the card. This operation can be done simultaneously with reproducing, gangpunching, summary punching, and mark-sensed punching.

Automatic Punches

There are four types of IBM automatic punches: the 514, 519, 528, and 549.

The IBM 514 Reproducing Punch is similar in appearance to the IBM 519 Document-Originating Machine illustrated in Figure 6-11. The Type 514 is designed to perform most of the functions that will be described later for the Type 519.

The IBM 528 Accumulating Reproducer is a high-speed punch that performs addition and subtraction in combination with any of the operations of gangpunch-ing, reproducing, and summary punching.

The IBM 549 Ticket Converter is used primarily for the purpose of converting or transcribing sales data from ticket stubs to punched cards. The Type 549 can also perform the functions of gangpunching, summary punching, and editing for double punches and blank columns.

The IBM 519 Document-Originating Machine illustrated in Figure 6-11 may be obtained with features that enable it to perform the functions of reproducing, gangpunching, emitting, summary punching, mark sensing, end printing, and double-punch and blank-column detection. The machine contains two feed units, the reading unit and the punching unit. Cards may be fed from one or both of the feed units depending on the operation being performed. The relation of the two units to each other and the sequence in which cards pass the operating stations in the two units are shown in Figure 6-12. Each feed unit holds approximately 800 cards which are normally placed in the feed hoppers face down with the 12-edges toward the throat. (The throat is the opening from the hopper into the machine.) Card feeding is initiated and ended by depressing the start key and the stop key. Once feeding is started, it continues automatically until a hopper becomes empty, the stacker is filled, cards fail to feed, or the comparing unit signals an error. All operations are performed at the rate of 100 cards a minute.

As cards are fed into the reading unit, they first pass the six read-X brushes, which can be set to read any six columns of the card. The purpose of these brushes is to read X (11 zone) punches that control the reading of selective information from the card. At the next station are 80 reproducing brushes corresponding to the 80 columns of the punched card. A card

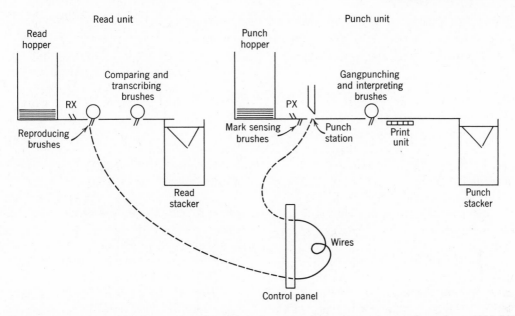

Figure 6-12. Schematic showing paths of cards during reproducing operation performed on IBM 519 Document-Originating Machine.

passes these two stations on a single cycle as it goes through the reading unit. The last station is a set of 80 comparing and transcribing brushes which represent the next cycle in the reading unit.

Cards fed into the punching unit first pass the six X brushes which can be set to read any six columns of the card. They read X (11 zone) punches which identify the master cards that control the subsequent punching and feeding operations. If the machine is equipped with a mark-sensing device, the mark-sensing brushes are the next station in the punching unit. These brushes read the marks on the card and punch the corresponding positions in the same card.

The next station is the punching mechanism which consists of 80 punch dies corresponding to the 80 card columns. Because the top of each card passes the punch dies first, the 12 position is the first to be punched. All 12 positions are

punched simultaneously, the 11 positions are punched next, and so on through the last or 9 positions. A card passes these three stations during one cycle in the punching unit. The next stations, the 80 gangpunching and interpreting brushes and the print unit (if end printing is installed), are the last stations in the punching unit.

When both feed units are being used, the cards feed simultaneously from both units. The comparing feature, if incorporated in the machine, provides for comparing the punching in two cards to see if it has been properly performed. Comparison may be made between one card in the reading unit and another card in the punching unit, or between cards at the two stations in the reading unit. When there is a difference between the punching in the two cards being compared, the compare light goes on, the machine stops, and the comparing indicator points out the position in which the error occurred. The compare light may be turned off by pushing the restoring lever on the comparing indicator.

The summary punch cable allows the document-originating machine to operate in conjunction with the accounting machine. This operation permits total or new-balance cards to be prepared automatically and simultaneously as summary totals are recorded on the accounting machine. When the machine is not being used in a summary punch operation, the cable must be disconnected and returned to the receptacle.

The automatic operation of the document-originating machine is made possible through the wiring of a control panel which fits into a rack on the front of the machine.

Applications

A description of several typical applications may help to illustrate the usefulness of automatic punches.

When data is recorded in the form of holes in a card, the Type 514 or 519 machine can transfer some or all of the data to another card. For example, if a company plans to participate in a fund-raising campaign, it may decide to prepare a deduction authorization card for each employee who wishes to contribute (Figure 6-13). The employee's name, department number, employee number, and shift number are available from his employee master card (Figure 6-14). By using the Type 514 Reproducing Punch or the Type 519 Document-Originating Machine, this data can be reproduced in the deduction authorization cards from the employee master cards at the rate of 100 cards a minute (Figure 6-15).

The wiring necessary for the IBM 519 Document-Originating Machine to accomplish the reproducing of the information from the employee master card (Figure 6-13) to the deduction authorization card (Figure 6-14) is shown in Figure 6-16. The following descriptions are numbered to correspond with the wiring illustration.

1. These connections cause the name from the employee master card to be re-

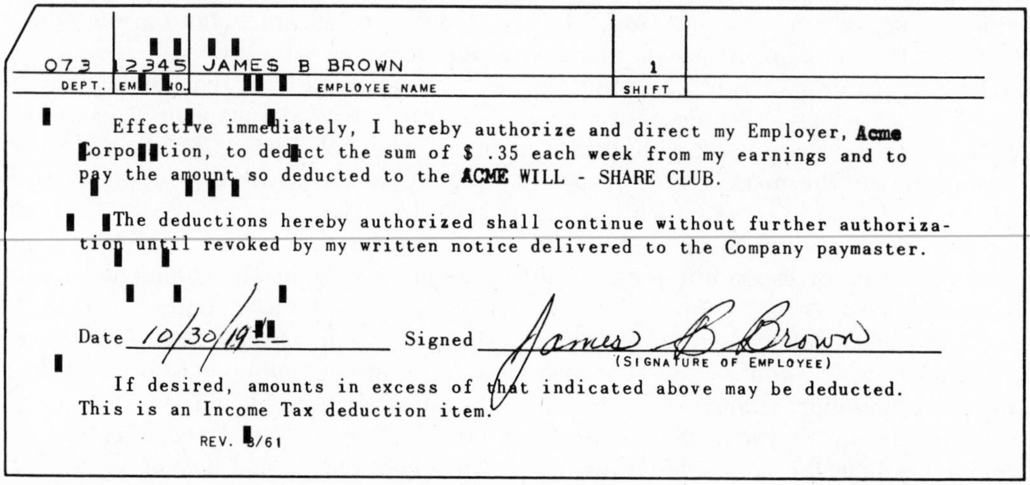

Figure 6-13. Deduction authorization card containing data automatically reproduced from another card.

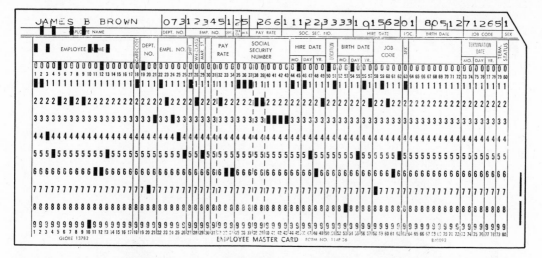

Figure 6-14. Employee master card used to reproduce name, employee number, department number, and shift into card shown in Figure 6-13.

produced into the deduction authorization card. The reproducing brushes read the information from the employee master card, and the punch magnets cause the data to be punched into the deduction authorization cards. The connection in the upper left-hand corner represents a wired switch that causes the reproduction function to take place.

2. After the employee name has been punched into the deduction authorization card, the employee name is read by the gangpunching and interpreting brushes. This information is transmitted to the comparing unit.

3. After the employee name has been read by the reproducing brushes for the purpose of reproducing (outlined in No. 1 above), it is again read by the comparing and transcribing brushes. This information is also transmitted to the comparing unit. Connections 2 and 3 permit the machine to compare the employee name punched in the employee master card with the employee name as punched in the deduction authorization card. If the information in the two cards agrees (compares), the machine process continues. If an error has been made in the reproducing process, the machine stops and indicates by means of an error light and indicators where the error has occurred.

The wiring for the reproduction of department number, employee number, and shift would be accomplished in the same way.

Another example of punching data into a card from a source that already contains some of the required data is shown in Figure 6-17. With the exception of the semester ending date, all the initial data required on student grade cards such as the one illustrated can be reproduced from the student class cards. Transferring names, identification numbers, program, master number, subject area, etc., from the student class cards to the grade cards is accomplished in the following manner:

1. The student class cards are placed in the feed hopper of the reading unit,

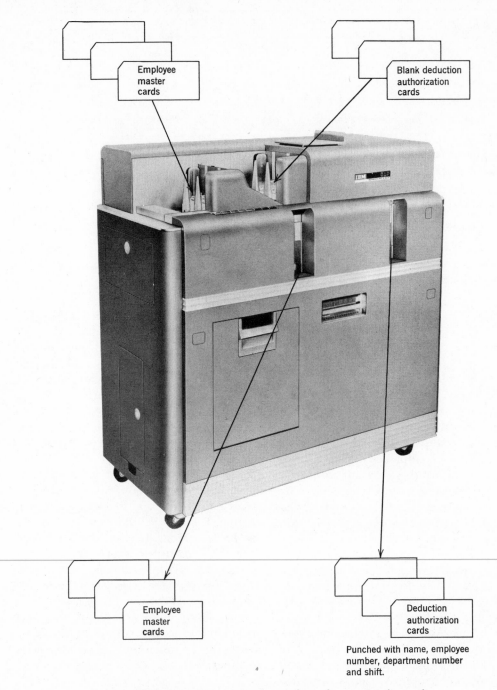

Employee master cards

Blank deduction authorization cards

Employee master cards

Deduction authorization cards

Punched with name, employee number, department number and shift.

Figure 6-15. Reproducing operation performed on automatic punch.

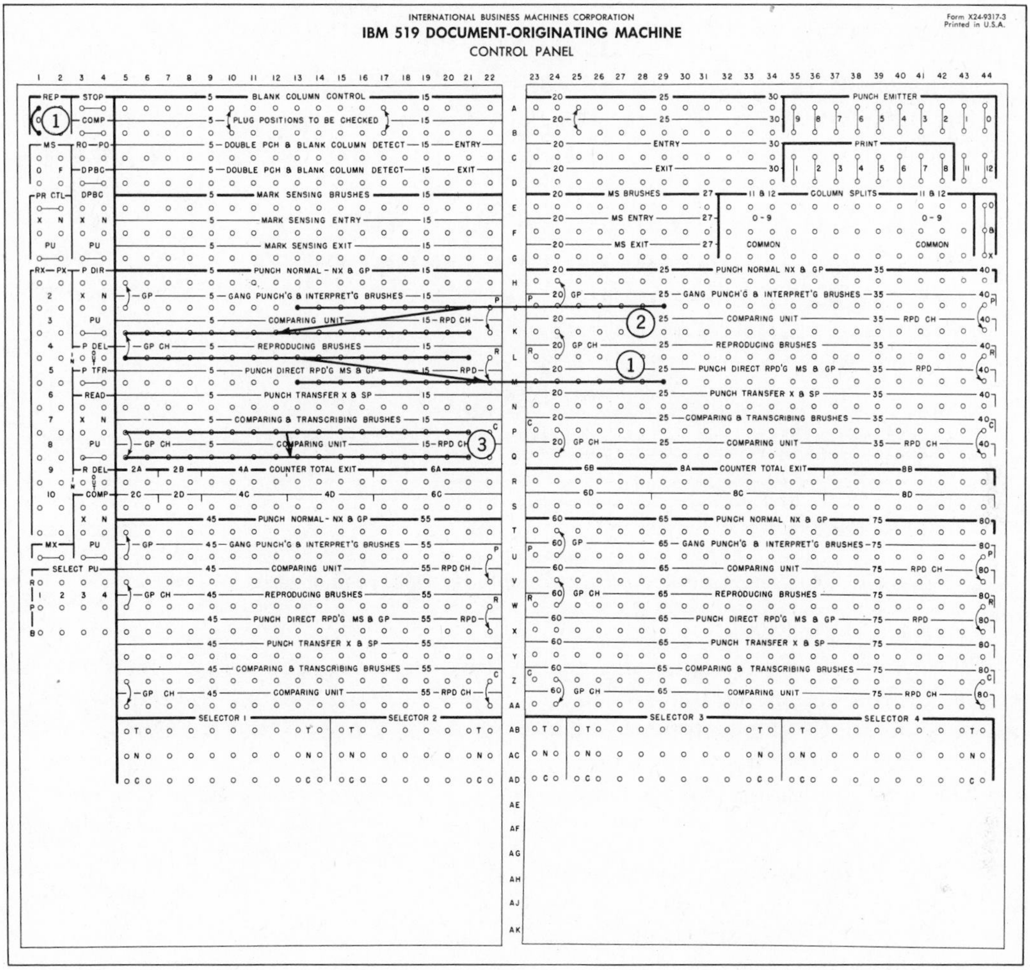

Figure 6-16. Wiring necessary to accomplish reproduction of employee name in the cards shown in Figures 6-13 and 6-14.

and the unpunched (blank) grade cards are placed in the feed hopper of the punching unit.

2. The cards in both hoppers are automatically fed after certain switches are set and the start button is depressed.

3. Feeding of the cards in both hoppers is synchronized so that as a student class card passes the first set of 80 reading brushes, a blank grade card simultaneously passes the 80 punching dies. As the identification number, name, and other data are read from each student class card, this data is transmitted by means of control panel wiring to the punch dies and the exact data is punched into the blank grade cards. A schematic of this operation is shown in Figure 6-12.

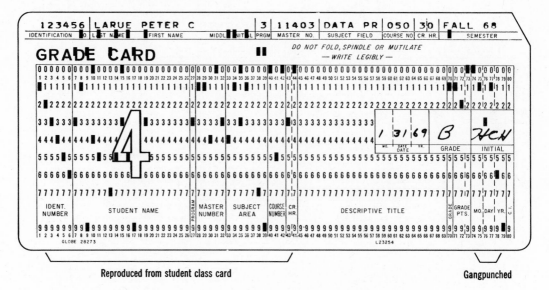

Reproduced from student class card   Gangpunched

Figure 6-17. 80-column card showing data reproduced from another card and gangpunched.

The semester completion dates that must be entered in field columns 74 to 79 can be entered by the technique called gangpunching (Figure 6-18). Gangpunching dates into the grade cards is accomplished as follows:

1. The grade cards are placed in the feed hopper of the punch unit. Only the first grade card is punched with the semester ending date.

2. The cards are automatically fed after certain switches are set and the start button is depressed.

3. As the first grade card passes the punch brushes, the second passes the punch dies. As the brushes read the punched date field in the first card, they create impulses that activate the dies to punch the date in the appropriate columns of the second card. As the card at the punch brushes moves on to the stacker, it is replaced by the card just punched; this card, in turn, is replaced by a blank

card from the hopper, at which time the reading and punching operations are repeated. Through this repetitive process the date on the first card is automatically reproduced on all cards that follow it. Figure 6-19 shows a schematic of the path cards follow in going from hopper to stacker in the Type 519 Document-Originating Machine.

INTERPRETING

It is possible for humans to determine the contents of a card by analyzing the punched holes. This, however, is a slow and tedious process that may be averted by the use of the *interpreter* (Figure 6-20). This machine is designed to read holes punched in a card and print the contents across the face of the same card or another card. Interpreting makes it possible to use the punched card method for many applications, such as bills or checks, that require visual reference to data included on the cards. Moreover, manual filing of cards is simplified if the cards in the file as well as those to be filed are interpreted. Generally, each card in a file is partially interpreted to facilitate quick reference to the contents.

IBM Interpreters

IBM interpreters include the Type 548 and the Type 557 machines. The IBM 548 Interpreter reads data punched in a card and prints at the rate of 60 cards a minute. As many as 60 characters can be printed on one of two lines on each card

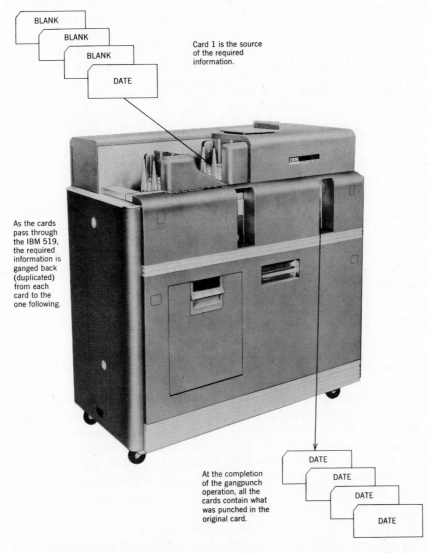

Card 1 is the source of the required information.

As the cards pass through the IBM 519, the required information is ganged back (duplicated) from each card to the one following.

At the completion of the gangpunch operation, all the cards contain what was punched in the original card.

Figure 6-18. Gangpunching operation performed on an automatic punch.

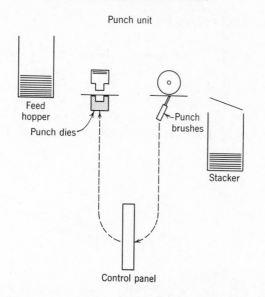

Figure 6-19. Schematic showing path of cards during gangpunching operation performed on IBM 519 Document-Originating Machine.

with a single pass through the machine. These lines, which can be selected by a manually operated dial, are located above the 12 zone and between the 12 and 11 zones on the card.

The IBM 557, illustrated in Figure 6-20, is designed to translate 60 columns of punched data into printed characters on any of 25 printing lines on the face of a card. The desired line is selected by a manually operated printing position dial. If more than 60 characters are required, two or more lines must be used.

The printing mechanism consists of 60 type wheels, each containing printing positions to accommodate 10 numerals (0 through 9), the 26 alphabetic characters, and up to 11 special characters (Figure 6-21). Since there are 80 columns of data recorded in a card and only 60 typebars, the ratio of typebars to card columns is 60 to 80. Thus printing is not directly related to the columns being interpreted.

The limit of 60 characters across the card results from the fact that the print on an interpreter is larger than that on the IBM 29 Card Punch.

On the IBM 557 a running indicator light goes on to show that the interpreter is ready for operation. Card feeding is controlled by depressing the start and stop keys. Cards are placed in the feed hopper face down with the 12-edges toward the throat of the machine. The feed hopper holds about 800 cards. The stacker is located at the left side of the front and holds about 900 cards. When the stacker becomes filled, the machine will automatically stop. However, cards may be removed from the stacker or added to the hopper without stopping the machine, thus permitting continuous operation.

Incorrect printing of valid 557 characters, failure to print for all characters, and the operation of repeat and suppress print may be checked with the installation of a special feature known as a *proof device*. Data printed on the card is checked by this device to assure accuracy. If an error is indicated, card feeding stops.

Applications

A large number of data processing applications require the printing of data from one card to another card or document. One of these applications is in the area of installment loan accounting. Each time a borrower makes a payment, a record of the date, present balance, payment amount, and new balance must be printed on a new line of the unit record or installment loan accounting ledger card. The interpreter accomplishes this by reading the data from the payment transaction card and interpreting the data on the ledger card (Figure 6-22).

The arrangement of printed data on a

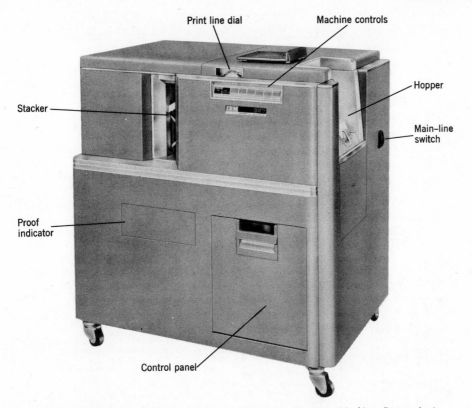

Figure 6-20. IBM 557 Interpreter. (*Courtesy International Business Machines Corporation.*)

card is determined and controlled through the use of a control panel. An example of the wiring required to control an interpreting operation is provided in Figure 6-23. Shown in the illustration is the wiring needed to interpret the identification number and name on the student attendance card that is superimposed on the wiring diagram. Descriptions of the wiring operations are as follows:

1. This connection causes the identification number from card columns 1 through 6 to be printed in *print entry* positions 1 through 6.

2. This connection causes the student name from card columns 7 through 26 to be printed in *print entry* positions 8 through 27.

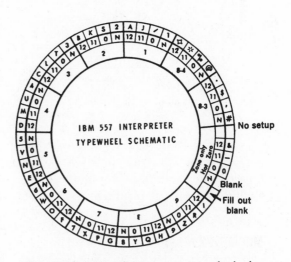

Figure 6-21. IBM 557 Interpreter typewheel schematic. (*Courtesy International Business Machines Corporation.*)

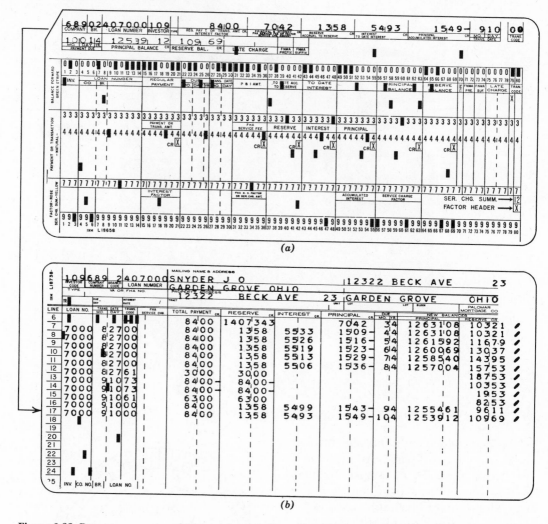

Figure 6-22. Data on payment card (*a*) posted to installment loan ledger card (*b*) by punched card interpreter.

3. This connection causes the unnecessary zeros in the high-order positions of the identification number to be eliminated from the printing.

MEDIA CONVERSION

Modern business applications sometimes require that machines be capable of communicating. For example, it may be desirable for data recorded in 80-column punched cards to be converted into punched paper tape, edge-punched cards, or stock identification tickets to facilitate other uses of the data. If the conversion from punched cards to such other media is demanded, the conversion from these media to punched cards must also be provided.

Media conversion involving punched cards consists of two basic processes: (1) *tape punching*, which is the process of feeding punched cards through a card-to-tape punch to convert the punched card into coded information in paper tape; and (2) *tape reading*, which is the process of feeding coded tapes through a tape-to-card punch to convert the coded information into punched cards.

Media Converters

The IBM 46 and 47 Tape-to-Card Punches (Figure 6-24) convert numerical or alphabetic data read from a punched paper tape into 80-column cards. Data can be read from either eight-channel or five-channel telegraphic tape by a paper tape reading unit that is permanently fastened to the reading board.

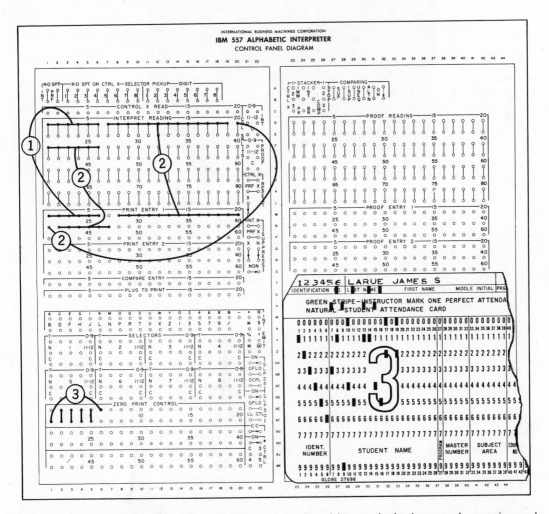

Figure 6-23. One section of IBM 557 Interpreter panel showing wiring required to interpret the superimposed card.

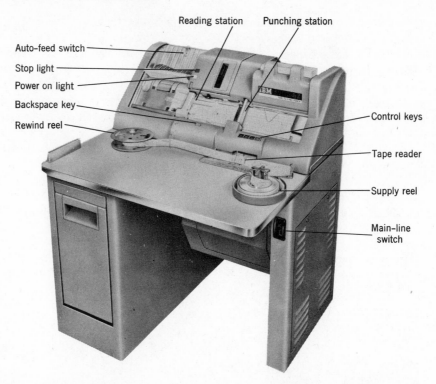

Reading station   Punching station

Auto-feed switch

Stop light

Power on light

Backspace key

Rewind reel

Control keys

Tape reader

Supply reel

Main–line switch

Figure 6-24. IBM 46 Tape-to-Card Punch. (*Courtesy International Business Machines Corporation.*)

The Type 46 machine has a card-punching unit similar to that on the Type 24 Card Punch, and the Type 47 has a unit similar to that on the Type 26 Card Punch. Either machine can be used as a manual card punch when not in use as a media converter if it is equipped with a keyboard that is available as a special feature.

The start key begins automatic operation of the machine provided the main line switch is on, tape is threaded in the paper tape reader unit, cards are inserted in the card hopper, and the control panel is wired and inserted in the machine. Once automatic operation has begun, the machine operates at a speed of 20 columns a second. Operation of the machine is terminated by a stop key.

The card hopper and the stacker each hold approximately 500 cards. Both the tape supply reel and the rewind reel have a capacity of about 300 feet of paper tape.

The IBM 63 Card-Controlled Tape Punch is a card-reading and tape-punching unit. It reads alphabetic and numerical data punched into cards and translates the data into paper tape. One roll of punched tape is equivalent to approximately 1,500 cards (Figure 6-25).

Cards are placed in the feed hopper of the IBM 63 face down with the 1's column toward the throat. Automatic operations begin with the depression of the release switch provided the control panel is wired and inserted, the main line switch is turned on, the feed hopper contains cards, and the paper tape is properly threaded in the tape-punching unit. The tape-punching unit, which operates at a speed of approximately 10 columns a second, is connected to the machine by means of a cable. The tape-punching unit and all machine operations are controlled by means of control panel wiring.

Applications

An example of the use of media conversion is provided by the following typical application. It is possible to transmit monthly physical inventories from each branch office of a large company to the home office by means of punched paper tape. The transmission is based on tally sheets given to the branch teletypewriter operator, who uses them to type a report and simultaneously prepare paper tape for transmission to the home office. When the transmission is received at the home office, the paper tape is automatically converted to punched cards by the use of a media converter (Figure 6-26). The punched cards representing the inventory at the branch office are then used for input to the central data processing system. A copy of the branch inventory report can also be prepared by the teletypewriter at the home office as the paper tape transmission is received.

This technique also makes it possible to prepare payroll checks for employees at distant locations from a central office with no loss of delivery time. To accomplish this, the information to be printed on each check is automatically punched into

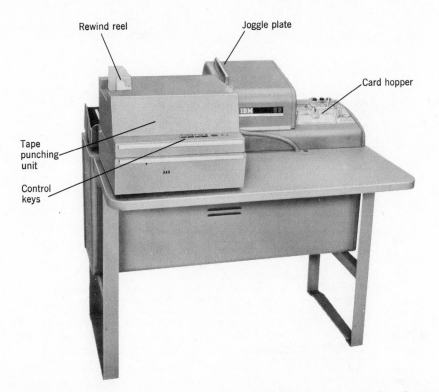

Figure 6-25. IBM 63 Card-Controlled Tape Punch. (*Courtesy International Business Machines Corporation.*)

WEEKLY INVENTORY REPORT

OFFICE CODE	DATE	OFFICE	OPERATOR
117	10/31/--	Branch Office One	JNB

Date Acq.	Purch. Order No.	Equip. Stock No.	Loc.	Cost	Serial Number	Description	Room No.	Ser. Code
10/64	018223	F1DI10000	280	365.00	63579	DICTATE MACH EDISON	A103	PRUC
10/64	09073	16T066115	182	109.00	9180447	UNDERWOOD PICA 15 IN	G108	DIST
10/64	046767	24TY67011	180	155.00	5943310	ROYAL ELITE 11 IN	F101	DIST
10/64	046767	F0CA23109	280	307.00	173085	CALC BURROUGHS 51035	B008	BURR

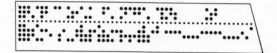

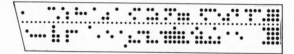

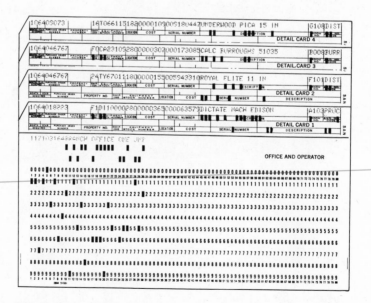

Figure 6-26. Example of media conversion involving inventory report, tape, and cards.

paper tape by a media converter from a punched card containing the employee's earnings data. The information on the paper tape is then transmitted by Teletype machine and the payroll check and earnings statement are prepared simultaneously by a teletypewriter at the destination point.

Review Questions

1. What two types of keyboards are available on card punches?
2. Explain the purpose and operation of the duplicating function on the card punch.
3. What is the purpose of the program unit on the card punch? What functions does it control?
4. What is the purpose of the IBM 59 Verifier? How does it differ from the 29 Key Punch?
5. Explain the manner in which original card punching is verified.
6. What does a notch on the top edge of a punched card indicate? What does a notch on the right edge of a card indicate?
7. Name the basic functions that can be performed by automatic punches.
8. Define the following functions: (a) reproducing, (b) gangpunching, (c) summary punching, (d) mark sensing.
9. What are the purpose and function of the IBM 519 comparing feature?
10. What is the reason for connecting the IBM 519 Document-Originating Machine to the accounting machine?
11. What is the purpose of the interpreting function?
12. How many type wheels does the printing mechanism of the interpreter contain?
13. How can the printing of an interpreter be distinguished from that of a printing card punch?
14. Describe the two basic processes of media conversion involving punched cards.

7

PUNCHED CARD
MANIPULATIVE FUNCTIONS

After source data has been properly recorded in punched card form, it must be processed to achieve the desired result, which may be an updated file, a report, or some other document. This generally entails the manipulation of data in one or more ways including sorting, comparing and analyzing, and calculating. All of these functions will be described in this chapter.

SORTING

Following the punching and verification of cards, they must be arranged in an orderly sequence to facilitate further processing. In addition, after initial arrangement, it may be necessary to rearrange cards in various ways for use in preparing special reports. These functions are performed on a machine called a *sorter* (Figure 7-1).

One of the greatest advantages of the punched card method is the ease with which cards can be arranged in sequence according to any field on the card. The field that is selected is called the *control field*. For example, sales data might be sorted according to region, salesman, commodity, or customer, each of which is recorded in a group of columns called a field.

It is often necessary to arrange cards in a sequence other than that in which they are stored. As an example, cards normally maintained in some numerical sequence may be required in alphabetical sequence for the preparation of a report. Or they may be filed in numerical sequence by one control field but may have to be rearranged into a different numerical sequence as required by another control field. They may have to be arranged in ascending sequence, that is, starting with the lowest control number or letters and proceeding to the highest, or they may have to be arranged in descending sequence. All of these operations are classified as sorting. Although a simple opera-

Pockets

Hopper

Column
selector
knob

Machine
controls

Selector
switch

Digit
suppression
switches

Main–line
switch

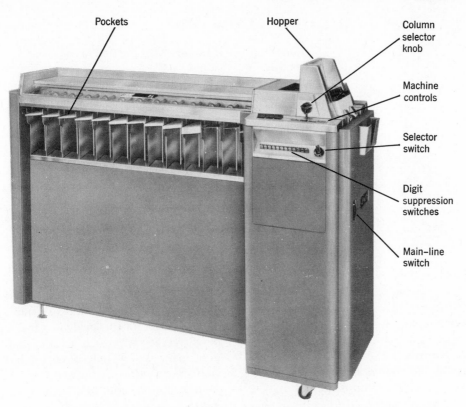

Figure 7-1. IBM 83 Sorter. (*Courtesy International Business Machines Corporation.*)

tion in itself, sorting requires a great deal
of skill in card handling when performed
on a sorter.

Sorting Operations

The various operations that can be
performed on a sorter can be classified
under four major categories, as follows.
Numeric Sorting. Cards can be arranged in numerical sequence by sorting
all columns of the control field one at a
time proceeding from right to left. A control field can be any field common to all
cards used in an operation, such as employee number, invoice number, or loan
number.

Upon completion of each pass (the
sorting of all cards on a selected card column), the cards are removed from the
sorter pockets in ascending sequence 0
through 9. (Pockets 0 to 9 on the sorter
are adequate for sorting cards in numerical sequence because the numerals 0 to 9
are represented by only one punch in a
column.) As shown in Table 7-1, after the
first pass the cards are arranged according to the low-order or units column of
the control field. The cards are replaced
in the machine, and it is adjusted to sort
on the second or tens column. Following
the second pass the cards are properly
arranged from 00 to 99 according to the
first two columns. This process is repeated

TABLE 7-1 SEQUENCE OF CARDS DURING A NUMERIC SORT

Random Order	End of First Pass	End of Second Pass	End of Third Pass
579	121	805	024
966	552	121	121
786	344	024	246
478	024	344	344
246	805	345	345
805	345	246	478
552	966	552	552
344	786	966	579
121	246	478	786
024	478	579	805
345	579	786	966

until all columns have been sorted. Thus a three-column field requires three passes, a five-column field five passes, and so on.

Alphabetic Sorting. Cards may be arranged in alphabetic sequence by passing them through the sorter twice for each column in the control field. Two sorts are necessary on each column since alphabetic characters are composed of two punches, a zone punch, and a digit punch.

Block Sorting. When the volume of cards is so great that it is inconvenient to finish all sorting in one operation, it is sometimes desirable to separate the cards into blocks. To accomplish this, the cards are first sorted according to the high-order digit of the control field which separates them into ten blocks. Each block is then sorted separately and can be forwarded to the next processing step before the remainder of the sorting has been completed. For example, if it were necessary to sort ten thousand cards, they could be sorted first into ten groups by the block sorting technique. This would allow the cards in the one thousand series to be sorted completely and forwarded, then the cards in the two thousand series, and so on. It also would allow blocks to be sorted on more than one machine at a time.

Digit Sorting or Selecting. In addition to sorting as described above, the sorter can also select specific items from a group of cards. Not all the cards in a file need to be sorted if only cards with a particular digit are needed. Selection switches provide a means of selecting certain items that require special attention without disturbing the sequence of the other cards in the file. Thus, if all credit transactions are needed to prepare a special report, it is possible to remove them from a file containing all types of transactions without affecting the remainder of the file.

Sorters

IBM sorters are divided into three types. The Type 82 sorts at the rate of 650 cards a minute. The Type 83 Sorter (Figure 7-1), similar in appearance and operation to the Type 82, operates at a speed of 1,000 cards a minute. The Type 84 Sorter has many of the same features as the Type 83 but operates at a speed of 2,000 cards a minute. The Type 84 has brushless sensing, radial stackers, a vacuum-assist feed, and solid-state circuitry, which provide for faster and more accurate sorting.

On the IBM 83 Sorter, sorting is accomplished by placing cards in the feed hopper, setting the sort brush to the desired column to be sorted, and depressing the start key. Once the start key is depressed, sorting continues until the feed hopper becomes empty, one of the stacker pockets is filled, or the stop key is depressed.

Thirteen receiving pockets are arranged from left to right as follows: 9, 8, 7, 6, 5, 4, 3, 2, 1, 0, 11, 12, and reject. Each pocket has a capacity of about 800 cards. Sorting is accomplished by directing cards to pockets corresponding to the particular digits punched in the cards. Some applications make it desirable to sort out only those cards containing certain digits, leaving the remaining cards in their original sequence. Digit suppression keys make this type of digit sorting possible.

The 12 digit suppression keys represent the 12 punching positions of the card. When either of the keys is depressed, cards punched with the corresponding digit will fall into the reject pocket. The sort selection switch located to the right of the digit suppression keys may be rotated to one of five positions to control the particular sorting operation involved. The function of each switch setting is described as follows:

1. N (numerical): Cards are sorted on the first punch read, and blanks are rejected.

2. Z (zone): Cards are sorted on zone punches only.

3. A-1 (alphabetic sort 1): Cards punched with a digit and a 12 zone (A through I) are sorted on the digits 1 through 9. Cards with an 11 zone sort into the 11 pocket and 0 zones into the 0 pocket.

4. A-2 (alphabetic sort 2): Cards punched with a 0 or 11 zone are sorted on the digits.

SORT SELECTION SWITCH SETTING	POCKETS												REJECTS REGARDLESS OF EDIT	ERRORS (When Edit or Edit-Stop is ON)
	9	8	7	6	5	4	3	2	1	0	11	12		
Numerical	9	8	7	6	5	4	3	2	1	0	11	12	Blanks	Multiple-punched cards (incl. letters)
Zone										0	11	12	Any card without a zone punch	Any card with more than one zone punch
Alpha-1	I	H	G	F	E	D	C	B	A	0 S–Z	11 J–R		Blanks and cards with a 12-zone punch but no digit punch. Digits 1 to 9.	Any card with more than one zone punch or with more than one digit punch
Alpha-2	R,Z	Q,Y	P,X	O,W	N,V	M,U	L,T	K,S	J 0–1				Cards with 0 or 11-zone only. Blanks. Letters A to I, and 12-zone spec. char. Digits 1 to 9.	Same as A-1
Alpha-Numerical	9	8	7	6	5	4	3	2	1	0 (digit)	11 J–R	12 A–I	Blanks, 0-zone (S–Z)	Same as A-1

This pattern is based on cards being fed face down, 9 edge first.

Figure 7-2. Summary of patterns established by each setting of the sort selection switches on an IBM 83 Sorter.

5. A-N (alpha-numerical): Cards containing digits 0 through 9, but no zone, are sorted into their respective pockets.

Figure 7-2 summarizes the sorting patterns established by each setting of the sort selection switches.

The actual sorting is controlled by a single sort brush. The brush may be set on any column desired by rotating the column selector.

Cards are placed in the feed hopper face down with the 9-edges toward the throat of the machine. The hopper has a capacity of approximately 1,200 cards.

As cards pass through the machine, the presence of a punch is detected by the sort brush dropping through the hole and making a contact with the roller. This establishes an electrical impulse that pushes down a selector pin and separates the chute blades, thus directing the card to the proper pocket (Figure 7-3).

A Typical Application

One of the most common applications of sorters is in arranging cards for the preparation of various reports. For example, the management of most companies requires sales reports to aid in determining the volume and trends of sales. Such reports are usually made up of sales lists grouped according to customer number, salesman number, or product number. In order to achieve such grouping the transaction cards must be arranged into the desired sequence (Figure 7-4).

As cards are completed by card punch operators they are ungrouped and in random sequence. Before any of the three sales analysis reports can be printed, the cards must be placed in proper sequence by the desired category. Sorting progresses one column at a time from right to left across the field. For example, in sorting the two-column customer number field,

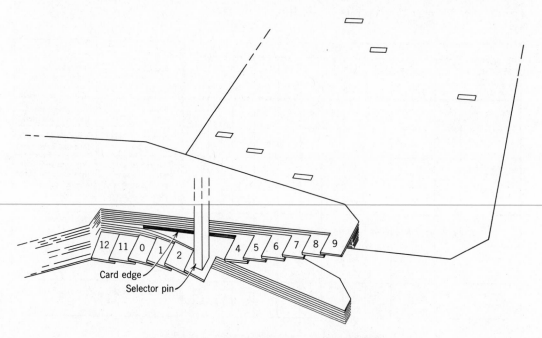

Figure 7-3. Chute blade schematic for IBM 83 Sorter.

C U S T NO	S A L E S	GROSS PROFIT
4	8 8 2 6	2 3 0 1
2 0	6 5 1 3	1 5 3 0
2 4	6 6 9 9 6	1 5 9 4 0
3 5	9 3 8 5 6	2 2 2 4 5
3 7	2 2 2 5 0	2 0 9 0
4 2	2 1 6 4 7 6	5 2 1 4 0
4 4	1 2 3 3 5	3 0 3 7
4 9	9 4 6 0 0	2 1 7 8 7
5 6	1 1 5 8 5 0	2 9 4 5 4

S L S M N NO	S A L E S	GROSS PROFIT
1	1 4 5 5 1	4 2 7 7
3	9 4 6 0 0	2 1 7 8 7
4	7 8 5 4 0	1 9 6 4 5
5	1 1 5 8 5 0	2 9 4 5 4
6	4 2 1 5 6 1	7 8 0 4 6
7	9 3 8 8 3	2 2 2 2 2
8	9 9 9 2 4	2 8 3 5 2

P R O D NO	S A L E S	GROSS PROFIT
1 1 2 0 2	9 6 1 8	2 6 3 2
1 5 1 0 2	4 8 3 0 0	1 1 9 7 0
1 6 4 0 2	3 0 6 0	6 1 0
1 7 2 0 3	3 8 0 7 0	7 5 2 0
2 1 1 0 3	1 0 7 6 3	2 6 0 5
2 3 3 0 2	1 9 7 0	4 5 2
2 3 7 0 2	1 5 5 4 0	3 5 7 0
2 6 1 0 4	9 7 6	2 2 4
2 6 3 0 2	2 4 2 1 0	6 8 9 4
3 3 2 0 2	1 9 5 3 0	4 5 2 3

Figure 7-4. Sales data grouped according to customer number, salesman number, and product number.

the right-hand or units column is sorted first. All of the customer numbers ending in zero, such as 20, 60, and 70, would be deposited in the 0 pocket. All of the customer numbers ending in 1, such as 61, 71, and 81, would be deposited in the 1 pocket, and so on. Cards are then removed from the sorter pockets in ascending sequence. It is then necessary to repeat this process for the second or tens column, after which the cards will be in proper order for the report based on customers. This entire procedure would have to be repeated twice in order to place the cards in proper sequence for the other two reports based on salesmen numbers and product numbers.

COMPARING AND ANALYZING

In the preceding section the importance of arranging cards in an orderly sequence was discussed and it was indicated that the basic arrangement of cards is performed on the sorter. There are, however, more complex arrangement and handling functions that cannot be done on the sorter. These functions are performed by the *collator* (Figure 7-5). Because the collator is capable of more types of operations, it supplements the sorter in many systems.

The basic function of the collator is to feed and compare two files of cards simultaneously in order to match them or combine them into a single file. At the same time the collator will automatically detect and separate cards from each file that do not have a matching card in the other file.

Collating Operations

Collators are used to perform the following types of operations:

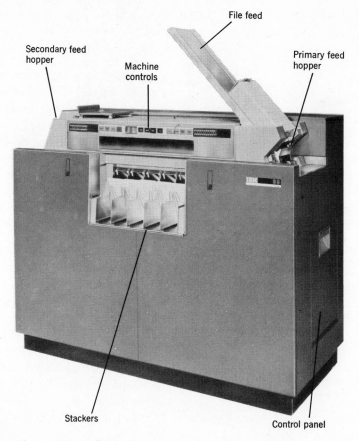

Figure 7-5. IBM 88 Collator. (*Courtesy International Business Machines Corporation.*)

Sequence Checking. After the sorter has been used to place a file of cards in a desired sequence, the file can be checked on the collator to determine if the sequence is correct. The collator does this by comparing each card with the one ahead of it. The machine may be directed to stop if an error is detected, or it may be directed to separate all cards that are out of sequence.

Merging. In this operation two files of cards already in sequence can be combined into one file. As cards from the two files are fed simultaneously, the card at the primary reading station is compared with the card at the secondary reading station and the one with the smaller number is dropped into a designated pocket. As a card advances to replace the one that has dropped, it is compared with the card remaining from the previous operation and the process is repeated.

Matching. In this operation instead of merging the two files, cards in either file that do not match the other can be separated, and cards that do match remain in the two original groups. Thus, as cards from the two groups simultaneously pass the primary and secondary reading stations and are compared, those that match are dropped side by side into the two center pockets. The primary cards for which there are no matching secondary cards are dropped into one outside pocket, and the secondary cards for which there are no matching primary cards are dropped into the other outside pocket. (Cards are called primary or secondary according to the feed hopper into which they are placed.) When the operation is completed there may be four groups of cards: two groups of matched and two groups of unmatched, as illustrated in Figure 7-6.

Merging with Selection. The operation of merging two files into one can be controlled so that if either file contains cards that do not match cards in the other, these cards can be separated. In effect, this operation represents a combination of the procedures described in the two preceding paragraphs. Here, matching cards are merged together rather than being left in their original two groups. As in the case of the matching operation, however, unmatched cards from the pri-

mary and secondary groups are deposited in separate pockets. Thus at the end of the operation, there may be three groups of cards: one group of merged cards and two groups of selected, or unmatched, cards.

Card Selection. The collator also has the ability to select certain types of cards from a file without disturbing the sequence of the others. The selecting task of the collator is similar to that of the sorter, except that the collator can select on more than one card column. Selected cards may be the first card of a group, a single card group, the last card of a group, a card with a particular number, or a card with numbers between two control numbers. Selected cards also may be X or no-X cards. To illustrate, in applications that require a distinction between male and female employees, all female employees might be identified with an X punch (11 punch) in a designated card column. In this case, card selection would consist of separating

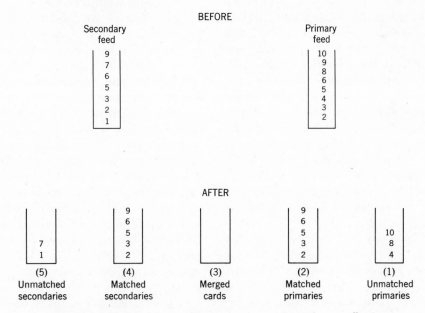

Figure 7-6. Results of a matching operation performed on a collator.

male from female employees as determined by the presence or absence of an X punch.

Collators

IBM collators can be divided into two general categories: numeric and alphabetic. Numeric collators, such as the Type 77, the Type 85, and the Type 88 illustrated in Figure 7-5, can process numerical data only, unless a special aphabetic collating device is installed. Alphabetic collators, such as the Type 87 and the Type 188, can process either numerical or alphabetic data. All collators, with the exception of the Type 88 and Type 188, are comparable both in operation and control panel wiring.

The Type 88 and 188 Collators are similar in appearance, basic operations, and speeds. Both machines perform the basic functions of sequence checking, merging, matching, merging with selection, card selection, or any combination of these. Speeds range from 650 to 1,300 cards a minute. Each machine is equipped with a file feed device holding 3,600 cards, and has five radial stackers of 1,000-card capacity each. The Type 188 is a fully transistorized solid-state machine that performs at high speed a variety of comparing, filing, selecting, and editing operations on either alphabetically or numerically punched cards.

The following operating features of the IBM 88 Collator are also typical of other models.

The feeding of cards is begun or ended by depressing separate start and stop keys. However, when the last card has been fed from either hopper, the machine stops automatically. In this case, several cards from the depleted hopper will remain in the machine. These are moved into the stacker by holding down the runout key.

When the machine senses an error condition by means of control panel wiring, the machine stops and the error lights go on. The reset key must be depressed in order to resume operation. Other indicators include a ready light which signals that the machine is ready for operation, and BCD (blank-column detection) lights which go on whenever a blank column is sensed in a card field wired for the detection of blank columns.

The two feed units on the collator are called the primary feed and the secondary feed. Cards are placed in the primary hopper face down with the 9-edges toward the throat of the machine, whereas those placed in the secondary hopper must be placed face down with the 12-edges toward the throat of the machine. The relationship of the two units is shown in Figure 7-8.

The primary feed is equipped with a file feed device. This magazine holds approximately 3,600 cards, which allows at least $5\frac{1}{2}$ minutes of continuous running time. Either unit can feed cards at the rate of 650 a minute. When using both feeds, the number of cards fed each minute will range from 650 to 1,300 depending on the function being performed.

As cards are fed from the primary feed hopper, they pass the primary sequence reading station and then the primary reading station. Each station consists of 80 reading brushes, which can be wired to read any of the card columns. Cards fed from the secondary feed hopper pass the secondary sequence reading station and then the secondary reading station consisting of 80 brushes.

After cards are read by the brushes, they can be directed to one of five pockets depending on the operation being performed.

Automatic operation of the collator is controlled by the wiring of a control panel that fits into a rack on the side of the machine.

A Collator Application

The following application illustrates several of the important functions performed by the collator.

It is sometimes necessary to obtain the data required for a report from two or more card files. Consequently, before the report or statement can be prepared, data from the individual files must be merged. For example, the preparation of W-2 tax forms may require the use of a name and address card and a year-to-date summary card for each employee (Figure 7-7).

The merging of the two sets of cards is, in itself, an easy operation. However, cards from each of the two files may be absent. Name and address cards, for example, may have been removed for the recording of address changes for certain employees. Thus, merging of two incomplete files would produce an incomplete W-2 report. By the use of the collator it is possible to be certain that there is a name and address card for each year-to-date summary card. If there is not, the collator prevents the unmatched cards from merging and singles them out for special attention.

This operation requires three stackers or pockets into which the cards from the feed hoppers can be directed. The merging operation for the name and address cards is accomplished as follows:

1. As cards are fed simultaneously from the primary and secondary feed hoppers, they are read by the primary and secondary read brushes. This automatically causes pocket 3 (merged cards) to receive both the matching name and address cards and the year-to-date summary cards (Figure 7-8).

2. Unmatched name and address cards from the primary feed are directed to the selected primaries pocket, and unmatched year-to-date summary cards from the secondary feed are directed to the selected secondaries pocket.

In addition to merging the applicable cards, the collator can check the sequence of the cards in the files to be merged. Cards that have been manually removed from the file for name and address changes are usually placed back into the file manually. In the event that a card was not put back in its proper location, an out-of-sequence condition was created. The collator can detect this condition during the merging operation by the process called *sequence checking*. If it senses this condition, the collator can be directed by means of control panel wiring to stop, thus permitting the operator to correct the out-of-sequence condition and resume the operation.

The wiring necessary for the IBM 88 Collator to accomplish the merging of the address and YTD summary cards shown in Figure 7-7 and the operation shown in Figure 7-8 is illustrated in Figure 7-9. The wiring is as follows:

1. These connections cause the employee numbers on the cards in the primary and the secondary feeds to be compared by (1) wiring the employee number (columns 6–11) of the name and address card from *primary read* to *primary comparing and DPBC* (double-punch and blank-column) *entry*, and (2) wiring the employee number in the year-to-date summary card

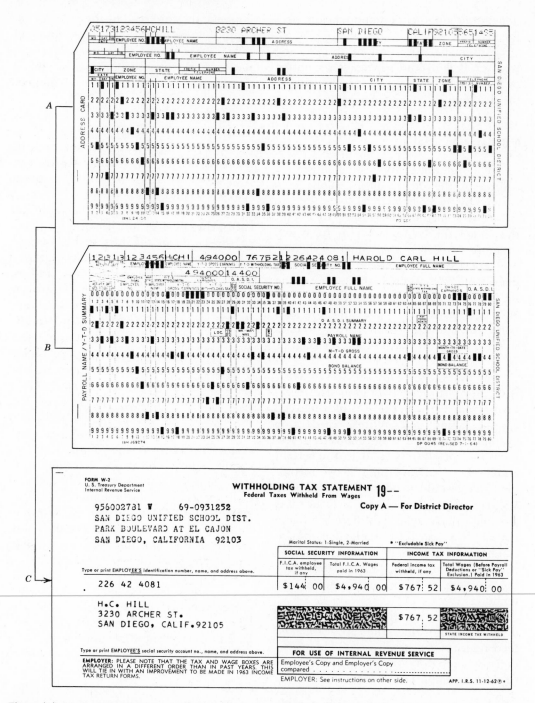

Figure 7-7. Name and address card (*A*) and year-to-date summary card (*B*) merged by collator for use in preparing Form W-2 (*C*).

from the *secondary read* to *secondary comparing and DPBC entry*. The cards in the primary feed are compared with each other by wiring from the *comparing DPBC* to *sequence entry 2* and from *primary sequence read* to *primary sequence entry 1*. The cards in the secondary feed are compared with each other by wiring from *comparing and DPBC* to *sequence entry 2* and from *secondary sequence read* to *secondary sequence entry 1*.

2. These connections cause card feeding to be controlled automatically.

3. These connections cause card feeding to stop for an error in ascending sequence in either feed. This condition would be recognized by the wiring in 1 above.

4. These connections direct all equal card groups to fall into the merge pocket (see Figure 7-8).

5. These connections will cause low primaries, name and address cards without corresponding secondary cards, to feed

into pocket 2; and low secondaries, YTD summary cards without corresponding primary cards, to fall into pocket 4 (see Figure 7-8).

CALCULATING

The only punched card machine that is able to perform all four arithmetic operations is the *calculating punch* (Figure 7-10). The arithmetic ability of the accounting machine, which will be described in the next chapter, is generally restricted to adding and subtracting. Calculating punches are designed to read several fields from a card containing factors to be calculated, perform calculations on the basis of these factors, and punch the results either in the card from which the factors are read or in designated cards that follow. Calculating encompasses various combinations of the basic processes of adding, subtracting, multiplying, and dividing.

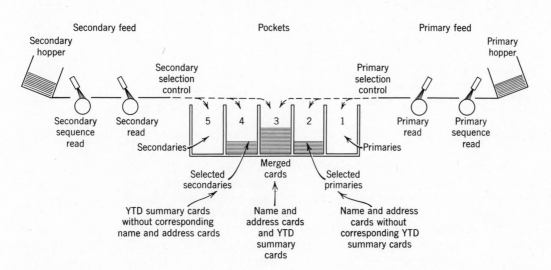

Figure 7-8. Schematic showing path of cards through the IBM 88 Collator in the merging of name and address cards with year-to-date summary cards.

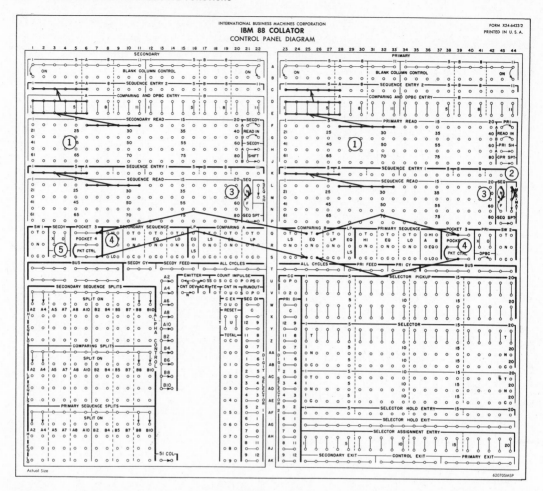

Figure 7-9. The IBM 88 Collator wiring necessary to accomplish the merging of the name and address cards and year-to-date summary cards shown in Figure 7-8.

Calculating Punches

Several types of IBM calculating punches are currently in use: The Types 602 and 604, and the Type 609 which will be discussed in detail.

The IBM 609 Calculator, illustrated in Figure 7-10, combines calculating and punching facilities in a single compact unit consisting of solid-state components. Complete operations are performed at a rate of 200 cards a minute (12,000 an hour), allowing 110 milliseconds for calculating. The IBM 609 can be instructed by control panel wiring to delay punching in any card that requires additional time for complex calculations.

Cards are placed in the feed hopper face down, 12-edges first. As cards feed through the machine, they pass three stations: an 80-column reading station, a punching station, and a second reading station. A schematic of these stations is shown in Figure 7-11.

Factors are read at the first reading station. In addition, certain punched holes on the card may be read for control purposes. Calculations are performed after the card is read and while it is moving to the punching station. As the card passes the punching station, the calculated results are punched into the card. As the card passes the second reading station, data can be read for the purpose of gang-punching or for double-punch and blank-column checking.

Program steps, which are controlled by a wired control panel, can be executed in any sequence. Steps may be repeated, and only those steps that are wired are executed. The maximum size of factors or result of calculations for any one program step is ordinarily six digits.

The console shown in Figure 7-10 is

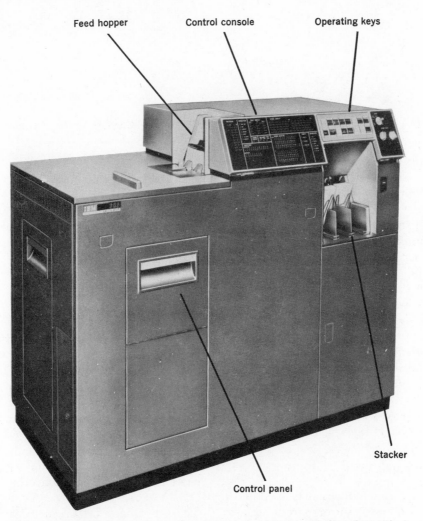

Figure 7-10. IBM 609 Calculator. (*Courtesy International Business Machines Corporation.*)

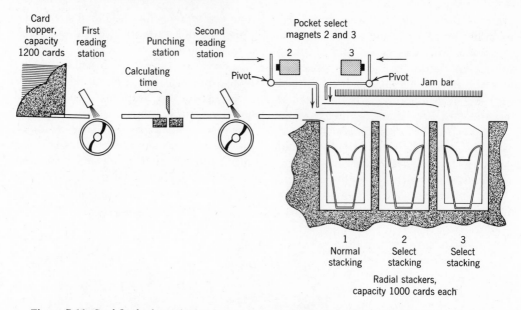

Figure 7-11. Card feed schematic showing card stations and stacker pockets in IBM 609 Calculator.

designed to assist the programmer in verifying the accuracy of the program, to display the progress of the program during calculation, and to display the data contained in storage.

Planning is the most important aspect of placing a calculator application into operation. Planning a problem on the 609 is similar in principle to planning a problem on other punched card calculators. A problem should first be analyzed to determine the most logical use of core storage and the sequence of steps to be executed by the machine. The technique of flow charting and the use of program sheets aid in planning the solution of problems. The necessary steps are executed by means of control panel wiring.

A Payroll Application

A calculating punch can be used in the following manner to prepare a weekly payroll. First, weekly earnings cards con-

taining hours worked and employees' accumulated earnings cards containing all necessary payroll data are merged on the collator. Then the merged cards are processed in the calculating punch where the weekly earnings for each employee are calculated as follows:

1. In calculating the gross pay, the hours are first accumulated in a register. Regular hours are separated from overtime hours if overtime is to be paid after eight hours. If overtime is to be paid after 40 hours, all the hours are stored in one register. A constant of 40, previously stored in the calculator, is subtracted from the total hours, thus indicating the amount of overtime to be paid. The calculation consists of multiplying regular hours and overtime hours, if any, times applicable pay rates to obtain gross pay.

2. After the gross pay is calculated, the year-to-date social security tax is read from the accumulated earnings card and

tested to see if the maximum amount has been reached. If not, this tax is computed and stored to be punched.

3. If the employee is subject to payment of disability insurance, these calculations are made in the same manner as those for social security.

4. The federal withholding tax is computed on the basis of the gross pay multiplied by the percentage factor on the accumulated earnings card.

5. Net pay is calculated by a crossfooting operation of gross pay minus current social security, federal withholding tax, and disability insurance.

6. When all the necessary calculations are completed, the weekly earnings card is moved to the punch position in the calculator where the stored data is punched into it.

OTHER FUNCTIONS

Statistical Machines

Statistics are important to many organizations and these statistics are often maintained in the form of punched cards. The preparation of a statistical report usually requires that cards be arranged into the desired sequence and tabulated. If only basic punched card equipment were available, it would be necessary to use several different machines and several steps to produce the desired result. Statistical machines, however, are able to combine into one operation the variety of operations required to produce statistical reports.

These elaborate machines are able to sense all 80 columns of a card on one pass through the machine and perform the following wide variety of functions.

Sorting. Cards can be arranged in any sequence desired, numerically or alphabetically.

Counting. The total number of cards sorted in one pass can be counted, or different groups can be counted selectively, without disturbing the sequence of the cards.

Accumulating. Amounts punched in the cards can be accumulated at the same time that the cards are being counted.

Editing. The editing feature enables a machine to review, check, and approve a card before it is sorted or counted. This is accomplished by directing the machine to check for predetermined punches in certain columns or for blank columns. This type of editing ensures that only wanted cards are retained and sorted appropriately. All other cards are dropped into the reject pocket. The sequence of cards can also be checked.

Printing. Final card counts and amount field totals which have accumulated during an operation can be printed on a report form along with the identification of the accumulated data.

Crossfooting. Crossfooting consists of horizontal addition or subtraction of factors in various columns. By this process totals in the different counters can be checked to assure that all of the items balance.

Equipment. There are two models of IBM electronic statistical machines: the Type 101 and the Type 108. The purpose and function of these two types are basically similar. The major difference between the Type 101 and the Type 108, which will be discussed in this section, is speed of operation. The IBM 101 Electronic Statistical Machine operates at a speed of 450 cards a minute. The basic operations that it performs are sorting, counting, accumulating, editing, printing, and crossfooting. The IBM 108 Card Proving Machine (Figure 7-12) operates at the rate of 1,000 cards a minute.

The IBM 108 Card Proving Machine detects errors and inconsistencies in cards and establishes totals. The functions include: normal sorting, selective sorting, multiple columns selection, numeric sequence checking, alphabetic sequence checking, comparing, and editing operations. Under arithmetic operations the 108 can perform adding, subtracting, manual totaling, automatic totaling, progressive totaling, total transfer, crossfooting totals, and balance testing. By addition of special features, total printing and summary punching can also be accomplished.

The IBM 108 Card Proving Machine is very similar in appearance to the card sorters. Cards are placed in the feed hopper face down, 9-edges toward the throat. The hopper holds approximately 1,200 cards which feed at the rate of 1,000 cards a minute.

Thirteen pockets are provided: twelve for sorting cards into groups and one normally used for rejects. Two 13-position switches can be used independently or together for selecting columns during specific runs of the cards. By means of control panel wiring, any one of 49 columns of a card can be sorted by using the two selection switches. The sort pattern switch can be set to one of eight positions to control the following operations:

ZN — Sorting zone portions of a card (0–12).

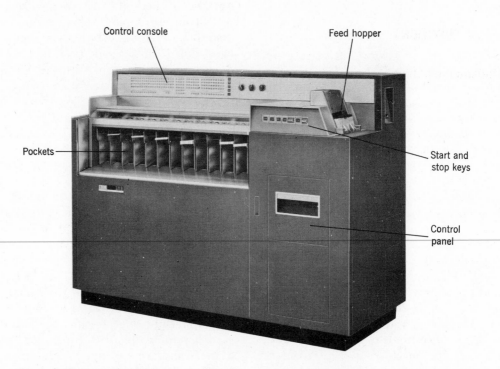

Figure 7-12. IBM 108 Card Proving Machine. (*Courtesy International Business Machines Corporation.*)

NOR — Normal sorting.

PROG. STACK — Stacking cards progressively from a full pocket on to the next pocket.

OFF — All cards are rejected.

1–4 — Selective sorting for different patterns.

During sorting operations cards move from right to left past two reading stations: card reading station 1 and card reading station 2 which are used for comparing purposes. Next, the cards pass under an arrangement of chute blades where they are directed to pockets as they move to the left (Figure 7-13).

A display panel provides a visual display that greatly facilitates control panel wiring and trouble shooting. If the machine stops because of error, the display panel can be used to readily locate the error.

The IBM 867 Output Typewriter and the IBM 534 Card Punch can be cable-connected to the IBM 108 Card Proving Machine for printing and summary punching. Both the 867 and 534 operate at a speed of 1,000 characters a minute. The operation of both machines, when cable-connected, is under control of the IBM 108 Card Proving Machine.

All operations performed by the IBM 108 are controlled by means of a control panel.

Applications. Under certain circumstances management may require information about particular characteristics of employees. One example of this type of study would be an age analysis of all employees according to sex, occupational classifications, and departments. Such a study could easily be prepared on the Type 101 Statistical Machine with several passes of the cards containing this type of employee data.

One of the most common applications of one of the machines in this category, the Type 108 Card Proving Machine, is the pre-editing of punched cards before their use as input to large-scale computer systems. To edit and correct all cards before the data is converted to magnetic tape, the cards can be checked by the 108 for double-punched columns, blank columns,

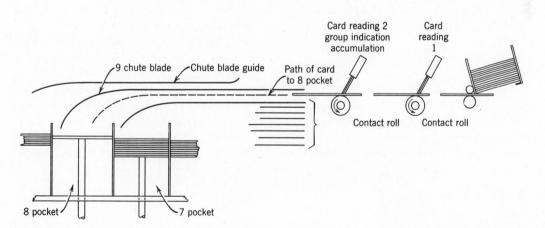

Figure 7-13. Card feed and chute schematic showing path of cards through IBM 108 Card Proving Machine.

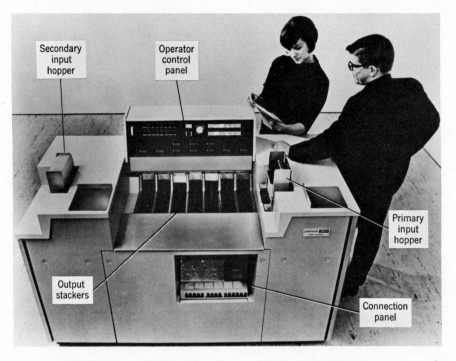

Figure 7-14. UNIVAC 1001 Card Controller. (*Courtesy* UNIVAC, *Division of Sperry Rand Corporation.*)

invalid codes, incorrect control totals, records out of sequence, and other types of errors and inconsistencies.

By the use of this pre-editing technique, costly conversion delays and lost computer time because of incorrectly punched cards can be eliminated.

Card Controller

The UNIVAC 1001 Card Controller (Figure 7-14) is a high-speed, multi-purpose machine whose principal function is to arrange card files into groups or sequences required for subsequent processing. It is equipped with two card-input stations, each capable of feeding cards at speeds up to 1,000 cards a minute. Seven output stackers permit a wide variety of selection as well as matching, merging, and other common collating operations.

The Card Controller has 256 characters of core storage and a variable sequence of program steps. Any or all information in any card may be selectively stored for one or more cycles and compared as required by the specific application. All operations are directed through wiring of a removable connection panel.

Review Questions

1. What is a control field?
2. Describe the process of numeric sorting.

3. How does the operation of alphabetic sorting differ from numeric sorting?
4. What is the purpose of block sorting?
5. How many pockets do sorters contain? Identify them from left to right.
6. Describe the purpose and operation of digit suppression keys on the sorter.
7. Describe the following functions of the collator: (a) sequence checking, (b) merging, (c) matching, (d) merging with selection, (e) card selection.
8. IBM collators can be divided into what two general categories?
9. Which basic arithmetic operations can be performed by a calculating punch?
10. What functions can electronic statistical machines perform in addition to sorting?

PUNCHED CARD SUMMARIZING AND REPORTING

Although punched card data processing encompasses a variety of operations, basically it is composed of three steps. First, source data must be converted into punched holes in cards. Second, these cards must be manipulated to produce a desired result. Third, a finished report or other document must be prepared. This last step is accomplished by the *accounting machine,* which automatically converts punched data into printed reports, printing a line for each card at the rate of 80 to 150 lines a minute (Figure 8-1).

ACCOUNTING MACHINE FUNCTIONS

The accounting machine is capable of performing a number of important functions which can be classified as follows:

Accumulating

Totals recorded in cards passing through a machine or a tabulation of the quantity of cards can be accumulated and stored in the counters of the machine until such time as it is desired to have these totals printed. Each of a series of counters can be directed to add or subtract data in specified card fields; to add, subtract, or disregard certain cards; and to print subtotals and totals at certain points.

Detail Printing

If it is desired to show detail about each transaction, the accounting machine will print data from each card that passes through the machine. The machine can be directed to print all columns of a card or to omit part of the data. It also can print

140

Figure 8-1. IBM 402-403 Accounting Machine. (*Courtesy International Business Machines Corporation.*)

the data in a sequence other than that in which it appears on the card.

Figure 8-2 illustrates this important function of the accounting machine. The application depicted is a common one: a detailed listing of inventory transactions showing beginning balances, receipts, issues, and closing balances.

Group Printing

If only a summary of data from each group of cards with a different classification is desired, the machine can be set up to print only the group identification data along with significant subtotals or totals that have been accumulated. Group printing is made possible by the machine's programming ability, as explained below.

Figure 8-3 illustrates group printing, the summarization of data by classification. In this case, the accounting machine has processed all of the inventory transactions that were printed in the detailed listing shown in Figure 8-2. However, the machine has been directed to accumulate the data in its counters and to print only the totals of each group of transactions.

Programming

By this process the machine can tell the difference between cards in one control group and those in another. This is accomplished by comparing the data in a specific field of a card at one reading station with data in the same field of a card at the following reading station. Impulses

PART NUMBER	PART NAME	UNIT	UNIT COST	TRANS DATE	T C	OPEN. BAL.	TRANSACTIONS RECEIPTS	ISSUES	ON HAND
11124	TRANSISTOR BG	EA	12 65	228	1	68			
11124	TRANSISTOR BG	EA	12 65	303	4			36	
11124	TRANSISTOR BG	EA	12 65	307	4			18	
11124	TRANSISTOR BG	EA	12 65	310	2		144		
11124	TRANSISTOR BG	EA	12 65	314	4			40	
11124	TRANSISTOR BG	EA	12 65	321	4			12	
11124	TRANSISTOR BG	EA	12 65	322	4		1		
11124	TRANSISTOR BG	EA	12 65	322	5			1	
11124	TRANSISTOR BG	EA	12 65	330	4			24	
						68	145	131	82
11211	LENS	777	8 33	228	1	84			
11211	LENS	777	8 33	301	4			6	
11211	LENS	777	8 33	304	4			15	
11211	LENS	777	8 33	307	6			1	
11211	LENS	777	8 33	321	4			36	
11211	LENS	777	8 33	325	4			6	
11211	LENS	777	8 33	329	4			18	
11211	LENS	777	8 33	330	2		156		
						84	156	82	158
11381	CONNECTORS XX1	EA	1 99	228	1	148			
11381	CONNECTORS XX1	EA	1 99	303	4			24	
11381	CONNECTORS XX1	EA	1 99	312	2		180	36	
11381	CONNECTORS XX1	EA	1 99	314	4			12	

UNITS: EA=EACH C=HUNDRED DZ=DOZEN GR=GROSS M=THOUSAND

INVENTORY TRANSACTION LISTING
DATE 3 / 31 /19 --

TRANSACTION CODES
1. BALANCE FORWARD 4. ISSUES FROM STOCK
2. RECEIPTS FROM VENDORS 5. RETURNS TO STOCK
3. RETURNS TO VENDORS 6. DEBIT ADJUSTMENT
7. CREDIT ADJUSTMENT

Figure 8-2. Detailed listing of inventory transactions.

resulting from an unequal reading between the two stations are used to start an automatic program cycle. This cycle consists of printing the accumulated total for the group being completed and spacing the form to prepare for the next entry.

Summary Punching

As indicated above, the accounting machine accumulates numerical data in its counters and prints totals as directed. It is often desirable to prepare new punched cards containing these summary totals for use in carrying balances forward to the next processing cycle. This is accomplished by connecting an automatic punch to the accounting machine by means of a cable. Thus as the accounting machine prints a total, the total and identifying data can be transferred to the automatic punch which simultaneously punches a summary card.

Figure 8-4 shows one of the new balance-forward inventory cards which was automatically produced by having the summary punch connected to the accounting machine during the operation illustrated by Figure 8-3. The printed data on the top of the card was obtained by processing the card through an interpreter.

IBM ACCOUNTING MACHINES

IBM accounting machines include the Types 402, 403, and 407. These three machines perform most functions similarly. The primary difference between the Types 402 and 403 is that the 403 is capable of printing three lines from one card, whereas the 402 can print only a single line. This operation is referred to as *multiple-line print*. The major difference between the Type 407 (Figure 8-5) and the other models is that the 407 is equipped with additional features that enhance its capability as an accounting machine. These additional features include:

STOCK STATUS SUMMARY

DATE ___3 / 31 /19 - -___

PART NUMBER	PART NAME	UNIT	UNIT COST	OPENING BALANCE	TRANSACTIONS		ON HAND
					REC-EIPTS	ISSUES	
1 1 1 2 4	T R A N S I S T O R B G	E A	12,65	68	145	131	82
1 1 2 1 1	L E N S 7 7 7	E A	8,33	84	156	82	158
1 1 3 8 1	C O N N E C T O R S X X 1	E A	1,99	148	180	175	153
1 1 3 8 2	C O N N E C T O R S X X 2	E A	1,38	75	288	184	179

Figure 8-3. Stock status summary resulting from a group-printing operation.

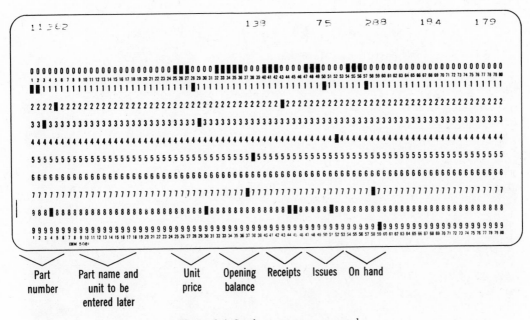

Figure 8-4. Stock status summary card.

1. 120 print wheels as opposed to a maximum of 88 on the 402-403.

2. Storage units for storing information to be used in later operations.

3. Multiple-line printing from one card.

4. A performance rate for all operations except multiple-line printing of 150 cards a minute.

The card feed hopper and stacker are located at the left end of the IBM 407 Accounting Machine. Approximately 1,000 cards can be placed in the hopper, face down, with the 9-edges toward the throat. As soon as the last card is fed, the machine stops automatically. The remaining cards in the machine must be run into the stacker by pressing the start key. The stacker is located directly above the feed hopper. When the stacker is full, feeding stops. Cards can be added to the feed hopper and removed from the stacker without stopping the machine.

The standard IBM 407 Accounting Machine can print 18,000 characters a minute. Cards are read at the rate of 150 a minute or 9,000 an hour. Printing is performed by 120 print wheels which form a solid bank 12 inches wide. Each print wheel has 47 different characters: all of the letters of the alphabet, all of the numbers, and 11 special characters. A print wheel schematic is shown in Figure 8-6.

In addition to printing, another main function of the accounting machine is *ac-*

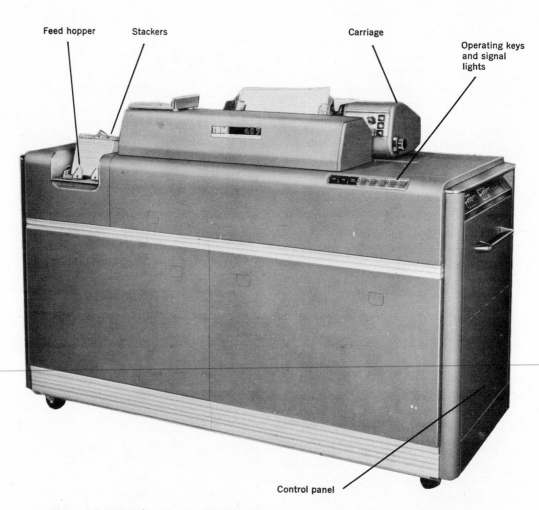

Figure 8-5. IBM 407 Accounting Machine. (*Courtesy International Business Machines Corporation.*)

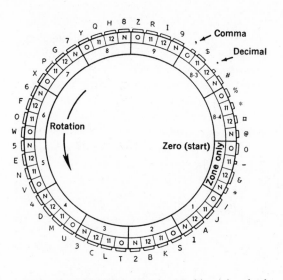

Figure 8-6. IBM 407 Accounting Machine print wheel schematic.

cumulation. This function is performed by counters similar to those used in adding or calculating machines. Thus the accounting machine is able to accumulate the results of adding or subtracting data in various columns of a report and to print totals.

The IBM 407 has a maximum of 112 counter positions. These 112 positions are made up of four 3-position counters, four 4-position counters, six 6-position counters, and six 8-position counters. A 3-position counter can total up to 999, a 4-position counter to 9,999, and so on. Counters can be used individually or combined in any manner to accommodate a larger number of digits. For example, if a counter large enough to hold a 10-digit total is needed, it may be made by combining a 6-position counter and a 4-position counter, or any other combination adding up to 10 positions.

Program control is a process by which the accounting machine is able to distinguish cards of one group from those of another. The factors in cards that initiate con-

trol operations are generally the factors of classification. For instance, each card included in the detailed list shown in Figure 8-2 contains a part number. Thus, a change from one part to the next would cause the 407 to recognize a difference in part number and to initiate a program step.

A standard IBM 407 can be made to take up to three program steps. These are generally referred to as *minor program, intermediate program,* and *major program.* Some of the things accomplished during a program step are the printing of totals, the punching of a card, and the advancing of the paper form to a particular printing line. For example, if automatic totals are desired by states, counties, and cities, state is the major group, county is the intermediate group, and city is the minor group. The impulse that initiates a program step is usually created when the machine detects a difference between the card at the first reading station and the card at the next reading station.

The automatic feeding and spacing of continuous forms is regulated by the

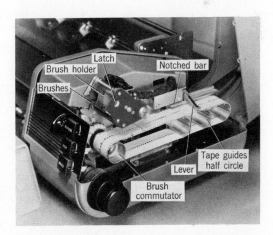

Figure 8-7. IBM 407 Accounting Machine tape-controlled carriage. (*Courtesy International Business Machines Corporation.*)

tape-controlled carriage together with control panel wiring. Tape control consists of punches in a narrow paper tape inserted in the carriage. Each tape corresponds to the exact length of the business form it is to control (Figure 8-7). Tapes control the feeding, spacing, and ejecting of forms, and the automatic skipping to various parts of a form.

The selection of printing positions

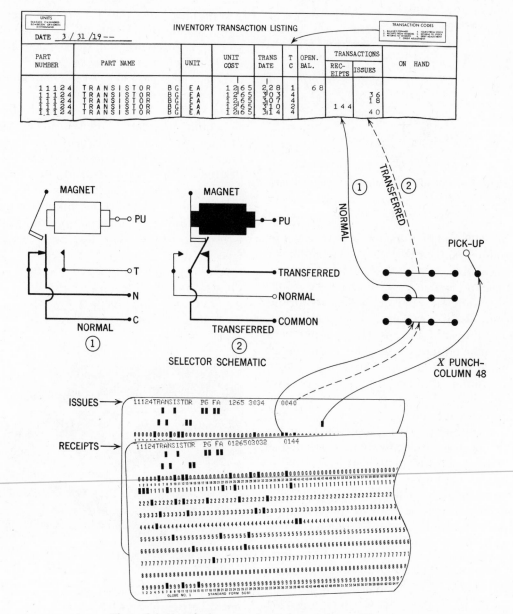

Figure 8-8. Use of selectors to determine printing positions.

on the report is accomplished through the use of *selectors*. For example, in Figure 8-8 the inventory transaction cards contain both receipts and issues in card columns 38 through 41. These need to be printed in different columns on the Inventory Transaction Listing. Therefore, some means must be provided for selecting the appropriate column. The selection of columns on the report is controlled by the use of an *X* (11) punch in card column 48 of the issues cards. If the pickup hub has not received an impulse, the selector is in a normal state, and the data in columns 38 through 41 of the card is transmitted through the common and normal hubs to the receipts column of the report. At this time there is an internal connection between the common hubs and the normal hubs directly above them. This is because any impulse wired to a common hub of a selector is available out of the normal hub of the selector when the selector is not energized.

If the card column that is wired to the pickup hub of the selector contains an *X* (11) punch, the punch causes the selector magnets to be energized. The selector is then in a transferred state and the data in card columns 38 through 41 of the card is transmitted through common and transferred hubs to the issues column of the report. At this time there is an internal connection between the common and the transferred hubs. This is because any impulse wired to a common hub of a selector is available out of the transferred hub when the selector is energized.

The principle of selection can be applied to operations performed with data processing machines through the proper wiring of selectors on the control panel. The use of selectors is similar in most data processing machines. Although operation of the selectors may differ slightly, the basic operating principle is the same.

The functions of detail printing, group printing, accumulating, and summary punching are also determined by control panel wiring. Varied formats of printed information can be achieved because of the flexibility that is attainable in control panel wiring. Control panels, which can be easily removed and inserted into the machine, are specially wired for different jobs. Because of the greater complexity of the wiring required to control accounting machine operations, no illustration of a completed wiring diagram is included here. However, an illustration of a wired control panel for an accounting machine appears in Chapter 5 (see Figure 5-9).

Review Questions

1. Discuss detail printing as opposed to group printing on an accounting machine.
2. Identify the three types of IBM accounting machines. What are the basic differences?
3. How many print wheels does the Type 407 Accounting Machine contain? How many different characters are contained on each print wheel?
4. What is the function of a counter on the accounting machine? How can a ten-digit total be accommodated if the largest counter has only eight positions?
5. Discuss the function of "program steps." How many can the Type 407 Accounting Machine be made to take?
6. What is the function of a control tape on an accounting machine?

PUNCHED CARD
PROCEDURE DEVELOPMENT

Chapters 6, 7, and 8 were devoted to the functions of punched card machines and to some of the typical applications of the different machines. Most of these applications were very specific since each was designed to illustrate the use of a single machine. However, business applications generally involve the use of several machines because most operations require the completion of more than one step in the data processing cycle. This will be evident in the punched card application appearing later in this chapter. Preceding the application, techniques of developing and documenting the procedures necessary to complete a business application will be described.

PROCEDURE DEVELOPMENT

Since the purpose of data processing is to transform source data into final reports and documents, it is evident that

the procedures necessary to effect this transition are of primary concern. Let us consider some of the steps that are involved.

Determining Objectives

Before a procedure is developed, the ultimate objectives must be determined. If a report is the main objective, a number of facts must be ascertained.

1. What information is needed in the report?
2. How detailed must the information be?
3. What form should the report take?
4. Who will receive and use the report?
5. When is it to be completed?
6. What priority is to be assigned to the report compared to other necessary reports?
7. What is the significance of the report to the organization?

Examining Source Documents

After the objectives have been established, it is necessary to examine the input required to start the procedure. In most cases basic data originates outside of the data processing department and must be key punched from some source document. Thus, it is necessary to assure that the source document contains all the items of data necessary to produce the final printed report. If the source data is not in the proper format for key punching, it must be rearranged or transcribed into some form of coded statement to facilitate the punching operation.

In most organizations it is customary to batch source documents and transmit them to the data processing department with control tapes or item counts to facilitate the handling and control of the documents.

Designing Cards

A number of considerations are important in determining how data is to be arranged on a card, including the relationship of the card to source documents and other unit records. Included are such factors as the following:

1. First and most important, the requirements of the finished reports must be listed. To this list should be added any information needed for control or reference purposes.

2. The number of columns needed for each item of information should be determined.

3. The fields of the card should be arranged so that data can be punched into the card in the order in which it is read from the source document. Data would normally be read from left to right or from top to bottom on the original document.

4. The alignment principle should be employed in designing a card to be used in various operations with other types of cards. That is, a given item of data in a new card should generally be placed in the same columns assigned to comparable data in other cards to which it is related.

5. Fields should be assigned according to the manner in which they are to be punched, i.e., manually punched by a card punch operator, or automatically punched by some other means. Automatic punching methods should be used as much as possible. Fields with similar punching operations should be placed in close relationship to simplify key punching and machine operations.

In addition to the arrangement of data on the card, the information to be interpreted and the order in which it is to be printed on the card should be determined.

After the preceding factors have been determined, the card should be designed with the aid of a card-layout form. Finally, the designed card should be checked with the planned procedure and the reports to make certain that all requirements have been met.

Cards as Source Documents

Before constructing the procedure, the use of punched cards as source documents should be considered. Punched cards may be used as source documents for such internal record-keeping functions as time tickets, inventory control cards, and production control cards. It may be possible to prepare the basic documents for these functions in the data processing department since most of these documents contain data that is available from the present punched card records.

Thus, the persons completing the forms are required to enter only the variable data such as hours worked, quantity on hand, or units completed.

Prepunching cards for use as source documents reduces the workload when the completed documents are returned to the data processing department. Other efficiencies include ease and flexibility of recording data on the documents and ease in handling because of uniform size.

Planning the Procedure

We have seen in previous chapters that punched card machines are designed to perform specific functions in the data processing cycle. To utilize personnel and machines most economically and effectively in completing the various recording, manipulating, and reporting procedures, it is necessary to:

1. Determine the job steps necessary to convert source data into final reports.
2. Determine which job steps can be performed mechanically.
3. Determine which machine operations and clerical functions will be used in the various steps.

After the procedures have been developed, it is necessary to translate the general plan into a graphic representation of the job steps and the sequence in which they must be performed to execute the plan. This is accomplished by the preparation of a *flow chart*.

Punched Card Flow Charts

A flow chart consists of a sequence of illustrative symbols representing documents, machines, or actions involved in a process. A flow chart aids in providing the designer, the user, and the managerial observer with a clear understanding of the major steps followed in a procedure. Certain criteria should be kept in mind in developing flow charts.

1. Any work that can be performed can be represented in a flow chart.
2. The flow chart should clearly show the flow of the work into the data processing department and the flow of work within the department.
3. The wording on the flow chart should be as brief as possible.
4. The type of work performed at each job step should be clear.
5. The chart should not be cluttered with details that might obscure the important parts of the procedure.
6. Keyed numbers or letters should be used to refer to sources of more detailed information concerning job steps and documents.

The development of a punched card procedure generally involves the preparation of an *operational* (detailed) *flow chart*. This type of flow chart depicts the specific steps necessary to arrive at the end result. It records in proper sequence each machine or clerical operation used throughout the procedure (see Figure 9-3). Thus the operational flow chart is useful to the analyst in designing the procedure, to the operator who performs the steps, and to the data processing supervisor.

To clearly indicate the various machine and clerical operations and to make flow charts more meaningful, a pictorial medium consisting of standard flow chart symbols is used. Ten of the available symbols are illustrated and explained in Figure 9-1. Special templates are available for use in drawing the various symbols required in flow charting (see Figure 20-7). In addition to the use of standard symbols,

Document symbol. Paper documents and reports of all varieties including source documents and ledgers.

Keying operation. An operation utilizing a key-driven device: card punching, card verifying, typing, etc.

Punched card. All varieties of punched cards.

Clerical operation. Manual off-line operation which does not require mechanical aid.

Off-line storage. Off-line storage of either paper tape or punched cards.

Transmittal tape. Proof or adding machine tape.

Auxiliary operation. Machine operation supplementing the main processing function.

Sorting or collating operation. Operation performed on sorting or collating equipment.

Perforated tape. Perforated tape, whether paper or plastic.

Processing. A major processing function.

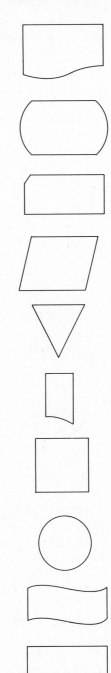

Figure 9-1. Punched card flow-charting symbols.

descriptive verbs or verb phrases are generally inserted within the symbols to further amplify their meaning. The movement of documents, cards, or data is generally from top to bottom and from left to right, and is represented by a solid line. Arrowheads must be used on flow lines that oppose these directions, although they may be used on all lines if desired.

Operators' Manuals

After a procedure has been planned and the necessary job steps have been flow charted, it is necessary to prepare operating and machine setup instructions as a guide for operators and as a source of reference in the performance of the work.

The type of procedures used may vary depending on the needs or preferences of the organization involved. However, one of the methods often used is the job step method, in which a separate instruction sheet is used to describe each step of the procedure. Special sheets are designed and preprinted for use in describing operations to be performed on each type of machine. These forms provide spaces for specific machine setup information as well as information concerning the sources of data, the time of receipt, forms to be used, instructions for performing various operations, the scheduled time for completion of the routine, and disposition of the resulting documents or reports. Figure 9-2 shows an example of operating instructions for a Type 407 Accounting Machine operation.

A PAYROLL APPLICATION

As indicated earlier, most punched card applications require the use of a se-

ries of machines to fulfill all processing requirements. However, most of the applications in the preceding chapters were limited to the completion of a single job step on one machine. Therefore, a more comprehensive application involving all of the basic machines will provide additional insight into the interrelationship and functions of punched card equipment. The application that has been selected for this purpose is a weekly payroll procedure.

Payroll may be defined as the process of reporting to the employee, to the employer, and to governmental organizations the amount of money paid for services rendered to the employer by the employee. Payroll is one of the most common accounting applications of data processing equipment. However, the details of the payroll process may vary considerably from one organization to another, depending on the size of the organization, the nature of the products, and the kind of data processing equipment used. In this application let us assume that the business concern employs several hundred people and performs its data processing on punched card equipment like that described in the preceding chapters.

A flow chart of the following application is shown in Figure 9-3. The steps on the flow chart are numbered or lettered to correspond with descriptions of the operations performed, the input documents accepted, and the output documents generated. Operational steps are keyed with operational numbers (e.g., *Operation 1, 2, 3,* etc.), and documents are keyed with alphabetic letters (e.g., *Document A, B, C,* etc.).

Document A. In the day or hourly rate type of payroll, an employee is paid according to the time spent on the job. The time may be entered on an employee work record by the worker, a timekeeper, or by the supervisor of the department or sec-

Alphabetical Accounting Machine

APPLICATION GENERAL LEDGER   STEP NO.   80

STEP DESCRIPTION TAB LISTINGS   CHART NO.   B06

                                                       MACHINE CODE   407

FROM   step 70   CONTROL PANEL NO.   T/007

CARD SEQUENCE:

	FIELDS	COLUMNS	PROGRAM
FIRST SORT	Acct. No.	15-21	Major
SECOND SORT			
THIRD SORT			
FOURTH SORT			
FIFTH SORT			

ARE SUMMARY CARDS REQUIRED? .... YES ____ NO X
NET TOTALS REQUIRED? .... YES X NO ____
PROGRESSIVE TOTALS? ....YES X NO ____
MULTIPLE LINE PRINT? .... YES ____ NO X

CARRIAGE TAPE: Receipts & Disbursement Journal

LENGTH		
CHANNELS	LENGTH	LINE NO.
1	3	69
2	8	74
3		
4		
5	55	121
6		
7		
8		
9		
10		
11		
12	60	126

SPACING:

SINGLE yes   DOUBLE no

OTHER no

LIST yes   TABULATE no

FORM: G.L. Special Detail Rpt.   PARTS 4 pt.

SWITCHES:

FORM .... INV. X CONV. ____
FINAL TOTAL .... ON X OFF ____
FORM STOP .... ON X OFF ____

RESET CHECK   CHECK X SET UP ____

MANUAL SETUP CHANGE SWITCHES				No Switches			ALTERATION SWITCHES		
1	2	3	4	5	6	7	8	9	10

OPERATION INSTRUCTIONS: Operator will select from cards the 600 & 700 series accounts (col. 15-17), and listing each group separately. Punch date header: Date Col. 2-7, X-38, Description 43-68.

HEADER INSTRUCTIONS   Label B06-2 G.L. Detail Report (Income or Expenses)

DISPOSITION OF CARDS Forward with B06-1 to Account Dept. Replace 600 & 700 series in their respective groups in file.

NEXT NO. ____

DATE PREPARED _____ June 11, 19 - _____   SP-120   NEXT STEP NO. 90

Figure 9-2. Operating instructions for a Type 407 Alphabetical Accounting Machine.

tion in which the work is performed (Figure 9-4). Individual job cards or tickets or punched card forms may also be used to record hours worked. For control purposes an adding-machine tape of the total hours worked usually accompanies each batch of records.

Document B. Every payroll procedure should be built using effective controls. Thus, all detailed records and reports are balanced against the payroll control register. The payroll control register establishes the predetermined totals to which all subsequent payroll reports and entries must balance. The series of checks and balances that make up the items appearing in the control register must begin with the entry of transactions into the data processing department and continue throughout the processing.

Operation 1. The data recorded in the employee work record is key punched into the work record card and key verified against the employee work record.

Document C. A work record card (Figure 9-5) is punched and verified in Operation 1 for each line on the employee work record. These cards serve as a basis for determining the employee's gross pay. Variations such as bonus payments and other adjustments are recorded in this card form and can be included in the calculation of gross pay.

Operation 2. The data punched into the work-record cards is tabulated and group printed by batch on the accounting machine.

Document D. The employee work-record proof listing is balanced back to the adding-machine tape that is received with the batch transmitting the employee work record. It is also used to post control data to the payroll control register.

Operation 3. The work-record cards are sorted in employee number sequence using the punched card sorter.

Operation 4. The work-record cards plus any bonus or other adjustment cards are calculated on the calculator to determine gross pay which is punched into the work-record card. The basic calculation involved is hours worked times hourly rate equals gross pay.

Operation 5. The work-record cards and other cards from Operation 4 are listed on the accounting machine to produce the gross pay proof listing.

Document E. The gross pay proof listing is balanced to the payroll control register.

Operation 6. The work-record cards from Operation 5 are sorted by department number.

Operations 7 and *8.* The cards from Operation 6 are listed on the accounting machine to produce the payroll summary register (Document F). At the same time this data is summary punched into the weekly earnings cards (Document G) by use of the document-originating machine.

Document F. The payroll summary register serves as a permanent record of all the current earnings data involved in the payroll calculation. This register becomes part of the permanent record of the payroll department.

Document G. The weekly earnings cards (Figure 9-6) which are summary punched contain the employee number and gross earnings data.

Document H. The employee work record, bonus, and adjustment cards used in Operations 7 and 8 are forwarded to the labor distribution procedure.

Operation 9. The weekly earnings cards (Document G) are listed on the accounting machine to produce the weekly earnings card listing.

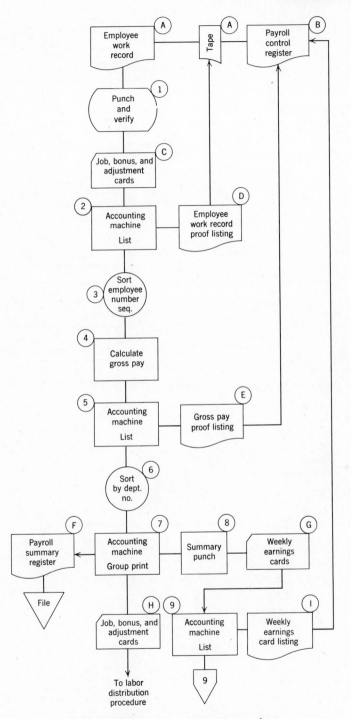

Figure 9-3. Flow chart of payroll procedure.

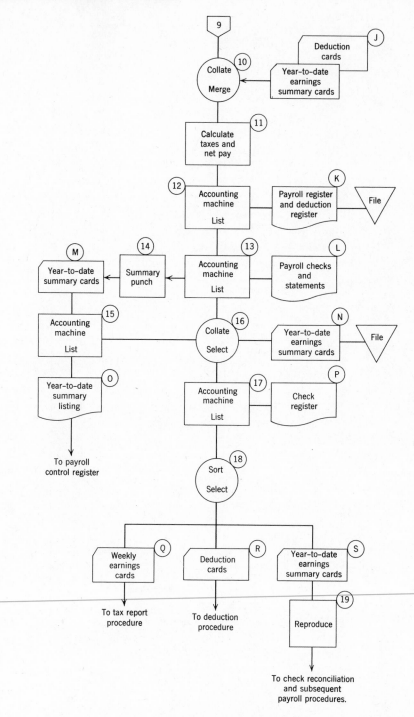

Figure 9-3 (continued)

Document I. The weekly earnings card listing containing the earnings for each employee is balanced back to the payroll control register. This establishes the accuracy of the summary punching in the weekly earnings cards.

Operation 10. The weekly earnings cards (Document G) and the year-to-date earnings summary cards and deduction cards (Document J) are merged into one file by use of the collator.

Operation 11. The weekly earnings cards (Document G), and the year-to-date earnings summary cards and deduction cards (Document J) are fed into the calculator for calculation of taxes and net pay, which are punched into the weekly earnings card.

Operation 12. The cards from Operation 11 are group printed on the accounting machine to obtain the payroll register and the deduction register (Document K).

Document K. Payroll register and deduction register (Figure 9-7).

Operations 13 and 14. The cards from Operation 12 are listed on the accounting machine to produce the payroll checks and statements (Document L). At the same time the year-to-date summary cards (Document M) for the current pay period are summary punched by the use of the document-originating machine.

Document L. Payroll checks and statements (Figure 9-8).

Document M. Current pay period year-to-date summary cards (Figure 9-6).

Operation 15. The current pay period year-to-date summary cards are listed on the accounting machine to produce the year-to-date summary listing (Document O).

Document O. The year-to-date summary listing includes the current year-to-date summary cards and is balanced to the payroll control register.

Operation 16. The year-to-date summary cards for the current pay period (Document M) are merged into the file from Operation 14 and the year-to-date summary cards for the previous pay period (Document N) are selected out of the file and stored.

Document N. Year-to-date earnings summary cards for the previous pay period are stored for future reference.

Operation 17. The merged file from Operation 16 is listed on the accounting machine to produce the check register (Document P).

Document P. The check register contains all the items appearing on the checks and statements. This document is retained as a permanent payroll record and as a research document for check reconciliation.

Operation 18. The merged file used in Operation 17 is separated by the use of the sorter into three groups: weekly earnings cards (Document Q), deduction cards (Document R), and current pay period year-to-date earnings cards (Document S).

Document Q. The weekly earnings cards (Figure 9-6) are forwarded to the tax report procedure.

Document R. The deduction cards (Figure 9-6) are forwarded to the deduction procedure.

Document S. The current pay period year-to-date earnings summary cards (Figure 9-6) are forwarded to Operation 19.

Operation 19. The year-to-date earnings summary cards for the current pay period (Document S) are reproduced on the document-originating machine for the check reconciliation procedure. The original file is retained for the next pay-period calculation.

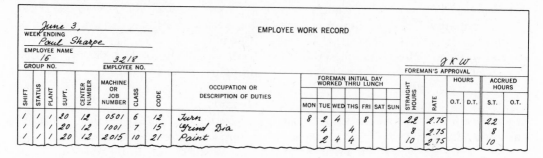

Figure 9-4. Employee work record. (*Courtesy International Business Machines Corporation.*)

Conclusion

The preceding application is designed to illustrate how different types of punched card machines can be combined to perform a variety of payroll accounting operations. The procedures illustrated here are intentionally simplified. Probably an actual payroll would consist of a number of related procedures including labor accounting, which uses many of the same input documents and involves many of the same computations. Nevertheless, this application does serve to illustrate the use of punched card machines in performing integrated functions.

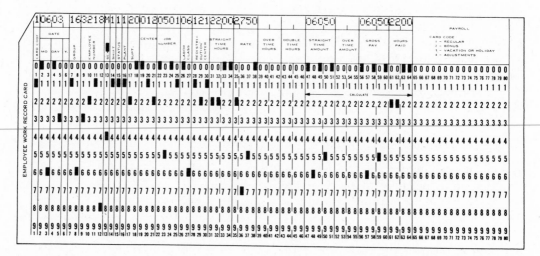

Figure 9-5. Employee work record card. (*Courtesy International Business Machines Corporation.*)

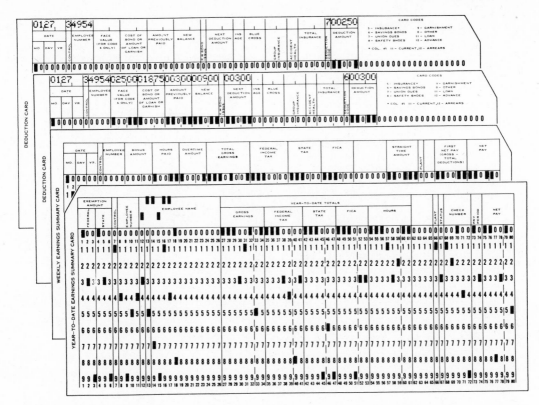

Figure 9-6. Deduction cards, weekly earnings summary card, and year-to-date earnings summary card. (*Courtesy International Business Machines Corporation.*)

PAYROLL REGISTER

DATE ______

Year-to-Date Earnings	Year-to-Date With. Tax	Employee Dept.	Employee Number	Name of Employee	Hours Worked	Base Rate	Earnings Regular	Earnings OT Prem.	Earnings Other	Earnings Total	Deductions FICA	Deductions With. Tax	Deductions Misc.	Net Pay
3002 38	267 68	01	206	W V ASTOR	44 0	2 250	99 00	4 50		103 50	3 11	13 95	8 75	77 69
2684 30	361 44	01	342	A F DUFFY	50 0	2 250	112 50	11 25		123 75	3 71	15 26	3 25	101 53
2432 71	255 24	01	518	B H ENGLISH	40 0	2 150	86 00			86 00	2 58	8 46	4 50	70 46
1807 50	266 22	01	615	F L FARELY	42 0	1 500	63 00	1 60	4 00	68 60	2 06	10 01	3 50	53 03
2175 64	269 82	01	703	J E GENDER	42 0	1 350	77 70	1 99	6 00	85 69	2 57	10 74	2 50	69 88
2231 27	342 54	01	893	F A HARRIS	44 0	1 900	83 60	4 06	5 75	93 41	2 80	14 47	3 75	72 39
1945 78											4 04	16 40	7 42	106 76
1870 32											3 38	8 70	5 80	94 92
2461 11											3 20	14 70	2 20	86 70
875 82											4 16	20 10	18 40	95 91
2521 12											4 08	21 00	21 61	89 47
2434 61											3 28	16 10	7 60	82 36
2220 02											3 85	25 60	17 41	

DEDUCTION REGISTER

TYPE
1-SINGLE PERIOD
2-SPECIFIC PERIOD
3-STANDING

WHEN MADE
1-FIRST WEEK
2-SECOND WEEK
3-THIRD WEEK
4-FOURTH WEEK
5-1ST AND 2ND WEEK
6-2ND AND 4TH WEEK
7-EACH WEEK

DATE ______

Employee Dept.	Employee Number	Name of Employee	Ded. Code	Type Code	When Made	Total Deductions	Savings Bond	Hospital Insurance	Group Life Ins.	Credit Union	Retire Annuity
01	206	W V ASTOR	4	3	4	8 75				8 75	
01	342	A F DUFFY	2	3	4	1 25		1 25			
01	342	A F DUFFY	4	3	4	2 00				2 00	
01	518	B H ENGLISH	1	3	6	2 00	2 00				
01	518	B H ENGLISH	5	3	4	2 50					2 50
01	615	F L FARELY	2	3	4	1 50		1 50			
01	615	F L	3	3	4	2 00			2 00		
01	703					2 50	2 50				

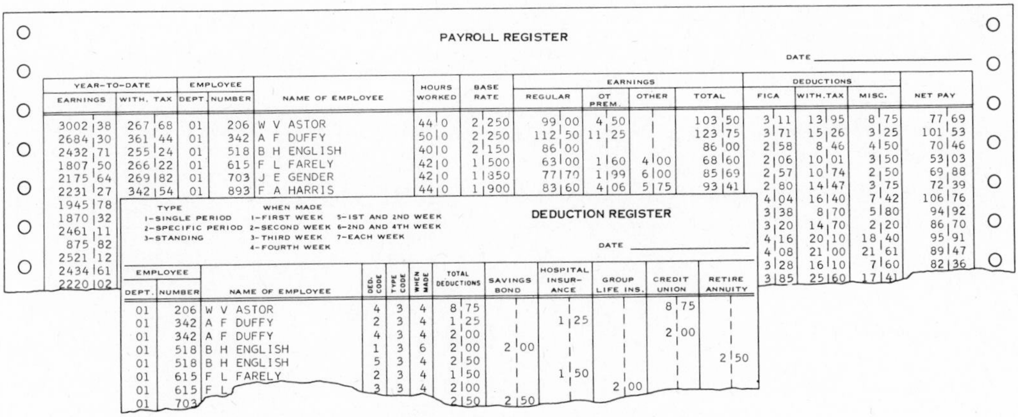

Figure 9-7. Payroll and deduction registers. (*Courtesy International Business Machines Corporation.*)

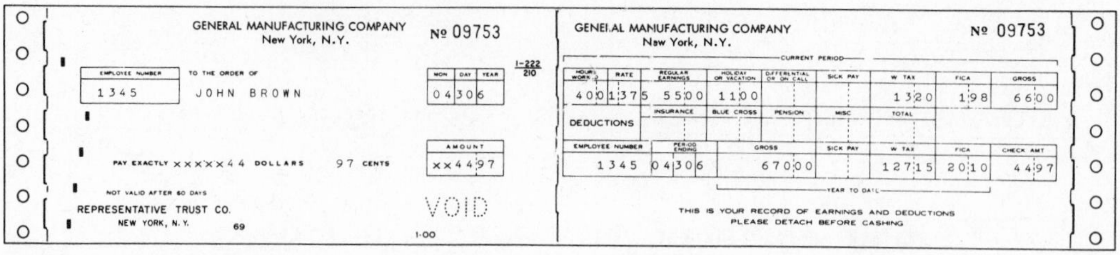

Figure 9-8. Continuous-form card check and statement. (*Courtesy International Business Machines Corporation.*)

Review Questions

1. What are the main steps in procedure development discussed in this chapter?
2. What major factors should be considered in determining how data is to be arranged on a card?
3. Discuss the advantages of using punched cards as source documents.
4. What are the nature and purpose of an operational flow chart?
5. What criteria should be kept in mind in developing flow charts?
6. What is the purpose of operating instructions? What information is included in operating instructions?

10

DATA COLLECTION

The ideal method of collecting data for processing in an automated system is to record it in a machine-sensible code at its point of origin. A machine-sensible code is a symbolic means of representing data in a medium such as punched tape, punched cards, or magnetic ink that can be sensed mechanically or electronically and, thus, transmitted automatically from one step to the next in a processing sequence.

Jean Emile Baudot took the first step toward the automation of source data when he built a paper tape punch and reader in the 1870's. Baudot, a French telegrapher, found that his messages were increasing faster than he could send them. In place of the telegraph key, he designed a keyboard similar to that of the typewriter. But, instead of typing on paper, his invention sent Morse code signals out over the wire. It was much faster and much easier to operate but, as the volume increased, the wire, the single link between remote points, was unable to handle the traffic. Baudot then devised an attachment to his keyboard for storing the Morse code signals in punched paper tape

which could then be used to transmit the messages as the line became available.

In punched code the letter *E*, a single dot in Morse code, became a single hole in the first row or channel of a five-channel punched paper tape. Other letters of the alphabet were represented by various combinations of holes in the five channels. This basic procedure, developed nearly one hundred years ago, is still used in Teletype and telegraph systems throughout the world.

Except for the use of punched cards, the development of techniques for automating source data progressed very slowly. The first accounting machine synchronized with a paper tape punch was developed in 1935. The first paper tape typewriter was introduced in the 1940's for use in automatic letter writing. A major advancement was made in the early 1950's when the concept of integrated data processing was introduced. The term *integrated data processing* was first used to describe systems involving paperwork that was mechanized from origination to completion. The large-scale application of IDP was pioneered by the United States

161

Steel Corporation and was first demonstrated at a special conference of the American Management Association in February, 1954. Five-channel punched tape was the machine-sensible code used in that system.

Originally, IDP involved the preparation of a machine-sensible code medium, generally punched paper tape, as part of a manual recording operation. However, developments in source data automation such as optical character recognition and magnetic ink character recognition broadened the scope of applications. In addition, translating devices such as tape-to-card converters extended the range of machines that could be included in performing a continuous series of data processing operations. To illustrate, let us assume that data has been punched into paper tape as a by-product of a recording operation performed on a typewriter with a tape-punching mechanism. This data could be transmitted to another city by a tape-transmitting device. The tape produced by the receiving unit could be converted to punched cards for processing on punched card equipment or as input to a computer. In either case, the processed information could be printed in characters that can be read by an optical character recognition (OCR) device. OCR devices can convert data into other forms including punched tape, the original recording medium of the data in this example.

This is merely one example of how data may be transferred among a variety of machines by the use of a common medium or by conversion from one medium to another. Later in this chapter we shall see additional samples of this technique.

The concept of integrated data processing became increasingly significant and resulted in two basic objectives that now dominate the field of data processing:

1. The recording of data at its point of origin in a machine-sensible code.

2. The completion of all processing on machines capable of reading the original code or a code to which it can be converted automatically.

These procedures are such a routine part of today's automatic data processing that they no longer require special identification. Thus, the descriptive term "integrated data processing" has become almost historical. However, the term "source data automation" is often used to describe the principle of recording information in a communicable medium at the point of origin.

When Jean Emile Baudot conceived the idea of a machine-sensible code, there was only one mode of recording data, the deliberate creation of punched paper tape by manually depressing the keys of a punching device. Now, as a result of today's varied equipment, three major modes are available for recording selected data in the languages of machines. Data may be recorded by deliberate action, as a by-product of another function, or by conversion from one medium to another. Some of the most commonly used codes, media, and machines used to collect data are discussed and illustrated in the following sections.

PUNCHED TAPE

Codes

Data is recorded in paper tape by a special arrangement of punched holes along the length of the tape. Since paper tape is a continuous recording medium, as compared to punched cards which are fixed in length, it can be used to record data in records of any length. The only limitation is that of the storage medium from which the data is received or the storage medium into which the data is to be placed.

Tapes using five, six, seven, and eight channels are available. However, only the five- and eight-channel codes will be described here since they are the most commonly used.

Five-Channel Code. Data is recorded (punched) in five parallel channels along the length of the tape. Each row of punches across the width of the tape represents one letter, digit, or symbol. Since the five punching positions allow only 32 possible combinations of punches, a shift system is used to double the number of available codes. A *letters* code punch at the start of a section of tape indicates to the printing or conversion device that the following characters are alphabetic. When the *figures* code punch appears, the following punches are interpreted as numeric or special characters.

Figure 10-1 illustrates the manner in which characters are interpreted, de-

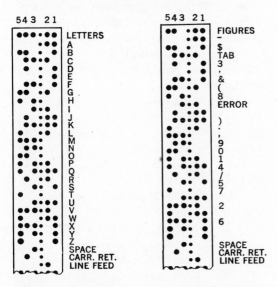

Figure 10-1. Punched tape showing five-channel code.

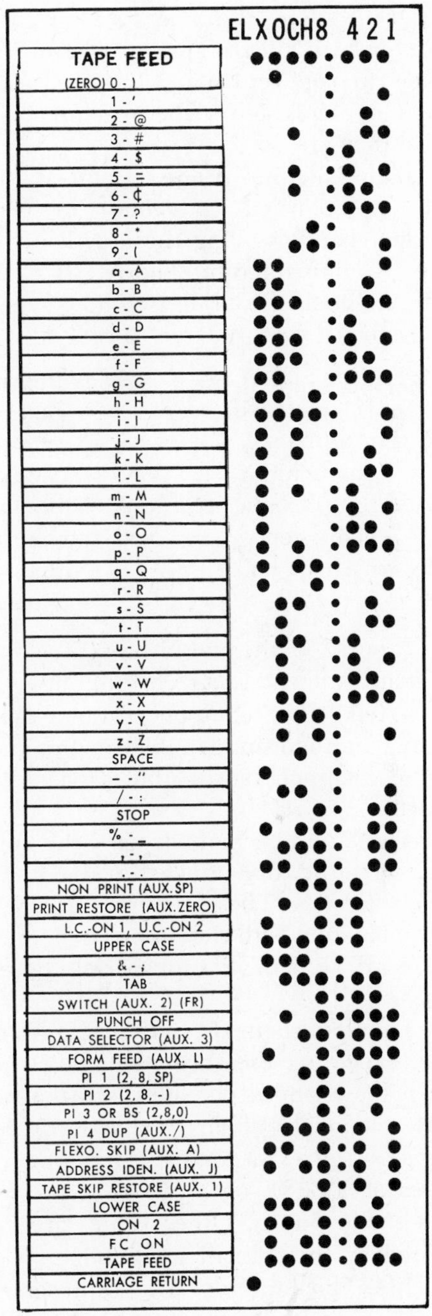

Figure 10-2. Punched tape showing eight-channel code (Friden).

pending upon the shift code preceding them. The function characters—space, carriage return, and line feed—are the same in both shifts. The actual function of the carriage return and line feed characters depends upon the machine with which they are used.

Eight-Channel Code. Data in this code is recorded (punched) in eight parallel channels along the length of the tape. As illustrated in Figure 10-2, the eight channels are used as follows, reading from left to right:

EL	End of Line (Carriage return)	8	Numeric channel
X	For alphabetic characters	4	Numeric channel
O	For alphabetic characters	2	Numeric channel
CH	For check bit	1	Numeric channel

A punch in the end-of-line (EL) channel marks the end of a record on the tape. On a typewriter equipped with a tape-sensing mechanism, a punch in the end-of-line channel causes the carriage to return.

The X and O channels serve the same purpose as the zone punches in 80-column punched cards. These channels are used in combination with the numeric channels to record alphabetic and special characters.

The four channels on the right of the tape, excluding the small feed holes between the 8 and 4 channels, are the numeric channels. When used alone these channels represent digits. The numeric values of 1, 2, 4, or 8 can be expressed by a single punch. Other values are expressed by the sum of a combination of punches. For example, 3 is represented by holes punched in the 2 and 1 channels; 7 is represented by holes punched in the 4, 2, and 1 channels, and so on.

The check bit channel (CH) performs a technical function. As a means of checking accuracy each column of the tape is punched with an odd number of holes. Since some characters are expressed by an even number of punches, it is necessary to add a check punch to produce an odd number of holes. Many tape-handling devices count the number of punched holes. If the number of punches in any column does not add to an odd figure, an error in transmission is indicated. This type of checking is known as *parity checking*.

Tape-Punching Devices

Automatic Typewriters. The automatic typewriter (Figure 10-3) can produce an original document and at the same time punch five-, six-, seven-, or eight-channel paper tape as an automatic by-product. Tape may be punched with all of the typewritten data or with selected items only. Tape can be coded to automatically control card punching, address plate embossing, communications machines, or electronic data processing machines. When placed on the reading mechanism of the typewriter, punched tape can be used to control the operation of the typewriter itself.

Punched tape may also be prepared on Teletype machines. On most models, punching of the tape is accompanied by simultaneous production of a ribbon (hard) copy of the data on plain paper or printed forms.

Accounting Machines. The accounting machine can be adapted to capture data in punched tape or punched card form as an automatic by-product of the basic accounting records prepared on the machine. It is often desirable to process basic accounting data further to obtain additional records and reports. Aux-

Figure 10-3. Flexowriter automatic writing machine. (*Courtesy Friden, Inc.*)

Figure 10-4. Accounting machine with paper tape perforator attachment. (*Courtesy Burroughs Corporation.*)

Figure 10-5. Add-punch capable of producing paper tape as a by-product of the adding function. (*Courtesy McBee Systems, A Division of Litton Industries.*)

iliary attachments to accounting machines capture automatically, in punched tape or cards, selected data computed or printed in the direct accounting operation (Figure 10-4). Such data, recorded in machine-sensible language, is then available as input for subsequent automatic data processing operations.

Add-Punches (Figure 10-5). The add-punch lists each item and total on a standard adding machine tape. At the same time complete or selected data may be automatically punched into tape for subsequent automatic processing or transmission by communication devices.

Cash Registers (Figure 10-6). Sales data may be captured at the point of origin by using a cash register equipped to automatically record transaction data in the form of punched paper tape.

Window Posting Machines. By connecting a punched paper tape recorder to a window posting machine it is possible to capture transaction data for subsequent machine processing and analysis. As the window posting machine records transactions such as charge sales, down payments, and installment payments in the

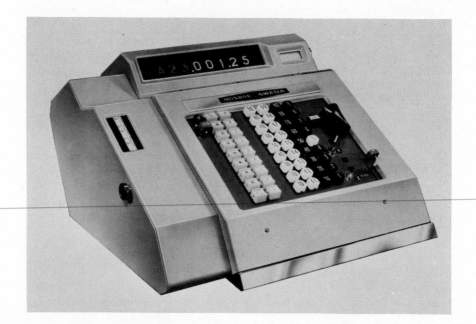

Figure 10-6. Cash register with attachment to record all transactions in the form of punched paper tape. (*Courtesy Sweda International, A Division of Litton Industries.*)

customer's passbook and ledger card, the data is also recorded on tape. The use of tape may eliminate the need for a ledger card at the window. (See Figure 4-21.)

EDGE-PUNCHED CARDS

Five- or eight-channel edge-punched cards may be punched with the same channel code that is used for recording information in paper tape (Figure 10-7). Edge-punched cards, also referred to as *wide tape*, are sometimes used as a substitute for paper tape because they are more durable and are easily filed in conventional card-filing equipment. Another advantage is that interpretation (translation of the punched holes) can be printed on the cards. Because of ease of handling, cards are advantageous for recording short bits of information used repetitively. For example, customers' names and addresses can be recorded on cards. By having a separate record for each customer, it is easy to extract the record from the file for

use in preparing invoices on an automatic typewriter whenever the customer sends in an order.

Edge-punched cards are prepared by automatic typewriters such as the one shown in Figure 10-3, and are also used to activate these devices.

PUNCHED CARDS

The punched card is one of the most useful media for communication with and between machines. The manner in which information is recorded by the use of standard card code was discussed in detail in Chapter 5. Therefore, further discussion of card code is not necessary.

Key punching of cards, which was described in Chapter 6, is still the most widely used manual method of recording data. Until recent years, the equipment needed to punch data into cards was mostly large and, thus, stationary. Such equipment was impractical for use by field personnel and others who moved

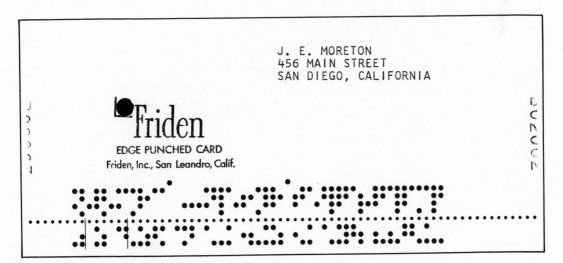

Figure 10-7. Edge-punched card with interpretation of punches.

Figure 10-8. Portable alpha-numeric printing punch (above), and portable card punch (below). (*Courtesy Wright Line.*)

from place to place in performing their jobs. Consequently, they were required to write their records in longhand (or on the typewriter) and send them somewhere to be key punched. Fortunately, this is no longer necessary because of the availability of portable card punches such as the ones shown in Figure 10-8.

A good example of the value of such devices is seen in the old and new way that source data is handled by the Plant Pest Control Division of the Agriculture Research Services, Department of Agriculture.* This department has the responsibility for controlling numerous plants and pests in 3,300 counties throughout the country. Formerly, over 200 forms were used at the county level and were transmitted to the central office in Washington through county, state, district, and regional channels. At each level copies were retained, statistics were extracted, and reports were prepared, thus,

---

* Raymond H. Eckenbach, "The Many Faces of SDA," *Business Automation,* December 1965, p. 36.

requiring up to 42 days for completed forms to reach the central office.

To expedite the collection of data, the Department of Agriculture installed a new system. Now the foreman of each field labor crew keeps a tally sheet of accomplishments. At the close of the day he punches the daily results into cards using a portable card punch which he keeps in the glove compartment of his truck. The punched cards are mailed directly to the central office and processed through a computer. Thus within 10 days after the work is completed in the field, the equipment produces all the reports needed for the county, state, district, regional, and central offices. As a result of the new system, it was possible to discard 200 different forms, and reports were available to the central office about 30 days sooner.

EDGE-NOTCHED CARDS

Edge-notched cards, previously discussed in Chapter 4 (see Figure 4-12), were originally used only for manual data processing operations. However, the development of tabulating punch and conversion devices has extended the usefulness of source data recorded in this medium. Edge-notched cards can now be read, tabulated, and summarized automatically. Unit records of this type can also be converted into punched tape or punched cards for computer input.

The code positions on cards may be notched individually by using a hand punch or in groups by using a hand-operated groover. Electric key punch devices (see Figure 4-13) and automatic tabulating punches are available for large operations.

PUNCHED TAGS

Another use of punched holes to automate source data is in the price-inventory tag attached to many items in modern department stores. The tag may be a single part or may consist of two or more detachable stubs. The tag generally contains a series of small holes as well as printed information indicating the price and identifying the user and the article to which the tag is attached. The holes in the tag represent selected data required by the user for automated record keeping (Figure 10-9).

The code structure used in tags is similar to the five-channel code structure used in punched paper tape. A combination of small holes in a vertical line represents a single digit of data. Punching is numeric only. In order to process data originating in tags, conversion to punched cards, paper tape, or magnetic tape is necessary.

Although print-punch tags have been used primarily in merchandising operations, applications are not limited to this field. They have also been used effectively for such purposes as inventory control, manufacturing records, production control, material inspection, and piecework payroll computations.

It is possible to create holes in tags by setting the dials of a print-punch recorder (Figure 10-10). Once the dials are set, many tags containing the same data may be made automatically at the rate of 200 stubs a minute without resetting the dials.

PERFORATED COUPONS

The average homeowner, car owner, or installment buyer is familiar with the perforated coupon as a method of automating source data. The perforated coupon has been used for a long time in banks, finance companies, mortgage companies, and department stores as a means of recording payments. The amounts, dates, payment numbers, and other data perforated in coupons are generally readable by the human eye since they form recognizable characters and figures (Figure 10-11).

Sorters are available to place randomly received coupons in account number order for processing. Special readers sense the language punched in the coupons and emit pulses for translation of the data into paper tape, punched cards, or magnetic tape. Beyond the sorting and reading of coupons, all other processing is done after conversion to another language.

Machine-sensible language is generally recorded in coupons by the use of a perfo-

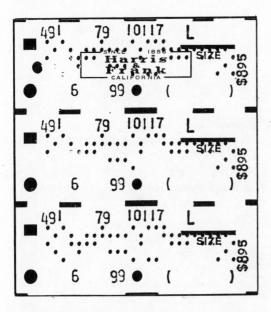

Figure 10-9. Three-section price ticket. (*Courtesy Harris & Frank Company.*)

Figure 10-10. Hopper-fed print-punch machine. (*Courtesy Dennison Manufacturing Company.*)

rator such as the one shown in Figure 10-12. Once set, these machines are able to gangpunch complete books of payment coupons, work tickets, or similar forms.

BAR CODE

Bar code is used extensively as a means of transferring data to sales transaction documents from plastic credit cards (Figure 10-13). An arrangement of bars is embossed on such credit cards to represent account numbers. The code structure consisting of short and long bars is used to encode numeric data only. Digits are represented by the varied positioning of one or two bars.

Bar code can be transferred from embossed credit cards to sales transaction documents using a device such as the one shown in Figure 10-14. Embossed cards and sales documents in the form of 51- or 80-column punched card unit sets can be easily inserted into the machine illustrated. By operating a simple lever or stamping mechanism, the identifying data on the card is imprinted on the original sales form and also on carbon copies. If the card contains both bar code and numeric characters, as shown in Figure 10-13, these are imprinted at the same time.

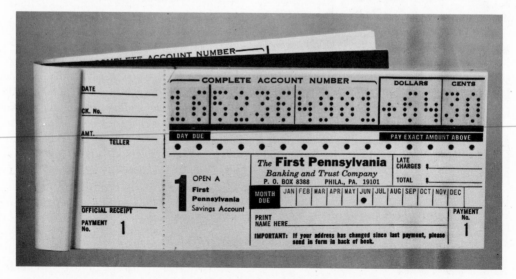

Figure 10-11. Book of perforated transaction coupons. (*Courtesy Cummins-Chicago Corporation.*)

Figure 10-12. Document perforator. (*Courtesy Cummins-Chicago Corporation.*)

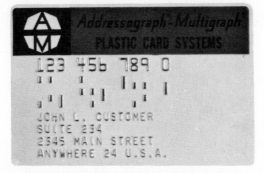

Figure 10-13. Embossed plastic plate used for credit or identification purposes. (*Courtesy Addressograph Multigraph Corporation.*)

transmission is the one that uses optical characters. Alphabetic as well as numeric data printed with specially designed type and hand-printed characters may be read by optical character readers through a scanning process.

Type style generally plays an important role in optical character reading. This is especially true in transferring data to

Variable numeric data such as the amount of sale or number of units may be recorded simultaneously on some devices by setting keys.

A special optical code reader and data converter reads documents imprinted with bar code and punches the information into cards or tape for further processing. The data may also be printed out in human-sensible language. The stylized numeric characters imprinted by plastic cards can be read and converted by other types of optical character readers.

OPTICAL CHARACTERS

An increasingly important method of recording for machine processing and

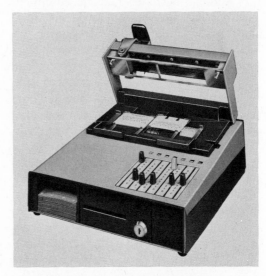

Figure 10-14. Data recorder used to imprint cards with both human- and machine-sensible characters. (*Courtesy Addressograph Multigraph Corporation.*)

sales documents from embossed credit cards such as the one shown in Figure 10-13. The embossed numbers on cards of this type are usually stylized to improve the print quality and facilitate machine recognition. For example, properly stylizing the numeral *6* prevents it from being read by a machine as the numeral *8* because of carbon or a poor impression. Some of the stylized type fonts are specifically designed for a particular method of machine reading. However, for other methods of reading, a stylized typeface may be helpful but not essential.

Optical characters are created by a variety of devices that print or type with a specially stylized typeface. For example, the type style shown in Figure 10-15, which meets the specifications of the U.S.A. Standards Association, is available on a special element designed for use with the IBM "Selectric" typewriter. Other typewriters can also be obtained with optically readable type styles.

Adding machines may be equipped with special type fonts to produce tapes that can be read by optical scanners as well as by humans. Cash registers can also be equipped with special type fonts. Thus, as a sales person records the original entry on the register, the data is printed on a journal tape in stylized type designed for optical scanning (Figure 10-16).

Special transaction recorders similar to that in Figure 10-14 are also used to prepare source documents in optically readable characters. Optical characters

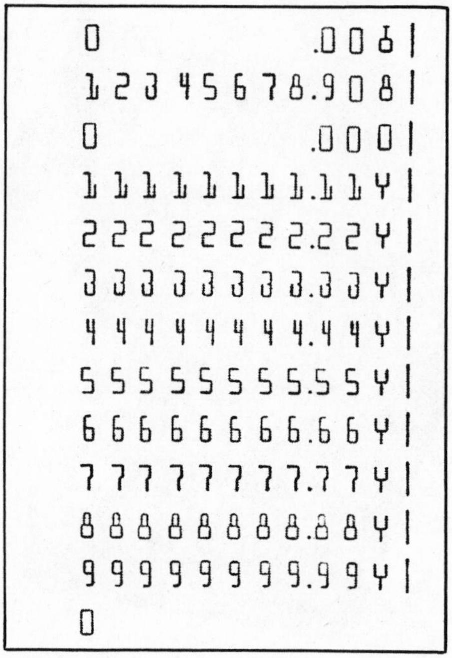

Figure 10-16. Cash register tape printed with optical characters.

embossed on credit cards are transferred to sales documents in the same manner as bar code.

Optical character readers eliminate the slow and costly process of manually key punching vast amounts of data from source documents in order to convert it into machine-sensible form. Depending on the model, the output of devices that read optical characters may include printed reports, magnetic tape, paper tape, or punched cards. Optical scanners may also enter data directly into a computer for immediate processing.

Figure 10-15. OCR type style prepared on an IBM "Selectric" typewriter. (*Courtesy International Business Machines Corporation.*)

MAGNETIC INK CHARACTERS

Magnetic ink character recognition, familiarly called MICR, is a machine-sensible code adopted by the American Bankers Association as a national standard for use by banks throughout the country. This code consists of numerals and symbols imprinted by machine in a distinctive type style and with magnetic ink containing particles of iron oxide. The MICR code consists of ten digits, zero through nine, and four special symbols. The numerals are readable by humans.

The documents on which MICR is used, primarily checks and deposit slips, may be paper or cards of various sizes. However, to make MICR a universal code, it was necessary to define a standard format for magnetic printing. The bottom $\frac{5}{8}$ inch of a check is reserved for encoding in MICR. A space of six inches, measuring from the right edge of the check, is specified as the universal printing area. Specific areas within the universal six-inch area are designated to contain certain types of data common to all banking operations (Figure 10-17).

All data except the amount can be printed before the bank issues a supply of checks to the user. Printing may be accomplished with standard duplicating or printing equipment using special iron-oxide bearing ink. Special key-operated devices are available to manually record amounts or other identifying data on checks. This data is encoded by the first bank receiving the check for processing.

The particles of iron oxide in the MICR ink are detected by reading heads

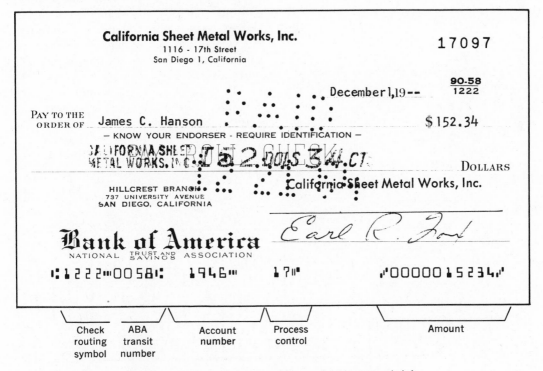

Figure 10-17. Check with characters inscribed in magnetic ink.

in magnetic scanning equipment. Scanned data may be entered directly into a computer, or the data may be recorded on punched cards, paper tape, or magnetic tape, which can then be used as input to the computer.

MAGNETIC TAPE

Codes

Magnetic tape looks very much like the tape used in home or office tape recorders except that it is normally $\frac{1}{2}$-inch wide and is manufactured to higher specifications. It is made of acetate or mylar coated with magnetizable material. Data is recorded in the form of magnetized spots or *bits* that create electrical impulses. Data recorded in this manner can be retained indefinitely.

Although it is impossible to see the magnetized spots that are recorded on magnetic tape, Figure 10-18 shows the arrangement in which the codes would appear if they were visible. Data is usually recorded in seven or nine parallel channels or tracks along the length of the tape depending on the code that is being used. Each channel can record from 100 to more than 3,000 bits an inch. Each character is represented by the presence or absence of bits in the channel positions of one column across the width of the tape.

As a means of verifying accuracy, each character may be checked for even or odd parity. Parity checking is a built-in self-checking feature utilized in most magnetic tape-coding methods. As in the case of paper tape coding, this consists of a channel in which a redundant bit is added whenever necessary to create either an odd or even parity for the character or digit represented. In some codes, each digit or character is represented by an even number of bits. Although different characters are made up of different combinations of bits, the number of bits in any valid character is always even. Thus, a character with an odd number of bits would be detected as an error. Similarly, a code may be used in which all characters must have an odd number of bits. In this case an even number of bits would indicate an error. Codes that use an odd number of bits are said to have an *odd parity*. Codes that use an even number of bits are said to have an *even parity*.

In contrast to the continuous recording of sound on tape, data is recorded as separate record units or groups of records. A record may consist of any number of characters, fields, or words. Records are separated from each other by a short segment of blank tape $\frac{6}{10}$- or $\frac{3}{4}$-inch in length

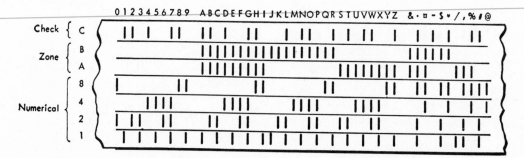

Figure 10-18. Representation of magnetic tape showing standard binary coded decimal interchange code.

for the majority of units. This blank tape is called an *inter-record gap* (Figure 10-19). During writing, a gap is automatically produced at the end of each record. During reading, the record begins with the first character sensed at the end of a gap and continues without interruption until the next gap is reached. Gaps allow the magnetic tape to stop between records and to attain proper speed before reading or writing is resumed. To save space a group of related records may be combined into a *multiple-record block*. Each of these blocks is also separated by an inter-record gap. The larger a block of records is, the more efficient the tape storage and data transfer rate will be.

Data Recorders

In the past, data was generally transferred to tape from some other medium by means of a conversion device. However, it is now possible to capture data on tape directly by using special tape recording devices. For example, the unit illustrated in Figure 10-20 permits an operator to record data onto 7- or 9-channel, $\frac{1}{2}$-inch magnetic tape via a keyboard. This model may also be used to verify data previously recorded on tape and to search a prerecorded tape for records specified by the operator.

Data that is keyed in by the operator is first entered into a storage device. This delay between keying and recording allows the operator to make changes in a record before it is actually written on tape. However, after data is recorded on tape, it may be easily changed by positioning the tape at the proper point and keying in new data that automatically replaces the data previously recorded. Automatic duplicating and skipping functions are performed by the use of a stored pro-

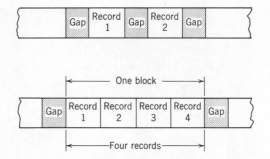

Figure 10-19. Representation of single records and multiple-record blocks recorded on magnetic tape.

gram analogous to the program drum card on card punch equipment.

Magnetic tape recording devices permit data to be recorded directly in a medium that has an input speed more nearly compatible with computer capabilities.

DATA CONVERSION

Every machine used in automatic data processing operates on a particular code. In a large system with a variety of equipment, several codes are likely to be found in use, each being related to a group of machines or a specific type of machine employed in the processing cycle. Thus, the code medium in which source data is originally recorded might not be acceptable to all machines in the system. Instead it would be necessary to convert the data from one medium to another to facilitate the flow of data through the system. This might occur once or perhaps several times.

The fact that the data was recorded originally in a machine-sensible form makes it possible to convert the data automatically. For example, credit card data recorded in bar code by the data recorder shown in Figure 10-14 can be automat-

Figure 10-20. Magnetic tape recording device. (*Reprinted with permission from Honeywell, Incorporated.*)

ically converted to punched cards. This is accomplished by the optical code reader shown in Figure 10-21. This device translates the machine-sensible language recorded on the transaction card by the data recorder into punched holes at the rate of 180 characters a minute. These punched cards are then available as input into a data processing system. Other equipment is available to convert bar code data into punched tape.

Journal tapes printed in optical characters by adding machines, accounting machines, or cash registers can be converted to punched tape by the use of the optical reader illustrated in Figure 10-22.

Figure 10-21. Optical code reader used to convert data recorded as bar code into punched cards. (*Courtesy Addressograph Multigraph Corporation.*)

This device scans the journal tape at the rate of 520 characters a second and transcribes the printed data into punched paper tape through the use of an auxiliary punch.

Figure 10-22. Optical journal reader used to read and convert journal tapes printed in optical characters by cash registers, accounting machines, and adding machines. (*Courtesy National Cash Register Company.*)

Other equipment can be used to convert data recorded in the form of optical characters or magnetic ink characters into punched cards or magnetic tape.

To facilitate the use of a variety of processing or transmittal equipment, conversion of data from one medium to another can be accomplished by many other special devices. In addition to the document to card or document to tape converters already mentioned, other combinations include the following.

Paper tape to:
- Magnetic tape
- Punched card
- Embossed card

Magnetic tape to:
- Paper tape
- Punched card

Punched card to:
- Magnetic tape
- Paper tape
- Embossed card

Print-punch tag to:
- Paper tape
- Punched card

Perforated coupon to:
- Punched card
- Paper tape
- Magnetic tape

Edge-notched card to:
- Punched card
- Punched tape

The large variety of machines available to complete the conversions listed above will not be described here. Instead, let it suffice to say that the code medium of almost any machine can be converted into the code media of other machines by the use of the proper converters. Furthermore, any new code that is developed is likely to be followed soon by devices to convert it to other forms.

Review Questions

1. What is a machine-sensible code?
2. List five machines that are capable of producing punched tape as a by-product of another operation.
3. In what ways are edge-punched cards preferable to punched tape?
4. Name two media other than punched tape and punched cards that use holes as a means of automating source data.
5. How is bar code imprinted on sales transaction documents?
6. List at least three types of machines that can be equipped with special type fonts to produce optical characters.
7. The output of devices that read optical characters may include what four media?
8. Magnetic ink character recognition is commonly used for what purposes?
9. What is the purpose of an inter-record gap on magnetic tape?

ELECTRONIC DATA PROCESSING: INTRODUCTION AND INPUT-OUTPUT DEVICES

Before the twentieth century was well on its way, electrically powered business machines were turning out great volumes of data for a world that was increasingly dependent on numbers and records. It was inevitable that electricity would be used to activate calculators and that an automatic computing machine would evolve. The age of the computer began in 1939 when Dr. Howard Aiken of Harvard University completed plans for a calculating machine that embodied many of the principles used in today's computers. Dr. Aiken's machine, called the Automatic Sequence Controlled Calculator, was completed in 1944. It combined in a single integrated device the ability to receive input data, perform a sequence of calculations, and record output.

In 1946 J. Presper Eckert and Dr. John W. Mauchly, faculty members at the University of Pennsylvania, completed the first actual electronic computer, called ENIAC, an abbreviation of Electronic Numerical Integrator and Computer. It was the first computer to use vacuum tubes instead of mechanical gears or electromechanical switches to do its calculating work. Also, it had a form of built-in machine logic enabling it to solve complete problems by making decisions or choices as it went along.

Succeeding advancements have been rapid and impressive and leave little doubt about the fact that the electronic computer is one of the most significant developments of this century. The purpose of this chapter and the ensuing six chapters is to survey the characteristics of this relatively new and important medium of processing data. The physical elements and functions of a computer system are outlined as well as basic programming techniques, programming systems, and electronic data processing operations.

CLASSIFICATION OF COMPUTERS

Computers are generally classified in three ways: by purpose, by type, and by capacity.

Purpose

Depending on their flexibility in operation, computers are either special purpose or general purpose. A *special purpose* computer is one that is designed to solve a restricted class of problems. Such a computer may even be designed and built to do one job only. In this case, the steps or operations that the computer follows may be built into the hardware. Many of the computers used for military purposes are of this type. Computers specifically designed to solve navigational problems on submarines or to track airplanes or missiles are good examples of special purpose equipment. Other examples include computers used for process control applications in such industries as oil refining, chemical manufacture, steel processing, and power generation. Special purpose computers are being increasingly used to control automated manufacturing processes.

General purpose computers are designed to solve a wide variety of problems. Theoretically a general purpose computer can be adapted by means of an easily alterable set of instructions to handle any problem that can be solved by computation. There are, of course, limitations imposed by memory size, speed, and type of input and output. The versatility of general purpose computers makes it possible to use them for such widely diversified tasks as payroll, banking, sales analysis, billing, cost accounting, labor distribution, manufacturing scheduling, and inventory control (Figure 11-1).

Capacity

In the early stages of electronic computer development, capacity was sometimes measured in terms of physical size. Today, however, physical size is not a good measure of capacity for late models have achieved compactness as a result of such developments as paper-thin monolithic silicon circuits, no larger than the letter o on a typewriter. These integrated circuits are chemically processed to perform the complete logic functions of a handful of transistors, diodes, and resistors previously used in second-generation computing systems (Figure 11-2). Integrated circuits also use less power and are more reliable and faster than the vacuum tubes or transistors used in previous models.

Another development, the magnetic core, makes it possible for computers to hold large amounts of data in storage, yet reach any single bit of information in a few billionths of a second. Microscopically thin metallic films built up in layers on glass or other material are another method used to reduce the size of computer storage. Thin-film components are often as small as a postage stamp, and can be switched at speeds of a few billionths of a second. Thus, as a result of miniaturization, capacity is expressed in terms of the volume of work that a computer can handle and is not necessarily evident in the physical size of the computer.

Computers are classified as small,

Figure 11-1. General purpose electronic data processing system. (*Courtesy International Business Machines Corporation.*)

medium, or large. A small computer generally consists of a central processing unit, storage capacity up to 65,000 positions, a card input-output device, perhaps two to four magnetic tape units, and a high-speed printer. This small computer configuration usually rents for under $7,500 a month, the average being around $4,000.

The medium-scale computer rents for over $7,500 and under $15,000 a month. It has more storage with faster access, and more and faster input-output devices.

Large-scale computers rent for over $15,000 and usually under $100,000 a month, and again are much faster and provide more storage than the medium-scale computers. Large-scale computers may contain up to several million positions of storage capacity. These computers as well as medium-scale computers may also provide for simultaneous operation of three or four input-output devices along with program monitoring and data transmission.

Rental costs are used here as a basis of comparison since most computers are rented. Some are purchased, however, and others are leased with options to purchase. Rental allows for maximum ease of change as improved equipment becomes available. Purchase or lease provides more economical operation over a period of several years if no major change in equipment is required.

Type

Electronic computers are basically of two types, analog and digital, according to the manner in which they represent data. An *analog computer* is so named because it performs by setting up physical situa-

Figure 11-2. Condensed circuitry on silicon chip in center ($\frac{1}{20}$ inch) performs functions previously requiring surrounding components. (*Courtesy Radio Corporation of America.*)

tions that are analogous to mathematical situations. An analog computer operates on data in the form of continuously variable physical quantities such as pressure, temperature, revolutions, speed of sound, or voltage. Thus, an analog computer is essentially a measuring device.

The automobile speedometer is a familiar device that utilizes information in analog form. It converts the rate of turning of a shaft into a numerical approximation of speed. A slide rule can also be classified as an analog device. Distances between points on the slide rule are read numerically in such a way that they provide approximate answers to multiplications, divisions, square roots, and so on.

Since analog data is acquired through a measuring process, analog computers

have the advantage of being able to accept data directly from measuring instruments without the need for an intermediate conversion to some symbol or code. This permits the high-speed collection of data at the point of origin. This feature, along with the analog computer's ability to process data at high speeds, makes these machines useful as controlling devices in oil refineries, paper mills, steel mills, and military weapons systems. Since the analog computer measures and compares quantities in one operation, it has no storage. The answers to problems are frequently read off on dials or cathode ray tubes.

Analog computers are far outnumbered in use today by digital computers. *Digital computers* operate on representations of real numbers or other characters coded numerically. The digital computer has a memory and solves problems by counting precisely, adding, subtracting, multiplying, dividing, and comparing. The ability of digital computers to handle alphabetic and numerical data with precision and speed makes them best suited for business applications. Therefore, the discussion in this book will be limited to computers of the digital type.

Although computers are basically of the analog or digital type, it should be recognized that a third type of computer is now being marketed. This is known as a *hybrid computer* which combines analog and digital capabilities in the same computer system. This capacity is most significant in a situation where the digital processing of data collected in analog form is desirable.

COMPUTER FUNCTIONS

The ability to compute is only one of the functions of an electronic data processing system. The other basic functions are data storage, control, and communication. These functions enable electronic computers to process data in the following steps:

1. The data to be processed and the instructions for processing it are recorded in an input medium such as punched paper tape, punched cards, magnetic tape, magnetic ink characters, or optical characters.

2. The instructions and data are fed into an input device where they are automatically converted into electrical impulses. The instructions and data are then routed to the main storage or memory unit where they are held until needed.

3. Instructions are accessed and interpreted by the control unit of the computer which directs the various data processing operations by issuing commands to all components of the system.

4. In accordance with instructions data is transferred from storage to the arithmetic-logical unit of the computer where arithmetic operations or comparisons are performed as directed by the control unit.

5. Processed data is routed to the storage unit where it may be held for further processing or moved to an output device, again as directed by the control unit.

6. Data emitted from storage is recorded by an output device in a medium such as punched tape, punched cards, magnetic tape, or printed documents.

The relationship of these functions is illustrated in Figure 11-3. This diagram depicts the significance of the storage unit as a common link between all units or components of the computer. It also shows that all units operate under the direction of the control unit as it receives and interprets one instruction at a time. These functions will be described in greater detail in the following chapters.

INPUT-OUTPUT

Communication with the data processing system is achieved through an input-output (I/O) device linked directly to the system. Data is entered into the system by means of an input medium that is sensed or read as it moves through an input device. The information is converted to a form usable by the system and is transmitted to main storage. Similarly, output involves converting processed data from main storage to a form or language compatible with an output medium and re-

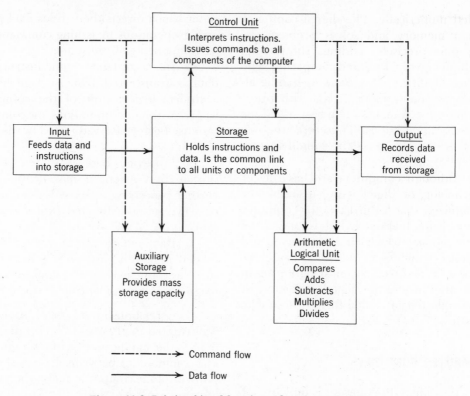

Figure 11-3. Relationship of functions of a computer system.

cording the data through an output device. The remainder of this chapter will describe these functions and the methods used for input and output of data.

The discussion of output at this point places this function out of sequence in relation to the data processing cycle. However, since many of the devices used for output are actually part of a combined I/O unit, it is more practical to consider the two functions simultaneously.

Input-Output Functions

Since the computer is an electronic device and input-output units are primarily electromechanical devices, the computer is capable of operating at much faster speeds. To enable the computer to operate as nearly as possible at full capacity, the transfer of data between I/O devices and the main storage unit usually takes place independently through an intermediary known as a *channel*.

The I/O channel and associated control and connecting units provide for the *buffering* (temporary storage), coordination, and transfer of I/O data. Thus, the central processing unit is relieved of the burden of communicating directly with I/O devices. This permits I/O operations to proceed concurrently with the processing of data. In other words, the computer can carry on high-speed computations while input data is being received and while output data is being transferred (Figure 11-4).

The channel that performs this function may be an independent unit complete with necessary logical and storage capabilities, in effect, a small special purpose computer capable of performing only I/O operations; or it may share central processing unit facilities and be physically integrated with the central processing unit. In either case, channel functions are identical.

In some cases a channel data path is shared by several low-speed devices such as card readers, punches, printers, and terminals. In other cases, a channel may accommodate higher data rates but may be limited to only one data transfer operation at a time.

Input-Output Devices

All standard I/O devices have certain common characteristics. They are auxiliary machines connected to the computer and under control of the central processing unit. Most I/O devices are automatic; once started, they continue to operate as directed by the stored program. These devices can transmit data to or receive data only from the main memory section of the central processing unit.

I/O devices may be used for both input and output or for just one of these functions. More than one form of input and output may be used, and different forms may be combined. For example, punched cards may be used as input and magnetic tape as output. The specific form of input and output depends on the configuration of the computer system and the functions it is designed to perform.

In addition to the standard I/O devices, the use of remotely located devices as I/O units is emerging as an important technique. Included in this category are transaction recorders, typewriters, and visual display units. Although they are remote from the computer, these devices can be operated on-line; that is, they may transmit data over conventional transmission facilities directly to a computer as the data is recorded at the point of origin. Traditionally, input has been regarded as the weakest link in computer

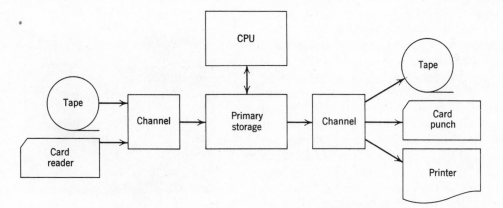

Figure 11-4. Representation of input-output channel functions.

systems because of the time required to record, convert, and read data for input. On-line transaction recorders, and other innovations such as optical character recognition and magnetic ink character recognition, are alleviating the "input bottleneck" by making it possible for data in machine-sensible language to be read directly into a computer.

Each of the I/O devices will be considered separately.

Punched Card Readers and Punches. The punched card is a versatile medium that can be key punched, verified, sorted, collated, and reproduced by punched card machines. It can also be read or punched by certain auxiliary computer devices. The major disadvantages of the punched card are the limit on the amount of data a single card can hold and the relatively slow data transfer rate of card readers and punches. Even so, punched cards are a very important source of data to the computer as well as a useful external storage medium.

Data to be processed is transferred from punched cards into the main storage of a computer system by means of a card reader. Output representing the results of processing may be a printed report or a new punched card file. The input file remains intact. Therefore, both the input and output files are available for further processing by the computer or by punched card machines.

As the punched card was discussed in earlier chapters, we are primarily concerned here with the card readers and punches used as computer input-output devices. Most card readers and punches use a mechanical picker knife and pinch rollers to transport cards under sensing brushes for reading and under die punches for punching. The majority of these devices read or punch an entire row at a time. Some card-reading machines use vacuum feed and belts to transport cards by the reading station. Certain card readers employ photoelectric reading stations. Most of these read the card serially a column at a time. The punch unit may be a separate device or may be combined with the read unit as a single card read-punch unit (Figure 11-5). Card-reading speeds vary from 100 to 2,000 cards a minute, and card-punching speeds vary from 100 to 300 cards a minute.

All card readers and punches operate at much slower data transfer speeds than the central processing unit. As this causes the central processing unit to lose some of its processing potential, many large installations use separate card-to-tape and tape-to-card converters to take advantage of magnetic tape's much faster data transfer speed. Another technique used to reduce this data transfer difference is the simultaneous operation of a number of input-output devices. To do this a computer must have the capacity to process several programs at the same time.

Punched Tape Readers and Punches.

Figure 11-5. Card read-punch unit. (*Courtesy International Business Machines Corporation.*)

Although punched tape is less widely used than cards in commercial electronic data processing systems, it has two distinct advantages over the punched card. First, punched tape record lengths are not limited as are the lengths of punched card records. Second, tapes lend themselves to use as a "common language" medium for communication between a variety of data processing devices and computers. In fact, input tapes generally originate as a by-product of other machine operations. Machines that can produce punched tape while simultaneously recording transactions or preparing documents in another form include automatic typewriters, accounting machines, cash registers, and window posting machines.

Punched tape has several disadvantages, however. Since tape is a continuous medium, records cannot be added or deleted very easily. Further, data punched in tape cannot be sorted or collated. Consequently, the use of punched tape for file applications is limited.

Most punched tape readers are either photoelectric or electromechanical. The speed of punched tape readers ranges from 10 to 2,000 characters a second. Mechanical readers can perform reliably at speeds up to 100 characters a second. For higher speeds, photoelectric sensing techniques are generally used.

Tape-punching equipment operates more slowly than tape readers. Because of the electromechanical action usually required to produce the holes in tape, the maximum speed is around 300 characters a second.

Magnetic Tape Units (Figure 11-6). A single magnetic tape transport can perform both input and output functions. In either case, magnetic tape has one of the best ratios of data transfer speed to central processing unit handling speed of any in-

Figure 11-6. Magnetic tape units. (*Courtesy International Business Machines Corporation.*)

put-output or auxiliary storage medium other than direct access storage devices. Magnetic tape can contain a large amount of data in a compact, easily erasable, and readily available form. The tape is relatively inexpensive, tolerant of many storage conditions, and usable for up to 50,000 passes through a tape read-write unit.

Magnetic tape provides a good means of storing information needed for particular computer runs. This may include programs, tables, and data needed for problem solving. Magnetic tape may also be used for storing intermediate results of computations. However, a more important use of tape is for storing large files of data. Although we are mainly interested here in the use of magnetic tape for input-output purposes, it should be noted that magnetic tape also serves as a major auxiliary storage medium.

Magnetic tape does have several disadvantages, however. First, data recorded on it cannot be read by people. Therefore, when used as output, it requires conversion to some other medium if it is to be visually readable. Second, when used as auxiliary storage, its fast stop-and-go requirements may cause equipment maintenance problems. Third, it is not a practical medium for random processing of data.

Magnetic tape drives can move tape at speeds of more than 100 inches a second. The data transfer rate for magnetic tape is governed by two factors: (1) data density (bits per inch), and (2) tape speed. Slow speed magnetic tape drives might have a data transfer rate of 15,000 characters a second, and high-speed tape drives, at 1,600 characters an inch, might have a data transfer rate of 180,000 characters a second. Many tape units can read tape as it moves in either direction, forward or backward.

All tape units require two tape reels. The one containing tape to be read or written is called a *file reel* and the other is called a *take-up reel*. Magnetic tape moves from the file reel through vacuum columns and past the read-write heads to the take-up reel. Each of the vacuum columns holds a loop of tape by a controlled vacuum. The purpose of the loop is to allow the tape reels to move independently and to allow some slack between the file reel and the take-up reel. If there were no slack tape, the fast starting and speed of the take-up reel would snap the tape. Because of the vacuum columns, the file reel can release tape and the take-up reel can automatically wind tape without maintaining a constant tension.

Magnetic tape reels are equipped with a file-protection ring that can be used to safeguard data recorded on the tape. When the ring is removed, data cannot be written on the tape, but the tape data can be read for processing.

Printers (Figure 11-7). Printing devices prepare permanent visual records of data received from the computer system. All printing devices have a paper transport that automatically moves the continuous manifold forms as printing progresses. The majority of printing devices are *impact printers* that print by pressing the paper and the ribbon against the proper type as it "flies by" in front of the paper. This method involves the use of type that is engraved and assembled in a chain or engraved on the face of a drum or wheels. During each print cycle, all of the characters in the print set move past each printing position and a magnetically actuated hammer presses the paper against an inked ribbon and piece of type at the instant the selected character is in position. This combination of mechanical and electronic technology is one of the marvels of the electronic data processing system.

Most high-speed printers can print 300 to 1,400 numeric lines containing 80

Figure 11-7. Printer. (*Courtesy International Business Machines Corporation.*)

to 160 print positions a minute. A few printers are slower and some can print as many as 1,200 alphanumeric lines a minute. Vertical spacing is usually controlled by a punched tape loop or by the program. The punched tape loop is known as a carriage tape, which is similar in design and function to the carriage tape used on a punched card accounting machine. (See Figure 8-7.) Vertical skipping of blank spaces or from one page to the next occurs at speeds ranging from 15 to 75 inches a second. Very often a *print buffer* that temporarily holds one line of data to be printed is provided in either the printer or central processor. This facilitates printer control and timing and frees the computer for other work while the line is being printed.

Nonimpact printers capable of printing about 5,000 lines a minute are sometimes used. These printers form an image, generally by electrical charges, and then transfer it to paper as a visible record. Although these devices are very fast, they presently have two disadvantages. They are unable to produce simultaneous multiple copies or to produce high-quality printing.

High-speed printers used to be considered as output devices exclusively. Now, however, impact printers are capable of printing data on forms such as utility bills, renewal notices, and other documents that are designed to be returned to the sender. Upon return the documents can be batched and fed into an optical scanning device capable of reading the data and automatically recording it on some magnetic storage medium. In view of this turn-around capability it can be said that impact printers are capable of preparing data in machine processable form and are, therefore, no longer limited in function to producing only human-sensible output.

Microfilm Systems. Considering the mechanical process that is involved, printers operate at speeds that are truly impressive. Nevertheless, even their maximum speeds are not compatible with the processing and output capacity of computers. This difference in speed between print out devices and computers can result in a serious loss of efficiency in some types of applications.

One technique that is emerging as a solution to this problem employs microfilm as an output medium. This process involves several basic steps: (1) computer output is converted to letters and numbers for display on a cathode ray tube, and (2) the data on the screen is then photographed on microfilm. In contrast to the 300 to 1,400 lines per minute capacity of impact printers, microfilm systems now in use can handle 7,000 to 30,000 lines a minute.

In addition to greater speed, this technique has the advantage of compactness which facilitates the storage and retrieval of data. For example, the microfilmed images of 1,600 pages of computer-generated information can be held in the palm of one hand. By the use of reader-printers, specific microfilm frames can be viewed and copies can be easily produced by depressing a button. (See Figure 4-26.)

Magnetic Ink Character Readers. Magnetic ink character recognition (MICR) is a high-speed data input technique that reduces manual keystroke operations and allows source documents to be sorted automatically. Magnetic ink reading heads produce electrical signals when magnetic characters are passed beneath them. These signals are analyzed by special circuits and compared with stored tables to determine what character has been sensed. The data is then transmitted to the memory of the computer for processing.

By the use of a combination reader-sorter it is possible to sort documents as they are being read to provide input to the computer (Figure 11-8). Such sorters may also be operated off-line, that is, independent from the computer. In a banking operation, for example, such a sorter might be used to arrange checks and deposits into customer account number order. Checks may also be sorted by Federal Reserve bank symbol or by American Bankers Association transit number. MICR reader-sorter units are capable of handling from 750 to 1,600 check-sized cards or paper documents a minute, with one line of printing on each document. The majority of MICR equipment is used by the banking industry to process checks and deposits.

Optical Character Readers (Figure 11-9). Optical character recognition devices are designed to handle sheets of paper, cards, or journal tapes. They have the ability to read marks, printed numerals, special characters, alphabetic characters, and more recently hand-printed letters or numerals.

There are many types and makes of optical character readers. Some of these can read only journal tapes, some read

Figure 11-8. Magnetic character sorter-reader. (*Courtesy National Cash Register Company.*)

Figure 11-9. Optical character reader. (*Courtesy Radio Corporation of America.*)

only numeric data and certain characters, some read alphabetic data as well as numerals, and some can read all of these forms of data as well as certain hand-printed characters. Some document readers can read only standardized type styles; therefore, the type styles and sizes approved by the U.S.A. Standards Institute are used by various equipment manufacturers to produce journal tapes and other kinds of documents that are widely acceptable.

As a source document moves past the scanning device of an optical character reader, the document is flooded with light and read by a photosensitive technique. Optical character readers translate each character into a code, and either transmit the coded data directly to a computer or transcribe it onto punched cards, punched tape, or magnetic tape. These techniques promise to reduce, and in many cases eliminate, the manual keystroke operations that have been required for the preparation of computer input data.

Optical scanning applications can produce great economies of time, manpower, and money in handling source and re-entry documents. For example, documents such as insurance premium notices, charge sales invoices, and utility bills can be prepared originally by a computer in a type style that can be read by an optical scanning device. Thus, upon return with the customers' payments the same documents can be validated and re-entered for further processing. These are referred to as *turn-around documents.*

Transaction Recorders. Point-of-origin transaction recorders may be operated off-line, i.e., not in direct communication with the computer, in which case the data is normally transmitted to a converter where it is recorded on punched cards or punched tape. However, we are primarily concerned here with the on-line use of transaction recorders, which enables them to transmit data directly to a computer storage unit.

Transaction recorders are generally equipped with slots into which the operator inserts prepunched cards, inventory tags, or badges containing such data as employee numbers, job numbers, stock numbers, and so on. Variable data, such as hours worked or amount of stock removed, may be entered by setting dials, keys, or levers. Other transaction recorders utilize keyboard arrangements into which the operator punches the data to be recorded (Figure 11-10).

Direct wire transfer of data from transaction recorders to a computer is an effective means of quickly updating account balances, payroll time records, inventory balances, and other records that must be maintained on a current basis.

Typewriter Terminals. Another type of on-line device capable of communication with the computer is the *printer-keyboard terminal.* These typewriter devices can be connected by cable to the

Figure 11-10. Teller terminal used to transmit transaction data. (*Courtesy International Business Machines Corporation.*)

computer system. Remote units can also be connected to a computer by a variety of data transmission techniques. Typewriter terminals can be used to inquire into a file of data under control of the computer. They can also receive data sent under computer control in response to either terminal commands or computer instructions.

A more detailed discussion of remote terminals and other data communications concepts will appear in Chapter 18.

Display Stations. Display stations are similar in operation to typewriter terminals except that instead of providing printed copy these devices display data on the face of a cathode ray tube. Display stations are preferred over typewriter terminals wherever printed copy is not required. As with typewriter terminals, data can be entered through the keyboard and sent to the computer. However, an advantage of display stations is that the data keyed in can be checked on the screen for accuracy before it is transmitted to the computer (Figure 11-11).

Another advantage of cathode ray

tube display stations is that they can display diagrams, drawings, graphs, and sketches. In the past it was often necessary for users of computers to convert drawings into numerical coordinates for computer input and to convert columns of numerical answers back into drawings or graphs in order to understand the answers. Through the use of special programming techniques and electronic controls, computer systems are now able to accept information and produce answers in graphical form.

When given a set of coordinates by the computer program, the cathode ray tube display will flash the corresponding spot on its face. Complete displays comprised of lines, curves, and letters can be formed with thousands of individual spots. With an appropriate feedback program and suitable attachments, a cathode ray tube display can also be used as an input device. This is accomplished through the use of a light pen, a device resembling a pocket flashlight. The pen has two uses: pointing at parts

Figure 11-11. Display station. (*Courtesy International Business Machines Corporation.*)

of a display, and drawing. By pointing, the operator is able to indicate to the computer which parts of a display to erase or move. Drawing is done with a tracking program. To move the end of a line, the operator points at the end and pushes a "move" button. The computer follows the course of the pen and redisplays the line in accordance with the pen's changing location. The light pen can be used alone or in conjunction with a keyboard to rearrange or delete displayed information, or to add lines from a base point already lighted by the cathode ray tube beam.

The use of a light pen with this type of display station is especially useful in scientific and technical applications. In engineering, for example, it is helpful in performing design work. This system may also be used for educational purposes. In this case the student station, or console, is connected by coaxial cable or telephone line to a computer that has been programmed for educational purposes. Depending on the situation, instructional material such as photographs, drawings, charts, tables, words, or equations may be displayed on the cathode ray tube. At his console the student may react to the display, respond to questions, or enter inquiries in two ways: (1) he may type responses or enter inquiries using ordinary English, numbers, or symbolic letters; (2) he may use the light pen to point to some part of the visual display. When the light pen is touched to the screen, the exact point of contact is communicated to the computer. In this way the correct answer to a multiple-choice question may be indicated, incorrect material may be erased by tracing the light pen over the undesirable portion of the image, or other functions may be performed.

Another type of cathode ray tube display device with an attached camera may be used to provide a permanent filmed record of displayed data. This technique is not too frequently used. However, it may be used for off-site display of an answer to a question manually keyed to the computer.

Voice Response Systems. Still another type of terminal communication device is the voice response system. This system is comprised of a message handling unit, a number of touch-tone telephone units, and standard telephone lines. The audio response unit is located near the computer and has a vocabulary tailored to the users' needs. The touch-tone telephone can be used to enter data or to inquire into a file under control of the computer (Figure 11-12). The inquiry is transmitted to the voice response unit and then accepted by the central processing unit. The computer processes the inquiry, composes a coded response, and returns the message to the voice response unit. Here the message is interpreted and the proper words are selected from the prerecorded stored vocabulary and sent to the inquirer's telephone headset.

Figure 11-12. Touch-tone telephone. (*Courtesy American Telephone and Telegraph Company.*)

The major advantage of the voice response system is that it provides quick verbal responses from a computer system by means of low-cost, remotely located, and multi-purpose telephone terminals. Such systems are used to provide stock quotation information, to relay weather information to airplane pilots, and to intercept incomplete telephone calls and tell the callers why their calls cannot be completed. Other voice response systems are in the planning stages or are in operation in such fields as banking, communications, transportation, retail sales, and hospitals. In banking, for example, bank account balances can be maintained in computer storage and used to provide clearance for persons desiring to cash checks. Thus, a telephone call to the automated system can produce a verbal clearance or indication of insufficient funds in response to the account number. In department stores a customer's credit standing can be verified in a similar manner by dialing the individual's account number and the amount of the sale.

Console. The console is, in effect, the external control center of a computer and is used mainly to monitor the system. The console is particularly important to

Figure 11-13. Console. (*Courtesy* UNIVAC, *Division of Sperry Rand Corporation.*)

the technician in testing for and locating computer failures.

The console control panel contains a series of lights which indicate to the operator the status of internal electronic switches and the contents of certain internal registers (Figure 11-13). Also included on the console control panel is a series of keys and switches which enable the operator to:

1. Start and stop the processing functions.

2. Change the selection of input-output devices.

3. Reset the computer when error conditions cause it to stop.

4. Manually enter data or cause data in storage to be visually displayed.

Some consoles contain a built-in or auxiliary electric typewriter that can be used by the operator to enter instructions into the control unit. The typewriter also enables the computer to print messages to the operator signaling that an error condition exists or that some device requires operator attention. In addition, the typewriter provides a means of printing totals or other information to assist the operator in monitoring the system.

As a result of advancements in computer design and programming techniques, the console is used less today as an aid to computer operations. Many of the functions once relegated to the console operator are now contained in the program or are performed by circuitry and components built into the computer.

Review Questions

1. What was unique about the ENIAC?
2. Briefly describe general purpose computers.
3. What is the main difference between analog and digital computers? Which one is generally used for business data processing?
4. Name several devices that utilize information in analog form.
5. Briefly describe a hybrid computer.
6. What are the four basic functions of an electronic data processing system?
7. What are the functions of the input-output channel?
8. Briefly describe the common characteristics of all standard input-output devices.
9. What are the advantages of punched tape as compared to punched cards?
10. Name three disadvantages of magnetic tape.
11. What is the purpose of the magnetic tape file-protection ring?
12. Why are high-speed printers no longer limited to producing human-sensible output?
13. What basic steps are involved when microfilm is used as computer output?
14. The majority of magnetic ink character readers are used by what industry?
15. Name two turn-around documents that could be read by an optical scanning device.
16. Describe the unique input-output capacity of display stations.
17. What is the major advantage of voice response systems?
18. What is the primary purpose of the console?

12

EDP
STORAGE DEVICES

The storage of data is a vital part of electronic data processing. After being recorded in one of the media previously described, data may be read by an input component and transferred to a main storage unit within the computer, or it may be stored in an external or auxiliary device. A method of representing data acceptable to the system is essential to this process. In this chapter we shall consider the various devices that are available for storing and handling data in an electronic data processing system, and also the methods of data representation that are used.

DATA REPRESENTATION

One prerequisite for understanding digital computers is a knowledge of the manner in which they handle data. Computers are made up of many electronic components: transistors, switches, magnetic cores, wires, integrated circuits, and so on. Data is represented in these components by the presence or absence of electronic signals or indications, much as the presence or absence of holes in a punched card represents data.

Each component in a computer has only two possible states: on or off. For example, transistors are in either a conducting or nonconducting state; magnetic materials are magnetized in one direction or in the opposite direction; relays and switches are open or closed; and voltage is present or absent. With this limited number of possibilities for each component part, the computer must be capable of accepting large volumes of numeric and alphabetic data, and must store, process, and produce data as output. Because of these design characteristics it is not feasible for the computer to utilize decimal arithmetic which would require components to have ten states for each digit. Instead, the computer uses a form of the two-digit numbering system known as the *binary numbering system*.

To aid in understanding the binary numbering system let us begin with the decimal system, which has a base of ten. Two important concepts in the decimal system, also applicable to other systems, are absolute value and positional value. The absolute values in the decimal system are the digits 0 to 9, and the positional values are powers of 10. As 10 is the base or radix of the decimal system, the first position to the left of the decimal point has a positional value of 10^0 (i.e., 1), the second position has a value of 10^1, the third 10^2, etc.

The value resulting from raising a number to a power, i.e., the value resulting from exponentiation, is the product of successive multiplications by the number, with the number of multiplications equaling the exponent. Therefore, $10^2 = 10 \times 10$ or 100; $10^3 = 10 \times 10 \times 10$ or 1,000, etc. Any number raised to the zero power has the value 1; any number raised to the first power has a value equal to that

of the number itself. Table 12-1 illustrates the positional-value and absolute-value concepts as applied to the decimal system.

Binary Numbering System

The binary system is comparable to the decimal system in using the concepts of absolute value and positional value. The difference is that the binary numbering system employs only two absolute values: 0 and 1. Because there are only two digits, the binary system has a base number of 2. This means that the positional significance of a binary number is based on the progression of powers of 2.

As shown in Table 12-2, the binary positional values are obtained by following the same rules discussed in the previous section on the decimal numbering

TABLE 12-1   THE DECIMAL NUMBERING SYSTEM

Positional significance:	10^5	10^4	10^3	10^2	10^1	10^0
Positional value:	100,000	10,000	1,000	100	10	1
Decimal number:			2	5	6	6

$$6 \times 10^0 = 6$$
$$6 \times 10^1 = 60$$
$$5 \times 10^2 = 500$$
$$2 \times 10^3 = \underline{2,000}$$
$$2,566$$

TABLE 12-2   THE BINARY NUMBERING SYSTEM

Positional significance:	2^7	2^6	2^5	2^4	2^3	2^2	2^1	2^0
Positional value:	128	64	32	16	8	4	2	1
Binary number:			1	0	1	1	1	

Binary-to-decimal conversion:

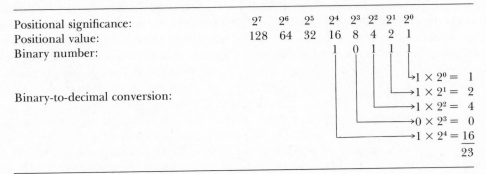

$$1 \times 2^0 = 1$$
$$1 \times 2^1 = 2$$
$$1 \times 2^2 = 4$$
$$0 \times 2^3 = 0$$
$$1 \times 2^4 = \underline{16}$$
$$23$$

system. Thus, the rightmost (least significant) position of a binary number represents the base number to the zero power and has a value of 1. The second position represents 2 raised to the first power, or 2. Progressing to the left, $2^2 = 2 \times 2$ or 4; $2^3 = 2 \times 2 \times 2$ or 8; etc. If the binary notations in Table 12-2 were continued to the left, they would have values of 256, 512, 1,024, 2,048, 4,096, 8,192, etc.

As indicated in Table 12-2, numbers are expressed in binary notation as a series of 0's and 1's, commonly referred to as bits. The 0 is described as no bit and represents an "off" condition. The 1 is described as a bit and represents an "on" condition. The lowest-order position in the binary system is called the 1-bit. The next position is called the 2-bit; the next, the 4-bit; the next, the 8-bit; and so on.

Other Computer Codes

To facilitate the recording and processing of data, most computers use one of the following codes based on the binary numbering system.

Binary Coded Decimal. This code is one of the most common variations of the binary system. It employs only the first four binary positions with the respective values of 1, 2, 4, and 8. Any decimal digit from 0 to 9 can be represented by a combination of these four values. In this system a separate binary equivalent is required for each digit of the decimal number being expressed. Thus, units, tens, hundreds, thousands, etc., can be expressed as follows:

Here are some additional examples of numbers expressed in the binary system:

Value of each bit							
64	32	16	8	4	2	1	
		1	0	1	0	1	= 21
	1	0	1	1	1	1	= 47
1	0	1	0	0	0	1	= 81
1	1	1	0	0	1	0	= 114

Since binary arithmetic requires the use of only two digits, binary numbers can be easily represented in the various two-state components of electronic computers. The on condition may represent 1, and off may represent 0. For example, transistors could be used to represent the quantity 5 electronically by the following combination of on and off conditions:

It is apparent that zero would be expressed if all circuits were in an off condition. Values other than 5 could be expressed by different combinations of on and off conditions. As indicated by the preceding illustration, four computer circuits are needed in this system to represent all of the decimal digits, 0 to 9, in binary form.

Standard Binary Coded Decimal Interchange Code (Table 12-3). This code, which is the one used by most second-generation computers, is an expansion of the

Thousands				Hundreds				Tens				Units				
8	4	2	1	8	4	2	1	8	4	2	1	8	4	2	1	
1	0	0	1	1	0	0	0	0	1	0	0	0	1	0	1	= 9,845
0	1	1	0	0	1	1	1	0	0	1	1	0	0	0	1	= 6,731

TABLE 12-3   COMPARISON OF SELECTED CODES

Character	Standard Card Code	Standard BCD Interchange Code		EBCDIC *		USASCII †	
0	0	100	1010	1111	0000	011	0000
1	1	000	0001	1111	0001	011	0001
2	2	000	0010	1111	0010	011	0010
3	3	100	0011	1111	0011	011	0011
4	4	000	0100	1111	0100	011	0100
5	5	100	0101	1111	0101	011	0101
6	6	100	0110	1111	0110	011	0110
7	7	000	0111	1111	0111	011	0111
8	8	000	1000	1111	1000	011	1000
9	9	100	1001	1111	1001	011	1001
A	12-1	011	0001	1100	0001	100	0001
B	12-2	011	0010	1100	0010	100	0010
C	12-3	111	0011	1100	0011	100	0011
D	12-4	011	0100	1100	0100	100	0100
E	12-5	111	0101	1100	0101	100	0101
F	12-6	111	0110	1100	0110	100	0110
G	12-7	011	0111	1100	0111	100	0111
H	12-8	011	1000	1100	1000	100	1000
I	12-9	111	1001	1100	1001	100	1001
J	11-1	110	0001	1101	0001	100	1010
K	11-2	110	0010	1101	0010	100	1011
L	11-3	010	0011	1101	0011	100	1100
M	11-4	110	0100	1101	0100	100	1101
N	11-5	010	0101	1101	0101	100	1110
O	11-6	010	0110	1101	0110	100	1111
P	11-7	110	0111	1101	0111	101	0000
Q	11-8	110	1000	1101	1000	101	0001
R	11-9	010	1001	1101	1001	101	0010
S	0-2	101	0010	1110	0010	101	0011
T	0-3	001	0011	1110	0011	101	0100
U	0-4	101	0100	1110	0100	101	0101
V	0-5	001	0101	1110	0101	101	0110
W	0-6	001	0110	1110	0110	101	0111
X	0-7	101	0111	1110	0111	101	1000
Y	0-8	101	1000	1110	1000	101	1001
Z	0-9	001	1001	1110	1001	101	1010

* Extended Binary Coded Decimal Interchange Code
† U.S.A. Standard Code for Information Interchange

binary coded decimal system. The significant difference in the standard BCD code is the use of zone bits as shown below:

Parity Zone   Numeric

C	B	A	8	4	2	1

The zone bits of an alphanumeric character perform a code function similar to the zone positions on a punched card. They are used in combination with digits to represent the letters of the alphabet or special characters.

The illustration above also shows a bit position on the extreme left labeled "Parity." It should be noted further that some of the codes in the third column of Table 12-3 contain a bit in the column on the extreme left and others do not. The bits recorded in this column are known as *check bits* which are used for verifying accuracy. Some computers have a built-in checking device that detects the loss or addition of bits during the transfer of data from one location to another in the computer. This process is known as a *parity check* and was explained earlier.

The addition of necessary check bits is accomplished automatically as input data is converted to binary codes. Further study of Table 12-3 will reveal that odd parity is being used in the code illustrated in the third column. Although check bits are not shown with the other codes, they are employed when these codes are used with most computers.

Whenever data is transmitted, the computer checks to determine if the necessary odd or even number of bits is present. If an error is detected, the computer will indicate that a parity error has occurred and will stop. Some computers make several attempts to transmit the data before stopping.

Extended Binary Coded Decimal Interchange Code (EBCDIC) (Table 12-3). This code, which is the one used by most third-generation computers, employs eight binary positions to represent a single character. The use of eight bits may seem to be inefficient. However, the extended code has some definite advantages over the standard BCD code:

1. Eight binary positions allow 256 different bit configurations (2^8) versus 64 provided by the six-position BCD code (2^6). This increase in possible bit configurations provides capacity for both upper and lower case letters, numerals, and many special characters as well as unused configurations for future use.

2. Each of the possible 256 bit combinations can be punched into one column of an 80-column card. This allows pure binary information to be punched into a card, with each column representing eight bits of binary information.

3. The eight-bit field can be used to store two decimal digits. This gives better utilization of storage facilities than the BCD format, which is capable of recording a single digit in a six-bit field.

As we have seen, most character codes are divided into zone and numeric parts. The extended binary coded decimal interchange code is no exception. To aid in understanding how this code is used, let us analyze a primary storage position typical of most third-generation computers. Each storage location is known as a *byte* and consists of eight bits plus a parity bit. The EBCDIC divides the eight bits of a byte as shown below:

Zone   Numeric

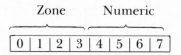

0	1	2	3	4	5	6	7

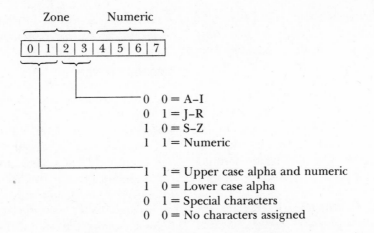

Figure 12-1. Uses of zone portion of EBCDIC byte.

Figure 12-1 illustrates how the zone portion, bits 0–3, of the EBCDIC byte is used to identify different characters. Bit positions 4–7 of the EBCDIC byte are the numeric portion and correspond to the numeric hole punches 0–9. Bits 4–7 are coded as a four-bit binary number. Note the similarity of the numeric portions of the standard BCD interchange code and the EBCDIC in Table 12-3.

Decimal data can be represented in binary form in either of two formats: zoned or packed. The zoned or unpacked format uses all eight bits of a byte to represent a digit as shown in Figure 12-2. The packed format uses the numeric portion of a byte to represent one digit and the zone portion to represent a second digit as shown below:

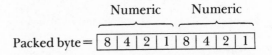

Figure 12-2 shows the decimal digits 1, 2, and 3 represented in binary form in

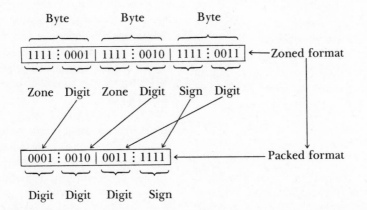

Figure 12-2. Decimal digits 1, 2, and 3 represented in binary form in both zoned and packed formats.

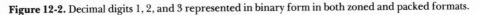

both zoned and packed formats. It should be noted in this example that the plus or minus sign is located in the zone portion of the low-order byte in the zoned format, and is located in the low-order digit position in the packed format. In this code the presence of the normal zone bits "1111" is an unsigned indication assumed to be positive. If this had been a negative quantity, the zone portion would have appeared as "1101" which is a minus indication.

Packing of digits leads to efficient use of storage, increased arithmetic performance, and improved rates of data transmission. Program instructions are available to cause the computer to either pack or unpack a numeric field.

U.S.A. Standard Code For Information Interchange (USASCII) (Table 12-3). This is a seven-bit binary code that can be processed by many third-generation computers. Also available is an eight-bit version of the USASCII code, which is not illustrated here. The bit identification for each format is as follows:

USASCII $\boxed{7\,6\,5\,4\,3\,2\,1}$

USASCII-8 $\boxed{8\,7\,6\,5\,4\,3\,2\,1}$

We should note that in the USASCII formats the bits are numbered from right to left, and in the EBCDIC format the bits are numbered from left to right. Today the USASCII format is most frequently used by data transmission devices.

STORAGE

Computer storage may be classified under three headings: (1) internal, (2) auxiliary, and (3) external, The most commonly used devices and the characteristics of each type are as follows.

Internal Storage

Internal storage is usually referred to as *main* or *primary* storage. This type of storage is an integral physical part of the computer and is directly controlled by the computer. Thus, data in main storage is automatically accessible to the computer. To be accessible, it is necessary that each data character be stored in an identifiable location. A sequential group of storage locations provides storage for one unit of data called a *word*. Each word consists of a certain number of digits or characters and may be fixed or variable in length depending on the computer. Each location is identified by an *address*. Addresses usually start with zero and continue sequentially to the highest number required.

An important characteristic of main storage units is that each position or word must be accessible on a random basis. In other words, the computer must be able to reach any position of main storage directly. Further, it must be possible to use the data as many times as desired without erasing it from storage until such time as it is no longer needed. Data in storage is not lost as a result of the writing out process unless the instruction is specifically a write-and-erase type. However, reading data into storage necessarily destroys data previously stored at the specified locations.

Main storage accepts data from an input unit, exchanges data with and supplies instructions to the central processing unit, and furnishes data to an output unit. Main storage is often temporary because in most business applications only part of the data in an application is put into main storage at one time while it is being processed. The usual procedure in computer operations is to store the bulk of data to be processed in an auxiliary or external storage device, transfer portions of the data to internal or working storage, process it, and then return it to auxiliary or external storage. This procedure is repeated until all of the data is processed.

Currently two major types of primary storage are in use: magnetic core and magnetic thin film.

Magnetic Core Storage. A vast majority of computers use magnetic core storage. The extensive use of magnetic core storage is based on the fact that it is comparatively inexpensive to build, pro-vides very fast access to data, and is very reliable. It requires little current and can be used on either a variable or fixed word length concept.

This medium is made up of thousands of magnetic cores, about the diameter of the head of a straight pin, strung on a grid of fine wires (Figure 12-3). Each grid of wires and cores is called a *plane*. Cores are mounted with wires running through each core at right angles to each other, and magnetized by sending electrical current through the wires. By sending half the current needed to magnetize a core through each wire, only the core at the intersection of the wires is magnetized. The act of magnetizing one or more cores

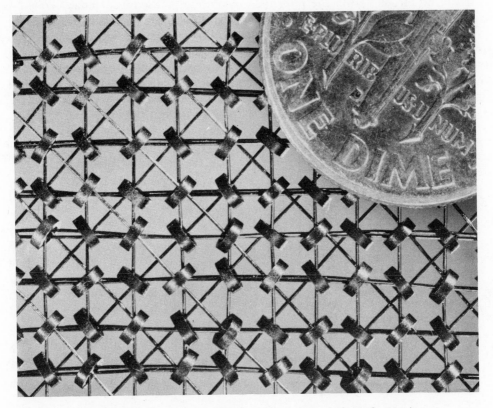

Figure 12-3. Magnetic core storage. (*Courtesy General Electric Company.*)

in a given line, called an address, causes all other cores in that address to be demagnetized. Cores are arranged so that combinations of charges representing data are instantly accessible.

Cores are magnetized positively or negatively depending on the direction of the current. By reversing the flow of current, the magnetic state, or polarity, of a core can be changed. Thus, the two states can be used in accordance with the binary system to represent 0 or 1, yes or no, or on or off conditions. Figure 12-4 illustrates the storage of both alphabetic and numeric data in magnetic cores using the extended binary coded decimal interchange code shown in Table 12-3.

It will be recalled from the punched card chapters that a card can be divided into segments called *fields*. Each field consists of a certain number of columns reserved for recording a specific type of data. When data is read into computer storage from punched cards or other media, it continues to be stored by fields. However, the term "word" is used to describe a group of characters that are handled by the computer as a complete unit.

Most third-generation computer instructions have the capacity to identify the location and length of a data field as well as the operation to be performed with the data. In this manner data in core storage can be accessed by addressing the high-order position of the data and stating the number of positions in the field or word. For example, if we wanted to use the word "clasp" in Figure 12-4, we would address storage location 1006 and state that the field contained four additional positions.

The majority of second-generation computers used the binary coded decimal coding system and employed an eighth storage position for the insertion of a word mark as a means of defining the length of the various fields in storage. In these computers the presence of a word mark at the left or high-order position of every word

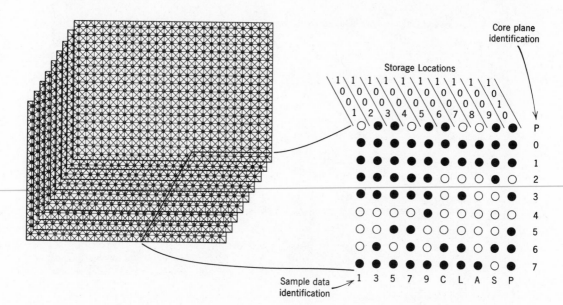

Figure 12-4. Representation of data stored in magnetic cores.

enables the computer to recognize the limit of each word. Thus, the computer is able to access and process data on a selective basis if desired.

In core storage a word mark is identified by a bit that has been turned on at the proper location in the word mark plane.

Magnetic Film Storage. Magnetic film storage functions in somewhat the same manner as core storage. However, instead of individual cores strung on wires, magnetic film is made of much smaller elements in a different form. One type of magnetic film, known as *planar film* or more commonly as *thin film*, consists of very thin, flat wafers made of nickel-iron alloy. These metallic spots are connected by ultra-thin wires and are mounted on an insulating base such as glass or plastic (Figure 12-5).

Magnetic film may also be in the form of plated wire. This is a type of cylindrical film, essentially the same as planar film, except that the film is wrapped around a wire. The wire is often made of beryllium-copper, plated with a magnetic alloy. Although cylindrical film is somewhat slower than planar film, it has technical properties that are advantageous. Wire may be assembled into planes by insertion into a grooved or holed frame or by a loom-weaving process.

Another type of cylindrical film is the plated rod. This technique, known as *thin-film rod memory*, consists of an array of tiny metal rods only a tenth of an inch long. The fine wire used for the rods is made of beryllium-copper plated with a thin magnetic film.

The operation of a magnetic film memory unit is similar in principle to that of a magnetic core unit as the storage elements in both are formed into planes that may be stacked. However, film memories have the advantages of compact-

Figure 12-5. Magnetic thin-film memory plane. (*Courtesy* UNIVAC, *Division of Sperry Rand Corporation.*)

ness and greater speed, along with reliability. These advantages are likely to result in the more extensive use of this storage medium.

Auxiliary Storage

Auxiliary storage supplements the main storage of a computer and usually holds much larger amounts of data than main storage. Auxiliary storage devices can store from several hundred thousand to several hundred million characters of data in either sequential or random sequence, depending on the medium. Random storage of such capacity is especially significant because of the greater freedom it allows in data handling.

The data paths of auxiliary storage devices are always connected to primary storage. However, since data moving from or to auxiliary storage must be routed through primary storage, it is not as rapidly accessible as the data in main storage.

Magnetic core and magnetic film

storage, two of the main storage devices described in the preceding section, may also be used for auxiliary storage. In addition, four other devices are available—magnetic disks, magnetic drums, magnetic cards and strips (mass storage), and magnetic tape.

Magnetic Disk Storage. The magnetic disk is a thin metal disk resembling a phonograph record. It is coated on both sides with a magnetic recording material. Data is stored as magnetized spots arranged in binary form in concentric tracks on each face of the disk. A characteristic of disk storage is that data is recorded serially bit-by-bit, eight bits per byte, along a track rather than by columns of characters as shown in the illustration of core storage (Figure 12-4).

Figure 12-6 shows data recorded serially using the extended binary coded decimal interchange code. The absence of parity bits in this illustration results from the fact that the technique of checking parity in each byte is generally not used with direct access devices. Instead these devices utilize a more efficient method of reliability checking, which will not be explained here because of its complexity.

Disks are normally mounted in a stack on a rotating vertical shaft. Enough space is left between each disk to allow access arms to move in and read or record data. Access arms are usually forked and have two recording heads. Thus, upon entry into a stack of disks a recording head is available to read or write on either side of a disk. Each track or sector of track on a disk is directly addressable.

A single magnetic disk unit is capable of storing several million characters. Usually more than one disk unit can be attached to a computer. Magnetic disk storage has an excellent cost-to-storage ratio and is very reliable. Although access speed is limited by the revolving action of disks and search movement of the arms, the average seek time (time it takes for the read-write heads to be positioned over a given track) is about 75 milliseconds, and the average rotational delay (time it takes for data within the track to reach the read-write head) is about 12.5 milliseconds. Once the data is located by the read-

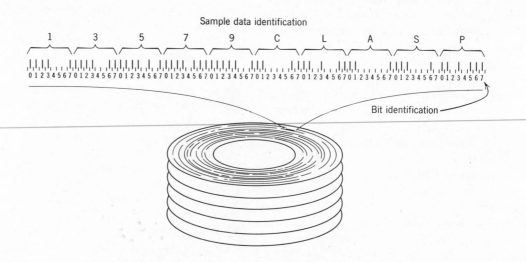

Figure 12-6. Representation of data recorded on a disk storage device.

Figure 12-7. Disk pack. (*Courtesy International Business Machines Corporation.*)

write head, the data transfer rate can be up to 312,000 bytes per second.

A major advantage of most disk storage devices is that disk packs, each consisting of a stack of disks, may be removed and replaced on the drive unit (Figure 12-7). This capacity is helpful in several ways. First, the pack required for a particular job may be mounted before the job is started, removed when the job is completed, and replaced with the pack necessary to perform the next job. Second, if the size of a file for a particular job exceeds the capacity of a single pack, multiple packs may be used.

Storage capacity may be extended further by the use of multiple disk units. For example, the direct access storage facility shown in Figure 12-8 contains eight independent disk storage units and their control unit. It also contains a ninth unit that can be brought into use if one of the eight normally used units requires maintenance.

Vast storage capacity, direct accessibility of data, and a relatively fast data transfer rate, along with other advantages, have made disk storage devices very common units on computers.

Magnetic Drum Storage (Figure 12-9). The magnetic drum has been used extensively as a means of storing data, especially in the early computers, many of which used the drum for primary storage. In today's larger computer systems the drum is used for rapid access to frequently used data and other auxiliary storage functions.

A drum is a cylinder with a magnetizable outer surface on which data is recorded serially in a series of bands around the drum in a manner similar to that utilized on disk storage. As the drum rotates at a constant speed, data is re-

Figure 12-8. Direct access storage facility. (*Courtesy International Business Machines Corporation.*)

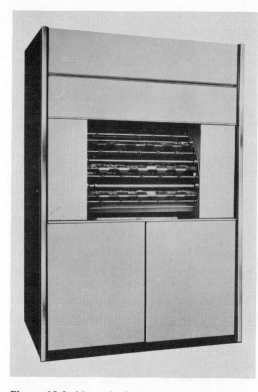

Figure 12-9. Magnetic drum storage unit. (*Courtesy* UNIVAC, *Division of Sperry Rand Corporation.*)

corded or sensed by a set of read-write heads. The heads are positioned close enough to the surface of the drum to be able to magnetize the surface and to sense the magnetization on it. The heads contain coils of fine wire wound around tiny magnetic cores. There may be one or more heads for each drum track or one or more heads that can be moved to the various tracks. The drum may rotate up to 3,500 revolutions per minute, and the data transfer rate to or from the processing unit may be up to 1,200,000 bytes per second. The rotational delay to a specific part of the track ranges from 0 to 17.5 milliseconds and averages 8.6 milliseconds.

Data is stored in the form of minute magnetized spots, arranged in binary form on the individual recording tracks. Spots are magnetized by sending pulses of current through the write coil. The polarity of a spot is determined by the direction of the current flow. Thus, depending on their polarity, spots can represent either 1's or 0's, the two binary digits.

Mass Storage. Magnetic cards and strips offer the advantages of disk storage plus the capacity to store a greater quantity of data at a lower cost per byte. In this medium, data is magnetically recorded in tracks or channels on the surface of cards or strips. Several hundred strips may be housed in a demountable cell or cartridge. Several manufacturers produce mass storage drive units that may contain from one to ten cells at a time and store from 125 million to more than 500 million bytes.

In the system illustrated by Figure

Figure 12-10. Card random access memory unit. (*Courtesy National Cash Register Company.*)

12-10, cards are filed in random order in cartridges holding 384 cards. Cards may be individually selected at random. A selected card is released from the rods on which it is suspended and is pulled by means of vacuum onto a rotating drum. While on the rotating drum, the card comes into contact with 36 read-write heads which read or record data magnetically. After a track of data has been read or written, the magnetic card may be recirculated so that data on the other tracks may be processed or it may be released. When released, the card is returned to its cartridge through a tunnel of moving air and is suspended until selected again. The physical movement of these cards from the cartridge to the rotating drum is relatively slow. However, once the card is

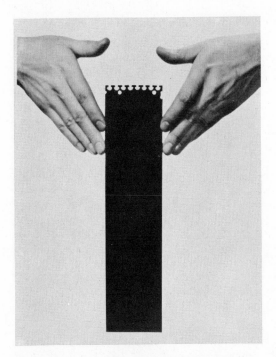

Figure 12-11. Magnetic card used in random access memory system. (*Courtesy National Cash Register Company.*)

ready to read or write, the data transfer rate is comparable to medium-speed magnetic tape devices. Figure 12-11 illustrates one of the magnetic cards used in this system.

The capacity for storing a large quantity of data on-line makes these devices ideally suited to very large files that will have a relatively low volume of transactions. Mass storage units are also accessible to remote terminals. A large inventory file that is batch updated daily and is inquired into from remote terminals is an example of an application that capitalizes on the advantages of this type of auxiliary storage.

Magnetic Tape Storage. Magnetic tape may be classified as auxiliary or external storage depending on the circumstances. Active tape records mounted on tape read-write units are considered as auxiliary storage during the time that they are connected to and controlled by the computer. However, when inactive tape records are removed from the tape read-write units and stored, they are classified as external storage. In other words, they hold data in a form prescribed for the computer but they are separated from the computer. The same could be said for magnetic disk packs and magnetic card cartridges.

Figure 12-12 shows how the same data represented in preceding illustrations would be recorded on magnetic tape in the extended binary coded decimal interchange code. Note that the channels on nine-track tape do not run in 0 to 7 sequence. The purpose of this is to place the most frequently used channels near the center of the tape, thereby reducing the chance of dust, dirt, or physical damage to the outer edge of the tape causing data to be lost. As shown in Figure 12-12, parity may be checked horizontally at the end of

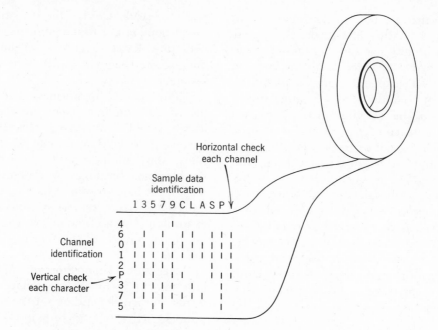

Figure 12-12. Representation of data recorded on magnetic tape.

each record on magnetic tape in addition to being checked vertically by each byte.

Another method of recording data on magnetic tape is called *phase encoding*. In this method, instead of recording only 1 bits, both 0 bits and 1 bits are recorded as magnetized spots that are opposite in polarity. This method of recording provides optimum performance and reliability with greater density and more rapid transfer of data.

Random versus Sequential Processing. Many authorities believe that in the future random access devices such as magnetic disks and magnetic strips will supplant magnetic tape as the major computer-storage medium for active files of data. Magnetic tape is, for all practical purposes, limited to sequential processing techniques. Since data on magnetic tape is processed serially, it might be necessary to read to the middle of a reel

of tape to gain access to a specific item of data located there. In locating record 20,001, for example, the computer must search each of the 20,000 earlier records before coming to record 20,001. This is a relatively time-consuming procedure which makes tape impractical in operations requiring frequent access to data on a random basis.

In addition, for economic reasons sequential filing techniques dictate that data must first be accumulated in sufficient quantity and batched for processing. In other words, a number of similar items are collected, sorted, and placed in sequence for processing together. Since sequential processing generally requires the batching of data, there are many applications that cannot be handled effectively on a sequential basis. Any applications requiring immediate posting of transactions to maintain up-to-date balances or current status, for example, are jobs that cannot be handled easily with the use of sequential access files.

When random access files are used, any record can be located directly without scanning all of the other records ahead of it in sequence. Instead, the access device proceeds directly to a specified location for the purpose of reading or recording data without regard to the sequence or location of data previously read or recorded. This ability to go directly from one record to another regardless of location gives random access devices an important advantage over sequential access devices.

Other significant features of random access are its abilities to process a variety of input in any order, to update all records affected by a transaction simultaneously, and to utilize input in many forms, including punched cards, paper or magnetic tape, optical scanning, magnetic ink character recognition, and keyboard. Furthermore, most random access devices have a data transfer rate that is faster and more reliable than that of magnetic tape. Thus direct access devices may be economical substitutes for magnetic tape as input-output devices for sequential data.

External Storage

External storage facilities provide a means of holding information before or after it has been processed by the computer. Although external storage contains data in a form suitable for entering into the computer, the storage device is not an integral part of the computer. In fact, external storage is not even under the control of the computer unless the medium containing the data is brought into direct contact with the computer system.

The media that are most commonly used for external storage are the ones that are also used for input-output purposes. These include punched cards, punched tapes, and magnetic tapes. Although originally designed for other purposes, these media provide an effective means of storing and transferring large amounts of data. However, data stored in this manner is not as readily accessible, since it must be batched and handled on a sequential basis rather than a random basis.

In addition to these well-known media, two newer input media may be classified as external storage. These are magnetic ink characters and optical characters. These media are designed primarily to be sensed or read by input devices. However, if retained, the documents containing the characters constitute in effect a form of external storage.

Two of the auxiliary storage devices—magnetic cards or strips and magnetic disks—may also be classified as external storage if the storage elements are removed from the drive units and are regarded as inactive.

Review Questions

1. What are the two symbols used in the binary number system?
2. What are the decimal equivalents of the following binary notations: (a) 1010011 (b) 11101 (c) 110010?
3. What are the binary notations for the following decimal values: (a) 255 (b) 83 (c) 37?
4. What is the difference between pure binary notation and the binary coded decimal notation?

5. Why are four binary positions required for binary coded decimal form?
6. Briefly describe odd parity.
7. What does EBCDIC represent?
8. How many bits are contained in a byte?
9. What are the advantages of a packed byte?
10. How does internal storage differ from other types of storage?
11. What are the two major types of internal storage?
12. Name four types of auxiliary storage.
13. How is the ability to remove disk packs helpful?
14. Briefly describe the mass storage medium. What advantages does it have over disk storage?
15. Why is magnetic tape limited to sequential processing?
16. What are the three most commonly used types of external storage?
17. Which auxiliary storage devices may also be classified as external storage?

13

EDP CENTRAL PROCESSING UNIT

The central processing unit (CPU) is the heart of an electronic data processing system. It controls and monitors the entire system and contains the facilities for addressing main storage, for storing or retrieving information, for accessing instructions in the desired order, for initiating the communications between main storage and all other devices, and for the arithmetic and logical processing of data. Before examining these functions, however, let us consider the type of arithmetic used.

COMPUTER NUMBERING SYSTEMS AND ARITHMETIC

In the preceding chapter we learned that a form of binary code is used in the internal operations of the computer because of design characteristics. Nevertheless, most computers can accept or deliver data in decimal form. In preparing input, data is written in standard decimal or alphabetic form. Computers automatically convert data into the proper mode for internal use. They also convert processed data into decimal and alphabetic characters when preparing output.

Because of this automatic conversion of data, a thorough understanding of the different notational systems is seldom required by business data processing personnel. However, to appreciate the manner in which computers manipulate numbers, we shall expand the discussion of numbering systems included in the preceding chapter and review some of the principles of binary computation.

Binary Computations

Arithmetic is performed with binary numbers following the same basic rules as in the decimal system except that the binary system requires more frequent "carries." In binary there is a carry to the next column whenever the total exceeds one. In the decimal system there is a carry to the next column whenever the total exceeds nine.

Addition. In binary addition the following rules apply:

1. 0 plus 0 equals 0.
2. 0 plus 1 equals 1.
3. 1 plus 1 equals 0, with a 1 carry.

Example   *Decimal*   *Binary*

$$
\begin{array}{rr}
9 & 1001 \\
+5 & +0101 \\
\hline
14 & 1110 \\
\end{array}
$$

Subtraction. In binary subtraction, which is equally simple, the following rules are used:

1. 0 minus 0 equals 0.
2. 1 minus 0 equals 1.
3. 1 minus 1 equals 0.
4. 0 minus 1 equals 1, with 1 borrowed from the left.

Example   *Decimal*   *Binary*

$$
\begin{array}{rr}
13 & 1101 \\
-6 & -0110 \\
\hline
7 & 0111 \\
\end{array}
$$

Complement Addition. Although subtraction can be performed as shown, computers usually execute subtraction by forming a *complement* of the subtrahend and by adding this number to the minuend. The procedure for complementing any number is to subtract each digit of the number from the highest digit value of the numbering system and add 1 to the low-order position. Therefore, the complement of binary numbers is obtained by subtracting each digit from 1 and adding 1 to the units position.

Example. To complement the binary number 1101:

$$
\begin{array}{r}
1111 \\
-1101 \\
\hline
0010 \\
+\quad 1 \\
\hline
0011 \\
\end{array}
$$

Another way of achieving the result in the preceding example is simply to invert each digit in the original number, i.e., replace all the 0's with 1's and all the 1's with 0's, and add 1 to the rightmost column.

The result of complement addition will be in one of two forms: true or complement. A carry from the leftmost column is used as a signal that the answer is in true form. The absence of a carry indicates that the answer is in complement form, i.e., negative.

Examples.

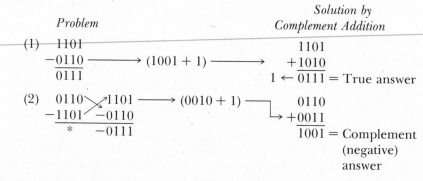

	Problem		*Solution by Complement Addition*

(1) 1101
  −0110 ⟶ (1001 + 1) ⟶
  0111

  1101
 +1010
 1 ← 0111 = True answer

(2) 0110 ⤫ 1101 ⟶ (0010 + 1) ⟶
 −1101   −0110
  *   −0111

  0110
 +0011
 1001 = Complement (negative) answer

---

* In subtraction, where the subtrahend is larger than the minuend, the positions of the minuend and the subtrahend are reversed; a subtraction is performed; and the difference is given a negative sign.

In the second of the preceding examples the absence of a carry indicates a complement answer. Thus the computer would have to recomplement the answer and change the sign. Recomplementing results in the true answer of -0111 which is obtained as follows:

$$
\begin{array}{r}
1111 \\
-1001 \\
\hline
0110 \\
+1 \\
\hline
-0111
\end{array}
$$

Although computers actually perform binary multiplication through a series of additions and division through a series of complement additions, the rules for multiplication and division are shown in the following paragraphs.

Multiplication. The rules for multiplying two binary numbers are:

1. 0 times 0 equals 0.
2. 0 times 1 equals 0.
3. 1 times 1 equals 1.

Example.

	Decimal	Binary
	6	110
	×5	×101
	30	110
		000
		110
		11110

Division. Binary division proceeds in the same manner as decimal division, except that the rules for binary multiplication and subtraction must be applied.

Example.

	Decimal	Binary
	6	110
	5)30	101)11110
	30	101
	00	0101
		101
		0000

Decimal to Binary Conversion. The conversion of a decimal number to its binary equivalent is accomplished by dividing the decimal number by two, the base of the binary system, until the quotient reaches zero. The remainder of each successive division is recorded to the right. The remainders, read in reverse, comprise the binary number.

Example.

$$
\begin{array}{l}
2)\underline{57} \\
2)\underline{28} \quad \text{with the remainder 1} \\
2)\underline{14} \quad \text{with the remainder 0} \\
2)\underline{7} \quad \text{with the remainder 0} \\
2)\underline{3} \quad \text{with the remainder 1} \\
2)\underline{1} \quad \text{with the remainder 1} \\
0 \quad \text{with the remainder 1}
\end{array} \right\} 111001
$$

Binary to Decimal Conversion. The conversion of a binary number to its decimal equivalent is accomplished by the following steps:

1. Multiply the high-order digit of the number by its base.
2. Add the next digit to the product.
3. Multiply the sum by the base.
4. Continue the process until the low-order digit has been added.

Example.

$$
\begin{array}{r}
1 \quad 1 \quad 0 \quad 1_2 \\
\times 2 \\
\hline
2 \\
+1 \leftarrow \\
\hline
3 \\
\times 2 \\
\hline
6 \\
+0 \leftarrow \\
\hline
6 \\
\times 2 \\
\hline
12 \\
+1 \leftarrow \\
\hline
13_{10}
\end{array}
$$

Hexadecimal Numbering System

Hexadecimal (a hexagon has six sides, and decimal means ten) stands for the base 16 numbering system. Most third-generation computers operate on a principle that utilizes the hexadecimal system as it provides high utilization of computer storage and an expanded set of characters for representing data.

As we have already seen, a numbering system requires as many different symbols as there are in the base of the system. Thus, base 10 (decimal) requires ten different symbols. Base 2 (binary) requires two. In base 16 (hexadecimal) sixteen symbols are required. Because only a single character is allowed for each absolute value, the hexadecimal system uses the ten symbols of the decimal system for the values 0 through 9, and the first six letters of the alphabet to represent values 10 through 15 (Table 13-1).

As illustrated in Table 13-2, the positional significance of hexadecimal symbols is based on the progression of powers of 16. The highest number that can be represented in the units position is 15. Therefore, we must carry 1 to the next position to the left to make the number 16. This then becomes the 16 position. The next number to the left is then 16 times as large, or 256; the next number is also 16 times as large, or 4,096; etc.

Since we think most readily in decimal terms, persons who plan to write programs for most modern computers will find it helpful to be able to convert hexadecimal to or from decimal. Although such conversions are usually performed with the aid of a table, the rules are presented in the following sections.

Decimal to Hexadecimal Conversion. Conversion of a decimal number to its hexadecimal equivalent can be accomplished by the following steps:

TABLE 13-1   DECIMAL, BINARY, AND HEXADECIMAL EQUIVALENTS

Decimal	Binary	Hexadecimal
10 1	8 4 2 1	1
1	1	1
2	1 0	2
3	1 1	3
4	1 0 0	4
5	1 0 1	5
6	1 1 0	6
7	1 1 1	7
8	1 0 0 0	8
9	1 0 0 1	9
1 0	1 0 1 0	A
1 1	1 0 1 1	B
1 2	1 1 0 0	C
1 3	1 1 0 1	D
1 4	1 1 1 0	E
1 5	1 1 1 1	F

TABLE 13-2   THE HEXADECIMAL NUMBERING SYSTEM

Positional significance:	16^5	16^4	16^3	16^2	16^1	16^0
Positional value:	1,048,576	65,536	4,096	256	16	1
Hexadecimal number:			1	A	3	C

Hexadecimal to decimal conversion:

$$C \times 16^0 = 12$$
$$3 \times 16^1 = 48$$
$$A \times 16^2 = 2,560$$
$$1 \times 16^3 = \underline{4,096}$$
$$6,716$$

1. Divide the decimal number by the new base (16).

2. The remainder becomes the low-order position of the base 16 number:

3. Divide the quotient by the new base (16).

4. The remainder becomes the next digit of the base 16 number.

5. Repeat steps 3 and 4 until a quotient of zero is obtained.

Example.

$$
\begin{array}{ccc}
42 & 2 & 0 \\
16\overline{)678} & 16\overline{)42} & 16\overline{)2} \rightarrow 2 \quad A \quad 6 \\
64 & 32 & \\
\overline{38} & \overline{10} & \\
32 & & \\
\overline{6} & &
\end{array}
$$

Hexadecimal to Decimal Conversion. The rules for hexadecimal to decimal conversion are:

1. Multiply the high-order digit of the hexadecimal number by the base (16).

2. Add the next digit to the product.

3. Multiply the sum by the base (16).

4. Repeat steps 2 and 3 until the low-order digit has been added.

Example.

$$
\begin{array}{r}
2 \quad A \quad 6 \\
\times \; 16 \\
\hline
32 \\
+ \; 10 \leftarrow \\
\hline
42 \\
\times \; 16 \\
\hline
252 \\
42 \\
\hline
672 \\
+ \quad 6 \leftarrow \\
\hline
678
\end{array}
$$

Binary – Hexadecimal Conversion. Conversion from binary to hexadecimal and vice versa is a simple process as there is a direct 4 to 1 relationship (2^4 to 2^1) between the base 16 and base 2 systems. Thus every four binary digits become a single hexadecimal digit and each hexadecimal digit becomes four binary digits.

Example. Convert hexadecimal 2A6 to binary:

$$
\begin{array}{ccc}
2 & A & 6 \\
\downarrow & \downarrow & \downarrow \\
0010 & 1010 & 0110
\end{array}
$$

Convert binary 001010100110 to hexadecimal:

$$0010 \quad 1010 \quad 0110$$
$$\downarrow \qquad \downarrow \qquad \downarrow$$
$$2 \qquad A \qquad 6$$

The hexadecimal to binary procedure illustrated above is also helpful in converting large decimal numbers to binary numbers. This procedure is usually accomplished by first converting decimal to hexadecimal and then converting hexadecimal to binary.

Hexadecimal Computations

Arithmetic is performed with hexadecimal numbers following the same basic rules used in the decimal system, except that hexadecimal addition does not result in a carry until the decimal value of 15 is exceeded.

Example.

Decimal: $9 + 1 = 10_{10}$
Hexadecimal: $F + 1 = 10_{16}$

Addition. Since the hexadecimal numbering system uses sixteen symbols, it has too many possible conditions to state all the rules regarding hexadecimal addition. Instead, we will illustrate hexadecimal addition with a series of problems.

Examples.

8	8	A	F	2A	AA	9A
+7	+8	+3	+F	+B1	+C6	+57
F	10	D	1E	DB	170	F1

Subtraction. Subtraction in hexadecimal is just like decimal subtraction, except that when borrowing from the position to the left the value transferred is 16 rather than 10.

Example.

Decimal

$$\begin{array}{r} 13 \text{ becomes} \quad 0(13) \\ -\ 8 \qquad\qquad -\ 8 \\ \hline 5 \end{array}$$

Hexadecimal

$$13 \text{ becomes} \quad 0(19) \leftarrow \binom{\text{Decimal}}{\text{value}}$$
$$-\ 8 \qquad\qquad -\ 8$$
$$\qquad\qquad\qquad \overline{\text{B}}$$

Another hexadecimal example:

$$F9A \text{ becomes} \quad F8(26) \leftarrow \binom{\text{Decimal}}{\text{value}}$$
$$-A8F \qquad\qquad -A8 \ \ F$$
$$\qquad\qquad \overline{50 \ \ B}$$

Complement Addition. The procedure for complementing a hexadecimal number is to subtract each digit of the number from 15 and add 1 to the units position. The complement of a hexadecimal number is usually called the "sixteens" complement.

Example. To complement the hexadecimal number 2B7:

$$\begin{array}{r} FFF \\ -2B7 \\ \hline D48 \\ +\ \ 1 \\ \hline D49 \end{array}$$

As with binary numbers, the result of complement addition will be in one of two forms: true or complement. Thus, a carry from the high-order position is used to signal that the answer is in true form, and the absence of a carry indicates that the answer is in complement form.

Examples.

	Problem	Complement	Solution by Complement Addition

(1)
$$
\begin{array}{r}
\text{E7A4} \\
-\text{A48E} \\
\hline
4316
\end{array}
\qquad
\begin{array}{r}
\text{FFFF} \\
-\text{A48E} \\
\hline
5\text{B}71 \\
+\quad 1 \\
\hline
5\text{B}72
\end{array}
\qquad
\begin{array}{r}
\text{E7A4} \\
+\ 5\text{B}72 \\
\hline
\text{C} \leftarrow 4316 = \text{True answer}
\end{array}
$$

(2)
$$
\begin{array}{r}
\text{ABCD} \\
-\text{EDCB} \\
\hline
-41\text{FE}
\end{array}
\qquad
\begin{array}{r}
\text{FFFF} \\
-\text{EDCB} \\
\hline
1234 \\
+\quad 1 \\
\hline
1235
\end{array}
\qquad
\begin{array}{r}
\text{ABCD} \\
+1235 \\
\hline
\text{BE02} = \text{Comple-} \\
\text{ment (nega-} \\
\text{tive) answer}
\end{array}
$$

Recomplement

$$
\begin{array}{r}
\text{FFFF} \\
-\text{BE02} \\
\hline
41\text{FD} \\
+\quad 1 \\
\hline
-41\text{FE} = \ \text{True answer}
\end{array}
$$

To verify the preceding solutions, the problems could be converted to decimal and solved. Then the answers could be converted to hexadecimal and compared with the original results. Thus, hexadecimal problems can be solved by converting the numbers to decimal. The method is optional; however, it is normally faster to solve hexadecimal problems in hexadecimal.

FUNCTIONAL ELEMENTS

The central processing unit contains a number of functional elements including registers, decoders, and adders.

Register

A *register* is a device capable of receiving data, holding it, and transferring it as directed by control circuits. Registers are named according to their function as shown by the following examples.

1. An *accumulator* is a register in which the results of arithmetic or logic operations are accumulated.

2. A *storage register* temporarily holds data taken from or being sent to storage.

3. An *address register* holds the address of a storage location or device.

4. An *instruction register* holds the instructions being executed.

5. An *index register* is used in address arithmetic, i.e., to modify an instruction address and for indexing. For example, the storage address of data could be increased by the length of the record each time the instruction is executed, thereby causing the computer to read sequential records one after the other.

6. A *general register* can perform the functions of several special registers such as accumulators, storage registers, address registers, and index registers.

7. A *floating point register* is used in floating point arithmetic operations.

Certain registers hold data while related circuits analyze the data. For example, an instruction may be held by one register while associated *decoder circuits* determine the operation to be performed and locate the data to be used. The contents of the more important registers may be displayed on the computer console through small lights associated with them.

Adder

Addition is the fundamental operation performed by a computer. When a computer subtracts, multiplies, or divides, it does so by adding and shifting. The adder constitutes a major part of the arithmetic unit circuitry and forms the basis of most of the computer's arithmetic and logical functions. It receives data from two or more sources, performs the arithmetic functions, and conveys the result to a receiving register.

CONTROL UNIT

The control unit directs and coordinates all activity of the computer including the following:

1. Control of input-output devices.
2. Entry and retrieval of information from storage.
3. Routing of information between storage and the arithmetic-logical section.

4. Direction of arithmetic-logical operations.

The performance of these operations requires a vast number of "paths" over which data and instructions may be sent. Routing data over the proper paths in the circuitry, opening and closing the right "gates" at the right time, and establishing timing sequences are major functions of the control unit.

All of these operations are under the control of a stored program. A *program* is a set of instructions indicating to the computer the exact sequence of steps it must follow in processing a given set of data. Each instruction usually includes two things:

1. An *operation code* which specifies what is to be done.
2. One or more *operands* which designate the address or addresses of the data needed for the specified operation.

The instructions and data that are required by a computer to solve a problem are generally entered through a regular input device and are stored sequentially within the computer's primary storage. The instructions must be stored in operating sequence in primary storage for the control unit to have access to them. To receive, interpret, and execute stored program instructions, the control section of the central processing unit must operate in a prescribed sequence. All stored program operations are executed in fixed intervals of time which are measured by regular pulses emitted from an electronic clock. The frequence of these pulses may be as high as a million or more each second. A fixed number of pulses determines the time of each basic machine cycle during which the computer can perform a specific operation.

The first machine cycle necessary to carry out an instruction is called an *instruction cycle*. The time for this cycle is known as *instruction time* or *I-time*. During *I*-time the following steps are completed:

1. An instruction is transferred from a specified primary storage location to the instruction register in the control unit. The instructions in primary storage are not destroyed or altered as a result of their being transferred to the control unit and, therefore, can be used an unlimited number of times.

2. The operation part of the instruction which tells the computer what is to be done is decoded by the control unit — that is, it activates the particular circuits needed to carry out the instruction.

3. The operands (location of data to be operated on) are placed in address registers. This indicates what data is to be used in performing the required operation.

4. The location of the instruction to be executed next is ascertained.

I-time is followed by one or more machine cycles referred to as *execution cycles* or *E-time*. During the execution cycle, the machine actually performs the specified operation. The number of execution cycles is determined by the instruction to be executed. For example, a computer would require more machine cycles to multiply "*A* times *B*" than it would to add "*A* plus *B*." The *E*-cycle begins by transferring from storage the data located at the address identified by the address register. This data is placed in a storage register where it is operated on according to the operation part of the instruction. In addition to the storage location of data, the address register may indicate the address of an input-output unit or a control function to be performed.

ARITHMETIC-LOGICAL UNIT

The arithmetic-logical unit performs the actual processing of data including addition, subtraction, multiplication, and division. This unit also performs certain logical operations such as comparing two numbers to see if one is larger than the other or if they are equal. In this way the computer is able to make simple decisions.

Arithmetic Operations

As indicated earlier, most computers now being produced are equally proficient at processing business or scientific problems. To satisfy both of these needs computers must be capable of handling fixed-length and variable-length data fields. They must also be capable of four classes of operations: fixed point arithmetic, floating point arithmetic, decimal arithmetic, and logical operations. Decimal arithmetic is generally associated with business applications, whereas fixed point and floating point arithmetic are generally used for scientific and engineering applications. The selection of the method to be employed is largely at the discretion of the programmer and is identified in the program instructions.

These classes of operations differ in the data formats used, the registers involved, the operations provided, and the way the field length is stated. To illustrate the four processing operations we will refer to Figure 13-1, a schematic of basic registers and data paths in the IBM System/360 computer.

Decimal Arithmetic. Computers perform decimal arithmetic on signed packed decimal numbers (see Figure 12-2) using the storage-to-storage concept employed by most business oriented second-generation computers. In the storage-to-storage

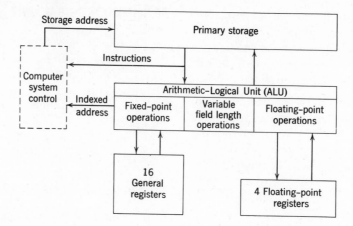

Figure 13-1. Schematic of basic registers and data paths in IBM System/360 computer.

concept, variable-length data fields are brought out of main storage, operated on by the arithmetic-logical unit, and the results are placed back into main storage. For example, let us assume that an instruction calls for the addition of a quantity in a field labeled A to the quantity in a field labeled B. As shown in Figure 13-2, the following operations would result.

1. The instruction "ADD A + B," the next instruction to be processed, is called from primary storage and goes to the computer system control unit where the operation code representing "ADD" is translated into commands.

2. The computer control system then commands the arithmetic-logical unit (ALU) to add the data stored at the locations identified as fields A and B and to store the result in the original location of field A.

As this concept is important, a more detailed discussion of a sample problem is justified. Let us assume that we wish to adjust the inventory of a certain stock item by adding the stock receipts and subtracting the stock issues. The following factors are involved:

Hammer, claw	170
Stock receipts	+ 50
Stock issues	− 95
Balance on hand	125

After the beginning inventory record for claw hammers has been read by an input device and transferred to primary storage, the computer would then be instructed to perform the following steps.

1. Add stock receipts to the quantity on hand. This is accomplished by one instruction, symbolically represented as ADD QTYHD + STKRCP, which causes the quantity on hand (170) and stock receipts (50) to be transferred to the arith-

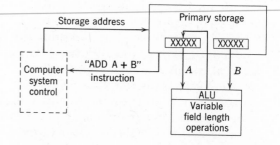

Figure 13-2. Schematic of decimal arithmetic data paths.

metic-logical unit where they are added together. The result (220) is returned to the quantity-on-hand field in primary storage. This causes the original quantity-on-hand amount in primary storage to be destroyed as the new quantity on hand is recorded.

2. After this ADD instruction is executed, the system control unit receives the next instruction, translates it and then executes it. During execution the series of operations described in step 3 would be performed.

3. Subtract stock issues from the quantity on hand. This is also accomplished by one instruction, symbolically represented as SUBT QTYHD — STKISS, which causes the quantity on hand (220) and the stock issues (95) to be transferred to the arithmetic-logical unit. Here the issues are subtracted from the quantity on hand and the result (125) is returned to the quantity-on-hand field in primary storage. Again this causes the previous quantity on hand (220) to be destroyed.

4. The new quantity-on-hand figure (125) is now available in primary storage for whatever use is to be made of it by the instructions that follow. Normally, the quantity on hand and its associated data would constitute a record that would be conveyed to an output device such as magnetic tape; or perhaps it would be formated into a print line and printed, or both. After the disposition of this updated record, the next instruction would cause the succeeding record to be read by an input device and transferred to primary storage. The process just described would then be repeated.

Fixed Point Arithmetic. Fixed point arithmetic is a method of calculation in which the computer does not consider the location of the decimal point. This is similar to the situation that exists in the use of desk calculators and slide rules which require the operator to keep track of the decimal point. With electronic computers the location of the decimal point is the programmer's responsibility.

Fixed point arithmetic uses the storage-to-accumulator or the accumulator-to-accumulator concepts that were used by most scientific oriented second-generation computers. Fixed point arithmetic operations are performed using fixed length binary data fields. The results of either the storage-to-accumulator or the accumulator-to-accumulator operation will be stored in either one or two general registers. Addition, subtraction, multiplication, division, and comparison operations take one operand (data field) from a register and another from either a register or storage and return the result to a general register. Figure 13-3 shows the data flow for the fixed point add instruction: "ADD field A to B." In this case let us assume that the

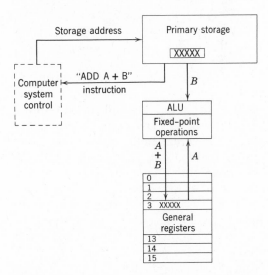

Figure 13-3. Schematic of fixed point arithmetic data paths.

A field quantity stored in general register 3 is to be added to the *B* field quantity stored in primary storage and that the result is to be returned to general register 3.

The stock inventory problem used to illustrate decimal arithmetic could also be performed using fixed point arithmetic.

Floating Point Arithmetic. For certain arithmetic operations, typically those in the scientific and engineering areas, it is helpful or even essential to let the computer assume the task of keeping track of decimal points. When using the fixed point binary or decimal instructions it is necessary to be aware of the maximum possible sizes of all data, intermediate results, and final results. It is often necessary to know the minimum sizes as well. This awareness is essential to avoid the possibility of exceeding the capacity of a register or of a storage location. Such knowledge about problem data is often difficult and sometimes impossible to develop. Furthermore, working in fixed point requires the programmer to align decimal or binary points correctly throughout the process of shifting and rearranging data in order to maintain significance while avoiding capacity overflow.

For these reasons, it is a great convenience to let the computer take over the clerical details of a complete accounting for number sizes and decimal point alignment. Floating point arithmetic saves programming time and makes possible the solution of complex problems that would otherwise be almost impossible.

The basic idea of floating point numbers is that each quantity is represented as a combination of two items: a numerical fraction and a power of 16 by which the fraction is multiplied to get the number represented. The 16 applies specifically to the IBM System/360; other floating point systems may use binary or decimal multipliers.

Floating point operations are performed with one operand from a floating point register and another one from either a floating point register or storage, with the result placed in a floating point register.

The details of floating point arithmetic are not within the scope of this book. The purpose here is merely to introduce the concept.

Logical Operations

Non-arithmetic data manipulations, generally referred to as *logical operations*, constitute a substantial portion of today's computing task. Logical operations such as *compare, move, translate, edit, bit test,* and *bit set* are used in extracting, categorizing, transforming, rearranging, and editing data. The operations are discussed in groups that possess similar functions.

Shifting. Left- and right-shift operations are used for many of the processes of isolating, eliminating, and aligning groups of contiguous bits. Shifting consists of moving data in one storage field to another location and realigning the data within the new field. For example, shifting is often used to drop excess digits beyond the decimal point that result from multiplication, or to align the decimal points in two data fields so that they may be arithmetically operated on.

Operand-Pair Logic. Logic operations on operand pairs are primarily used for extracting, testing, modifying, and recombining bit groups. The *load, store, insert,* and *move* type of operations are the easiest to understand. The compare logical operations result in the setting of a condition code to one of three states: low, equal, or high. The program can check the condition code setting and as a result either branch to an alternate series of instructions or continue to process the series of instructions being processed at the time the condition code was tested.

Editing. The editing operations are generally those that perform the following:

1. The *move zones* or *move numeric* operations permit the separation or recombination of zone and numeric data.

2. The *pack* and *unpack* operations are used for packing and unpacking decimal data fields.

3. The *edit* operations permit editing of packed decimal data for printing. These operations can suppress or protect leading zeros, provide punctuation such as commas and periods, and control printing of credit or minus signs.

Conversion. The *convert to binary* and *convert to decimal* operations provide for radix conversion of address and data values.

In the next chapter we will cover many of the logical operations from a programming point of view.

Review Questions

1. In what manner do computers usually perform subtraction?
2. What is the highest hexadecimal number that can be represented in the units position?
3. What are the sums of the following hexadecimal values: 7 + 7; 8 + 8; A + 4; and C + D?
4. How many binary digits are there in each hexadecimal digit?
5. What are the functions of a register?
6. What four types of activities are directed and coordinated by the control unit?
7. Define a stored program.
8. What are the functions of the arithmetic-logical unit?
9. What three classes of arithmetic operations are performed by computers?
10. Name four types of logical operations.

14

EDP PROGRAM DEVELOPMENT

Computers are automatic, which means that they are able to perform long sequences of operations without human intervention. In fact, a computer may perform millions of operations without aid from an operator. A computer does, however, require instructions to direct its operations. These instructions define each basic operation to be performed and identify the data, device, or mechanism needed to carry out the operation.

The purpose of this chapter is to consider the manner in which instructions are developed, stored, and executed.

STORED PROGRAM INSTRUCTIONS

One of the most significant characteristics of electronic computers is that of internal storage. As indicated earlier, all data to be processed is initially entered into storage. In order to be processed, this data must be transmitted electronically to the other internal component, the arithmetic-logical unit. The results of the operations performed in the arithmetic-logical unit must then be routed electronically back to storage. When the results are desired, they are forwarded electronically from storage to an output device. A schematic diagram of these operations was presented in Figure 11-3.

All of these operations are under the control of a stored program. A *program* is a set of instructions indicating to the computer the exact sequence of steps it must follow in processing a given set of data.

The instructions and data that are required by a computer to solve a problem are both stored within the computer's main memory in numbered locations called *addresses*. Instructions are usually grouped together in main memory. They generally can be placed in any area of storage. Sequential instruction computers generally access each instruction from left to right. Therefore, each succeeding instruction is to the right of the last instruction executed unless a change in sequence of operations is dictated.

When not being operated on by the computer, a program may be stored as a deck of punched cards, or on punched tape, magnetic tape, or a random access device. When the program is required for operation it can be read into the computer memory from any of these external storage devices. After the program is loaded into memory, the computer locates the first instruction of the program and proceeds through the sequence of instructions operating on the data until it reaches the end of the job or is instructed to stop.

A stored program instruction is treated like any other information while stored in the computer. An instruction is not identified as an instruction until it is placed in the control section where it is divided into its various operational segments, decoded, and then executed.

Instruction Format

Most instructions are composed of two basic parts: (1) an operation part and (2) one or more operands.

The *operation* part designates the action to be taken such as read, write, add, subtract, compare, move data, and so on. This information is coded to have a special meaning for the computer. For example, in the programming system to be used for illustrative purposes later in this chapter, the letter A is interpreted by the computer as "add," the letter C as "compare," the letter D as "divide," SIO as "start input/output," and TR as "translate." These are, of course, merely representative of the many instructions used in this system. Furthermore, other computers may use different methods of coding to define operations

An *operand* designates the location of data, an instruction, or an input-output unit or other device that is to be used in the execution of an operation. Thus the operand says what to add, where to store, what to compare, and so on. The operand does not actually give the number to be added or compared. Instead, it is a symbol or label consisting of several characters or bits that give the address in storage where the data to be added or compared will be found.

There are three types of addresses:

1. An *instruction address* is the address in memory where the instruction is located.

2. A *data address* is the address in memory of data that is to be operated upon.

3. A *device address* is the identification of a particular input-output device; it also may refer to a certain location within the device.

A computer instruction may have more than one operand. Most computers have two and some have three. Generally, multiple operand instructions require less storage and fewer instructions to complete a given procedure since they result in more than one operation being performed with a single instruction.

To illustrate instruction format we will use a simple *add* instruction which appears as follows:

$$A \quad 5 \quad 1443$$

The *A* part of this instruction is the operation code that tells the computer it is to perform an add operation. The operand portion of the instruction contains two addresses. The first is the address of a general register and the second is a location in primary storage. Thus the computer is instructed to add the data at storage location 1443 to the contents of register 5.

Instruction Classifications

Some computers use over 200 types of operation codes in their instruction formats and provide several methods for doing the same thing. Other computers employ fewer (20–50) operation codes and have the capacity to perform more than one operation with a single instruction. Although all instructions will not fit into a single class, there are four basic types of instructions: (1) input-output, (2) arithmetic, (3) branching, and (4) logic and test (decision making).

Input-Output Instructions. Input instructions direct the computer to a particular input device. Input instructions also tell the computer to read the next record and to put it into the storage locations specified. Output instructions tell the computer to send data from storage to an output device and to record it on the output medium. All input-output instructions must necessarily identify the device to be used. In some cases the device is specified by the operation part of the instruction and in other cases it is controlled by both the operation and operand.

Other types of input-output instructions are those used in *editing*. This is the process of putting data into a more useful format. The two major editing functions are extraction of particular parts of a record for computer use or for output, and the alteration of a record into a different format. The primary editing function is the preparation of quantitative data. For example, the digits 0100135 would have limited significance if printed without editing which would bring about the following result: $1,001.35.

The editing of quantitative data may include:

1. Eliminating all zeros to the left of the high-order significant digit.

2. Retaining zeros both to the right and left of significant digits when required.

3. Punctuating quantitative amounts with decimal and commas, and if required with the minus or credit sign. If the amount to be punctuated is expressed in dollars, then in addition to the decimal and commas, the dollar sign will be shown in accordance with accepted accounting practice. Amounts are seldom punctuated at the time of input or while operated on in the storage unit in order to conserve as much space as possible within a field or data word.

Editing may require only one instruction but will often require two or more. Usually editing is effected by first moving into the print storage area an edit word consisting of (1) the standard punctuation signs for the type of data to be printed, and (2) an indication of the point to the left of which zeros are to be dropped. This is then followed by an edit instruction that moves the data into the print storage area and eliminates the unnecessary zeros and punctuation marks.

Arithmetic Instructions. All of the basic arithmetic operations can be performed by a computer. All computers have instructions for adding and subtracting and most have instructions for multiplying and dividing. In those computers that do not have multiply or divide instructions, these arithmetic operations can be performed through a series of additions and/or subtractions. The instructions required to perform multiply-divide operations in this manner are usually contained in a utility program called a *subroutine*. A subroutine is a set of instructions designed to direct the computer to carry out a well-defined operation—in this case an arithmetic calculation. After a self-contained subroutine of this type is written and checked, it can be used in any program that requires the operations that it will perform. Sets of these subroutines are generally provided by the manufacturer of each computer as a programming aid.

Thus, when multiply or divide cannot be achieved by a standard instruction, the programmer can utilize an appropriate subroutine. This enables him to accomplish the same results without having to write all the program steps that otherwise would be required each time he found it necessary to multiply or divide. In other words, the subroutine automatically executes a series of instructions that produce the desired calculation.

In every arithmetic operation at least two factors are involved: multiplier and multiplicand, divisor and dividend, and so on. These factors are operated on by the arithmetic unit of the computer to produce a result such as a product or quotient. Therefore, at least two storage locations are needed for every calculation. Depending on the type of computer involved, these may be provided in main storage, by storage registers, accumulators or a combination of these.

A computer has the capacity to perform numerous calculations on many factors during a series of instructions. For example, a factor may be multiplied and then other factors may be added to or subtracted from the product. The computer also has the ability to shift and round a factor or result. Shifting and rounding operations are used for adjusting, lengthening, or shortening results; and for placing the decimal point. All computers have some provision for recognizing and storing the sign associated with a factor, and for operating algebraically with the factor.

The exact rules governing the placement of factors, size of results, and so on vary somewhat from one system to another. In all cases where it is anticipated that a result will exceed the capacity of the field or word, the programmer must arrange his data to produce partial results.

Branch Instructions. Branch instructions cause the computer to switch from one point in a program to another point, thereby controlling the sequence in which operations are performed. When a branch is executed regardless of existing conditions, it is known as an *unconditional branch* When the execution of a branch instruction is contingent upon certain conditions being met, it is known as a *conditional branch.* Conditional branches will be discussed more fully in the following section.

Logic Instructions. Logic (decision-making) instructions enable the computer to deviate from the normal sequence of instructions in accordance with the existence or nonexistence of certain conditions. If instructions always had to be followed sequentially in a fixed pattern, this would limit the computer to a single path of operation. The computer would not have any method of dealing with exceptions to a procedure and would be unable to select alternate paths, known as *branches,* based on conditions encountered while processing data. Moreover, a complete program would be necessary to process each record if it were not possible to repeat a given set of instructions

The simplest of logic instructions is the *data transfer* type. Data transfer instructions are used to move data from one storage location or register to another. Included are such instructions as *plain move, move numeric data only, move zone only,* and *store address.*

A more complex type of logic operation is the *shift.* Shifting consists of moving the characters in a word columnwise to the right or left; that is, each character is moved from one column to the next. Shift operations are used to line up the characters of two words before comparing them or to line up two sets of numerals before adding them.

Shifting also may be used to isolate data. This operation is necessary in a fixed word length computer where two items of data may be stored in one computer word to save space. For example, in a computer with a fixed word length of ten characters, the assignment of a four-character item of data to a storage location would leave six unused character positions. These six positions could be used to store another item of data. However, it would be necessary to separate the items in order to isolate the one needed for a particular operation.

Another type of logic operation is to *compare* the data at one storage location with data in a register, accumulator, or other storage location. The two fields can be compared and evaluated in a specified sequence and one of four possible results will be indicated. The four results of comparisons are:

1. *A* is smaller than *B*.
2. *A* is equal to *B*.
3. *A* is not equal to *B* (the opposite of 2).
4. *A* is larger than *B* (the opposite of 1).

The comparison instruction should be followed by a *conditional branch* instruction with a provision that the branch instruction is to be executed if the comparison indicates the existence of the condition requiring the branch (Figure 14-1). If the condition does not exist, the computer executes the next in the regular sequence of instructions.

It should be noted that computers do not actually make decisions in the normal sense of the word. Instead, they follow directions that are explicitly set forth in the program. In other words, the programmer decides what exceptions can arise

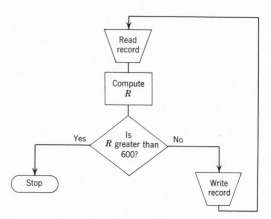

Figure 14-1. Flow chart of a conditional branch.

during a program. He then establishes a set of comparisons which enable the computer to recognize the exceptions. Finally, he specifies the exact procedure that the computer is to use in processing each exception.

The *test* for a certain condition is another type of logic operation involving the same techniques as the comparison instruction. Tests may be made for such conditions as a positive or negative sign for a quantity, zeros or blanks, last card, end of file, or end of job. If the condition being tested is met, the result is a branch to the designated location of another instruction. If the test is not met, the branch instruction is ignored and the next sequential instruction is accessed. Thus branching is conditional, that is, it is dependent on the condition tested for being met.

In addition to the branching instructions which can be used to vary the path that the computer will follow through a program, there are other programming techniques that can be used to accomplish this type of alteration. No attempt will be made here to explain these techniques; however, for reference purposes, they are known as *instruction modification, address modification, indexing,* and *indirect addressing.*

PROGRAM DEVELOPMENT

As indicated previously, the entire series of instructions needed to complete a given routine or procedure is called a *program*. The development of this sequence of steps is referred to as *programming*. The person who writes computer programs, a process that most authorities consider to be an art, is called a *programmer*.

The development of a computer program requires six basic steps:

1. Analyzing the problem.
2. Preparing program flow charts.
3. Writing the program.
4. Assembling or compiling the object program.
5. Testing and correcting the program.
6. Preparing the program for production.

Each of these steps will be discussed in the pages that follow.

Analyzing the Problem

The first step in preparing an application for a computer is to define the problem precisely. In addition, program planning requires a very thorough analysis of all facets of the problem. This includes analysis of source data, the logical and practical procedures that will be needed to solve the problem, and the form of the final output. This analysis must take place before actual preparation of the program can begin. Otherwise, time may be wasted in preparing a program that will be subject to major change before completion.

The methods used to identify the various requirements as well as the inputs into the system will be discussed in the chapter on systems study and design.

Preparing Program Flow Charts

After the problem to be solved has been defined and thoroughly analyzed, it is possible to list the steps that must be followed in solving it. These steps may be written out in detail. It is more likely, however, that they will be represented by a *program flow chart*, which is a graphic illustration of what the computer is supposed to do. The flow chart is a precise and convenient means of outlining the various steps in a program. Flow charts are not as apt to be misinterpreted as an entirely verbal presentation. Furthermore, they provide the programmer with an easy means of trying out and comparing several approaches to a problem.

The three basic symbols of the program flow chart are (1) the *flow direction*, a connecting line between two symbols with an arrow indicating direction if required; (2) the *input-output symbol* denoting any function of an input-output device; and (3) the *processing symbol* representing actual processing operations. The other six symbols shown in Figure 14-2 are optional and may be used to make a flow chart more illustrative.

Some program flow charts flow from left to right across the paper; however, most flow from top to bottom. The main considerations in flow chart preparation are:

1. A conventional technique for flow charting should be used so that others may be able to follow it.
2. The program should have a clearly defined beginning and ending.
3. The flow of the chart generally should be in the same direction, as this reduces confusion and makes it easier to follow the main flow.
4. No flow line should be unconnected at any point.

Processing. A group of program instructions which perform a processing function of the program.

Input-output. Any function of an i/o device (making information available for processing, recording processing information, tape positioning, etc.).

Decision. Points in the program where a branch to alternate paths is possible, based upon variable conditions.

Program modification. An instruction or group of instructions which changes the program.

Predefined process. A group of operations not detailed in the particular set of flow charts.

Terminal. The beginning, end, or a point of interruption in a program.

Connector. An entry from, or an exit to, another part of the program flow chart.

Off-page connector. Used instead of the connector symbol to designate entry to or exit from a page.

Annotation. The addition of descriptive comments or explanatory notes as clarification. The broken line may be drawn on either the left or right, and connected to a flow line where applicable.

Figure 14-2. Program flow chart symbols.

5. The person drawing a flow chart should try to prepare it so that another person could program from it even though this may not actually occur.

6. Side notes should be used to describe complex logic or unique computer program concepts.

Flow charts may be either descriptive or symbolic. As can be noted in Figure 14-3, the descriptive flow chart, has a brief statement in each box and the symbolic flow chart has symbols, usually in a for-

mula concept. Both types have certain advantages. Generally, the descriptive flow chart is employed in business applications and the symbolic is employed in engineering or scientific applications.

To illustrate the manner in which a flow chart is used in planning a program, let us assume that we wish to develop a means of preparing a current stock status report. Basically this involves the following steps:

1. Determining the beginning balance.
2. Adding stock receipts.
3. Deducting stock issues.
4. Printing the new balance.

A program flow chart of the solution to this problem is shown in Figure 14-4.

The following is a description of the steps shown in the flow chart:

Step 1. For each program written there are certain preliminary steps such as (a) define where in primary storage the program will be located, (b) identify input-output devices, (c) reserve storage areas and assign names to the areas, and (d) generate constant data in primary storage. Following these preliminary steps and before actual processing is started, most programming systems require that the files be opened. In this example opening the files consists of informing the program compiler that the input records in the form of punched cards are to be read by the punched card reader.

Step 2. Instructs the computer to determine if the last card has been processed. If the answer is no, the computer is directed to the next step. This function is automatically taken care of in some programming systems by an input-output control system (IOCS). It might at first glance appear strange that the very first step taken is to test for a last card. The primary reason for this is that if there were no data

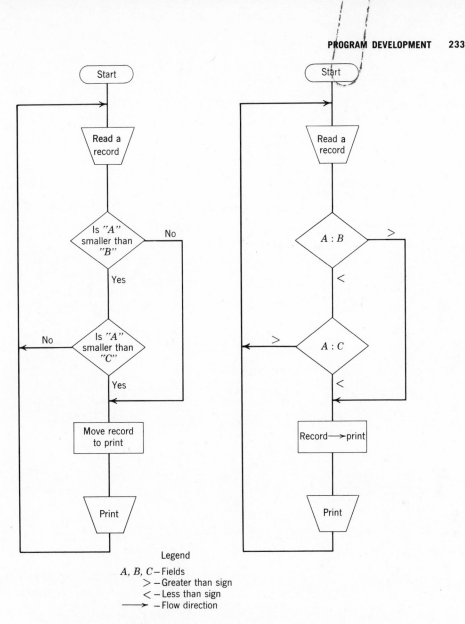

Figure 14-3. Comparison of descriptive and symbolic flow charts.

cards to be read after the program is loaded, we would not want the computer to continue with the process. The last card test in this illustration is also used to determine when the last card in the file has been processed.

Step 3. Instructs the card reader to read a card provided the last card has not been read.

Step 4. Instructs the computer to add the quantity on hand to the primary storage field labeled CTR; to add the stock

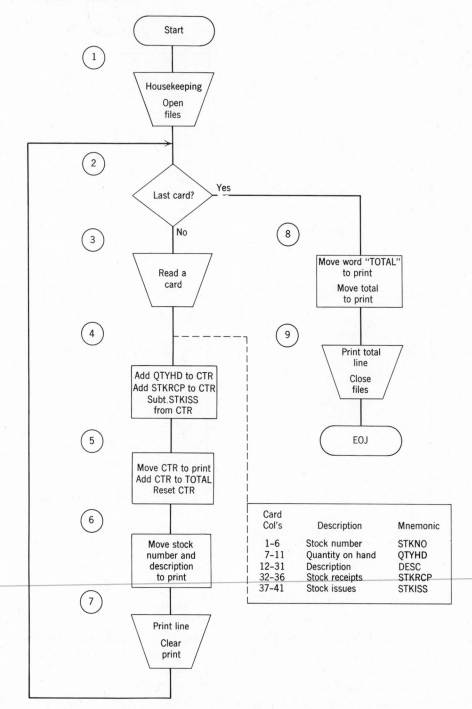

Figure 14-4. Program flow chart.

receipts to the field labeled CTR; and to subtract stock issues from the field labeled CTR. In this case the label CTR is used by the programmer to identify a group of storage positions reserved to hold the factors and results of the arithmetic operations specified.

Step 5. Moves the result stored at CTR to the print area and adds it to a final total field labeled TOTAL.

Step 6. Moves the stock number and description to the print area.

Step 7. Instructs the printer to print a line and clears the print area after printing.

Step 8. If the last card indicator shows that the last card has been read and processed, the program will branch out to the end-of-job routine. This moves the final (accumulated) total to print. (This total is significant only for control purposes since it includes unrelated items.)

Step 9. Instructs the printer to print a line.

It should be pointed out that this problem was designed to illustrate certain facets of developing a program rather than to illustrate a typical stock status application.

It is essential to check each program to assure that it provides a means for handling every condition that might be encountered. For example: (1) each decision box must have at least two alternatives, and each possible result of the test must be represented by a flow line; and (2) each loop must have at least one test which can terminate it and a method for passing on to the next case if the end is not reached.

The first opportunity to perform such checking is usually when the program flow chart is complete. A thorough check of the flow chart before programming begins, perhaps by a second person, will usually reveal major defects when it is most convenient to correct them. If obscurities are detected in the review process, it is advantageous to be able to correct them before programming is started.

The checking of the flow chart does not end at this point, as minor flaws will often be revealed during the process of writing the program. These flaws are often detected during the programming process because of the need to concentrate on one part of the program at a time. For this reason, however, programming seldom helps in detecting the larger flaws in the program.

Writing the Program

After the steps for solving a problem have been set down, usually in a flow chart, a detailed series of instructions called a *program* is written. The stored program is man's method of conveying to the computer, in a language that the computer can interpret, the operations it is to perform.

Only during the first few years were computer programs prepared in actual machine language or codes. Today most computer programs are first written in some symbolic language convenient to the programmer and then translated by the computer to machine-processable codes.

The program written in symbolic form is called the *source program.* This program is usually punched into cards and read into the computer where it is translated into machine language by a *processor program,* commonly called a *compiler* or *language translator,* previously stored in the computer. The machine-language program produced as output from the compiler is called the *object program.* The object program is used in operation of the routine or procedure that was programmed originally in symbolic form.

Types of Source Program Statements. A computer is directed to perform its operations by a series of actual machine instructions stored in primary storage following their translation from the source program. These instructions usually originate as one-line statements on the coding form. There are three types of source program statements:

1. *Machine-instruction statements* are one-for-one symbolic representations of machine instructions.

2. *Macro instruction statements* cause the compiler to retrieve a specially coded symbolic routine from the macro library, modify the routine according to the information in the macro instruction, and insert the modified routine into the source program for translation into machine language. A macro may be defined as "involving large quantities." Thus, for one macro instruction, many instructions may be assembled.

3. *Processor instruction statements* specify auxiliary functions to be performed by the processor and, with a few exceptions, do not result in the generation of any machine-language code. The auxiliary functions assist the programmer in checking and documenting programs, in controlling storage-address assignments, in program sectioning and linking, in data and storage-field definition, and in controlling the processor program.

In order to go into greater detail about writing a program we will use a specific programming system. As the IBM System/360 Assembler Language is the most popular machine-oriented programming language now in use, we have selected it to illustrate basic programming concepts. Although the System/360 Assembler Language is a very complete and powerful language, we will use a very limited number of its instructions as the goal here is

to illustrate the basics of programming and not the capacity of the language.

Coding Forms. Figure 14-5 illustrates the coding of the procedure depicted by the program flow chart in Figure 14-4. To assist the reader in understanding the program shown in Figure 14-5, let us first describe the various fields and columns on the form used for coding in this language.

1. The intended use of the various sections in the form heading should be obvious. The reason for the punching instructions is to identify for the card punch operator how certain graphics are to be punched. The instructions indicate, for example, that the $\emptyset$ represents a zero and the unslashed 0 represents the letter *O*. This prevents errors in reading and key punching these similar characters. Since modern programming languages of this type use more letters than numerals, the programmer has chosen to slash zeros as this requires less effort. It should be noted, however, that other programmers may prefer to use the opposite approach and to slash letters rather than numerals. In this case, Z's may also be slashed to distinguish them from 2's.

2. The name field is used to assign a symbolic name to a statement. A name allows other statements to refer to the statement by that name. If a name is given, it must begin in column 1 and must not extend beyond column 8. SAMPLE and START in Figure 14-5 are examples of names in the name field.

3. The operation field is used to specify the mnemonic operation code of a machine or assembler instruction or a macro. This field may begin in any column to the right of column 1 if the name field is blank. If the name field is not blank, at least one blank must separate the name and operation fields. In our ex-

```
IBM                          IBM System/360 Assembler Coding Form              X28-6509-3 U/M050
                                                                               Printed in U.S.A.
PROGRAM  SAMPLE                              PUNCHING   GRAPHIC   Ø  O            PAGE  1  OF 3
                                            INSTRUCTIONS
PROGRAMMER                          DATE                PUNCH   NUM ALPHA         CARD ELECTRO NUMBER
                                  STATEMENT                                      Identification-
  Name      Operation      Operand                      Comments                 Sequence
SAMPLE    START   X'Ø'                    START PROG RELATIVE TO CORE LOC Ø       SAMØ1ØØØ
START     BALR    9,Ø                     LOAD BASE REG WITH PROG LOC            SAMØ1Ø1Ø
          USING   *,9                     DEFINE REG 9 AS BASE REGISTER          SAMØ1Ø2Ø
          B       PROC                    BRANCH AROUND DTF TABLES               SAMØ1Ø3Ø
CARDIN    DTFCD   DEVADDR=SYSØØ7,                                               X SAMØ1Ø4Ø
                  IOAREA1=RECIN,                                                X SAMØ1Ø5Ø
                  BLKSIZE=8Ø,                                                   X SAMØ1Ø6Ø
                  DEVICE=254Ø,                                                  X SAMØ1Ø7Ø
                  EOFADDR=LCARD,                                                X SAMØ1Ø8Ø
                  RECFORM=FIXUB,                                                X SAMØ1Ø9Ø
                  TYPEFLE=INPUT                                                   SAMØ11ØØ
PRTOUT    DTFPR   DEVADDR=SYSØØ9,                                               X SAMØ111Ø
                  IOAREA1=PRLINE,                                               X SAMØ112Ø
                  BLKSIZE=133,                                                  X SAMØ113Ø
                  DEVICE=14Ø3,                                                  X SAMØ114Ø
                  CTLCHR=ASA,                                                   X SAMØ115Ø
                  RECFORM=FIXUNB                                                  SAMØ116Ø

RECIN     DS      ØCL8Ø            DEFINE CARD INPUT AREA                         SAMØ2ØØØ
STKNO     DS      CL6              STOCK NUMBER COLS 1-6                          SAMØ2Ø1Ø
QTYHD     DS      CL5              QUANTITY ON HAND COLS 7-11                     SAMØ2Ø2Ø
DESC      DS      CL2Ø             DESCRIPTION COLS 12-31                         SAMØ2Ø3Ø
STKRCP    DS      CL5              STOCK RECEIPTS COLS 32-36                      SAMØ2Ø4Ø
STKISS    DS      CL5              STOCK ISSUES COLS 37-41                        SAMØ2Ø5Ø
BLANK     DS      CL39             REST OF CARD COLS 42-8Ø                        SAMØ2Ø6Ø
PRLINE    DS      ØCL133           DEFINE PRINT LINE                              SAMØ2Ø7Ø
CTLCAR    DC      CL1' '           DEFINE CONTROL CHARACTER                       SAMØ2Ø8Ø
RECOUT    DC      CL132' '         DEFINE PRINTER OUTPUT AREA                     SAMØ2Ø9Ø
PQTY      DS      CL3              RESERVE 3 BYTES FOR QTY (PACKED)               SAMØ21ØØ
PSRCP     DS      CL3              RESERVE 3 BYTES FOR RCP (PACKED)               SAMØ211Ø
PSISS     DS      CL3              RESERVE 3 BYTES FOR ISS (PACKED)               SAMØ212Ø
CTR       DC      P'+ØØØØØØØØ'      DEFINE 4 BYTE PACKED DEC COUNTER              SAMØ213Ø
TOTAL     DC      P'+ØØØØØØØØ'      DEFINE 4 BYTE PACKED DEC TOTAL CTR            SAMØ214Ø
TOTCON    DC      CL5'TOTAL'       DEFINE A CONSTANT OF TOTAL                     SAMØ215Ø

PROC      OPEN    CARDIN,PRTOUT    OPEN THE CARD & PRINTER FILES                  SAMØ3ØØØ
GETCD     GET     CARDIN           READ A CARD                                   SAMØ3Ø1Ø
          PACK    PQTY,QTYHD       CONVERT QTY ON HAND TO PACKED DEC             SAMØ3Ø2Ø
          PACK    PSRCP,STKRCP     CONVERT STOCK RECPT TO PACKED DEC             SAMØ3Ø3Ø
          PACK    PSISS,STKISS     CONVERT STOCK ISSUE TO PACKED DEC             SAMØ3Ø4Ø
          AP      CTR,PQTY         ADD QTY ON HAND TO COUNTER                    SAMØ3Ø5Ø
          AP      CTR,PSRCP        ADD STOCK RECEIPTS TO COUNTER                 SAMØ3Ø6Ø
          SP      CTR,PSISS        SUBTRACT STOCK ISSUES FROM COUNTER            SAMØ3Ø7Ø
          UNPK    RECOUT+79(6),CTR UNPACK CTR INTO PRINT AREA                    SAMØ3Ø8Ø
          AP      TOTAL,CTR        ADD COUNTER TO TOTAL COUNTER                  SAMØ3Ø9Ø
          SP      CTR,CTR          CLEAR COUNTER                                 SAMØ31ØØ
          MVC     RECOUT+24(6),STKNO   MOVE STOCK NO TO PRINT AREA               SAMØ311Ø
          MVC     RECOUT+39(2Ø),DESC   MOVE DESCRIPTION TO PRINT AREA            SAMØ312Ø
          PUT     PRTOUT           PRINT A LINE                                  SAMØ313Ø
          MVI     RECOUT,X'4Ø'     MOVE A BLANK TO PRINT AREA                    SAMØ314Ø
          MVC     RECOUT+1(131),RECOUT MOVE 131 SPACES TO CLEAR PRINT AREA       SAMØ315Ø
          B       GETCD            BRANCH TO READ THE NEXT CARD                  SAMØ316Ø
LCARD     MVC     RECOUT+89(5),TOTCON  MOVE THE WORD TOTAL TO PRINT AREA         SAMØ317Ø
          UNPK    RECOUT+99(7),TOTAL   UNPACK TOTAL INTO PRINT AREA              SAMØ318Ø
          PUT     PRTOUT           PRINT TOTAL LINE                              SAMØ319Ø
          CLOSE   CARDIN,PRTOUT    CLOSE CARD & PRINTER FILES                    SAMØ32ØØ
          EOJ                      END OF JOB                                    SAMØ321Ø
          END     START                                                         SAMØ322Ø
```

Figure 14-5. Source program written in IBM System/360 Assembler Language (related to Figure 14-4).

ample we have consistently started the operation codes in column 10 as this makes the program easier to follow and is in fact the technique used by most programmers.

4. The operand field provides the assembler with additional information about the instruction specified in the operation field. If a machine instruction has been specified, the operand field contains information required by the assembler (processor program) to generate the machine instruction. The operand field specifies registers, storage addresses, input-output devices, and storage-area lengths. The operand field may begin in any column to the right of the operation field, provided at least one blank space separates it from the last character of the operation mnemonic. If there is no operand field but there is a comments field, the absence of the operand field must be indicated by a comma, preceded and followed by one or more blanks.

Depending on the instruction, the operand field may be composed of one or more subfields called operands. Operands must be separated by commas and a blank space must not intervene between operands and commas as a blank space sets the limits of the field. Note on the illustration that each operand field has been started in column 16. Again this is a preferred technique and not required.

5. The comments field is provided for the convenience of the programmer and permits any number of lines of descriptive information about the program to be inserted into the object program list which is printed out after the program is assembled (Figure 14-18). Comments appear only in the program list and have no effect on the assembled object program. The comments field must appear to the right of the operand field and be preceded by at least one blank. The entire line can be used for comments by placing an asterisk in column 1. The comments fields in the program illustration have been very liberally used in order to make the program as easy as possible to follow. A programmer would not normally be so verbose.

6. The X in column 72 is used to identify the continuation of entries on the following line. Notice that lines 1040 through 1090 have X's in column 72 and that the last DTFCD entry on line 1100 does not have an X in column 72.

7. The identification-sequence field may be used for program identification and statement sequence numbers. (Each line on the coding form is a statement.)

Program Coding. Now that the assembler coding form has been described, we shall consider the program coding illustrated in Figure 14-5. The program shown is an actual program written in accordance with the program flow chart in Figure 14-4. This flow chart should serve as an aid in following the program. The operation codes and mnemonic operands, which are intended to aid the programmer, should also be helpful in interpreting the program. This is because they may be easily associated with the operations they actually represent. For example, the operation code B on line 1030 of the sample program represents a branch instruction, and the operand "PROC" is a mnemonic operand selected by the programmer to represent the beginning of the actual procedure that starts on line 3000.

The following numbered comments can be related to each block on the flow chart in Figure 14-4 by the corresponding numbers. To facilitate reference to particular lines on the coding sheets, excerpts from the coding sheets will be shown on the pages where the specific instructions are described. However, an occasional reference to the complete coding sheets in Figure 14-5 may be necessary to fully comprehend explanations involving other sections of the program.

1. The first three lines are standard assembler coding entries that tell the processor program the beginning storage location for this program (Figure 14-6). The next statement on line 1030 is a branch instruction that will cause the computer to jump to the instruction with the name PROC shown on line 3000. In other words, as the compiled program is first executed the branch instruction causes the computer to go around the series of processor instructions to the first procedure instruction on line 3000.

The next series of instructions, 1040 through 1160, are standard instructions used to define the characteristics of the specified file to be processed. There are many prescribed DTF (define the file) macro names which include additional symbols identifying the specific type of file. In this case the macro named DTFCD on line 1040 stands for "define the file–card," and the statements on lines 1040 through 1100 define the characteristics of that card file for the processor program (Figure 14-7).

The macro name DTFPR stands for "define the file–printer," and the statements on lines 1110 through 1160 define its characteristics (Figure 14-8). These two series of statements will cause the processor program to insert a series of instructions and constants into the object program.

The statements on lines 2000 through 2150 are used to reserve areas of primary storage and to define and enter constant data into the program (Figure 14-9). DS

```
SAMPLE   START X'Ø'               START PROG RELATIVE TO CORE LOC Ø      SAMØ1ØØØ
START    BALR  9,Ø                LOAD BASE REG WITH PROG LOC            SAMØ1Ø1Ø
         USING *,9                DEFINE REG 9 AS BASE REGISTER          SAMØ1Ø2Ø
         B     PROC               BRANCH AROUND DTF TABLES               SAMØ1Ø3Ø
```

Figure 14-6

```
CARDIN   DTFCD DEVADDR=SYSØØ7,                                          XSAMØ1Ø4Ø
               IOAREA1=RECIN,                                           XSAMØ1Ø5Ø
               BLKSIZE=8Ø,                                              XSAMØ1Ø6Ø
               DEVICE=254Ø,                                             XSAMØ1Ø7Ø
               EOFADDR=LCARD,                                           XSAMØ1Ø8Ø
               RECFORM=FIXUNB,                                          XSAMØ1Ø9Ø
               TYPEFLE=INPUT                                             SAMØ11ØØ
```

Figure 14-7

```
PRTOUT   DTFPR DEVADDR=SYSØØ9,                                          XSAMØ111Ø
               IOAREA1=PRLINE,                                          XSAMØ112Ø
               BLKSIZE=133,                                             XSAMØ113Ø
               DEVICE=14Ø3,                                             XSAMØ114Ø
               CTLCHR=ASA,                                              XSAMØ115Ø
               RECFORM=FIXUNB                                            SAMØ116Ø
```

Figure 14-8

Name	Operation	Operand	Comments	Identification-Sequence
RECIN	DS	ØCL80	DEFINE CARD INPUT AREA	SAMØ2ØØØ
STKNO	DS	CL6	STOCK NUMBER COLS 1-6	SAMØ2Ø1Ø
QTYHD	DS	CL5	QUANTITY ON HAND COLS 7-11	SAMØ2Ø2Ø
DESC	DS	CL2Ø	DESCRIPTION COLS 12-31	SAMØ2Ø3Ø
STKRCP	DS	CL5	STOCK RECEIPTS COLS 32-36	SAMØ2Ø4Ø
STKISS	DS	CL5	STOCK ISSUES COLS 37-41	SAMØ2Ø5Ø
BLANK	DS	CL39	REST OF CARD COLS 42-8Ø	SAMØ2Ø6Ø
PRLINE	DS	ØCL133	DEFINE PRINT LINE	SAMØ2Ø7Ø
CTLCAR	DC	CL1' '	DEFINE CONTROL CHARACTER	SAMØ2Ø8Ø
RECOUT	DC	CL132' '	DEFINE PRINTER OUTPUT AREA	SAMØ2Ø9Ø
PQTY	DS	CL3	RESERVE 3 BYTES FOR QTY (PACKED)	SAMØ21ØØ
PSRCP	DS	CL3	RESERVE 3 BYTES FOR RCP (PACKED)	SAMØ211Ø
PSISS	DS	CL3	RESERVE 3 BYTES FOR ISS (PACKED)	SAMØ212Ø
CTR	DC	P'+ØØØØØØØ'	DEFINE 4 BYTE PACKED DEC COUNTER	SAMØ213Ø
TOTAL	DC	P'+ØØØØØØØ'	DEFINE 4 BYTE PACKED DEC TOTAL CTR	SAMØ214Ø
TOTCON	DC	CL5'TOTAL'	DEFINE A CONSTANT OF TOTAL	SAMØ215Ø

Figure 14-9

stands for "define storage" and is used to reserve storage areas and to assign names to the areas. For example, statement 2000 assigns the name RECIN to an 80-position card input area and statement 2010 assigns the name STKNO to a six-position field within the 80-position area. The DC statements are used to generate constant data and to place it in primary storage. For example, the DC statement on line 2130 assigns the name CTR to a four-position packed field containing seven zeros and a plus sign. The statement on line 2150 assigns the name TOTCON to a five-position field containing the word TOTAL. The comments field should be helpful in understanding the other DS and DC statements.

The statement on line 3000 prepares the card reader and printer for operation (Figure 14-10). This completes all of the "housekeeping" functions, and we are now ready to begin the procedure or processing part of the program.

2. The last card test is made by the input-output control system (IOCS) as instructed by the statement on line 1080. Since this statement automatically instructs the IOCS to insert into the object program

all of the necessary instructions for this operation, no other statements need be entered by the programmer.

3. The statement on line 3010 has a GET macro and a CARDIN operand (Figure 14-11). This instruction makes the next consecutive record from the file named CARDIN available for processing. The mnemonic CARDIN will refer the processor program to the statement with the name CARDIN. This statement is on line 1040 and is the first of several statements describing the card-read device.

4. Before performing decimal arithmetic we must pack the data as decimal arithmetic instructions are intended for use only with packed decimal data. Therefore, the instructions on lines 3020 through 3040 will cause the decimal data just read into storage to be packed and placed at new locations (Figure 14-12). For example, the pack instruction on line 3020 will cause the data located at QTYHD to be packed and stored at location PQTY. The operand QTYHD represents the "quantity on hand" field in card columns 7 through 11 as it is named and described on line 2020. The operation AP on line 3050 represents an "add packed decimal" in-

Name	Operation	Operand	STATEMENT	Comments	Identification-Sequence
PROC	OPEN	CARDIN,PRTOUT		OPEN THE CARD & PRINTER FILES	SAM03000

Figure 14-10

GETCD	GET	CARDIN		READ A CARD	SAM03010

Figure 14-11

PACK	PQTY,QTYHD	CONVERT QTY ON HAND TO PACKED DEC	SAM03020
PACK	PSRCP,STKRCP	CONVERT STOCK RECPT TO PACKED DEC	SAM03030
PACK	PSISS,STKISS	CONVERT STOCK ISSUE TO PACKED DEC	SAM03040
AP	CTR,PQTY	ADD QTY ON HAND TO COUNTER	SAM03050
AP	CTR,PSRCP	ADD STOCK RECEIPTS TO COUNTER	SAM03060
SP	CTR,PSISS	SUBTRACT STOCK ISSUES FROM COUNTER	SAM03070

Figure 14-12

UNPK	RECOUT+79(6),CTR	UNPACK CTR INTO PRINT AREA	SAM03080
AP	TOTAL,CTR	ADD COUNTER TO TOTAL COUNTER	SAM03090
SP	CTR,CTR	CLEAR COUNTER	SAM03100

Figure 14-13

MVC	RECOUT+24(6),STKNO	MOVE STOCK NO TO PRINT AREA	SAM03110
MVC	RECOUT+39(20),DESC	MOVE DESCRIPTION TO PRINT AREA	SAM03120

Figure 14-14

struction. The operand CTR represents a reserved storage location defined on line 2130, and the operand PQTY represents the reserved storage location defined on line 2100. This statement on 3050 is translated into program instructions by the processor program which causes the computer to add the sum at the location named PQTY to the sum at the location named CTR. With this understanding it should be possible to follow the statements on lines 3060 and 3070.

5. To print a packed-decimal sum we must first change it to an unpacked or zoned format and move it into the assigned print area. The statement on line 3080 causes the sum at the storage location named CTR to be unpacked and placed in the print area named RECOUT (record out) plus 79 (Figure 14-13).

RECOUT + 79 identifies where in the print output area the six-position sum should be placed. RECOUT + 79 is translated by the processor program into an actual storage address 79 greater than the actual address of RECOUT.

The statement on line 3090 causes the sum at CTR to be added to the sum at TOTAL. The following instruction on line 3100 causes the sum at CTR to be subtracted from itself; thus the storage location named CTR will be reset to zero.

6. The statement on line 3110 will cause the data at the storage location named STKNO to be moved to the print area at RECOUT + 24. The next statement will cause the data at the storage location named DESC to be moved to the print area at RECOUT + 39 (Figure 14-14).

7. The PUT macro on line 3130 is

```
      PUT    PRTOUT                        PRINT A LINE                    SAM03130
      MVI    RECOUT,X'40'                  MOVE A BLANK TO PRINT AREA      SAM03140
      MVC    RECOUT+1(131),RECOUT          MOVE 131 SPACES TO CLEAR PRINT AREA  SAM03150
      B      GETCD                         BRANCH TO READ THE NEXT CARD    SAM03160
```

Figure 14-15

the opposite of the GET macro on line 3010 (Figure 14-15). The PUT macro causes the output device named PRTOUT (print out) to print a line. The statements on lines 3140 and 3150 will cause a blank first to be placed at RECOUT and then to be moved to the other 131 print-area positions. These operations clear the 132-position print area of the data just printed. As shown on the flow chart, the next step should be to test for a last card and, if the last card has not been read, to read a card. The B operation on line 3160 is a branch (jump) instruction telling the computer to get its next instruction at GETCD, the name of the statement on line 3010.

8. When the input-output control system (IOCS) recognizes that the last card has been read it will cause the computer to branch to the instruction named LCARD. This name was given to the EOFADDR (end of file address) statement on line 1080 as part of the DTFCD specifications. The statement named LCARD is on line 3170 and will cause the constant (TOTAL) named TOTCON to be moved to the print area at RECOUT + 89 (Figure 14-16). The next instruction will cause the sum at storage location named TOTAL to be un-

packed and moved to the print area at RECOUT + 99.

9. The statement on line 3190 will cause the output device named PRTOUT to print a line (Figure 14-17). The close statement on line 3200 is the opposite of the open statement and will cause the card reader and printer devices to discontinue service as input and output file processing devices for this job. The statement on line 3210 signals "end of job" and will cause the computer to go to the next job.

The last statement on the coding sheet (3220) causes two functions to be performed. First, it instructs the processor program to terminate the assembly of the object program. Second, it designates a point in the program to which control will be transferred after the object program has been loaded. In this program, control will be transferred to the point identified by the operand START, which is the name of the statement shown on line 1010.

Assembling or Compiling the Object Program

After the program has been written and checked, and usually punched into

```
LCARD MVC    RECOUT+89(5),TOTCON          MOVE THE WORD TOTAL TO PRINT AREA    SAM03170
      UNPK   RECOUT+99(7),TOTAL           UNPACK TOTAL INTO PRINT AREA         SAM03180
```

Figure 14-16

```
      PUT    PRTOUT                        PRINT TOTAL LINE                SAM03190
      CLOSE  CARDIN,PRTOUT                 CLOSE CARD & PRINTER FILES      SAM03200
      EOJ                                  END OF JOB                      SAM03210
      END    START                                                        SAM03220
```

Figure 14-17

cards (note that each line can contain a maximum of 80 characters), it is ready for translation into an object program.

As indicated above, a source program is prepared in a language that is convenient to the programmer but that is not meaningful to the computer. Consequently, it is necessary to translate the source program from symbolic language to a machine language. This is accomplished by a program called a *processor* which is usually furnished by the computer manufacturer for use with his computer.

The processor is loaded into the computer prior to the reading of the source program, which is written in a language common to the programmer and the processor. Then as the source program is read, the processor automatically translates it to a machine-language program known as an *object program* (Figure 14-18). In other words, the processor treats the source program as input data and produces an object program as output data. The object program may be recorded on punched cards, magnetic tape, or another auxiliary storage medium. Since the object program is in a language that is meaningful to the computer, it may then be loaded into memory and used by the computer to perform the planned operations.

After the object program has been assembled, a printed list of the program is usually prepared. This program list is a helpful programming aid as it lists, in addition to the information contained on the coding sheets, the machine-language instructions and the addresses in storage where the instructions are located. These storage locations are assigned automatically by the processor. The program list also flags many of the programmer errors by listing an error notification code on any line that has an error in the source statement.

Figure 14-18 illustrates the assembled program list of the program shown on the flow chart in Figure 14-4, and on the coding sheets in Figure 14-5. At the top of the System/360 program lists are field headings which are defined as follows:

1. The field headed LOC (location) contains the high-order byte storage address assigned to each machine-language instruction generated by the processor. Storage addresses are actually in binary form; however, for ease of reading, they are printed on these lists in hexadecimal.

2. The field headed OBJECT CODE, ADDR 1 ADDR 2 (addresses 1 and 2) contains all of the actual machine instructions generated by the processor program in hexadecimal representation.

3. The STMT (statement) field is used to number sequentially all the statements in the program. The statements inserted by the processor program are flagged with a plus sign at the right of the number; all other statements are those originally written by the programmer.

4. The SOURCE STATEMENT field contains each statement line as it was key punched from the coding form and also the source statements inserted by the processor program. Note that the statements beginning with statement 5 (identification sequence 1040 through 1100) have been assigned only one statement number. The reason is that this group of entries made by the programmer is regarded as one continuous statement since all but the first statement have an X in column 72. Statements 6 through 25 are all inserted by the processor program to meet the specifications dictated by the DTFCD (define the file—card) macro statement. No effort should be made to interpret these macro-generated instructions as they are meaningful only to experienced systems pro-

grammers who are knowledgeable in the development of processor programs. However, this is a good example of how one statement can cause many machine-language codes to be generated. Macro instructions will be covered in greater detail in the next chapter.

With the aid of the flow chart in Figure 14-4, it should be possible to follow most of the program steps. It should be noted that the location and object code data are represented in hexadecimal and that the procedure part of the program actually starts with statement 63.

Most program lists are accompanied by a supplemental list such as a cross-reference list or symbol table. This list will show, usually in alphabetical order, the name given a statement, the length of the field represented, the location in storage where the definition appears, the statement number of the definition entry, and the statement number of each statement making reference to it. This list is another helpful aid to the programmer when he is reviewing the program, locating errors, and correcting or making a change in the program.

```
                                                                            PAGE   1

 LOC   OBJECT CODE      ADDR1 ADDR2   STMT     SOURCE STATEMENT                              DOS CL2-4 02/16/68

000000                                  1 SAMPLE   START X'0'          START PROG RELATIVE TO CORE LOC 0    SAM01000
000000 0590                              2 START    BALR  9,0           LOAD BASE REG WITH PROG LOC          SAM01010
000002                                   3          USING *,9           DEFINE REG 9 AS BASE REGISTER        SAM01020
000002 47F0 915A       0015C             4          B     PROC          BRANCH ARROUND DTF TABLES            SAM01030
                                         5 CARDIN   DTFCD DEVADDR=SYS007,                                    SAM01040
                                                          IOAREA1=RECIN,                                    XSAM01050
                                                          BLKSIZE=80,                                       XSAM01060
                                                          DEVICE=2540,                                      XSAM01070
                                                          EOFADDR=LCARD,                                    XSAM01080
                                                          RECFORM=FIXUNB,                                   XSAM01090
                                                          TYPEFLE=INPUT                                      SAM01100
                                         6+** 360N-CL-453 CHANGE LEVEL 2-4     DTFCD
000006 0000
000008                                   7+          DC    0D'0'
000008 00008000000000                    8+CARDIN    DC    X'000080000000' RES. COUNT,COM. BYTES,STATUS BTS
00000E 01                                9+          DC    AL1(1) LOGICAL UNIT CLASS
00000F 07                               10+          DC    AL1(7) LOGICAL UNIT
000010 00000028                         11+          DC    A(IJCX0001) CCW ADDRESS
000014 00000000                         12+          DC    4X'00' CCB-ST BYTE,CSW CCW ADDR.
000018 00                               13+          DC    AL1(0)
000019 000000                           14+          DC    VL3(IJCFZIZ0) ADDRESS OF LOGIC MODULE
00001C 02                               15+          DC    X'02' DTF TYPE (READER)
00001D 01                               16+          DC    AL1(1) SWITCHES
00001E 02                               17+          DC    AL1(2) NORMAL COMM.CODE
00001F 02                               18+          DC    AL1(2) CNTROL COMM.CODE
000020 00000070                         19+          DC    A(RECIN) ADDR. OF IOAREA1
000024 000001D6                         20+          DC    A(LCARD) EOF ADDRESS
000028 0200007020000050                 21+IJCX0001 CCW   2,RECIN,X'20',80
000030 412E 0000       00000    00000   22+          LA    2,0(14) LOAD USER POINTER REG.
000034 4700 0000       00000            23+          NOP   0 MOVE IOAREA TO WORKA
000038 0000                             24+          DC    X'0000'
00003A                                  25+IJJZ0001 EQU   *
                                        26 PRTOUT   DTFPR DEVADDR=SYS009,                                    XSAM01110
                                                          IOAREA1=PRLINE,                                    XSAM01120
                                                          BLKSIZE=133,                                       XSAM01130
                                                          DEVICE=1403,                                       XSAM01140
                                                          CTLCHR=ASA,                                        XSAM01150
                                                          RECFORM=FIXUNB                                     SAM01160
                                        27+** 360N-CL-453 CHANGE LEVEL 2-5     DTFPR
00003A 000000000000
000040                                  28+          DC    0D'0'
000040 00008000000000                   29+PRTOUT    DC    X'000080000000' RES. COUNT,CUM. BYTES,STATUS BTS
000046 01                               30+          DC    AL1(1) LOGICAL UNIT CLASS
000047 09                               31+          DC    AL1(9) LOGICAL UNIT
000048 00000068                         32+          DC    A(*+32) CCW   ADDR.
00004C 00000000                         33+          DC    4X'00' CCB-ST BYTE,CSW CCW ADDRESS
000050 00                               34+          DC    AL1(0)
000051 000000                           35+          DC    VL3(IJDFAZZZ) ADDR. OF LOGIC MODULE
000054 08                               36+          DC    X'08' DTF TYPE  (PRINTER)
000055 30                               37+          DC    AL1(48) SWITCHES
000056 09                               38+          DC    X'09' NORMAL  COMM. CODE
```

Figure 14-18. Assembled program list (related to Figure 14-5).

```
LOC  OBJECT CODE     ADDR1 ADDR2  STMT   SOURCE STATEMENT                                DOS CL2-4 02/16/68

000057 09                          39+         DC    X'09' CONTROL COMM. CODE
000058 000000C1                    40+         DC    A(PRLINE+1) ADDRESS OF DATA IN IOAREA1
00005C 0000C000                    41+         DC    4X'00' BUCKET
000060 0700                        42+         NOPR  0 PUT LENGTH IN REG12 (ONLY UNDEF.
000062 4700 0000          00000    43+         NOP   0 LOAD USER POINTER REG
000066 0000                        44+         DC    2X'00' NOT USED
000068 099000C120000084            45+         CCW   9,PRLINE+1,X'20',133-1
000070                             46+IJJZ0002 EQU   *
000070                             47 RECIN    DS    0CL80                    DEFINE CARD INPUT AREA            SAM02000
000070                             48 STKNO    DS    CL6                      STOCK NUMBER COLS 1-6            SAM02010
000076                             49 QTYHD    DS    CL5                      QUANTITY ON HAND COLS 7-11      SAM02020
00007B                             50 DESC     DS    CL20                     DESCRIPTION COLS 12-31          SAM02030
00008F                             51 STKRCP   DS    CL5                      STOCK RECEIPTS COLS 32-36       SAM02040
000094                             52 STKISS   DS    CL5                      STOCK ISSUES COLS 37-41         SAM02050
000099                             53 BLANK    DS    CL39                     REST OF CARD COLS 42-80         SAM02060
0000C0                             54 PRLINE   DS    0CL133                   DEFINE PRINT LINE               SAM02070
0000C0 40                          55 CTLCAR   CL1' '                        DEFINE CONTROL CHARACTER         SAM02080
0000C1 4040404040404040            56 RECOUT   DC    CL132' '                 DEFINE PRINTER OUTPUT AREA       SAM02090
000145                             57 PQTY     DS    CL3                      RESERVE 3 BYTES FOR QTY (PACKED) SAM02100
000148                             58 PSRCP    DS    CL3                      RESERVE 3 BYTES FOR RCP (PACKED) SAM02110
00014B                             59 PSISS    DS    CL3                      RESERVE 3 BYTES FOR ISS (PACKED) SAM02120
00014E 0000000C                    60 CTR      DC    P'+0000000'              DEFINE 4 BYTE PACKED DEC COUNTER SAM02130
000152 0000000C                    61 TOTAL    DC    P'+0000000'              DEFINE 4 BYTE PACKED DEC TOTAL CTR SAM02140
000156 E306E3C1D3                  62 TOTCON   DC    CL5'TOTAL'               DEFINE A CONSTANT OF TOTAL       SAM02150
                                   63 PROC     OPEN  CARDIN,PRTOUT            OPEN THE CARD & PRINTER FILES    SAM03000
                                   64+* CHANGE LEVEL 2-0
00015B 00                          65+         CNOP  0,4
00015C                             66+PROC     DC    0F'0'
00015C                             67+         LA    1,=C'$$BOPEN '
00015C 4110 9206          00208    68+IJJ00003 BAL   0,*+4+4*(3-1)
000160 4500 916A          0016C    69+         DC    A(CARDIN)
000164 00000008                    70+         DC    A(PRTOUT)
000168 00000040                    71+         SVC   2
00016C 0A02                        72 GETCD    GET   CARDIN                   READ A CARD                      SAM03010
                                   73+* CHANGE LEVEL 2-0
00016E 5810 9216          00218    74+GETCD    L     1,=A(CARDIN) GET DTF TABLE ADDRESS
000172 58F1 0010          00010    75+         L     15,16(1) GET LOGIC MODULE ADDRESS
000176 45EF 0008          00008    76+         BAL   14,8(15) BRANCH TO GET ROUTINE
00017A F224 9143 9074 00145 00076  77          PACK  PQTY,QTYHD               CONVERT QTY ON HAND TO PACKED DEC SAM03020
000180 F224 9146 908D 00148 0008F  78          PACK  PSRCP,STKRCP             CONVERT STOCK RECPT TO PACKED DEC SAM03030
000186 F224 9149 9092 0014B 00094  79          PACK  PSISS,STKISS            CONVERT STOCK ISSUE TO PACKED DEC SAM03040
00018C FA32 914C 9143 0014E 00145  80          AP    CTR,PQTY                 ADD QTY ON HAND TO COUNTER       SAM03050
000192 FA32 914C 9146 0014E 00148  81          AP    CTR,PSRCP                ADD STOCK RECEIPTS TO COUNTER    SAM03060
000198 FB32 914C 9149 0014E 0014B  82          SP    CTR,PSISS                SUBTRACT STOCK ISSUES FROM COUNTER SAM03070
00019E F353 910E 914C 00110 0014E  83          UNPK  RECOUT+79(6),CTR         UNPACK CTR INTO PRINT AREA       SAM03080
0001A4 FA33 9150 914C 00152 0014E  84          AP    TOTAL,CTR                ADD COUNTER TO TOTAL COUNTER     SAM03090
0001AA FB33 914C 914C 0014E 0014E  85          SP    CTR,CTR                  CLEAR COUNTER                    SAM03100
0001B0 D205 90D7 906E 000D9 00070  86          MVC   RECOUT+24(6),STKNO       MOVE STOCK NO TO PRINT AREA      SAM03110
0001B6 D213 90E6 9079 000E8 0007B  87          MVC   RECOUT+39(20),DESC       MOVE DESCRIPTION TO PRINT AREA   SAM03120
                                   88          PUT   PRTOUT                   PRINT A LINE                     SAM03130
```

```
LOC  OBJECT CODE     ADDR1 ADDR2  STMT   SOURCE STATEMENT                                DOS CL2-4 02/16/68

                                   89+* CHANGE LEVEL 2-0
0001BC 5810 921A          0021C    90+         L     1,=A(PRTOUT) GET DTF TABLE ADDRESS
0001C0 58F1 0010          00010    91+         L     15,16(1) GET LOGIC MODULE ADDRESS
0001C4 45EF 000C          0000C    92+         BAL   14,12(15) BRANCH TO PUT ROUTINE
0001C8 9240 90BF          000C1    93          MVI   RECOUT,X'40'             MOVE A BLANK TO PRINT AREA       SAM03140
0001CC D282 90C0 90BF 000C0 000C1  94          MVC   RECOUT+1(131),RECOUT MOVE 131 SPACES TO CLEAR PRINT AREA SAM03150
0001D2 47F0 916C          0016E    95          B     GETCD                    BRANCH TO READ THE NEXT CARD     SAM03160
0001D6 D204 9118 9154 0011A 00156  96 LCARD    MVC   RECOUT+89(5),TOTCON      MOVE THE WORD TOTAL TO PRINT AREA SAM03170
0001DC F363 9122 9150 00124 00152  97          UNPK  RECOUT+99(7),TOTAL       UNPACK TOTAL INTO PRINT AREA     SAM03180
                                   98          PUT   PRTOUT                   PRINT TOTAL LINE                 SAM03190
                                   99+* CHANGE LEVEL 2-0
0001E2 5810 921A          0021C    100+        L     1,=A(PRTOUT) GET DTF TABLE ADDRESS
0001E6 58F1 0010          00010    101+        L     15,16(1) GET LOGIC MODULE ADDRESS
0001EA 45EF 000C          0000C    102+        BAL   14,12(15) BRANCH TO PUT ROUTINE
                                   103         CLOSE CARDIN,PRTOUT            CLOSE CARD & PRINTER FILES       SAM03200
                                   104+* CHANGE LEVEL 2-0
0001EE 0700                        105+        CNOP  0,4
0001F0                             106+        DC    0F'0'
0001F0 4110 920E          00210    107+        LA    1,=C'$$BCLOSE'
0001F4 4500 91FE          00200    108+IJJC0007 BAL  0,*+4+4*(3-1)
0001F8 00000008                    109+        DC    A(CARDIN)
0001FC 00000040                    110+        DC    A(PRTOUT)
000200 0A02                        111+        SVC   2
                                   112         EOJ                           END OF JOB                       SAM03210
                                   113+* 360N-CL-453   EOJ     CHANGE LEVEL   2-0
000202 0A0E                        114+        SVC   14
000000                             115         END   START                                                   SAM03220
000208 5B5BC2D6D7C5D540            116         =C'$$BOPEN '
000210 5B5BC2C3D3D6E2C5            117         =C'$$BCLOSE'
000218 00000008                    118         =A(CARDIN)
00021C 00000040                    119         =A(PRTOUT)
```

Figure 14-18. (continued)   245

Testing and Correcting the Program

Flow chart preparation and program coding are major steps in developing a program. The other major step is to test the program by processing test data. Often the preparation of test data will require more time than the writing of the program. Therefore, an experienced programmer will usually make test data notes as items to be tested come to mind during the design of the flow chart and writing of the program.

A good test will contain examples of every conceivable condition that could occur during actual operation. Test material may include (1) copies of the actual data that the program is intended to process, (2) hypothetical data designed to simulate conditions that will be encountered in processing actual data, or (3) a combination of actual and hypothetical data.

In testing the larger or more complicated programs, it is usually best to first test a segment (module) of the program at a time and then test the complete program. Segmenting large programs for testing aids the programmer in finding errors as the more errors there are in a program, the more difficult they are to find since one error may obscure clues to another error. A test, whether it is designed for a segment or the entire program, should first test the organization of the program with a simple test that follows the typical flow of the program. It should then test all of the normal conditions in the program. The exceptions should be tested next and finally the extreme cases, usually related to incomplete or incorrect input. An error in a program can be identified through incorrect output or more frequently through the computer stopping as a result of trying to operate on an invalid instruction.

The primary aid to locating the cause of an error is to print out the data in storage related to the program being tested. This process, which is called a *storage dump* or sometimes a *storage print*, produces a "snap shot" image of the following:

1. The contents of the permanently assigned storage area. These are the first few positions of primary storage.

2. The contents of the registers.

3. As much of the primary storage above the permanently assigned storage as is allowed to print. This should include the entire program and all of the data as it existed in primary storage at the time the dump occurred.

The storage dump is used by the programmer as an aid in detecting the program error without tying up the computer. This procedure of getting the bad program off the computer is better than trying to locate and correct the error through manual operation at the computer console. Locating an error can often be more challenging to the programmer than programming itself.

Many programs will suddenly fail after being in production for as long as several months. This is invariably the result of a condition occurring that was not anticipated while preparing the program or during program testing. Thus, program testing can be every bit as important as program preparation.

Preparing the Program for Production

The final step is the preparation of the program for production. This consists

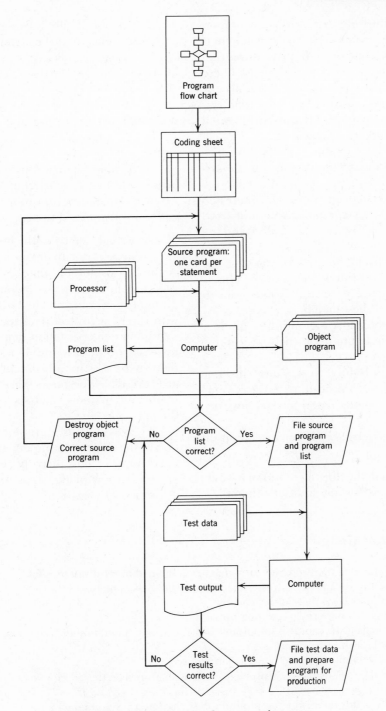

Figure 14-19. Relationship of programming steps.

of completing the system documentation and the run manual. Normally a system is comprised of one or more procedures that may contain one or more programs. These programs may be run individually or grouped into one or more jobs. The system documentation and the run manual usually contain the following:

1. A narrative description of the system. This is usually a general description of the total system and is used by interested persons such as computer operators and programmers who need to understand the system.

2. A system flow chart showing the flow of data through the system. This is helpful because it relates various data to its origin and destination.

3. A procedure definition. This is a narrative description of each procedure in the system.

4. A procedure flow chart showing the steps for each procedure in the system.

5. Job definition and job step instructions.

6. Job control cards for execution of the job.

The system documentation usually contains the following additional items.

1. Copies of all the correspondence and notes relative to the system.

2. Copies of all card layouts, record layouts, storage layouts, input-output analysis layouts, and file analysis layouts.

3. Program flow charts and/or decision tables for each program.

4. A program list for each program written.

5. Sample reports, report layouts, and printer carriage tape if required.

6. Source program, object program, and job control card decks.

As we can see from the list of items in the systems documentation and run manual, considerable time and effort are required in their preparation. Most programmers would much rather proceed with the next project than spend the time that good documentation requires. Therefore, one of the responsibilities of management is to see that documentation standards are developed and that all programmers and systems analysts comply with them.

Figure 14-19 is a graphic representation of the programming steps discussed in this chapter. This may be helpful as a general review of the steps in developing a computer program.

Review Questions

1. Name and define the two basic parts that are contained in most instructions.
2. Name the three types of addresses that an operand may contain.
3. Name the four basic types of instructions.
4. Briefly describe the primary editing function.
5. Why are logic instructions so important to the successful operation of a computer?
6. What is a branch instruction?
7. When is a conditional branch instruction ignored?
8. What are the various facets of problem analysis that precede the development of a computer program?
9. What are the advantages of the program flow chart as a programming aid?

10. What three basic program symbols are used in a program flow chart?
11. Why are most of today's programs written in some sort of symbolic language?
12. Distinguish between a source program, a processor program, and an object program.
13. How does the programmer distinguish between a zero and an alphabetic 0?
14. What is the purpose of the comments field on the coding form?
15. How is an object program produced?
16. What will a good program test contain?

PROGRAMMING SYSTEMS

In the preceding chapter it was stated that even though a computer program can be written in machine language, very few of them actually are. Writing a program in machine language is difficult for the following reasons:

1. Each instruction must be written using actual machine codes. For those computers that use pure binary representation this is almost impossible.

2. The instructions must be arranged in the exact sequence in which they are to be executed. Each time an instruction is omitted through error or oversight, all succeeding instructions must be relocated to make room for the insertion in storage of the omitted instruction. This requires the programmer to keep a detailed record of where in storage each instruction is located.

3. Revising an existing program is usually impractical and very time consuming because of the need to reassign the locations of the instructions affected.

4. The programmer must fully understand the basic operations of the computer and the functions of each operation code.

5. Including proven routines or segments of other programs in a new program is quite difficult unless each instruction can be automatically located in storage in proper sequence within the new program. When a machine language is used, the programmer must assign the storage locations for the routine.

ELEMENTS OF PROGRAMMING SYSTEMS

Many of the difficulties and objections to writing a program in actual computer codes have been eliminated by the development of programming systems. These systems were made possible by the use of symbolic languages which enable the programmer and the computer to communicate in a language that is much simpler for the programmer to use. A programming system consists of two parts, a *language* and

250

a *processor,* which are described in the following sections.

The Programming Language

The basic purpose of a programming language is to allow a data processing program to be written with a minimum of burden on the programmer and a maximum of burden on the computer. Thus the language is composed of abbreviated words or symbols that can be easily associated with the regular language of the programmer and that also can be translated into machine language by the computer. The use of symbolic language also makes it easier for persons who are not familiar with the program to read and understand it. All programming languages, like other languages, have certain established rules of grammar and punctuation. Each one also has a vocabulary of its own.

A data processing procedure is first written in the programming language; this is called a *source program.* The source program must be written in precise form according to the rules of the language to convey to the computer exactly what it is to do. The source program is then recorded on a computer input medium such as punched cards and read into the computer for translation by the processor.

The Processor

A *processor,* frequently called a *compiler* or *translator,* is a program usually supplied by the equipment manufacturer for creating machine-language programs. A processor previously stored in the computer receives the source program written in symbolic language by the programmer and translates the instructions into machine-language instructions that are acceptable to the computer. This machine-language program is called an *object program.*

While translating the source program into an object program, the processor performs these functions:

1. Refers to a table containing all mnemonic abbreviations used by the programmer to specify operations and selects the equivalent machine codes.

2. Assigns storage locations to mnemonic names (labels) and indexes them for future reference. This relieves the programmer of a great amount of clerical work in assigning memory.

3. Calculates the amount of storage needed to store each instruction and assigns the necessary storage addresses.

4. Refers to stored constants and other data as required by the source program.

5. Prints messages that note names that are not referenced elsewhere in the program, references to nonexistent names, invalid mnemonic operations, and other discrepancies. This aids the programmer in the development of an operable program.

6. Usually prepares the instructions necessary to load the object program into computer storage and refers the computer to the first step in the program after it is loaded.

As the object program is developed, it is recorded on a storage medium as explained in the preceding chapter.

The more powerful the computer, the more assistance the programming system can provide in the preparation of programs. For example, in the more powerful systems, previously written routines for checking, input-output, restart, etc., may be inserted into the object program by the processor as specified by the programmer.

Because of characteristics such as those described above, as well as others to be described later, a good programming system offers the following advantages:

1. The programmer can concentrate more fully on the problem being programmed rather than on the computer.

2. Program preparation time is reduced thus making a programmer many times more productive.

3. The man-machine communication problem is overcome, and there is less opportunity for human error.

4. The programmer is able to utilize program techniques and routines that have been developed previously by himself or by other programmers and that have proved to be satisfactory.

5. It is easy for a program to be modified as the need arises.

6. Program testing requires far less machine time since a programming system aids in reducing programming errors.

All programming systems are translators since they translate language written by the programmer into language understood by the computer. All of these translators treat the source program as input data, manipulate it, and create a machine program. There are, nevertheless, different levels of sophistication in the method of operation and effectiveness of programming systems. This will be apparent in the following discussion.

PROGRAMMING SYSTEM AIDS

The complexities of equipment and the development of powerful programming systems have resulted in programming subspecialties. Although there is and probably always will be an overlap, *application programmers* write programs designed to do specific jobs, for example, the one illustrated in the preceding chapter. *Systems programmers* write the programs that run the computer system and aid the application programmer in performing his task. Most of these programs are originally developed by the manufacturers of the various computer systems. The programs are usually written in a generalized fashion encompassing all of the necessary components or features of the equipment marketed in a given product family and are supplied along with the equipment. The user's systems programmers then modify or tailor these vendor-supplied programs to meet unique requirements and to give maximum efficiency of computer operation. Many of these programs, commonly referred to as *software,* will be described here or in later chapters.

Subroutines

A *subroutine* is a standard sequence of instructions designed to direct the computer to carry out a specified operation. Originally these basic routines recorded in a computer input medium were included in the source program at the proper place and assembled along with the rest of the program. In other words, the subroutines had to be inserted at each point that they were needed in a routine as shown in Figure 15-1. As a result they were included in the main operational sequence of the object program. These are known as *open subroutines.*

A *closed subroutine* is one that requires programming only once since it may be entered several times during a program. As a means of avoiding repetition of the same sequence of instructions in different places in the main routine, control may be transferred to a closed subroutine from more than one place in the main routine.

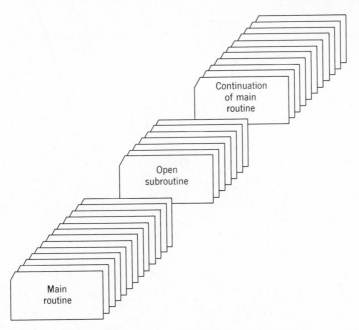

Figure 15-1. Program using an open subroutine.

Multiplication is a typical example of an operation that can be performed whenever needed by the use of a subroutine.

To utilize a closed subroutine it is necessary to provide linkage from the main routine to the subroutine. This is accomplished by means of a *branch instruction*. Since a subroutine may be entered several times, some provision must be made for returning to the main program each time the subroutine is used. Consequently, before branching occurs, the return instruction in the subroutine must be modified so that at the end of the operation it will effect a return to the appropriate point in the main routine (Figure 15-2).

Macro Instructions

Instructions that have the capability of generating more than one machine-language instruction are called *macro instruc-*

tions. A macro instruction is a method of describing in a one-line statement a function, or functions, to be performed by the object program. Macro instructions enable the programmer to write one instruction such as "read a tape," and the processor will then automatically insert the corresponding detailed series of machine instructions. In this manner the programmer avoids, in still a better way, the task of writing one instruction for every machine step. This increases programmer productivity because sequences of instructions that are repeated frequently can be called for by a simple macro statement, thereby relegating still another clerical task to the computer.

A macro instruction is actually a *pseudo instruction* which is not translated into a machine instruction. Instead, the macro instruction causes the automatic insertion of an open subroutine. The

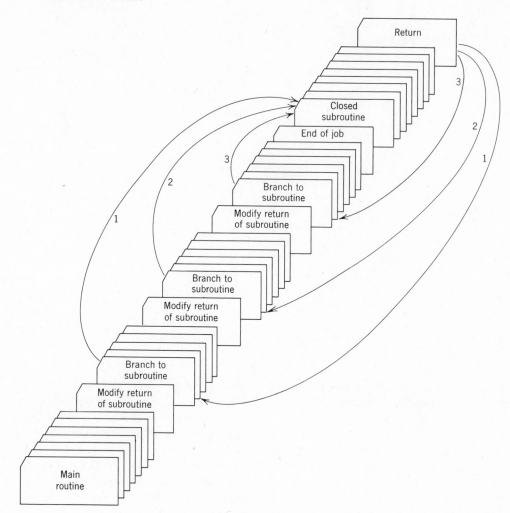

Figure 15-2. Program using a closed subroutine.

macro routine may differ from the standard subroutine, however. The standard subroutine is a self-contained routine that is available in a fixed form. The macro routine, on the other hand, may be formed when the macro instruction is encountered and may be tailored to meet the data requirements of the program being processed. Such routines are inserted in the source program automatically wherever a macro statement appears. The basic sub-

routines that are used in this process are drawn from a library of subroutines usually held in auxiliary storage until called for.

In its simplest form, a macro instruction may result in merely including in the main program a fixed subroutine from a library. This is known as *macro substitution*. The use of this type of macro generally imposes upon the user the task of designing or selecting the proper library routine.

Subroutines are typically used to perform detailed operations such as multiplication and division.

By the use of a more advanced technique known as *macro generation,* the user need only specify the type of function he wishes to perform. In other words, he merely describes in a one-line statement an operation to be performed at a certain point by the object program. The statement does not indicate how the operation is to be performed. This is determined by the compiler which selects the proper routine and generates a set of instructions tailored to meet the specific requirements of the program.

The subroutine that results from the use of either a substitute or generative macro consists of a sequence of symbolic instructions. These symbolic instructions are merged into the source program as it is assembled. The processor then produces the object program by translating the symbolic instructions into machine instructions.

Input-Output Control Systems

A computer program can be divided into three segments:

1. Input—the entering of data into the computer.
2. Processing—the internal manipulation of data.
3. Output—the writing of the results.

A large portion of each program deals with the input-output segments. Therefore, *input-output control systems* (IOCS) were developed to relieve the programmer of all equipment and timing considerations involved in these functions, thus allowing him to concentrate on the processing portion of his program. The input-output control system accomplishes this by means of a group of programmed routines that control the reading of input data and the writing of output data. The IOCS also performs the following functions:

1. Checks for equipment error while reading or writing and initiates reread or rewrite procedures if possible.
2. Generates end of reel (EOR) and end of file (EOF) procedures as required.
3. Checks the labels on input tapes and writes the labels on output tapes. Labels can also be written and checked on disk files.
4. Controls the organization and transfer of records to and from magnetic tape or disk files.
5. Allows simultaneous reading, computing, and writing on those computers capable of simultaneous processing.
6. Provides for priority processing, and when requested prepares records to indicate the point at which an interrupted program should be restarted.

The ability of IOCS to perform the preceding functions reduces the programmer writing, checking, and testing effort required to produce a working program. The use of IOCS also produces standard input-output routines and formats that are most helpful when several programmers are working on different parts of the same program or on several programs within an application. IOCS can also be most helpful in adapting existing programs to a different configuration of the same computer or to an entirely new computer system.

To use IOCS the programmer first must describe in coded form the equipment on which the program will be processed. Then the files must be defined, also in coded form. Following this, the programmer can employ certain macros such as *get, put, open,* and *close* to generate instructions that make a record available to the object program for input or output. Some IOCS also provide other features such as priority interrupt, checkpoint for restart, and real-time routines that will be described later.

IOCS are especially important in the utilization of random processing techniques. Random access storage devices can provide vastly increased storage capacity to a computer system. They also present a greater challenge in the effective storage and retrieval of data. IOCS provide the special techniques necessary for the optimum processing of data stored on a random basis.

Sort and Merge Programs

Sort Programs. Sorting files consumes a large percentage of computer time in any application requiring the sequential processing of records. It is fairly easy to sort punched cards and other individual documents because the records can be physically rearranged. However, the problem of rearranging the sequence of items on magnetic tape or disks is somewhat different. Fortunately, it is possible to use the computer itself to perform the complex sorting and merging operations necessary to arrange records on such media in either ascending or descending sequence.

Nearly every computer has a *generalized sort program* consisting of two parts: the assignment program and the actual sort program. The *assignment program* converts the generalized sort program to a specific program that will efficiently sort a particular file of records. In other words, the generalized sort program has an overall structure that can be modified to handle files of various formats. Variable characteristics such as record length, location, and length of control fields (keys), and number of records in each block may be entered into the computer. This data may then be used to modify the structure of the basic program, thereby producing a program to do the specific sort.

The *sort program* is normally divided into three operating sections called *phases*.

Phase 1. As most files being sorted are too large to fit into main storage at one time, the sort program causes as many records to be read into storage as capacity will permit. The records are sorted internally and written out onto intermediate work tapes, or disk areas if this type of storage is being used. The next batch of records is then read from the input file, and the process continues until the entire file has been read, partially sorted, and rerecorded on intermediate work tapes or disk areas. After phase 1 is completed, two or more tapes or disk areas containing many series of sequenced records are ready for the merge passes to be performed during phases 2 and 3.

Phase 2. During phase 2 all merging except the last merge takes place. Through a series of merges the relatively small strings of sequenced records are merged into successively longer strings. A two-way merge is the minimum merge possible. Depending on the number of tape drives available, three- or four-way (or more) merges are possible. The more tapes used in the merge process, the faster the sort will be.

Phase 3. During phase 3 the final merge of two or more strings of information into a single sequence takes place. At the same time most programs provide for the restoration of each record to its original format. This would be necessary if the original record format was rearranged during phase 1 to facilitate the sorting operation. It is also possible through added programming for records to be summarized, deleted, or altered during phase 3.

To illustrate the process of sorting on magnetic tape, let us assume that the key words in Figure 15-3 are recorded on a tape in the order shown. It should be recognized that these are only the control words and that in actual practice each would be associated with an entire record. Our objective is to sort the records so that they will be in sequence according to the key words.

Tape *A*

```
519
676
017
773
372
348
301
526
416
888
255
101
```

Figure 15-3

In phase 1 the records on Tape *A* are sorted, three records at a time, and placed alternately on Tapes *C* and *D* as shown in Figure 15-4.

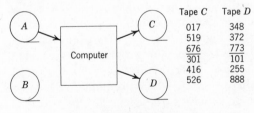

Tape *C*	Tape *D*
017	348
519	372
676	773
301	101
416	255
526	888

Figure 15-4. Phase 1 sort.

Phase 2 merges Tapes *C* and *D* and alternately places them on Tapes *A* and *B* as shown in Figure 15-5. It should be noted that in writing records a change is made from one tape to another when a stepdown occurs. A stepdown is a number followed by a smaller number. Thus rec-

ords were written on Tape *A* until a stepdown, occurred between key words 773 and 101, at which time output was switched to Tape *B*.

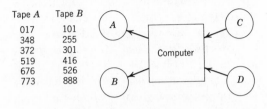

Tape *A*	Tape *B*
017	101
348	255
372	301
519	416
676	526
773	888

Figure 15-5. Phase 2 sort.

As illustrated in Figure 15-6, phase 3 is the final merge of all records into a single string of records in sequence. Records may also be prepared for the next operation as this final pass is completed.

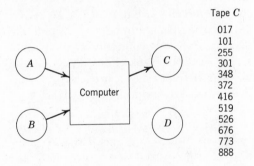

Tape *C*

```
017
101
255
301
348
372
416
519
526
676
773
888
```

Figure 15-6. Phase 3 sort.

At the end of phase 1 the tapes ordinarily would have to be rewound in order to become input to phase 2. During phase 2 the tapes would have to be rewound before each of the many passes necessary to complete the merging process. There are, however, some computers that can read records from tape in either direction and can merge records without rewinding. In an actual sort, phase 1 would handle many more records on each sort, and phase 2 would require many passes to complete the merge.

In the next few years more and more

data sorting will be accomplished on some random access device. Since all of the strings of records in a random access device are readily available, it is possible to use other sorting techniques that may be more efficient than tape-sorting procedures like the one described above.

Merge Programs. Merge programs are similar to phase 3 of the sort program. They are generalized and also have an assignment phase during which they may be modified in accordance with user specifications. Merge programs can be used to merge many strings of records and at the same time check the sequence of the records on each file as it is merged. Examples of how a merge program might be used are:

1. Files that are too large to be sorted on the available equipment as a single file may be sorted in sections and then merged.

2. Several transaction files may be merged at the end of a processing period such as weekly, monthly, or quarterly.

Sort and merge programs are usually classed as utility programs. However, they have been covered here separately because of the major role sorting plays in most computer facilities.

Utility Programs

Utility programs relieve the computer user of the need to prepare his own programs to do the routine things such as clear disk storage, write from disk to tape or tape to card, and test programs. The functions of a data processing facility are to compile and test programs, and to perform production runs. Utility programs are used to support and augment both of these functions.

Utility programs are general purpose programs that can be grouped into the following six general classifications.

1. *Sorting* and *merging* programs perform the functions described in the preceding section.

2. *Simulators* are routines that run on one computer and imitate the operations of another computer.

3. *Translators* are programs whose input is a sequence of statements in some language and whose output is an equivalent sequence of statements in another language.

4. *Housekeeping routines* are used to set storage to an initial condition (blanks or zeros) or to cause data to be placed into or read out of storage. For example, *clear storage, print storage,* and *punch storage* are the names of some of the more common housekeeping routines.

5. *File conversion routines* are used to move data from one external or auxiliary storage device to another. *Tape to disk, card to tape,* and *tape duplicate* are the names of three of the more common file conversion routines.

6. *Program-testing aids* are designed to make program testing easier and to aid in error detection. Most medium- to large-scale computers have utility programs that provide automatic program testing. That is, when the computer is under control of this program it may assemble and load a new program, then feed in the test data, and test the program. Any errors during assembly or test are indicated as printed output, and the computer automatically produces a display of storage (storage dump) at end of job or at point of error. The computer then automatically assembles and loads the next program to be tested.

TYPES OF PROGRAMMING LANGUAGES

Machine-Oriented Programming Languages

Instructions written in a computer-oriented language reflect the composition of the machine instructions required by the particular computer being used. The number of letters that can be used in a word, the set of acronyms such as BAL (branch and link), and the order of fields within an instruction are fixed in accordance with the order and size of the fields in a machine instruction. In short, a machine-oriented language is designed for a specific computer and is not intended for use on other types of computers. The assembler language discussed in the preceding chapter exemplifies a machine-oriented programming language.

A machine-oriented programming language allows the programmer to take advantage of all the features and capacities of the computer system for which it was designed. It also is capable of producing the most efficient object program insofar as storage requirements and operating speeds are concerned. For these reasons, most vendor-supplied software is written in a machine-oriented language.

The primary reasons that most application or production programs are not written in a machine-oriented language are:

1. Being such a complete language, it is a more difficult language to learn, to use, and to debug.

2. Being machine oriented, any extensive additions or deletions of equipment on which the program is to be run will usually cause considerable reprogramming to be done before the program will operate on the changed configuration. This is one of the major reasons for using a problem-oriented language in writing application programs.

Problem-Oriented Programming Languages

In a problem-oriented language, the notations reflect the type of problem being solved rather than the computer on which the program is to be run. For example, the notations used to write a program in COBOL resemble English; FORTRAN notations resemble the language of mathematics; PL/1 notations combine the features of both COBOL and FORTRAN.

Just as restrictions exist in the notation of English and of mathematics, there also exist restrictions in the notation of problem-oriented languages. Only a specified set of numbers, letters, and special characters may be used in writing a program; and special rules must be observed for punctuation and for the use of blanks. Nevertheless, a program written in a problem-oriented language is written in a more flexible form than a machine-oriented language.

The problem-oriented processor is designed to scan the source program, character by character, recognize the intended meaning of the words or symbols, and generate the instructions required to perform the designated functions. In doing this, the compiler uses techniques that enable it to produce a number of machine-language instructions from a single statement in the source program. This is known as a one-to-many translation as opposed to the one-to-one translation that generally occurs in a machine-oriented program.

Problem-oriented programming languages have several advantages.

1. They are easier to use than most machine-oriented languages and, therefore, generally enable the programmer to finish his job much sooner.

2. They are easier to learn, thus, enabling specialists other than programmers to write computer programs.

3. They are more durable because they are easier to modify. This is especially helpful if the program must be modified by someone other than the original programmer.

4. They can be compiled and run on a variety of computers. In addition, they may require only minor modification and recompiling when major changes are made in the computer configuration.

Some of the most widely used problem-oriented languages will be discussed and illustrated in the next chapter.

Review Questions

1. A programming system consists of what two parts? Describe the basic purpose of each part.
2. Distinguish between application programmers and systems programmers.
3. How does a closed subroutine differ from an open subroutine?
4. What is a macro instruction?
5. What are the primary purposes of input-output control systems? How do they aid the programmer?
6. Outline briefly the magnetic tape-sorting procedure described in this chapter.
7. What is the basic purpose of utility programs? Name the six general classifications of utility programs.
8. What are the two basic types of programming languages? What is the main difference between the two?
9. Most application or production programs are not written in a machine-oriented language for what reasons?
10. What are the advantages of problem-oriented programming languages?

16

PROBLEM-ORIENTED
PROGRAMMING LANGUAGES

In the preceding chapter the character-istics and advantages of problem-oriented programming languages were discussed. In this chapter, four of the most widely used problem-oriented languages will be described and illustrated. Included are FORTRAN, COBOL, Programming Language I, and Report Program Generator.

The program used to illustrate each of these languages is based on the same problem used to illustrate programming in Chapter 14. Therefore, the program flow chart shown in Figure 14-4 should be helpful in interpreting each program. Furthermore, a comparison of the four programs in this chapter with each other and with the 360 Assembler Language program shown in Figure 14-18 will provide an opportunity to compare five different methods of programming the same problem.

FORTRAN

The name FORTRAN is a derivative of the original title, *Formula Translation*.

FORTRAN is a programming system that makes it possible to state a problem to be programmed in terms approximating mathematical notation. Except for a general knowledge of computer operating principles and the types of input and output that can be handled, the programmer need not be concerned with the characteristics of the computer while writing a FORTRAN program. The advantage of the FORTRAN programming system is that it provides a language in which any mathematical problem can be stated and then compiled and executed on many kinds of computers. As a result, several hundred thousand people are currently using the FORTRAN programming language as their primary method of communicating with a computer.

A FORTRAN source program is composed of statements that may cause data to be read, processing to be performed, and results to be recorded. These statements in the source program provide information to the FORTRAN processor for object program preparation. The FORTRAN programming language is composed of statements consisting of operation symbols (+ or −) and expressions (A + B − C). Statements may be divided into the following groups:

1. *Input-output* statements describe the operations that are necessary to bring in data and to write or punch the results of the program.

2. *Control* statements may determine the sequence in which statements will be followed or may provide the program with the ability to handle predefined exceptions to the procedure.

3. *Arithmetic* statements specify the mathematical calculations to be performed. These statements very closely resemble a conventional arithmetic formula; for example, $X = Y + Z$ is a valid statement.

4. *Specification* statements provide certain additional facts such as the size of the input data that is read by the program, or the placement of alphabetical and numerical information on the printed page.

5. *Subprogram* statements are available in many systems. These statements enable the user to name and define functions and subroutines that are to be included in the object program.

Unless the FORTRAN processor provides for source language program checkout, the programmer will need the ability to check-out and remove errors in the object program. This requires that the programmer know the details of the computer and materially reduces one of the primary advantages of any programming system.

The process of converting the source program into a machine-language (object) program is called *compiling*. As there are probably no two compilers that use identical logic, it is difficult to describe a FORTRAN processor without identifying it with a particular machine. The most com-

mon compiling technique is to first convert the source program notations into a one-for-one symbolic program. This program is then converted to an object program by an assembly system. Other compilers convert the FORTRAN language directly to machine language in one pass.

Figure 16-1 shows a printed list of a short program written in FORTRAN. As mentioned earlier, this program is based on the same problem used for illustrative purposes in Chapter 14. A flow chart of the problem appears in Figure 14-4.

During the period when FORTRAN was developed in this country, ALGOL was being developed in Europe. They are similar as some exchange of ideas occurred during the development of these two programming systems. FORTRAN, in a general sense, is an engineering language and ALGOL is more nearly a true mathematical language. International Algebraic Language (IAL) was the forerunner of the Algorithmic Oriented Language (ALGOL). Today the language is most frequently referred to as ALGOL and on occasion IAS/ALGOL.

A very large library of FORTRAN programs has resulted from the fact that FORTRAN is the most widely used language. However, those using the ALGOL language contend that it is easier to learn, capable of expressing a wide variety of problems, and superior to FORTRAN in all respects.

COBOL

The name COBOL is derived from Common Business Oriented Language. The COBOL system was developed in 1959 by a committee composed of government users and computer manufacturers. Additional organizations have since par-

```
‡‡FOR

*FANDK0810
C 1620 FORTRAN  2-D
        TOTAL=0.
    2 IF(SENSE SWITCH 9)10,1
    1 READ 90,SN,QUAN,IDES1,IDES2,IDES3,IDES4,RCPTS,XISS
   90 FORMAT (F6.0,F5.0,4I10,2F5.0)
        CTR=QUAN + RCPTS - XISS
        TOTAL= TOTAL + CTR
        PRINT 91,SN,IDES1,IDES2,IDES3,IDES4,CTR
   91 FORMAT (E7.0,F10.0,3X,4I10,F12.0)
        GO TO 2
   10 PRINT 92, TOTAL
   92 FORMAT (7HTOTAL =,F14.0)
        END
00009 0000000099
00019   TOTAL
00029      SN
00039    QUAN
00049   IDES1
00059   IDES2
00069   IDES3
00079   IDES4
00089   RCPTS
00099    XISS
00109     CTR
0002 00134
0001 00154
0090 00280
0091 00540
0010 00618
0092 00660
00724 CORES USED
19999 NEXT COMMON
END OF COMPILATION
```

Figure 16-1. Printed list of program written in FORTRAN.

ticipated in the refinement, improvement, and maintenance of COBOL. COBOL is the first major attempt to produce a truly common business oriented programming language. It has not fully met that goal. For example, the COBOL programming approach for a binary or octal computer differs from that for a binary coded decimal computer. Even so, it is a very useful programming language.

The COBOL character set is composed of the 26 letters of the alphabet, the numerals 0 through 9, and 12 special characters. The COBOL language consists of names to identify things; constants and literals; operators that specify some action or relationship; key words essential to the meaning of a statement; expressions consisting of names, constants, operators, or key words; statements containing a verb

and an item to be acted on; and sentences composed of one or more statements properly punctuated.

A COBOL program list is illustrated in Figure 16-2. This sample program list shows that source statements may start at either of two margins. In general, margin A (the leftmost margin) is used to locate major subdivisions of the program, while margin B (the indented margin) locates subordinate items and continuations of items from one line to another. Thus, the names of divisions, sections, and paragraphs are placed at margin A, as are the main entries of the data division. Most other items are placed at margin B. Names may contain from 1 to 30 characters and must not contain blanks. For this reason names very frequently contain one or more hyphens as this allows for the

```
LINE NO. SEQ. NO.              SOURCE STATEMENT              CBD CL 2-4 02/15/68

    1    001000 IDENTIFICATION DIVISION.                              SAMPLE01
    2    001010 PROGRAM-ID.                                           SAMPLE01
    3    001020    'SAMPLE'.                                          SAMPLE01
    4    001030 REMARKS.                                              SAMPLE01
    5    001040    SAMPLE COBOL PROGRAM.                              SAMPLE01
    6    001050    READS CARDS AND ADDS STOCK RECEIPTS TO QTY ON HAND BAL  SAMPLE01
    7    001060    SUBTRACTS STOCK ISSUES AND DEVELOPS A NEW ON HAND BAL.  SAMPLE01
    8    001070 ENVIRONMENT DIVISION.                                 SAMPLE01
    9    001080 CONFIGURATION SECTION.                                SAMPLE01
   10    001090 SOURCE-COMPUTER.                                     SAMPLE01
   11    001100    IBM-360.                                          SAMPLE01
   12    001110 OBJECT-COMPUTER.                                     SAMPLE01
   13    001120    IBM-360.                                          SAMPLE01
   14    001130 INPUT-OUTPUT SECTION.                                SAMPLE01
   15    001140 FILE-CONTROL.                                        SAMPLE01
   16    001150    SELECT CARD-INPUT ASSIGN TO 'SYS007' UNIT-RECORD 2540R.  SAMPLE01
   17    001160    SELECT PRINT-OUTPUT ASSIGN TO 'SYS009' UNIT-RECORD 1403.  SAMPLE01
   18    001170 DATA DIVISION.                                       SAMPLE01
   19    001180 FILE SECTION.                                        SAMPLE01
   20    001190 FD  CARD-INPUT,                                      SAMPLE01
   21    001200    RECORDING MODE IS F,                              SAMPLE01
   22    001210    RECORD CONTAINS 80 CHARACTERS,                    SAMPLE01
   23    001220    LABEL RECORDS ARE OMITTED,                        SAMPLE01
   24    001230    DATA RECORD IS RECORD-IN.                         SAMPLE01
   25    002000 01  RECORD-IN.                                       SAMPLE01
   26    002010    05  STOCK-NUMBER      PICTURE   X(6).             SAMPLE01
   27    002020    05  QTY-ON-HAND       PICTURE   9(5).             SAMPLE01
   28    002030    05  DESCRIPTION       PICTURE   X(20).            SAMPLE01
   29    002040    05  STOCK-RECEIPTS    PICTURE   9(5).             SAMPLE01
   30    002050    05  STOCK-ISSUES      PICTURE   9(5).             SAMPLE01
   31    002060    05  FILLER            PICTURE   X(39).            SAMPLE01
   32    002070 FD  PRINT-OUTPUT,                                    SAMPLE01
   33    002080    RECORDING MODE IS F,                              SAMPLE01
   34    002090    RECORD CONTAINS 133 CHARACTERS,                   SAMPLE01
   35    002100    LABEL RECORDS ARE OMITTED,                        SAMPLE01
   36    002110    DATA RECORD IS PRINT-LINE.                        SAMPLE01
   37    002120 01  PRINT-LINE.                                      SAMPLE01
   38    002130    05  FILLER            PICTURE   X(25).            SAMPLE01
   39    002140    05  PRT-STOCK-NUMBER  PICTURE   X(6).             SAMPLE01
   40    002150    05  FILLER            PICTURE   X(9).             SAMPLE01
   41    002160    05  PRT-DESCRIPTION   PICTURE   X(20).            SAMPLE01
   42    002170    05  FILLER            PICTURE   X(19).            SAMPLE01
   43    002180    05  PRT-NEW-BALANCE   PICTURE   9(6).             SAMPLE01
   44    002190    05  FILLER            PICTURE   X(4).             SAMPLE01
   45    002200    05  PRT-WORD-TOTAL    PICTURE   X(5).             SAMPLE01
   46    002210    05  FILLER            PICTURE   X(5).             SAMPLE01
   47    002220    05  PRT-TOTAL         PICTURE   9(7).             SAMPLE01
   48    002230    05  FILLER            PICTURE   X(27).            SAMPLE01
   49    003010 WORKING-STORAGE SECTION.                             SAMPLE01
   50    003020 77  WORKING-COUNTER      PICTURE   9(6)  VALUE ZEROES .  SAMPLE01
   51    003030 77  TOTAL-COUNTER        PICTURE   9(7)  VALUE ZEROES .  SAMPLE01
   52    003040 PROCEDURE DIVISION.                                  SAMPLE01
   53    003050 START-PROG.                                          SAMPLE01
   54    003060    OPEN INPUT CARD-INPUT, OUTPUT PRINT-OUTPUT.       SAMPLE01
   55    003070    MOVE SPACES TO PRINT-LINE.                        SAMPLE01
   56    003080 READ-A-CARD.                                         SAMPLE01
   57    003090    READ CARD-INPUT, AT END GO TO LAST-CARD.          SAMPLE01
   58    003100    ADD QTY-ON-HAND TO WORKING-COUNTER.               SAMPLE01
   59    003110    ADD STOCK-RECEIPTS TO WORKING-COUNTER.            SAMPLE01
   60    003120    SUBTRACT STOCK-ISSUES FROM WORKING-COUNTER.       SAMPLE01
   61    003130    MOVE WORKING-COUNTER TO PRT-NEW-BALANCE.          SAMPLE01
   62    003140    ADD WORKING-COUNTER TO TOTAL-COUNTER.             SAMPLE01
   63    003150    MOVE ZEROES TO WORKING-COUNTER..                  SAMPLE01
   64    003160    MOVE STOCK-NUMBER TO PRT-STOCK-NUMBER.            SAMPLE01
   65    003170    MOVE DESCRIPTION TO PRT-DESCRIPTION.              SAMPLE01
   66    003180    WRITE PRINT-LINE AFTER ADVANCING 1.               SAMPLE01
   67    003190    MOVE SPACES TO PRINT-LINE.                        SAMPLE01
   68    003200    GO TO READ-A-CARD.                                SAMPLE01
   69    003210 LAST-CARD.                                           SAMPLE01
   70    003220    MOVE 'TOTAL' TO PRT-WORD-TOTAL.                   SAMPLE01
   71    003230    MOVE TOTAL-COUNTER TO PRT-TOTAL.                  SAMPLE01
   72    003240    WRITE PRINT-LINE AFTER ADVANCING 1.               SAMPLE01
   73    004000    CLOSE CARD-INPUT, PRINT-OUTPUT.                   SAMPLE01
   74    004010    STOP RUN.                                         SAMPLE01
```

Figure 16-2. Printed list of program written in COBOL.

```
1    001000 IDENTIFICATION DIVISION.                                          SAMPLE01
2    001010 PROGRAM-ID.                                                       SAMPLE01
3    001020    'SAMPLE'.                                                      SAMPLE01
4    001030 REMARKS.                                                          SAMPLE01
5    001040    SAMPLE COBOL PROGRAM.                                          SAMPLE01
6    001050    READS CARDS AND ADDS STOCK RECEIPTS TO QTY ON HAND BAL         SAMPLE01
7    001060    SUBTRACTS STOCK ISSUES AND DEVELOPS A NEW ON HAND BAL.         SAMPLE01
```

Figure 16-3

use of descriptive names without violation of the rules, e.g., QTY-ON-HAND.

The source program for this problem was written in COBOL and was key punched into cards that were used to produce the program list shown in Figure 16-2. In this case the source program written by the programmer is not shown because in COBOL there is very little difference between the source statements and the statements appearing on the printed list. Again, the program flow chart in Figure 14-4 may be helpful in following the COBOL program discussion since the same problem is being used for all programming illustrations.

COBOL programs are divided into four divisions. The functions of these divisions and the program instructions for this problem that fall within each division are described below.

1. The *identification division* is used to attach a unique identification such as program name, program number, program version, etc., to the program.

In the sample program excerpt shown in Figure 16-3, the identification division contains the name of the program on line 3 and a brief description of the program. These remarks can be very helpful to someone trying to comprehend the program for the first time.

2. The *environment division* is used to acquaint the processor with the computer on which the program is to be compiled and executed.

The configuration section of the environment division in the sample program, lines 9 through 13, identifies the IBM 360 as the computer that will be used to compile the program and to operate the object program (Figure 16-4).

The input-output section, also shown in Figure 16-4, is used to name each file, identify its media, and assign it to one or more input-output devices. The statements on lines 14 through 17 identify the card-input device as a card reader known as SYS007 and the print-output device as a line printer known as SYS009.

3. The *data division* is used to define the characteristics and format of the data to be processed. Every data name referred to in the procedure division except figurative constants must be described in the data division. Items and

```
8    001070 ENVIRONMENT DIVISION.                                            SAMPLE01
9    001080 CONFIGURATION SECTION.                                           SAMPLE01
10   001090 SOURCE-COMPUTER.                                                 SAMPLE01
11   001100    IBM-360.                                                      SAMPLE01
12   001110 OBJECT-COMPUTER.                                                 SAMPLE01
13   001120    IBM-360.                                                      SAMPLE01
14   001130 INPUT-OUTPUT SECTION.                                            SAMPLE01
15   001140 FILE-CONTROL.                                                    SAMPLE01
16   001150    SELECT CARD-INPUT ASSIGN TO 'SYS007' UNIT-RECORD 2540R.       SAMPLE01
17   001160    SELECT PRINT-OUTPUT ASSIGN TO 'SYS009' UNIT-RECORD 1403.      SAMPLE01
```

Figure 16-4

records are described by record description entries, and files are described by file description entries. The data division of this program is composed of two sections, the file section and the working-storage section.

The file section, lines 19 through 48, has two file description (FD) entries. The first, statements 20 through 24, describes the card-input as a fixed form, 80-character record without labels identified as RECORD-IN (Figure 16-5).

The card-input file, statements 25 through 31, contains records identified as RECORD-IN (Figure 16-6). The record is subdivided into its various fields such as STOCK-NUMBER and described by a picture clause. The term "picture" is used to identify a coded description of a data item (field). For example, the picture clause X(6) on line 26 describes STOCK-NUMBER as a six-position field containing alphanumeric data. The picture clause 9(5) on line 27 identifies QTY-ON-HAND as a five-position field containing numeric data. The remainder of the RECORD-IN statements should be easy to translate.

The statements on lines 32 through 48 describe the print-output file named PRINT-LINE (Figure 16-7).

The working-storage section, lines 49 through 51, identifies reserved storage locations for two fields known as WORKING-COUNTER and TOTAL-COUNTER, and describes them as numeric fields originally containing zeros (Figure 16-8).

4. The *procedure division* is used to describe the internal processing that is to take place. All input-output operations, logical decisions, data movement, and computing operations must be defined in the procedure division.

Just as verbs in the English language designate action, so it is with the COBOL verbs. Whereas the entries in the other divisions of a COBOL source program describe or define things, the verbs specify action, or procedures, to be carried out. Accordingly, the COBOL verbs form the basis of the procedure division of a source program.

The smallest unit of expression in the procedure division is the statement. Sentences, paragraphs, and sections are the larger units of expression. A statement consists of a COBOL verb or the word IF or ON, followed by any appropriate operands (data-names, file-names, or literals) and other COBOL words that are necessary for the completion of the statement. There are four types of statements:

1. Compiler-directing statements direct the compiler to take certain actions at compilation time.

2. Imperative statements specify unconditional actions to be taken by the object program.

3. Conditional statements contain a condition that is tested to determine which alternate path in the program flow is to be taken.

4. Note statements (comments) make it easier for programmers to understand and follow the program. These statements are not included in the object program.

A sentence is a single statement or a series of statements terminated by a period and followed by a space. Paragraphs consist of one or more sentences. A section is composed of one or more successive paragraphs and must begin with a section-header.

In the sample program the procedure division starts on line 52 and ends on line 74. There are no section headings in the sample program. The first paragraph

```
18   001170 DATA DIVISION.                                                    SAMPLE01
19   001180 FILE SECTION.                                                     SAMPLE01
20   001190 FD  CARD-INPUT,                                                   SAMPLE01
21   001200     RECORDING MODE IS F,                                          SAMPLE01
22   001210     RECORD CONTAINS 80 CHARACTERS,                                SAMPLE01
23   001220     LABEL RECORDS ARE OMITTED,                                    SAMPLE01
24   001230     DATA RECORD IS RECORD-IN.                                     SAMPLE01
```

Figure 16-5

```
25   002000 01  RECORD-IN.                                                    SAMPLE01
26   002010     05  STOCK-NUMBER       PICTURE   X(6).                        SAMPLE01
27   002020     05  QTY-ON-HAND        PICTURE   9(5).                        SAMPLE01
28   002030     05  DESCRIPTION        PICTURE   X(20).                       SAMPLE01
29   002040     05  STOCK-RECEIPTS     PICTURE   9(5).                        SAMPLE01
30   002050     05  STOCK-ISSUES       PICTURE   9(5).                        SAMPLE01
31   002060     05  FILLER             PICTURE   X(39).                       SAMPLE01
```

Figure 16-6

```
32   002070 FD  PRINT-OUTPUT, .                                               SAMPLE01
33   002080     RECORDING MODE IS F,                                          SAMPLE01
34   002090     RECORD CONTAINS 133 CHARACTERS,                               SAMPLE01
35   002100     LABEL RECORDS ARE OMITTED,                                    SAMPLE01
36   002110     DATA RECORD IS PRINT-LINE.                                    SAMPLE01
37   002120 01  PRINT-LINE.                                                   SAMPLE01
38   002130     05  FILLER             PICTURE   X(25).                       SAMPLE01
39   002140     05  PRT-STOCK-NUMBER   PICTURE   X(6).                        SAMPLE01
40   002150     05  FILLER             PICTURE   X(9).                        SAMPLE01
41   002160     05  PRT-DESCRIPTION    PICTURE   X(20).                       SAMPLE01
42   002170     05  FILLER             PICTURE   X(19).                       SAMPLE01
43   002180     05  PRT-NEW-BALANCE    PICTURE   9(6).                        SAMPLE01
44   002190     05  FILLER             PICTURE   X(4).                        SAMPLE01
45   002200     05  PRT-WORD-TOTAL     PICTURE   X(5).                        SAMPLE01
46   002210     05  FILLER             PICTURE   X(5).                        SAMPLE01
47   002220     05  PRT-TOTAL          PICTURE   9(7).                        SAMPLE01
48   002230     05  FILLER             PICTURE   X(27).                       SAMPLE01
```

Figure 16-7

```
49   003010 WORKING-STORAGE SECTION.                                          SAMPLE01
50   003020 77  WORKING-COUNTER        PICTURE   9(6)  VALUE ZEROES .         SAMPLE01
51   003030 77  TOTAL-COUNTER          PICTURE   9(7)  VALUE ZEROES .         SAMPLE01
```

Figure 16-8

```
52   003040 PROCEDURE DIVISION.                                              SAMPLE01
53   003050 START-PROG.                                                       SAMPLE01
54   003060     OPEN INPUT CARD-INPUT, OUTPUT PRINT-OUTPUT.                   SAMPLE01
55   003070     MOVE SPACES TO PRINT-LINE                                     SAMPLE01
```

Figure 16-9

heading appearing on line 53 in the procedure division reads START-PROG. In this paragraph the input and output files are opened, and the PRINT-LINE is cleared of any data that may be there at the time the program is loaded (Figure 16-9).

In the next paragraph headed READ-A-CARD the following steps are programmed:

1. The statement on line 57 says to read a card and, when the last card has been read, to go (branch) to the LAST-CARD paragraph (Figure 16-10).

2. The next three statements (lines 58 to 60) say to add quantity on hand to the storage area named WORKING-COUNTER, add stock receipts to WORK-ING-COUNTER, and subtract stock issues from WORKING-COUNTER (Figure 16-11).

3. The next statements (lines 61 and 62) say to move the sum stored at WORK-ING-COUNTER to a storage field known as PRT-NEW-BALANCE, and to add the sum stored at WORKING-COUNTER to the storage field known as TOTAL-COUNTER. The next statement (line 63) says to clear the storage field known as WORKING-COUNTER by moving zeros into that field (Figure 16-12).

4. The next two statements (lines 64 and 65) cause indicative data in the RECORD-IN file section to be moved to the PRINT-OUTPUT PRINT-LINE (Figure 16-13). It should be noted that the statement names shown on lines 64 and 65 can be related to the names in the file section of the data division.

5. The next three statements (lines 66, 67, and 68) cause the paper to be spaced, a line to be printed, the print line to be cleared, and the program to branch to the paragraph headed READ-A-CARD (Figure 16-14).

6. The instructions in the LAST-CARD paragraph (lines 69 to 74) will be activated by a branch operation which occurs after the last card has been read. This LAST-CARD paragraph says to move the literal TOTAL to the print line, move the data at TOTAL-COUNTER to the print line, space the paper, write the PRINT-LINE, close the CARD-INPUT and PRINT-OUTPUT files, and stop the job (Figure 16-15).

In addition to the list shown in Figure 16-2, the COBOL compiler may also produce a data division map showing each data name and the storage address it represents, and a procedure division map showing machine-language instructions and their storage addresses. These instructions are also referenced to their source statement line number. In most cases several machine-language instructions are generated for each source statement.

Although COBOL has not attained perfect commonality, there are advantages to its use as a programming system. Among these advantages are:

1. The chance for clerical errors is reduced, as the program is written in a language familiar to the programmer.

2. Internal processing functions are stated in English. This eliminates the need for the programmer to be familiar with the machine instructions.

3. The processor will automatically insert the required input-output control system segments into the object program.

4. Standard input-output format definitions improve communications between programmers working on several interdependent programs.

Most of the arguments against the use of COBOL in its present form are:

1. A good programmer can write a more efficient program in a machine-oriented language than in COBOL, although it may require more programming time.

2. Since COBOL processors are very complex, they require more computer time to compile the program. Even though the more powerful computers require less time for compiling, the time consumed is still relatively greater than that required for less complicated processors.

```
56    003080 READ-A-CARD.                                              SAMPLE01
57    003090     READ CARD-INPUT, AT END GO TO LAST-CARD.             SAMPLE01
```

Figure 16-10

```
58    003100     ADD QTY-ON-HAND TO WORKING-COUNTER.                  SAMPLE01
59    003110     ADD STOCK-RECEIPTS TO WORKING-COUNTER.               SAMPLE01
60    003120     SUBTRACT STOCK-ISSUES FROM WORKING-COUNTER.          SAMPLE01
```

Figure 16-11

```
61    003130     MOVE WORKING-COUNTER TO PRT-NEW-BALANCE.             SAMPLE01
62    003140     ADD WORKING-COUNTER TO TOTAL-COUNTER.                SAMPLE01
63    003150     MOVE ZEROES TO WORKING-COUNTER.                      SAMPLE01
```

Figure 16-12

```
64    003160     MOVE STOCK-NUMBER TO PRT-STOCK-NUMBER.               SAMPLE01
65    003170     MOVE DESCRIPTION TO PRT-DESCRIPITON.                 SAMPLE01
```

Figure 16-13

```
66    003180     WRITE PRINT-LINE AFTER ADVANCING 1.                 SAMPLE01
67    003190     MOVE SPACES TO PRINT-LINE.                           SAMPLE01
68    003200     GO TO READ-A-CARD.                                   SAMPLE01
```

Figure 16-14

```
69    003210 LAST-CARD.                                               SAMPLE01
70    003220     MOVE 'TOTAL' TO PRT-WORD-TOTAL.                     SAMPLE01
71    003230     MOVE TOTAL-COUNTER TO PRT-TOTAL.                     SAMPLE01
72    003240     WRITE PRINT-LINE AFTER ADVANCING 1.                 SAMPLE01
73    004000     CLOSE CARD-INPUT, PRINT-OUTPUT.                      SAMPLE01
74    004010     STOP RUN.                                            SAMPLE01
```

Figure 16-15

3. Failure to fully understand the limits of the so-called computer independence of COBOL has led some into thinking that once a problem has been programmed in COBOL it can be used with any computer without reprogramming. In reality, if a COBOL program is to be efficient, the programmer writing the program must be familiar with the characteristics of the specific computer to be used.

PROGRAMMING LANGUAGE I

Programming Language I (PL/I) is a multipurpose, high-level programming language that enables the programming not only of business and scientific applications but also of real-time and systems applications. Program preparation is simpler because PL/I does not impose rigid form rules on the programmer. In addition, no special coding forms are required. This free form reduces transcription errors because programs are not bound by card column restrictions as in previous languages.

PL/I uses basic building blocks called procedures. A procedure is a block of instructions designed to perform a specific function such as the calculation of overtime pay in a payroll application. Programmers build application programs by employing procedures as functional blocks. The use of procedures as functional blocks simplifies the programmer's task because he can revise an existing program by changing individual procedures without having to change others. He can also write a number of short procedures and combine them into a complete program.

Certain procedures may be applicable in different programs. Thus, seldom-used procedures can be held in auxiliary storage and called into main storage when needed. This conserves working storage for operations of higher priority.

A PL/I program consists of words and/or delimiters. *Words* belong to one of two categories: identifiers or constants. An *identifier* can be a word used to identify a file, a data item, or all or any part of a program. This type of identifier is known as a *key word*. An example of a key word would be the word DECLARE shown in card 1020 in the sample program (Figure 16-16). *Constants* name data items that will actually appear within a PL/I program and, consequently, are immediately available for use in the program. The word TOTAL on line 2160 of the sample program is an example of a constant.

There are two types of *delimiters:* separators and operators. *Separators* include the comma, semicolon, colon, period, and parenthesis. They are used to separate elements of a list, terminate statements, separate name qualifiers, and enclose lists. *Operators* are comprised of a series of the following:

1. Arithmetic operators are the signs used to denote the various arithmetic functions such as add, subtract, multiply, and divide.

2. Comparison operators are the signs used to denote greater than, not greater than, greater than or equal to, equal to, etc.

3. Logical operators are the signs used to denote *and, not,* and *or.*

Comments may be used anywhere that a blank is permitted, except within a character-string constant or a picture specification. Comments must be preceded by a slash and an asterisk and must be followed by an asterisk and a slash. The first line of the sample PL/I program is an example of how comments are bracketed (Figure 16-16).

Figure 16-16 shows the PL/I source text for the problem flow charted in Figure 14-14. Although PL/I can be written in free form, it is written in this example on a standard sheet designed for key punching the data into 80-column cards. Card columns 2 through 72 are used for source text and 73 through 80 are used to identify the program and as a sequence number field. To demonstrate the flexibility of the PL/I language, the first part of the program ending on line 2070 is written in a blocked format similar to that of COBOL; the remainder of the program is written in a formula format similar to that of FORTRAN.

The sample PL/I program shown in Figure 16-16 is described in the following paragraphs.

Explicit descriptions of data characteristics are written in the form of DECLARE statements used to describe named data as it is represented within the internal storage of a computer. The properties that characterize a data item are called attributes and are specified by key words. The DECLARE statements shown in cards 1020 through 1206 describe the CARDIN, PRTOUT, and PRTTOT records as they will exist in the primary stor-

IBM GENERAL PURPOSE CARD PUNCHING FORM

JOB	SAMPLE		PUNCHING INSTRUCTIONS

WRITTEN AS:	Ø	O						
PUNCH AS:	NUM	ALPHA						

BY		DATE	

NOTES:

FIELD IDENTIFICATION

```
SAMPLE: PROCEDURE OPTIONS (MAIN); /* SAMPLE PROG. IN PL/I. */         SAMØ1Ø1Ø
     DECLARE 1 CARDIN,   /* CARD INPUT AREA */                        SAMØ1Ø2Ø
             2 STOCKNO        CHARACTER (6),                          SAMØ1Ø3Ø
             2 QTYONHD        PICTURE '99999',                        SAMØ1Ø4Ø
             2 DESC           CHARACTER (2Ø),                         SAMØ1Ø5Ø
             2 STKRCPTS       PICTURE '99999',                        SAMØ1Ø6Ø
             2 STKISS         PICTURE '99999',                        SAMØ1Ø7Ø
             2 FILL           CHARACTER (39),                         SAMØ1Ø8Ø
           1 PRTOUT,   /* PRINTER OUTPUT AREA */                      SAMØ1Ø9Ø
             2 FILL1          CHARACTER (24),                         SAMØ11ØØ
             2 PSTOCKNO       CHARACTER (6),                          SAMØ111Ø
             2 FILL2          CHARACTER (9),                          SAMØ112Ø
             2 PDESC          CHARACTER (2Ø),                         SAMØ113Ø
             2 FILL3          CHARACTER (19),                         SAMØ114Ø
             2 PTOT           PICTURE '999999',                       SAMØ115Ø
             2 FILL4          CHARACTER (48),                         SAMØ116Ø
           1 PRTTOT,   /* FINAL TOTAL LINE */                         SAMØ117Ø
             2 FILL5          CHARACTER (88),                         SAMØ118Ø
             2 TOTWORD        CHARACTER (5),                          SAMØ119Ø
             2 FILL6          CHARACTER (5),                          SAMØ12ØØ

             2 FTOT           PICTURE '9,999,999',                    SAMØ12Ø3
             2 FILL7          CHARACTER (27),                         SAMØ12Ø6
     /* THE NEXT TWO FIELDS ARE USED AS COUNTERS */                   SAMØ121Ø
           WCTR       FIXED DECIMAL (6),                              SAMØ122Ø
           FCTR       FIXED DECIMAL (7),                              SAMØ123Ø
     /* FILE DECLARATION FOR CARD AND PRINTER FILES */                SAMØ124Ø
           CARD FILE INPUT RECORD BUFFERED                            SAMØ125Ø
             ENVIRONMENT (F(8Ø) MEDIUM (SYSØØ7,254Ø)),                SAMØ126Ø
           PRINT FILE OUTPUT RECORD BUFFERED                          SAMØ127Ø
             ENVIRONMENT (F(132) MEDIUM (SYSØØ9,14Ø3));               SAMØ128Ø
     /* END OF DATA DECLARATIONS. LOGIC OF PROGRAM BEGINS */          SAMØ129Ø
/* INITIALIZE CTRS TO ZERO */                                        SAMØ2Ø1Ø
     START:    FCTR = Ø;                                              SAMØ2Ø2Ø
/* OPEN RECORD FILES EXPLICITLY */                                    SAMØ2Ø3Ø
       OPEN FILE (CARD), FILE (PRINT);                                SAMØ2Ø4Ø
       ON ENDFILE (CARD) GO TO EOJ;                                   SAMØ2Ø5Ø
/* READ CARD AND PROCESS */                                          SAMØ2Ø6Ø
     GETCARD: READ FILE (CARD) INTO (CARDIN);                         SAMØ2Ø7Ø
       WCTR = QTYONHD + STKRCPTS - STKISS;                            SAMØ2Ø8Ø
       PTOT = WCTR;                                                   SAMØ2Ø9Ø

       FCTR = FCTR + WCTR;                                            SAMØ21ØØ
       PSTOCKNO = STOCKNO;                                            SAMØ211Ø
       PDESC = DESC;                                                  SAMØ212Ø
       WRITE FILE (PRINT) FROM (PRTOUT);                              SAMØ213Ø
       GO TO GETCARD;                                                 SAMØ214Ø
/* END OF JOB ROUTINE */                                             SAMØ215Ø
     EOJ: TOTWORD = 'TOTAL';                                          SAMØ216Ø
       FTOT = FCTR;                                                   SAMØ217Ø
       WRITE FILE (PRINT) FROM (PRTTOT);                              SAMØ218Ø
       CLOSE FILE (CARD), FILE (PRINT);                               SAMØ219Ø
END; /* END OF PROG */                                               SAMØ22ØØ
```

Figure 16-16. Source program written in PL/I.

age unit of the computer (Figure 16-17).

The WCTR and FCTR statements on lines 1220 and 1230 name two counters, identify their attributes, and fix their size (Figure 16-18).

Cards 1250 and 1260 contain the DECLARE statements defining the card file as buffered and read by a model 2540 card reader with the system name SYS007. ("Buffered" indicates that data in a record being transmitted to and from a file is to be placed into an intermediate storage area known as a buffer.) The statements also identify the records (cards) as being 80-characters in length and in a file with no label (Figure 16-19).

Cards 1270 and 1280 contain the DECLARE statements defining the printer file as buffered with 132-position records printed by a 1403 model printer with the

system name SYS009 (Figure 16-20). The semicolon at the end of the statement on card 1280 indicates the end of a statement or a series of statements; in this case it marks the end of the DECLARE statements.

The processing part of the program actually starts with card 2020. The first step in this problem is to be sure that the FCTR counter is set to zero by stating that the counter is to be made equal to zero (Figure 16-21).

Cards 2040 and 2050 specify that the card and print files are to be opened and that after the last card has been processed the computer is to go to the EOJ (end of job) routine (Figure 16-22). The file-opening statements cause about the same instructions to be inserted into the PL/I object program as were generated by the

```
 SAMPLE  PROCEDURE  OPTIONS  (MAIN);  /* SAMPLE  PROG  IN PL/I */            SAM01010
      DECLARE  1, CARDIN,  /* CARD  INPUT  AREA */                          SAM01020
                2, STOCKNO,       CHARACTER  (6),                           SAM01030
                2, QTYONHD,       PICTURE  '99999',                         SAM01040
                2, DESC,          CHARACTER  (20),                          SAM01050
                2, STKRCPTS,      PICTURE  '99999',                         SAM01060
                2, STKISS,        PICTURE  '99999',                         SAM01070
                2, FILL,          CHARACTER  (39),                          SAM01080
            1, PRTOUT,  /* PRINTER  OUTPUT  AREA */                         SAM01090
                2, FILL1,         CHARACTER  (24),                          SAM01100
                2, PSTOCKNO,      CHARACTER  (6),                           SAM01110
                2, FILL2,         CHARACTER  (9),                           SAM01120
                2, PDESC,         CHARACTER  (20),                          SAM01130
                2, FILL3,         CHARACTER  (19),                          SAM01140
                2, PTOT,          PICTURE  '999999',                        SAM01150
                2, FILL4,         CHARACTER  (48),                          SAM01160
            1, PRTTOT,  /* FINAL  TOTAL  LINE */                            SAM01170
                2, FILL5,         CHARACTER  (88),                          SAM01180
                2, TOTWORD,       CHARACTER  (5),                           SAM01190
                2, FILL6,         CHARACTER  (5),                           SAM01200
                2, FTOT,          PICTURE  '9999999',                       SAM01203
                2, FILL7,         CHARACTER  (27),                          SAM01206
```

Figure 16-17

```
        /* THE NEXT TWO FIELDS ARE USED AS COUNTERS */                     SAM01210
            WCTR,      FIXED, DECIMAL  (6),                                 SAM01220
            FCTR,      FIXED, DECIMAL  (7),                                 SAM01230
```

Figure 16-18

```
/* FILE DECLARATION FOR CARD AND PRINTER FILES */              SAM01240
           CARD FILE INPUT RECORD, BUFFERED                    SAM01250
           ENVIRONMENT (F(80), MEDIUM (SYS007,2540)),          SAM01260
```

Figure 16-19

```
      PRINT FILE OUTPUT RECORD BUFFERED                        SAM01270
           ENVIRONMENT (F(132), MEDIUM (SYS009,1403),);        SAM01280
      /* END OF DATA DECLARATIONS. LOGIC OF PROGRAM BEGINS */  SAM01290
```

Figure 16-20

```
/* INITIALIZE CTRS TO ZERO */                                 SAM02010
     START:   FCTR = 0;                                        SAM02020
```

Figure 16-21

```
/* OPEN RECORD FILES EXPLICITLY */                            SAM02030
     OPEN FILE (CARD), FILE (PRINT);                           SAM02040
     ON ENDFILE (CARD) GO TO EOJ;                              SAM02050
```

Figure 16-22

```
/* READ CARD AND PROCESS */                                   SAM02060
     GETCARD: READ FILE (CARD) INTO (CARDIN);                  SAM02070
     WCTR = QTYONHD + STKRCPTS - STKISS;                       SAM02080
     PTOT = WCTR;                                              SAM02090
     FCTR = FCTR + WCTR;                                       SAM02100
     PSTOCKNO = STOCKNO;                                       SAM02110
     PDESC = DESC;                                             SAM02120
     WRITE FILE (PRINT) FROM (PRTOUT);                         SAM02130
     GO TO GETCARD;                                            SAM02140
```

Figure 16-23

COBOL and Assembler Language processors.

Card 2070 states that a card record is to be read into the primary storage location named CARDIN (Figure 16-23). The next statement specifies that QTYONHD and STKRCPTS are to be added and the result entered into the area named WCTR, and that STKISS is to be subtracted from the sum at WCTR. Card 2090 specifies that the sum at WCTR is to be moved into PTOT. The next statement specifies that the sum at WCTR is to be added to the sum at FCTR and the result is to remain at FCTR. The next two state-

ments, cards 2110 and 2120, cause STOCKNO to be moved to PSTOCKNO and DESC to be moved to PDESC. The next two statements, cards 2130 and 2140, cause a line to be printed as formated in the PRTOUT declarations and the program to branch back to GET-CARD, the statement that causes the computer to read a card.

The program will continue to move through this loop—read a card, process, print a line, branch to read-a-card, and so on—until the last card has been read. After the last card has been processed, the IOCS will cause the program to branch to the

```
/* END OF JOB ROUTINE */                                    SAM02150
   EOJ: TOTWORD = 'TOTAL';                                  SAM02160
        FTOT = FCTR;                                        SAM02170
        WRITE FILE (PRINT) FROM (PRTTOT);                   SAM02180
        CLOSE FILE (CARD) , FILE (PRINT);                   SAM02190
END; /* END OF PROG */                                      SAM02200
```

Figure 16-24

end-of-job routine statements starting in card 2160 (Figure 16-24). The end-of-job statements cause the word TOTAL to be moved to TOTWORD, FCTR to be moved to FTOT, the line to be printed, and the files to be closed.

PL/I has not been as widely used as COBOL or FORTRAN because it is a relatively new programming system developed by one equipment manufacturer, IBM. However, it is likely that the advantages of PL/I will cause it to become the most universally used programming system.

REPORT PROGRAM GENERATOR

Report Program Generator (RPG) is designed to provide users with an efficient, easy-to-use technique for generating programs. RPG uses a set of simple and largely self-explanatory specification sheets on which the user makes entries. Although technically RPG may not be considered a programming system, it is a very important program producing technique. As its vast capabilities include many functions in addition to report preparation, its name is a misnomer and fails to do it justice. When RPG is used, the computer actually performs two separate functions: (1) program generation, and (2) data processing.

In the first function, program specifications, defined by the user, produce machine-language instructions. Storage areas are automatically assigned; constants or other reference factors are included; and linkage to routines for checking, for input-output operations, and for other functions are produced.

In the second function, the machine-language instructions created in the first function are executed under control of the RPG. The user's input data files are utilized to produce the desired reports or output files.

The preparation of a report by means of RPG consists of the general operations illustrated in Figure 16-25 and described in the ensuing paragraphs.

The programmer must evaluate the report requirements to determine the format of the input files and the desired appearance of the finished report. Then he must make the required entries on the various specification sheets. To illustrate this we have prepared RPG specification sheets for the same basic problem programmed in each of the previously discussed programming systems. The functions of the RPG specification sheets are as follows.

The *file description* sheet is used to describe all files used by the object program: input files, output files, table files, etc. (Figure 16-26). In the sample problem there are two files: a card input file and a printed report. The entries in columns 15 through 27 of line 10 indicate that the card input file named CARDIN is an input type file, is a primary file, is to be checked for end-of-file condition, is in ascending se-

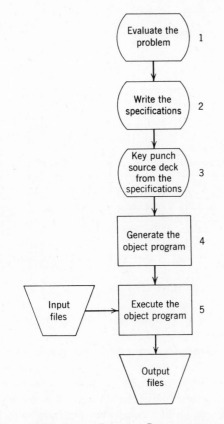

Figure 16-25. Report Program Generator preparation steps.

quence, and has a fixed file format containing 80-position unblocked records.

Columns 40 to 52 of line 10 show that the device is a model 2540 card reader assigned the symbolic name SYS007. The report output file named PRINTOUT is identified on line 20 as an output file containing a variable number of positions up to 132. The printer is assigned the symbolic name SYS009.

The *input specification* sheet is used to describe the input: record layouts, field used, etc. (Figure 16-27). The first two lines on the sample input sheet identify the record as an 80-column card with the name CARDIN. Lines 30 through 70 define and name the various fields in the card record.

The *calculation specification* sheet is used to describe the processing steps: add, subtract, multiply. The sample sheet specifies that QTYHD is to be added to CTR; STKRCP is to be added to CTR; STKISS is to be subtracted from CTR; and CTR is to be added to TOTCTR (Figure 16-28).

The *output-format specification* sheet is used to identify the printing positions, carriage control, etc. which will establish

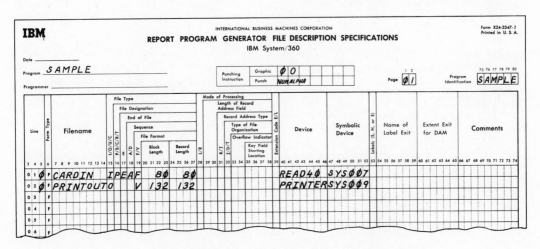

Figure 16-26. RPG file description specifications.

IBM — INTERNATIONAL BUSINESS MACHINES CORPORATION
REPORT PROGRAM GENERATOR INPUT SPECIFICATIONS
IBM System/360
Form X24-3350-1 Printed in U. S. A.

Date
Program SAMPLE
Programmer
Punching Instruction — Graphic: Ø O; Punch: NUM ALPHA
Page Ø2
Program Identification SAMPLE

Line	Form Type	Filename	Sequence	Resulting Indicator	Record Identification Codes 1: Position	Not (N)	Character	Field Location From	To	Decimal Positions	Field Name
01Ø	I	CARDIN	AA	11	8Ø		C				
02Ø	I		OR	11	8Ø	N	C				
03Ø	I							1	6		STKNO
04Ø	I							7	11	Ø	QTYHD
05Ø	I							12	31		DESC
06Ø	I							32	36	Ø	STKRCP
07Ø	I							37	41	Ø	STKISS
08	I										

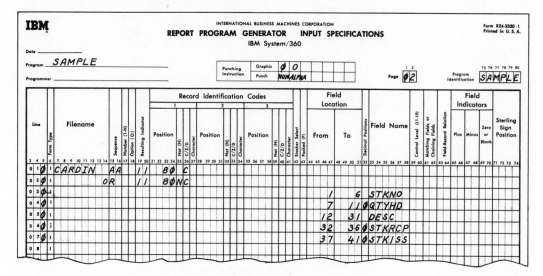

Figure 16-27. RPG input specifications.

the format of the report (Figure 16-29). In the sample, the file named PRINTOUT obtains its data from a detail record or from the result of calculations and causes the data in the fields named STKNO, DESC, and CTR to print as specified. The entries on lines 50 through 70 state that the word TOTAL and the sum in the field named TOTCTR with zeros suppressed are to be printed after the last record has been processed.

Note that mnemonic names similar to those used in the Assembler Language may be used in RPG. This is one of the important features that help to make RPG the valuable program-generating technique that it is.

After the specifications have been

IBM — INTERNATIONAL BUSINESS MACHINES CORPORATION
REPORT PROGRAM GENERATOR CALCULATION SPECIFICATIONS
IBM System/360
Form X24-3351-1 Printed in U. S. A.

Date
Program SAMPLE
Programmer
Punching Instruction — Graphic: Ø O; Punch: NUM ALPHA
Page Ø3
Program Identification SAMPLE

Line	Form Type	Indicators	Factor 1	Operation	Factor 2	Result Field	Field Length	Decimal Positions
01Ø	C	11	CTR	ADD	QTYHD	CTR	6	Ø
02Ø	C	11	CTR	ADD	STKRCP	CTR		
03Ø	C	11	CTR	SUB	STKISS	CTR		
04Ø	C	11	TOTCTR	ADD	CTR	TOTCTR	7	Ø
05	C							
06	C							
07								

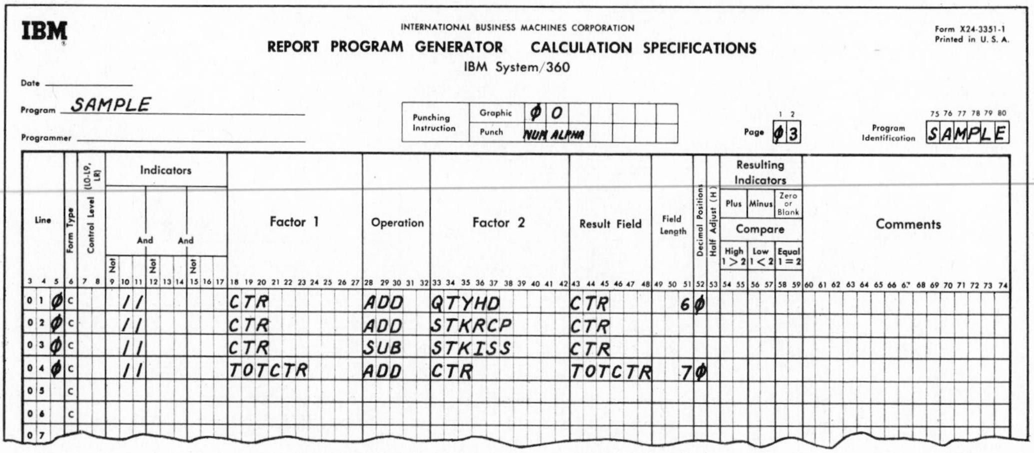

Figure 16-28. RPG calculation specifications.

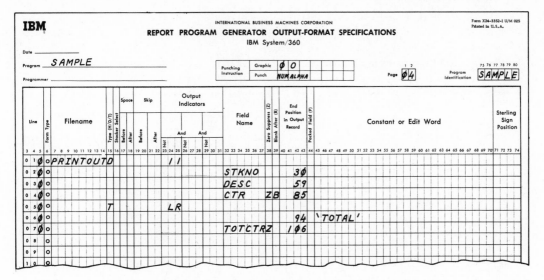

Figure 16-29. RPG output-format specifications.

written on the appropriate forms, cards are key punched with the data from the forms. These punched cards, called a *source deck,* are combined with the processor control card and the job control cards. The source deck and the control cards are supplied to an input device and are processed.

At the end of the processing run, known as a *compilation run,* a program capable of preparing the report specified by the programmer has been produced. This program, known as an *object program,* contains all of the computer instructions and linkages to the control system necessary to prepare the desired report.

The input files can then be read into the system, and processing of the program will begin. This is known as the *object run.* At the end of the object run, the report has been prepared and any other functions, such as file updating, are completed. Figure 16-30 shows the results of the sample run produced by the RPG program shown in the four preceding illustrations.

```
// EXEC
              123456      HAMMER,BALL PEAN                125
              123457      HAMMER,CLAW                      55
              123458      HAMMER,SLEDGE 20 LB               8
              123459      HAMMER,SLEDGE 10 LB              10
                                                                  TOTAL     198
```

Figure 16-30. Report resulting from RPG program.

Review Questions

1. What is the primary advantage of a FORTRAN programming system?
2. Name the four divisions of a COBOL program.

3. In which COBOL division is the computer that will be used identified?
4. Name the four types of COBOL procedure division statements.
5. What are the advantages of the use of COBOL?
6. What are the arguments against the use of COBOL?
7. What types of applications can be programmed with PL/I?
8. Briefly describe the functions performed by Report Program Generator.

17

ELECTRONIC DATA PROCESSING OPERATIONS

Although electronic data processing organizations may vary in structure, they all must perform comparable functions. These functions can be divided into five major categories: systems planning, research, training, programming, and the actual operation of EDP equipment.

Electronic data processing operations encompass many important activities: data is transcribed from human-sensible documents to machine-language documents, machine operations are performed, files of data are maintained, and accuracy controls are exercised. These and other facets of EDP operations will be considered in this chapter.

THE DATA PROCESSING FACILITY

An electronic data processing facility consists of one or more processing units and associated input-output devices, as well as certain auxiliary support equipment and files. Insofar as the arrangement of the equipment is concerned, most manufacturers have a suggested layout. The computer components should be arranged close so as to keep operator travel to a minimum and yet spread out so as not to cause congestion of personnel, documents, or supplies.

In addition to the equipment, the facility will have a certain amount of space for the supervisors, document control group, programming personnel, card punch operations, storage of records and supplies, and equipment maintenance. The arrangement of the various activities should be one that is most ideal from a total performance point of view.

As the components of a computer system have interconnecting cables for supply of power and transmission of data, it is advisable that the equipment be placed on a raised floor 12 to 18 inches above the regular floor. This provides room for all of the cables to run under the raised floor. Air conditioning and humidity control equipment that will meet computer manufacturers' specifications is also essential.

DATA FLOW

Input Preparation and Control

The majority of data entering business data processing systems must be converted to machine-language documents. The bulk of this transcribing from human-sensible documents to machine language is performed by operators using card punch machines. Most documents are received by data processing in groups or stacks called *batches.* These batches should have associated with them a *control* or *batch ticket* that shows from whom the documents were received, the date, perhaps the time, and a document count (Figure 17-1).

Control totals of quantitative data may also be provided. A *control total* is the sum of the quantitative data recorded in a common field of each record in a batch of records. In Figure 17-1, for example, the control total is the sum of the amount fields in the accompanying purchase orders and material requisitions. If control totals are not provided, then they should be developed by the control clerks in the data processing facility. Normally the control clerks check the source documents for completeness and accuracy. The clerks also protect the source documents and batch or control tickets against loss or destruction while they are in the custody of the EDP

County of San Diego
Dept. of Public Works

TRANSMITTAL SHEET

BATCH NO. 2-125
DATE 2-26

DESCRIPTION	HOURS OR MILES	AMOUNT
LABOR AND EQUIPMENT		$
PURCHASE ORDERS Numbered 21101 thru 21121		5,174 19
MATERIAL REQUISITIONS Various		1,315 62
CLAIMS		
ADJUSTMENTS		
OTHER (DESCRIBE)		
total		6,489 81

COMMENTS
This is the last of these transactions for the month of Feb.

TRANSMITTED:	RECORDED:	RECEIVED:
L. Meers ACCOUNTING DIV.	Peggy IBM	E. Boland ACCOUNTING DIV.

FORM DPW - 143

Figure 17-1. Combined batch ticket and transmittal sheet.

facility. Finally the control clerks see that the input and output schedules stated in the procedures are met.

Input Handling Procedures

After the source data has been converted into machine-language documents, both are usually conveyed to the machine room. Each batch of machine-language documents should have some sort of human-language identification (Figure 17-2). Each batch may also have some sort of machine-language identification, usually in the form of a leader card containing all of the batch control data including quantitative totals. These batches can first be audited and balanced by the computer. All batches that do not balance can be flagged and returned to the control section for corrective action.

Another and often preferred approach is to have the computer list on an error sheet during the edit run the items of input data that do not have valid indicative data or the quantitative totals that do not equal the batch control totals. This ap-

proach allows the computer to continue with the normal process without operator intervention and allows the control clerks at a later time to adjust for the errors by creating new entries, one to revise out the error, and another to reenter the transaction correctly. Whatever the approach, all reasonable effort should be made to insure the accuracy of the machine-language input. Invalid or inaccurate data can quickly destroy user confidence in the reliability of the output of the system.

Once the accuracy of the input data is established, there may be a limited amount of auxiliary processing required before the actual production run. This may include sorting, sequencing, merging, or interpreting. All data, whether in tape, card, or other form, should be clearly identified at all times. The identification should show what it is and what the next step should be.

With EDP procedures it is important that processed data be retained as long as required to replace current to-date records in the event they are lost or destroyed. Most organizations maintain a

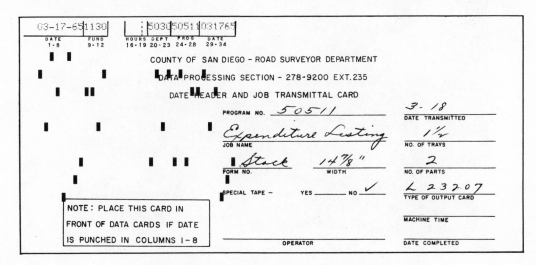

Figure 17-2. Date header and job transmittal card.

log reflecting data in storage and use this for aid in replacing records or as a basis for purging stored data no longer required. Control must also be maintained over data that is temporarily stored for scheduled use at a later date.

Output Handling Procedures

Computer output can be in the form of human-sensible information to be distributed to users, or machine-language records to be retained in the data processing facility for a following operation or for reuse at a later date. If data is in printed form, it may be balanced to control totals. Printed forms may also need to be prepared for distribution to the users. This may include separating carbon paper from multicopy forms, detaching or bursting continuous forms, and possibly inserting them into envelopes. If it were

necessary to separate and detach hundreds or thousands of multicopy forms by hand, the task would be tedious and costly. To solve this problem a variety of forms-handling equipment is available, including the following.

Separator (Figure 17-3). This machine separates multicopy continuous forms and refolds the parts continuously into individual sets. At the same time, carbon paper is removed and wound individually on removable spindles. Certain models will remove one copy and one carbon from a multicopy set and leave the remainder of the set intact.

Burster or Detacher. This type of equipment splits individual sets of continuous forms into single forms. This operation is known as "bursting." Excess margins can be removed by a power slitter.

Detacher-Sorter. The model illustrated (Figure 17-4) is a detacher with a

Figure 17-3. Multicopy continuous forms separator. (*Courtesy Moore Business Forms, Inc.*)

built-in optical character reading unit which permits it to random sort a continuous form during the detaching operation. The machine performs as follows:

1. Margins are removed from the documents by a power slitter.

2. The machine bursts the one-part form into individual units.

3. A scanning device reads each form and detects the presence of one or more horizontal dash (–) lines printed in a specific location during the completion of the form. The pattern of this printing determines which pocket is to receive the detached form. One dash signifies "sort 1," two dashes "sort 2," and so on. When no mark is present the form goes into the reject pocket.

Imprinter. This device imprints on continuous forms a limited amount of constant data such as dates, consecutive numbers, or signatures. For example, a series of pay checks in continuous form could be signed automatically on an imprinter by using a signature plate. Imprinting may be performed as a separate operation or on certain models it may be combined with bursting.

Storage of Machine-Language Data

Machine-language output is usually entered in a log and stored in or near the data processing facility in the space provided. This may be a magnetic tape vault, a card file, or storage rack for removable random storage units. Again, all output media require some sort of control as to date and time of completion and accuracy.

Most recently the tendency is to meet

Figure 17-4. Detacher-Sorter detaches continuous forms and sorts detached sheets by optical scanning process. (*Courtesy Moore Business Forms, Inc.*)

the larger output requirements by providing machine-language data instead of, or in addition to, human-language data. This can be very beneficial to the receiver of the data as he will be saved the cost of converting the human-sensible data to machine-language data. It also reduces the opportunity for discrepancies between the originator and the user of the data. Examples of this are the fulfillment of certain federal and state information requirements such as quarterly reports on earnings, social security deductions, and unemployment insurance contributions by sending this data to the governing agencies on magnetic tape.

Scheduling

Scheduling can be the most arduous and frustrating part of managing an EDP operation unless a carefully conceived plan for scheduling is installed and followed with integrity. Too often EDP management expects the input always to be on schedule, and yet shows no concern if the output is delayed. If dependability of input is to be required, there must be comparable reliability of output. Some of the problems that make scheduling so difficult are:

1. Users often require their reports at about the same time, generally at the end of the month, quarter, or year.

2. The volumes of data to be processed tend to vary from one time to the next.

3. A minimum of input and output devices is usually all that is available for reasons of economy. Therefore, any increase in volume of one job may cause a delay in the start of the next job.

4. Machine breakdowns cannot be scheduled, even though with the best of equipment they occasionally do occur. In some critical operations a second standby computer may be justified in order to insure continuity of performance.

The total computer time available must be scheduled for reruns and restarts, program assembly and testing, and preventive maintenance in addition to the regular scheduled and nonscheduled production runs. One method for successful scheduling is to assign a certain period of time each day to program assembly and testing, and another to reruns. Also, a definite period may be set for preventive maintenance. The majority of the remaining time should be available for scheduling of production runs. Another plan for handling the scheduling problem is to schedule most of the production runs during the second shift and thereby leave the prime shift open for program assembly and testing, maintenance, reruns, and high-priority special runs.

CONSOLE OPERATION

The operator console is often a part of the central processing unit. However, on the larger systems especially, the console may be a separate unit at which the computer operator can sit. The power on and off switches are located on the console. In addition to the regular power off switch, there is also an emergency off switch that is to be used only in the event of a real emergency such as a fire. The start key is used to initiate or resume machine operations. The stop key is used to stop the machine at the completion of the instruction in process. On many computers additional start and stop keys are located on other input-output units for operator convenience.

Other control switches on the computer console start or stop various operations including the loading of a program from cards, tape, etc. Some consoles also contain a built-in or attached electric typewriter that can be used by the operator to enter instructions into the control unit (Figure 17-5).

The setting of the mode switch or switches determines the mode of operation; that is, run, alter, character display, storage print out, address stop, etc. Most computers have a set of switches or dials for manual address operations. For example, they may be used to cause data at a specific location to be displayed on the console. The manual address switches can be used only in conjunction with certain mode switch settings. Those computers that employ parity and/or validity check usually have a switch for manual restoration of the computer after the error has been identified. Usually these systems also have a switch that can be used to tell the machine to ignore the errors.

Computers generally provide a method for manually entering data into storage. This is usually accomplished through a series of switches that are used to set up the character to be entered. These switches or dials are generally operated after the destination in storage is identified in a storage address register.

Various types of registers are capable of receiving information from primary storage, storing it, and transferring it as directed by control circuits within the system. The condition of these registers at

Figure 17-5. Computer central processing unit and console with typewriter. (*Courtesy International Business Machines Corporation.*)

COUNTY OF SAN DIEGO
360 PRODUCTION RUN SETUP

PROCEDURE NAME: San Diego Municipal Court
Prior Violation File Daily
Process

JOB NAME: Daily Update

FREQUENCY Daily   AVG. RUN TIME 2.5 Hours

JOB NUMBER	M	C	1	4	0	0	1	0

PROGRAMS								
PROGRAMMER	NUMBERS							
H. Ferguson	M	C	1	4	0	5	6	1
DOS Utility	D	E	S	O	R	T		
H. Goodwin	M	C	1	4	0	5	6	2

MAGNETIC STORAGE DEVICES

VOL. I.D. NO.	64983	63921				
DEVICE NO.	1A1	1A2	1A3	1A3	1A3	
		(1)	Cell 7	Cell 8	Cell 9	

COMMENTS: (1) The pack on drive 1A2 will change from time to time and the packs will be identified on the console typewriter.

LABEL INSTRUCTIONS:

1403 PRINTER

STANDARD STOCK PAPER: YES [X] NO [ ]   FORM THICKNESS: [ ]   STANDARD CARRIAGE TAPE: YES [X] NO [ ] NO._____

CARRIAGE TAPE: CUT AT LINE NO. _____

CHANNEL NO.	1	2	3	4	5	6	7	8	9	10	11	12
LINE NUMBER												
LINE NUMBER												

REPORT NAME: Batch Control Report (Note 1)   NO. OF PARTS 2   LINES PER INCH 6 [X] 8

ALIGNMENT: 1st line to print 1 inch from top of form.

Note 1: This report should go to Step 15 immediately after EOJ.

SPECIAL FORMS: 11 x 14-7/8 2-part white 20# stock lined 3 to inch

DISTRIBUTION:

2540 READER

FILE NAME Prior Violation File Transactions   AVERAGE CARD VOLUME_____

SPECIAL INSTRUCTIONS

FORM NO. 0306-096

Figure 17-6. Production run setup sheet.

any particular time during processing can be displayed by lights and keys on the console. The *I*-address containing the address of an instruction, the data addresses of the information to be operated upon, and the storage location affected on each machine cycle all may be displayed on the console for operator use as required. In addition to the address registers there may be single character registers that can be displayed.

Normally there is another group of lights that signal adder error conditions, arithmetic overflow, and results of a comparison. These are usually called logic lights. Still another set of lights indicates that an input or output device requires operator attention.

Console Operating Procedures

The console operator has control over the computer and all of its input or output devices. He usually is the one who coordinates the input process and output operations of each procedure. The console operator generally follows the procedures as set out on the production run setup sheet (Figure 17-6). This sheet serves as a check list of operations to be performed in preparing the computer for performance under control of the proper program.

The production run setup sheet is prepared by the programmer and is his means of conveying to the operator what he must know to proceed with the processing operation. For example, the run sheet tells the operator which program deck, tape reels, or disk packs to use; which forms to use in the printer; and how to continue with the processing when departures from conventional procedures are necessary.

The console operator usually is responsible for having the computer read in the correct program, read in the correct input data, and produce the proper output. The console operator also must cause the proper procedures to be performed in the event of computer malfunctions, input inaccuracies, operator errors, or program mistakes.

If the computer stops because of a program or machine malfunction, a storage print out (dump) at the point of failure should normally be made. If the computer stopped because of a program error, the output, storage print out, and console readings at the time of the machine stop should be recorded and delivered to the programmer; and another job should be put on the machine immediately. In case of machine failure, the machine must be repaired and tested before the operation can continue. Some computers have more internal checking systems than others. Those with good checking systems will stop at the point of malfunction, which makes the problem easy to diagnose.

The console operator should also keep a computer operations log (Figure 17-7). This log should show the start, stop, and lapsed time for each job. The log may require other information deemed of value to management. This may include such things as maintenance, rerun times, and card volumes. Time recording machines may be used by the operator to record the various times.

Those computers with printer keyboard consoles that operate under control of an operating system may automatically prepare the computer operations log. This type of log usually shows the job number, job name, job start time, any interruptions to the process, and job stop time. In addition to providing operating information, this type of log may also be used for job accounting and job auditing activities. It also provides a means of communication

AUDITOR AND CONTROLLER
DATA PROCESSING DIVISION

DATE	WORK WEEK	SHIFT	SECTION	SUPERVISOR
3-1	36	1ST	4	

CLOCK TIME		METER TIME		EMPLOYEE NUMBER	JOB NUMBER			ACT. CODE	TYPE CODE
START	STOP	START	STOP		DEPT.	PROC.	FQ.		
7.8	7.9	263403	263404	16104	0302	06		1401	0
7.9	8.3	263404	263418	16104	5600	22			0
8.3	8.5	263418	263421	16104	0001	06			0
8.5	8.9	263421	263430	16104	0600	01			0
8.9	9.3	263430	263437	16104	0305	01			0
9.3	9.5	263437	263440	16104	0001	09			0
9.5	9.7	263440	263443	16104	0001	06			0
7.7	9.7	263443	263444	80960	0001	06			0
9.7	9.8	263444	263445	80960	0001	06			0
9.9	10.3	263445	263454	16104	0001	07			0
10.3	10.5	263454	263460	16104	0001	28			0
10.5	10.5	263460	263463	16104	0305	01			0
10.6	10.8	263463	263470	16104	6111	02			0
10.8	10.9	263470	263474	16104	0306	405			0
10.9	11.1	263474	263478	16104	0306	433			0
11.1	11.2	263478	263482	16104	0306	272			0
11.2	11.3	263482	263483	16104	0306	434			0
11.3	11.7	263483	263510	16104	5600	01			0
11.7	12.0	263510	263519	16104	5100	01			0
12.2	12.8	263519	263552	90500	0304	13			0
12.8	12.9	263552	263555	27049	0500	03			0
12.9	13.5	263555	263567	27049	0500	97			0
13.5	13.8	263567	263576	16104	5600	21			0
13.8	14.8	263576	263607	16104	0304	13			2

MACHINE ACTIVITY CODES		NON MACHINE ACTIVITY CODES	
024 Key Punch	519 Reproducer	805 Supervision, Training and Instruction	99700 Machine Operation
026 Key Punch	557 Interpretor	806 Conferences	99800 Machine Maintenance
056 Verifier	615 Burster	807 Housekeeping	99900 Machine Down Time
083 Sorter	1201 Inscriber	808 Assembly and Testing	
084 Sorter	1401 CPU	809 Control	
088 Collator	1402 Read Punch	810 Manual	
117 Decollator	1403 Printer	811 Scheduling	TYPE CODES
407 Tabulator		815 Telephone	
		816 Correspondence	0 Prime Time
		878 Procedures	1 Dual Time
		899 General	2 Rerun Time

Form 9

Figure 17-7. Computer operations log.

between the computer and the operator and between the computer and the programmer. The communication between computer and operator may occur from the computer to the operator or from the operator to the computer via commands issued by the operator at the printer keyboard.

Even though a console might technically be classed with the input-output devices to be discussed in the next section, it has been covered separately because of its special relationship to the whole EDP system.

OPERATION OF INPUT-OUTPUT UNITS

Card Readers and Punches

Card readers and punches may be either separate or combined machines. They all require operator attention. That is, the operator must place cards in the hopper where the machine may pick, feed, and read one card at a time. Further, when the stacker becomes full, the operator must remove the cards that were placed there after being read. Some card readers have a file feed device capable of holding up to 3,000 cards at a time. However, many card readers and punches have hoppers that can hold only about 1,000 cards at a time.

Most card readers and punches provide easy access to a jammed card in the hopper or transport mechanism. The operator need only remove or dismantle certain parts to gain access to the one or more cards fouled in the feed mechanism. After removal of the fouled cards, the removed transport parts are replaced, the damaged cards are made over and inserted in their proper place, and the job is restarted at the point of interruption. The majority of card readers and punches provide for restarting at the point of failure rather than requiring that the job be started over at the beginning. At the end of a job, the operator may have to run out the last one or two cards inside the unit by depressing the appropriate key. Many card readers and punches have an end-of-file button that may be depressed after the last cards have been placed in the hopper or file feed.

Magnetic Tape Units

The various makes and types of magnetic tape units are similar in general appearance and operation. They differ primarily in the speed at which the tape is moved past the read-write heads, and in the quantity of data recorded on an inch of tape (Figure 17-8).

Figure 17-8. Magnetic tape units. (*Courtesy Honeywell, Incorporated.*)

Various keys and switches are used to open and close the head assembly, to position the tape for reading or writing the first record, and to rewind the tape onto the file reel for unloading. A dial may be used to assign a number to the tape unit in order to associate the unit with the tape-drive number specified in the stored program. This dial setting should never be changed while a tape operation is in progress. Also, no two tape drives should ever have the same number at one time.

Many magnetic tape drives have a fixed three-character device address. The first character refers to the input-output channel, and the second and third characters identify the specific tape drive. This device addressing technique and a standard set of symbolic names used by the programmers allows a symbolic name to be assigned to, or identified with, any available magnetic tape drive.

Tape unit heads write and erase information by magnetizing extremely small areas on the tape. Because of the speed at which tape moves past the heads and because of the small size of these areas, magnetic tape requires careful handling to protect it from foreign particles, nicks, and kinks. The following are standard rules for proper tape handling.

1. Each reel of tape should be kept in a dust-proof container when it is not in use on a tape unit. It should be stored in a suitable cabinet, elevated from the floor and away from paper and cards which may be sources of dust.

2. The top of a tape unit should not be used as a work area as this exposes tape materials to heat and dust from the blowers in the tape drives and might interfere with the cooling of the drive unit.

3. A label material, such as adhesive stickers, that can be removed without leaving a residue should be used to externally identify a reel of tape. An eraser should never be used to alter the identification on a label.

4. File-protection rings should be removed carefully.

5. The tape reel should be handled near the hub or center of the reel. Pinching the reel or contacting the exposed edge of the tape should be avoided.

6. The tape surface should never be touched except in the leader area when threading the tape onto the take-up reel.

7. The tape drive heads should not be touched except for cleaning and maintenance.

8. The power should never be turned on when the tape head is down as this may erase valuable information from the tape.

9. Smoking should not be permitted in the machine room. Ashes can contaminate tape.

10. The entire machine room should be vacuumed every 24 hours, and the floor should be damp-mopped every day. Waxing should be kept to a minimum, and steel wool should never be used.

Mounting a magnetic tape on one of the most common types of tape units is accomplished in the following manner.

1. Open the hub latch and place the tape reel on the hub with the finger hold side out. Press the reel back until it is seated firmly against the stop, and close the hub latch.

2. Unwind about four feet of tape leader and thread the tape through the mechanism and onto the take-up reel.

3. Hook the tape onto the take-up reel and turn the take-up reel clockwise until the tape is wrapped around on itself. Continue to wind more tape on the take-up reel until the load point marker is several turns past the read/write heads.

4. Close the access door and depress the load rewind push button. This action pulls the tape into the vacuum columns, lowers the head, and rewinds the tape to the load-point marker.

5. Depress the start push button to place the tape unit under automatic control.

Disk Storage Units

As disk unit heads write and erase information by magnetizing extremely small areas on the disk surface, careful disk pack handling procedures are required. The following are standard rules for proper disk pack handling.

1. Each disk pack should be kept in its container when it is not in use on a disk drive. The container should be kept closed whenever it is not actually being handled.

2. The disk edges or surfaces should never be touched or left exposed.

3. A label material, such as adhesive stickers, that can be removed without leaving a residue should be used to externally identify a disk pack.

4. The exterior surface of the container should be kept clean and dust free.

5. The disk pack should always be handled with great care as the disk surfaces can easily be damaged through rough treatment or by being dropped. If the disk pack is even slightly damaged, the data on it will be lost forever as a damaged pack cannot be mounted on a disk drive.

6. The disk unit cover should never be opened unless the disk drive is stopped.

Every demountable disk pack is kept in a plastic container that resembles a cake cover. In loading a disk pack the following steps should be followed.

1. Hold the disk pack container firmly by the top handle, turn the locking knob on the bottom plate, remove the bottom plate, and set the plate aside.

2. With the disk unit stopped and the cover open, place the disk pack (still in the cover) on the spindle.

3. Rotate the cover in the direction of the "on" arrow until firm resistance is met, and lift the cover off.

4. Store the empty closed container.

5. Close the cover on the disk unit.

6. Move the start/stop switch on the disk unit to start. This action starts the disk pack rotating, causes the pack surfaces to be cleaned, and positions the read/write heads.

7. Move the enable/disable switch to enable. This makes the unit available to the system.

Magnetic Character Readers

Magnetic character readers operate in three basic modes: (1) reader off-line, (2) reader on-line, and (3) central processing unit on-line. In the off-line mode, document feeding, reading, and sorting are controlled by the keys on the operator's panel of the magnetic character reader. In the on-line mode, the central processing unit controls document feeding and reading while document distribution remains under the sorter operator's control. In the CPU on-line mode, document feeding, reading, and distribution are all under control of the stored program.

Magnetic character readers handle intermixed card and paper documents. Except for the document-feeding methods and the advanced technique used to read and recognize characters, the operating principles closely parallel those of conventional punched card sorters.

Printers

Most impact printers have knobs, dials, or switches that enable manual adjustment of vertical and lateral print alignment, print density, continuous forms feeding, and starting point alignments. Normal spacing during printing is in increments of six lines or eight lines an inch. This adjustment is controlled by a knob located on the printer or tractor feed device. Line spacing can be either single, double, or triple and is under control of the program.

Any movement of paper other than normal spacing is controlled by a paper or plastic tape with its two ends attached in the form of a belt. The tape with the proper punched holes for control of the form must be installed on the printer before the job can be started. The tape moves around the tape read mechanism in unison with the feeding of the continuous form. The punched holes in the tape, under program control, cause the tape and form to skip or stop skipping as instructed in the program.

All forms are moved past the print area by a forms tractor with pins that fit into marginally punched holes in the form. Forms are started into the printer by the operator and when the printer has run out of paper, another stack of forms can be started with a minimum of effort and delay. Printers also provide controls for forms feeding and stacking. Most printers are designed so that the operator can change the inked ribbon when it needs replacing (Figure 17-9).

The main operations involved in readying line printers are:

1. Loading the paper forms. All forms have two common features: they are assembled in continuous form with the pages separated by perforations, and both

Figure 17-9. High-speed printer. (*Courtesy International Business Machines Corporation.*)

side margins are punched with sprocket holes.

2. Aligning the forms so that printing is in the correct area.

3. Setting the printing controls to obtain the best quality printing.

4. Installing the carriage control tape.

5. Setting up the paper stacker.

6. Checking the first few forms printed for alignment and legibility.

THE OPERATOR'S DUTIES

To operate a computer system the operator must be knowledgeable in three areas:

1. The mechanical details of each component or unit. He must know how to load a reel of tape on a tape unit, how to load a disk pack into the disk unit, how to load blank forms into the line printer, and how to operate any of the other auxiliary units. These tasks are basic and easily learned. After the operator has performed such tasks once or twice he can perform them without difficulty.

2. The particular job being run on the computer. Information concerning the nature of each program and what is required of the operator is supplied in the run book.

3. Computer manufacturer supplied programs. The operator must know how to use compiler programs, utility programs, and control programs. The control program and the associated processing programs supplied by the vendor are commonly called a programming system. If the programming system has the ability to monitor the relatively uninterrupted execution of a number of programs, it is called an *operating system* which will be discussed in the following section.

EDP OPERATING SYSTEMS

During the past few years the trend in computer systems has been toward higher speeds, increased storage, and greater problem solving capability. These improvements in machine capabilities and their associated costs have created a great deal of interest in the efficiency with which systems are operated.

In many computer installations idle processing time may run as high as 65 per cent of the total available time. The input-output devices and associated control units often are utilized only 5 to 30 per cent of the time. These percentages of utilization should make it obvious that the processing speed for which the user is paying will seldom be properly exploited without some sort of internally stored master control program. Such a program is more commonly known as an *operating system*.

The operating system is designed to control the processing of various jobs individually or concurrently. An operating system is basically a program that super-vises the running of other programs. It includes such programming aids as program compilers, program testers, an input-output control system, a report program generator, a generalized sort-merge program, and various utility programs. In general, the operating system integrates these various types of programs into a single consistent system.

The primary purpose of operating systems is to reduce the cost of running problems (production) by increasing the utilization of the various computer components and by avoiding lost time. The main sources of lost time that all operating systems are designed to reduce are:

1. Job changing and the mounting and removal of files. This source of lost time is especially apparent when the setup time exceeds the processing time required by a small job.

2. Operator intervention to analyze error conditions and to initiate corrective action. If the operator is required to determine the cause of an error by consulting either the operator's manual or the programmer and then to initiate corrective action, this is certain to result in lost computer time.

3. Operator intervention required in the processing of service routines such as tape handling, program selection, and data or program correction routines.

4. Imbalance between the time required for central processor and input-output functions.

Some of the secondary objectives of an operating system are:

1. Increased programmer productivity.

2. Adaptability of programs to changing system components.

3. Expandability of the functional

capabilities of the operating system to meet changing circumstances.

4. Improved response times that will more readily meet real-time requirements.

Operating System Functions

Through the use of operating systems, part of the burden of improved electronic data processing efficiency is delegated to the computer itself. For an operating system to achieve the high efficiencies that present-day electronic data processing systems are capable of, it should:

1. Provide for efficient utilization of the processing unit as well as all input-output devices on the system. The operating system accomplishes this by scheduling jobs in such a way that their input-output and processing time requirements are balanced, thus reducing idle processing unit time.

2. Provide for the automatic scheduling and loading of programs into memory.

3. Provide for the processing of jobs in the input job file, in accordance with control card instructions, by (a) scheduling jobs, (b) overlapping jobs requiring operator action with jobs requiring no operator action, and (c) issuing messages to the operator.

4. Provide for the queueing and dispatching of input-output results.

5. Provide for the receiving, processing, and dispatching of remote messages.

6. Provide a means of exercising control after a program is interrupted, saving the status of the interrupted program, and determining the routine required to process the interrupt condition.

7. Include, as part of itself, standard error handling procedures, thus assuring that operator intervention is kept to a minimum. It should also include a method whereby programs that require long processing times need not be restarted from the beginning when an error occurs, but only from a previous checkpoint. This allows programs with errors to be interrupted and saved until the error condition is corrected. Other programs can then be processed pending continuance of the interrupted program.

8. Furnish a record (log) of what happened during processing for all programs and the time required for each job.

9. Include the ability to generate and maintain an operating system that meets the requirements of a particular installation. For example, if certain segments of the operating system have not been used recently, it will cause them to be stored in more remote areas thereby making that prime storage area available for more useful routines.

10. Provide a program tester that enables a program or part of a program to be loaded and tested in accordance with simple and concise specifications. The specifications are comprised of symbols and definitions appearing in the original source program.

11. Provide an interruption-handling program that coordinates transfer of control between programs after an interruption. The five types of interruption that must be covered are input-output, external, program, machine, and those that are required by the operating system. The interruptions should aid the operating system in optimizing use of all the peripheral equipment as well as the processing unit. A comprehensive interrupt system allows many programs to share memory at the same time. Idle processing unit time is reduced to a minimum and input-output operations for several jobs can be proc-

essed simultaneously while processing of another job is taking place.

Programs that are to be used with an operating system may be written without regard to absolute memory locations and physical input-output units. Thus, should the user add any peripheral equipment to his system, the operating system adjusts to the change automatically. This provides maximum benefits from the increased input-output capacity without necessitating any change in the program.

The Operating System in Operation

The operating system is actually a composite of many programs which can be united in a variety of combinations. Therefore, before the operating system is ready for operation it must be tailored to the requirements of the installation and the jobs to be performed. This tailoring of the operating system is achieved by a segment of the system generally referred to as a *system librarian*. The system librarian also has the ability to modify, add, delete, and replace programs in the system to reflect changes in the installation's input-output equipment and storage size, the user's objectives, and other needs.

Once the operating system is generated and stored in the computer it is ready for operation. The sequence of events required to compile and execute a typical job might be:

1. Clear the computer for the next job to be processed.

2. Read control cards and make input-output and scratch (working) tape assignments.

3. Load the program compiler into primary storage.

4. Process the source program, generate the object program, store the object program in the system library maintained in auxiliary storage, and transfer the object program from the system library to primary storage for execution. This is an exception to the procedure of recording the object program in an external storage medium such as punched cards or magnetic tape.

5. Pass control to the object program which reads data, performs the necessary processing, and produces output.

6. Return control to the operating system upon completion of the object program.

This is a "job-at-a-time" or one-phase illustration. A similar cycle would be entered for the next job to be processed.

Another concept is the three-phase system. As almost all computer programs involve three functions, input data reading, computation or processing, and output result writing, it is logical for the operating system to handle each job in three separate phases. During phase one, input data is converted if necessary — decimal to binary, for example. Conversion requirements are specified by control cards or control codes in the data cards. Also, program translation may take place during phase one.

During phase two the programs go into execution, and the results are recorded on a medium such as magnetic tape or disk in a language basic to the computer.

During phase three the output results recorded during phase two may be converted for printing or punching. Also, debugging (error identification) data may be converted to symbolic formats to facilitate analysis by the programmer.

Other operating system features, in addition to the ability to execute programs in any of the three phases, include tape error recovery procedures, data input-output channel supervision, and standard or special handling of automatic computer branches (called traps) and error conditions. All of these utilize overlap features of the computer without detailed concern by the programmer. In short, the operating system enables the stacking and overlapping of jobs and computer functions.

Multiprogramming with the Operating System

Multiprogramming is the technique whereby more than one program can reside in primary storage at the same time and be executed concurrently. Although only one program can be executed at a time, the supervisor program rapidly switches control between the programs and gives the effect of simultaneous operation. For example, one program might be processing a batch job, another program might be performing a utility function, and a third program might be handling a remote terminal operation. The supervisor program would monitor the concurrent processing of these three programs so that the utility program would be executed with minimal interruption to the processing of the batch program, and the remote terminal program would be executed on request by the terminal operator.

To accomplish this interleaving of programs, the control program and equipment must be capable of recognizing the point at which a program being executed must wait for the completion of some auxiliary processing phase. At that point, the control program begins another processing task that is ready for execution. When that is done, the control program must be able to proceed to another task or return to the previous unfinished program, if it is ready to continue. Since several programs may be in stages of partial completion, multiprogramming usually requires that levels of priority be specified for different tasks.

Remote Message Processing with the Operating System

The efficient operation of most organizations depends on a consistent flow of a wide variety of timely information. For effective decision making the right kind of information must be at the right place, in the right form, and at the right time. To speed the information flow and reduce the data-to-decision time to a minimum in a large organization, an efficient remote message processing network is necessary.

Remote message processing is, in effect, an extension of the full power of the data processing and programming facilities of the operating system to remote locations. By extending the services of the operating system directly to the user of a remote terminal, the turnaround or response time of the system is reduced to seconds. Consequently, the system can directly control and participate in activities taking place in various parts of an organization. Remote message processing has the additional advantage of enabling centralized records to be updated instantaneously as transactions occur at different locations.

The operating system has the ability to process messages received from remote locations by means of communication lines and special equipment. Processing of remote messages differs from other types of data processing mainly in the way in which information enters and leaves the computer. Messages from remote locations enter the system in random order at unpredictable intervals and often demand a response within a few seconds. This ability to receive and process data so rapidly that the results are available in time to influence operations that are still in progress is commonly called *real-time* data processing.

The EDP system may be engaged in performing other functions when a remote message is received. Therefore, some means must be provided for interrupting the program in operation to allow the receipt and processing of the remote message and the dispatch of a return message, if necessary. As indicated before, the interrupt procedure and control of the interrupted program are functions of the operating system. The operating system will on command:

1. Interrupt the job in process provided it has a lower priority than that of the request.

2. Cause the interrupted program and its restart point to be temporarily stored outside of the main memory in an auxiliary storage.

3. Cause the proper program for handling the interrupt request to be loaded into main memory.

4. Process the requirements of the request.

5. Return the interrupted program to main memory.

6. Restart the program at its point of interruption.

All of this process, known as *roll-out* and *roll-in,* could take place within a very few seconds.

The real-time processing concept is illustrated in the banking application that follows.

Today's EDP system provides to the user a vast accumulation of technology and experience. A system with the right amount of direct access storage under control of an operating system is capable of handling concurrently several extremely large and complex data processing applications on a truly real-time basis. This capability to reflect the status of several applications as the factors affecting their operation are fed into the EDP system can bring to management with unprecedented speed and accuracy the information required to operate today's complex business organization. Real-time processing has made possible the prompt consideration of interactions between the various facets of business such as sales and production, or production and purchasing. This is a great step toward the *total system concept* in business data processing.

AN EDP BANKING SYSTEM

A large bank with many branches using centralized processing and filing of banking data has been selected to illustrate the capacity and versatility of today's EDP systems. The system used in this illustration could fulfill all of the data processing requirements of a large banking organization and still have time to provide services to outside organizations. To make this possible an EDP system similar to the following would be required (Figure 17-10).

1. Two central processing units with simultaneous control and a processor switching unit.

2. Two mass random storage units.

3. Several magnetic tape drive units.

4. One high-speed printer.

5. One punched card read-punch unit.

6. Two magnetic ink character sorter reader units.

7. Several transmission control units.

8. Many teller terminals (window posting machines). (See Figure 11-10.)

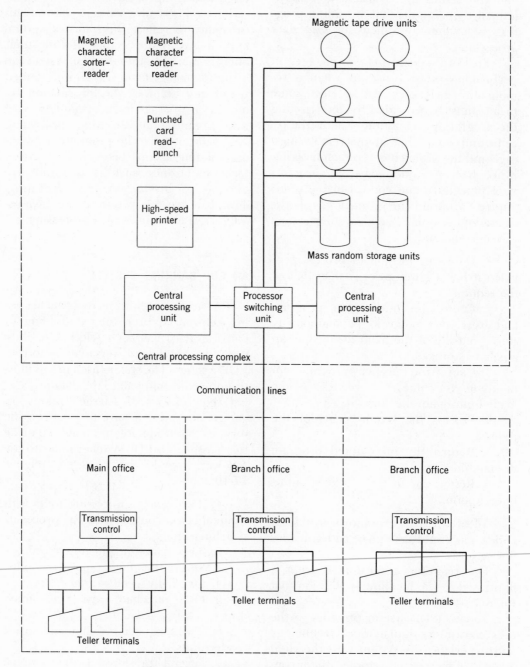

Figure 17-10. Schematic of EDP banking system.

During normal business hours one of the processing units is occupied handling teller terminal transactions on an on-line basis. The second processing unit is used to process off-line jobs. In the event of failure of the first processing unit, the second unit is available for temporary handling of on-line transactions.

An on-line savings system makes the savings records stored on the random storage device available to tellers in the main office or branches whenever needed. For example, a step-by-step processing of a savings withdrawal transaction occurs as follows:

1. Reading from the passbook, the teller enters the customer's account balance on the terminal keyboard.

2. The teller enters the amount of the withdrawal on the terminal keyboard.

3. In this system the entering of the customer's account number through the terminal keyboard signals the computer that this is the end of the message. At this point the EDP processing unit takes control and the terminal keyboard is locked out against further manual entries.

4. After receiving the withdrawal transaction from the terminal, the processing unit first checks the message to ensure that it has been transmitted accurately. The processing unit informs the teller of any error that is detected by turning on the error indicator light. If such a condition should occur, the teller would merely reenter the data.

5. Once the processing unit is satisfied that the message is accurate, it accesses the customer's account status in the working file stored in the random storage unit.

6. The processing unit then makes several tests of the account in memory and the transaction data to ascertain the following:

a. Does the balance entered by the teller agree with the record in memory? If not, the processing unit signals the teller that an error has been made and instructs him to reenter the data.

b. Does the withdrawal transaction exceed the customer's available balance? If so, the processing unit signals the teller that an overdraft would occur if this transaction were processed.

c. Has any type of hold condition been placed on this account? If so, the teller is informed.

d. Are any unposted entries such as interest included in the stored record? If so, they are prepared for transmission to the terminal for posting to the customer's passbook.

7. After all the tests have been completed, the processing unit instructs the terminal to update the customer's passbook. It also rewrites the updated version of this account back on the working file and stores certain data about the transaction in a separate section of the random storage file. This data is used at the end of the day to update the master file and to prepare reports.

8. As the message to update the customer's passbook is flashed to the terminal, the message is automatically checked for accuracy of transmission.

9. In addition to posting the transaction to the customer's passbook, the terminal accumulates the necessary individual teller's totals and prints the entries on an audit journal.

The teller terminals also may be used to handle deposits, mortgage payments, money order preparation, check cashing, and other transactions suited to terminal use.

The EDP system performs many off-line processing functions for the bank. For example, at the end of the day the current day's teller terminal transactions that were stored on the random storage device are read into the processing unit, sorted into account number order by branch, and re-written onto the random storage device in new sequential order. At the same time, a printed record of the day's activity is prepared in the sequence in which the transactions occurred. Next, the savings master file is updated and a trial balance is printed by branch. Any necessary reports relative to uncollected funds, significant balance changes, new accounts, etc., can be prepared.

The central EDP system is also used at the close of each business day to process the MICR encoded items received from each branch bank. Through the magnetic character sorter-reader, the encoded documents are read into the computer system at a rate of over 1,200 a minute. During this input operation, many results are achieved.

1. Batches of items are proved to control totals established by each branch bank.

2. Completeness and validity of magnetic encoding are verified.

3. The data on the items is written out on magnetic tape.

4. Controls are established for the various types of accounts.

5. An input journal is created to provide a complete audit trail of the items that enter the EDP system.

Miscellaneous items such as change of address, change of account status, etc., are read into the computer by the punched card reader.

After all of the data from the encoded documents and punched cards has been read into the EDP system, the random items stored on magnetic tape during the input operation are sorted into account number and transaction code order. In addition to providing a file of sequenced items, this operation provides a printed transaction journal showing in account number order the amount of each transaction and the transaction code.

Next, the master file of checking accounts maintained on magnetic tape for the main office and each branch bank is updated. The EDP system accomplishes this by posting the sequenced transactions to their respective accounts in the master file. This updating operation produces the following results:

1. The active accounts are updated to reflect the daily transactions.

2. A new updated master file is written, and the old one is retained for backup in the event of damage to the current master file tape.

3. A complete daily trial balance is printed.

4. Controls are established to prove the accuracy of the posting.

5. Statement information is generated and written out on magnetic tape.

6. Exception report data is generated and written out on magnetic tape.

Following the daily updating procedure, the EDP system prepares for the main office and each branch bank a complete trial balance of checking accounts and other management reports. These reports, along with checks and deposits sequentially sorted by account number, are delivered by messenger before the banks open for business each day.

Customer statements are prepared on a cycle basis designed to spread the workload evenly throughout the month. These statements are mailed to each customer along with the sequentially sorted canceled checks.

Loan accounting, trust accounting, and safe deposit income accounting are some of the other financial activities that can be processed as off-line applications. In addition to other internal applications, such as general accounting, payroll, budgetary control, and trust investment control, the EDP system has made possible the processing of certain management information. Economic forecasting, retail market analysis, bank bond portfolio analysis, bond bidding, and asset management are some of the areas where management has been helped by computer information analysis.

As mentioned earlier, the processing of all these jobs would not consume all of the computer time available. Therefore, many banks have been making their EDP facilities available to other financial institutions such as correspondent banks, savings banks, mutual funds, and security brokers. Banks also have been providing EDP services to local businesses. These services include payroll accounting, account reconcilement, accounts receivable accounting, and inventory control, to name a few.

Applications of this magnitude are a clear indication of the capacity of today's EDP systems to handle a great variety and large volume of operations both rapidly and efficiently.

Review Questions

1. What is the function of batch tickets?
2. What are the functions of forms separators and forms detachers?
3. Briefly describe one method for successful scheduling.
4. What are the principal responsibilities of the console operator?
5. How may data be manually entered into storage?
6. Why does magnetic tape require careful handling?
7. What is an operating system?
8. How do operating systems improve data processing efficiency?
9. What is the function of the operating system librarian?
10. What is multiprogramming?
11. How does remote message processing reduce the data-to-decision time to a minimum?
12. Define the term "real-time data processing."

18

DATA COMMUNICATIONS

Much of man's progress has depended and will continue to depend on his ability to communicate. For over a hundred years electrical communication has been one of the most useful methods employed. Traditionally, electrical communication services such as the telephone and the telegraph have served primarily as a means of transmitting information between people. However, modern man, confronted with an ever-increasing need for rapid, accurate transmission of data between widely scattered business offices, government offices, and industrial plants, has had to develop new methods of communicating. As a result, electrical communication has assumed a new role—now it is serving as a link between machines, and between people and machines.

A link of this type, consisting of devices for sending and receiving data and the medium by which the data is transmitted, is known as a *data communications system*. A data communications system represents the merging of two technologies: high-speed electrical communication and electronic data processing. The pur-

pose of this chapter is to provide an introduction to the concepts and techniques of this rapidly growing field.

SIGNIFICANCE OF DATA COMMUNICATIONS

In today's complex and vigorous society, an enormous amount of information is generated daily by the activities of both public and private organizations. To achieve maximum usefulness, much of this information needs to be transmitted promptly to one or more points remote from its origin. Thus, every organization with activities in more than one location, or complex activities in a single location, must provide a system of communications for effective performance, operational efficiency, and management control. The extent to which business, government, and other large organizations are dependent on information and the movement of information is briefly discussed in the following paragraphs.

Data Communications in Government

National Defense. The U.S. Department of Defense employs what is undoubtedly the largest combination of computer and communications systems in the world. NMCS, National Military Command System, comprises more than forty Army, Navy, and Air Force systems that provide up-to-the-second information about our military status anywhere in the world.

A striking example of a huge information and control center also involved in defense is NORAD, North America Air Defense Command, at Colorado Springs. NORAD's Combat Operations Center maintains close vigil on the air and sea space surrounding the North American continent. Information from hundreds of sources is transmitted to the center's thirteen computers by means of a vast communications network. Among the sources are huge Ballistic Missile Early Warning Systems (BMEWS) at Clear, Alaska, at Thule, Greenland, and at Fylingdales Moor, England; the Distant Early Warning (DEW) Line, consisting of an unbroken radar wall across the top of the continent; and hundreds of other radars strategically located throughout the United States and Canada.

Data regarding more than 200,000 flights daily in North America is fed into this huge computerized warning center, with special attention being given to the 800 to 1,200 flights that originate overseas. In addition, NORAD's Space Defense System (SDS) keeps up-to-the-instant on everything happening in space. By means of data transmitted over communications lines from a variety of detection devices, NORAD maintains a comprehensive record of the positions of all orbiting objects. The future orbits of satellites are calculated by the computers and anticipated tracks can be displayed on a screen in the Combat Operations Center. As a result, the staff can see the paths a satellite will follow for as many as 12 revolutions in the future. Figure 18-1 shows the course of a U.S.-launched weather-reconnaissance satellite as charted on the screen by an electronic computer. The traces indicate its present position as well as the course it will follow for its next two trips around the globe.

NORAD's giant computer and communications systems have the ability to cope with staggering amounts of information. Incoming information is received by an input-output data controller which converts signals into data that can be used by the computers or stored until needed. The converter can reverse the procedure by taking data already stored and converting it back into signals for transmission to distant sites. Information processed by the center's thirteen computers is translated into language symbols which may be projected in seven colors on wall-size, transparent display boards of Eurasia and North America spread out before the observers. Between the observation of an event, its digestion and interpretation by the computers, and its display on consoles, there is an insignificant delay that can be measured in millionths of a second. Thus the observers are provided at every moment with real-time information concerning the continent's status.

Federal Agencies. The federal government employs a number of very large data communications networks in addition to those used for military purposes. For example, the United States Weather Bureau maintains an extensive network to collect and disseminate weather information to the Federal Aviation Agency, commercial airlines, agricultural organizations, and the general public. The Federal Aviation Agency, the Social Security Administration, and the Veterans Administration have established extensive facilities for transmitting both voice and data communications between their various locations.

The National Aeronautics and Space Administration uses a large communications network for data acquisition and tracking in connection with its activities. The success of the many phases of each space mission—design, development, test, preflight checkout, launch, injection into orbit, stabilization and control, guidance, reentry, recovery, and subsequent

analysis of data—is largely dependent on the vast communications facilities that are employed and the power of computers to process data.

Law Enforcement. Law enforcement activities in the United States are divided among a great many state, county, and municipal organizations that are highly interdependent. Effective law enforcement requires a flow of information between these organizations. To achieve rapid communications and ready access to records, many of the most advanced data communications techniques are used. Many states today have installed extensive

Figure 18-1. Course of weather-reconnaissance satellite charted on screen by electronic computer. (*Courtesy North American Air Defense Command.*)

communications networks to send various messages including reports of suspects and stolen property. These networks are interconnected with those of other states to facilitate the rapid exchange of information throughout the country.

Trends in law enforcement indicate increasing dependence on data communications. This is especially evident in the tendency toward automation of police information systems and the establishment of regional record centers.

Data Communications in Business

Business is recognizing, at an ever-increasing rate, the advantages of company-wide data communications networks as a means of effectively managing widespread operations. Consequently, it has been estimated that by 1975, 60 to 75 per cent of the amount spent annually on computer systems will be spent for communications terminal equipment and communications services. It has also been predicted that the volume of information transmitted in the form of digital data will eventually equal the volume transmitted by voice.

As companies grow in size, become more widely dispersed, and more diverse in their operations, and at the same time try to give better service at lower prices, the problems of effective internal communications increase. Data communications plays an important role in keeping a company in touch with its own divisions as well as with its customers and suppliers. The rapid collection and transmission to a central point of data from outlying facilities such as manufacturing plants, warehouses, regional sales offices, and other branch offices provides the management of large organizations with timely information about overall operations. This tech-

nique also reduces the number of times and places at which data must be manually handled and transcribed, thus, reducing clerical costs and the possibility of errors. Data generated and/or processed at a central facility can also be transmitted rapidly to outlying locations. Just as the prompt collection of data is important to a large organization, the prompt dissemination of information also plays a vital role in effective operations.

Data communications also serves to reduce operating expenses. Companies with decentralized plant operations often find it advantageous to handle payroll, purchasing, billing, and other functions on a centralized basis. By means of data communications, all branch time cards, invoices, bills, etc., can be processed at a central location, thus, improving efficiency and reducing clerical operations at each of the plants.

Data communications plays an especially important role in the management of large enterprises. As a result of advances in electrical communications, business executives have almost immediate access to detailed data concerning widespread operations, formerly delayed by distance, traffic, or technical limitations. It is now possible to send information anywhere in the nation, in almost any form, with speed and accuracy. In just a few minutes, a sales, inventory, production, or financial report can be transmitted wherever needed so that a management decision can be based on timely information. Data communications can also deliver promptly all types of information vital to forecasting. Thus an efficient communications system assures that overall planning and control are based on information that is accurate, comprehensive, and up-to-date.

Efficient data communications has been an essential element in the widespread development of on-line and real-time data processing. *On-line* means that all elements of the system, including remote terminals, are interconnected with and perform under control of a computer. Many organizations find it advantageous to establish central data files that can be randomly accessed to provide prompt responses to inquiries from outlying locations. Thus the basic data flow pattern is in both directions. Inquiry messages are transmitted from remote terminals to the central processing facility. Appropriate responses are generated and transmitted back to the inquiring terminals.

The on-line inquiry processing function is often combined with real-time functions. *Real-time* means the ability of a system to collect data about transactions as they occur, and to process that data so rapidly that the resulting new information is available in time to influence the process being monitored or controlled. In a system designed for real-time updating, the central data files are modified each time a transaction occurs so that the central files always reflect the true current status of the situation involved. This provides an accurate, up-to-the-minute basis for responding to succeeding inquiries and influencing further events such as transactions, operations, special reports, or manufacturing processes.

Real-time inquiry systems are especially useful to organizations such as banks, brokerage firms, hotels, and airlines, where prompt servicing of customer inquiries is of primary importance. The reservation systems of airlines are good examples of on-line real-time information systems. When a customer wishes to make a reservation on a particular flight, the ticket agent, using a special keyboard terminal that is on-line to the computer, questions the computer about the availability of seats

on that flight. The computer responds with the necessary information. If a seat is available, the agent then keys in an order for one seat. The computer records the reservation immediately and revises the inventory of seats for that flight so that following inquiries will show one less available seat.

FUNCTIONS OF DATA COMMUNICATIONS

Because system requirements differ from one organization to another, the data communications systems in use today vary widely in their functions, their structures, and their degree of complexity. However, systems generally follow three basic patterns which are illustrated in Figure 18-2. In this illustration a circle represents a

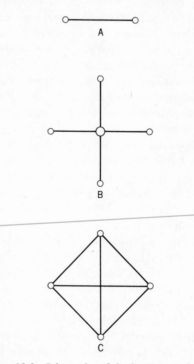

Figure 18-2. Schematic of basic communications networks.

terminal that can send messages, receive messages, or both. The connecting lines represent the communications channel or circuit, which can be a wire, cable, radio or microwave.

Network *A* represents a simple point-to-point network, i.e., two computers or other terminal devices connected by a channel. Organizations with two or more computers in different locations may find it advantageous to connect them by a communications line of this type to facilitate computer load balancing. Thus, if one computer experiences a slack period while the other has an excessive work load, some of the excess work can be transferred to the less active computer. In addition to providing more effective utilization, communications links also make it possible for one or more computers to take over another computer's work load in the event of a breakdown. Furthermore, since each computer in such an arrangement has access to the data stored in the memory of other units, it is unnecessary to duplicate the contents of all the storage units. In this way the total amount of information that can be stored in the system is increased.

Network *B* illustrates a situation in which two terminals can communicate over channels only by passing through a third terminal. Network *B* also describes a system in which a central office can transmit data to outlying locations. A weather broadcast network that transmits weather reports to many stations is an example of this type. Conversely, outlying branches can communicate with a main office. For example, sales offices may transmit orders to a centralized data processing center for further processing.

Another example of the use of a *B* type network is for computer time sharing. The purpose of a time-sharing system is to furnish continuous computing service to many users through the simultaneous use of a single facility. To accomplish this a large-capacity computer at a centralized location is tied to terminals at various remote locations by a communications link. Each remote terminal has direct and immediate access to the entire capability of the data processing facilities at the centralized location. Programs and other data can be entered into the system through each of the remote terminals. The system provides the user with a response so rapidly that he feels he has exclusive use of the computer. Actually, however, the computer services users in sequence with the operating system allocating short "slices of time" to each user in the order of microseconds or milliseconds. Generally, when a participant's time allotment is used up, his job goes into the waiting line for a fraction of a second until its turn arrives again. This is controlled by the operating system which causes the interrupted program and its restart point to be temporarily stored outside of main memory in an auxiliary storage unit until processing is resumed. In spite of interruptions, the high speed of the computer makes it appear that all of the users are being served simultaneously.

The basic data flow pattern in a time-sharing system is necessarily bidirectional; operating instructions and input data are transmitted from the terminals to the central computer facility and the results of processing are transmitted back to the appropriate terminals. It is entirely possible that in the future this capability will result in the widespread development of large centralized computer utilities providing services to a great many users.

Network *C* is the most complex of the basic distribution patterns. This is a multi-terminal system in which each terminal is able to exchange information with every other point in the system.

COMMUNICATIONS MEDIA AND CODES

Data to be transmitted may originate from a number of physical forms or media. Included are handwritten or printed pages, punched cards, punched paper tape, magnetic tape, imprinted magnetic ink characters, microfilm, or computer memory, all of which have been described in preceding chapters. Although the data at the sending end may be in a form that can be transmitted, it may not satisfy the requirements at the receiving end. For example, data on a printed page might be needed at the receiving office in punched card form. Thus, the data would have to be recorded on punched cards before transmission, or it could be transmitted in its original form by a facsimile system and transcribed by a card punch operator at the receiving end.

Most of the data that is transmitted is recorded in coded form. The exceptions are visual display, facsimile, and handwriting transmissions. One of the codes that has been most commonly used for communications is the five-level Baudot Code. A number of variations of the five-level code are in use as well as six-, seven-, and eight-level codes. However, a recently developed standard code provides the basis for achieving coding uniformity of data interchanged between data processing and communications systems. In June 1967 the United States of America Standards Institute adopted a new data processing code, known as USASCII (U.S.A. Standard Code for Information Interchange) (see Table 12-3). Although the adoption of this seven-level code by installations is voluntary, it is anticipated that its use will become widespread.

The various codes other than US-ASCII were designed for certain types and makes of equipment and certain applications. These codes have been useful. However, with the ever-increasing scope of data processing, their differences become more restrictive because of the growing need for interchange between diverse types of equipment. For example, many data processing applications now require computer centers to process data collected from various remote points. Information at those locations may be originated by different methods and machines. Furthermore, data communications requirements may involve a wide range of terminals and multiplexers that may not be fully compatible.

Since it is generally not possible for data to be recorded in the same medium and code throughout a system, some conversion is essential. It may be necessary to convert from a paper tape code to a card code, from a card code to magnetic tape code, or from magnetic tape code to paper tape code (Figure 18-3). It is desirable to capture original data in a machine-sensible language at the source if possible. In this way any further processing, transfer, or conversion of the data can be handled automatically by machines. USASCII has made it possible to achieve eventual standardization of the specifications and formats of each of the media used to record data, thus, facilitating the conversion and general interchange of data among all kinds of data processing systems, communications systems, and associated equipment.

DATA COMMUNICATIONS EQUIPMENT

Data transmission of a basic point-to-point type is generally accomplished in

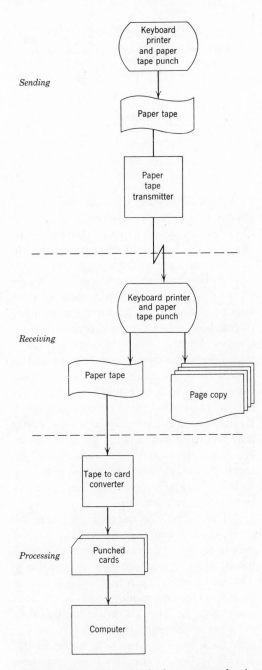

Figure 18-3. Data communications system showing conversion of transmitted data for use as computer input.

five stages. The data goes from (1) an input device to (2) a transmitting terminal, then through (3) an electrical transmission link to (4) a receiving terminal and, finally, to (5) an output device. The functions performed and the facilities used in each of these stages (illustrated in Figure 18-4) are described in the following sections.

Input-Output

In most cases, data that is entered into a transmitting system is captured in an independent operation and then physically moved to the input terminal unit. This is true of such media as cards, magnetic tape, and paper tape. However, certain transmitting units may also accept data from a computer storage device, or data that is entered manually through a keyboard, by dialing, or by inserting a coded badge or card into a reading device. Thus, the input device at the transmitting terminal may be a paper tape reader, card reader, magnetic tape unit, keyboard, computer, or special data collection device.

The output device at the receiving terminal may be a tape punch, card punch, printer, magnetic tape unit, display device, or computer.

Transmitting-Receiving Terminals

Data communications terminals differ widely with respect to input-output media, compatibility with other equipment, speed, flexibility, and operating characteristics. However, the components of different terminals are essentially the same. As shown in Figure 18-4, these include input-output control units, error control units, synchronization units, and

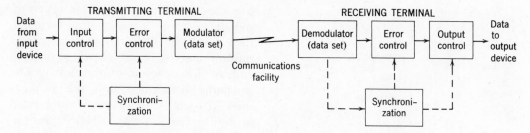

Figure 18-4. Data flow in a typical data communications system.

modulation-demodulation units. Although several of these units are generally contained in a single cabinet and sold as a single communications terminal device, their individual functions will be described briefly.

The *input control unit* at the transmitting terminal controls and accepts data from the input device at a rate generally determined by the speed of the input device. The control unit stores the data temporarily by means of a buffer device and transmits it at a speed suitable to the communications facility. At the receiving terminal, the *output control unit* accepts the data that is received, stores it temporarily, and transfers it to the output device at an appropriate rate.

Not all data communications terminals contain buffered input-output control units. If no buffers are used, the input, data transmission, and output functions occur simultaneously and at the same speed.

Error control units are used to detect, indicate, and possibly correct errors that occur during transmission. In most error control systems the digital data at the transmitting terminal is encoded according to some set pattern. At the receiving terminal, the data is decoded and checked to see if the data pattern meets standard requirements.

The two commonly used methods for automatic checking of data are validity checking and parity checking. A *validity check* assures the accuracy of character representation. Thus, any code configuration that does not represent a legitimate member of the character set being used is recognized as an error. *Parity checking* consists of determining whether the number of one bits in the characters received meets the established odd or even standard.

Since data signals are transmitted at precise time intervals, some means must be provided to assure synchronization between transmitting and receiving stations. By means of *synchronization units,* sending and receiving instruments are able to operate continuously at substantially the same frequency and are maintained, by means of correction if necessary, in a desired phase relationship.

The signals generated by terminal input devices usually have to be modified before they can be transmitted over common-carrier communications facilities. The unit used at the transmitting terminal to complete this modification is called a *modulator*. At the receiving terminal a *demodulator* is needed to convert the signals back into a form acceptable to the output device. Typically, both functions are performed by a modulation-demodulation unit used for two-way data communications. This unit is commonly called a *data set* or *modem* (Figure 18-5).

Figure 18-5. DATA-PHONE data set. (*Courtesy American Telephone and Telegraph Company.*) ·

Data sets can not only convert input signals into tones the communications channels can handle but also can provide a means for dialing and setting up the connection. Data sets are furnished by the common carriers for use with many different types of communications terminals. The following section is devoted to a description of some of these terminals.

Data Transmission Terminal Equipment

Keyboard-Only Devices. Keyboard-only devices are generally used to transmit data for input to a device such as a computer or card punch. The push-button telephone is a good example of a keyboard-only device. Instead of a rotary dial, this telephone model has push buttons. These push buttons generate tones that direct calls through the telephone network (Figure 18-6).

Calls are placed by depressing the buttons corresponding to the desired telephone number. When the call has been completed the telephone can be used to carry on a conversation or to transmit data by means of the push buttons. For example, let us assume that a call is placed from a push-button telephone to a receiving set connected to a card punch. The receiving set automatically accepts the call, transmits an answer tone, and connects the card punch to the line. Data is then entered by depressing the appropriate buttons on the telephone. Depressing the buttons creates tones that are transmitted over the line to the receiving data set. The data set converts the tones to electrical signals that are transferred to the card punch. The card punch reproduces the original data by punching holes in a card.

The telephone model illustrated in Figure 18-6 also permits automatic dialing by using punched plastic cards. Data may also be punched in the cards and transmitted to computers or other receiving devices. For example, some whole-

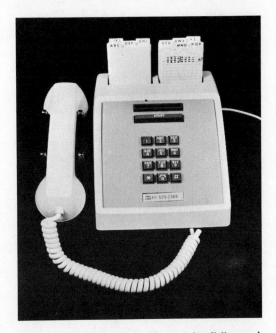

Figure 18-6. A telephone that permits dialing and transmission of data by means of push buttons or punched card. (*Courtesy American Telephone and Telegraph Company.*)

salers have installed systems that allow customers to enter orders quickly and easily. When a customer wishes to place an order, he dials the phone number of the wholesaler and identifies his company by feeding a prepunched identity card into the reading device attached to the telephone. He then feeds into the reader a punched card describing the first item he wishes to order. On a signal that the contents of the card have been transmitted, he enters the quantity desired through keys on the keyboard of the transmitting device. He then feeds in the next item card, and so on through the entire order. At the receiving end an automatic key punch, connected to the receiving device, produces a set of cards describing the complete order. No written purchase order is transmitted. At the end of the month the wholesale firm provides each customer with a listing of all orders entered.

The following example indicates how the push-button telephone is used in an audio response system at the Rohr Corporation plants in Chula Vista and Riverside, California. The system has as its basic elements the touch-tone telephone and the computer. If an employe wants to know the present location of an order for parts or material, he lifts the touch-tone receiver and on the phone keyboard presses a predetermined digit code for an order location inquiry. The audio response unit, with a prerecorded female voice, responds with a request for the "register number." The employee then enters the order register number by pressing the proper keys on the touch-tone keyboard, sending a question to the computer in the form of a series of electronic impulses. The computer then checks the register number on its disk files for status information and instructs the prerecorded voice

drum to respond with appropriate and up-to-date data on the status of the order. If the order is in transit, the voice drum responds with "from location," "date," and "time," plus "to location," "date," and "time." The system could also give priority ratings for the order.

The foregoing is a simple example of a system which is much more expansive in its capabilities. It can deal with many facets of manufacturing such as new order inputs, history of an order, the moving of an order to a new location, quantity adjustments, and so on. It can also be applied to financial and other management problems. This use of large-scale computers coupled with audio response systems has greatly improved data processing flexibility, thus, permitting current status reports and progress to be determined on a real-time basis.

Keyboard Printers. Teletype machines were among the earliest and are now probably the best known of the units available for wire transmission. Teletypewriter service does for written data what the telephone does for spoken data. It is a versatile written communication system that permits transmission and receipt of messages and data between two points by telephone lines. Teletype machines will transmit direct from a four-row keyboard similar to that of a typewriter (Figure 18-7). Printed copy can be produced at both the sending and receiving ends. In addition, data can be transmitted and received in eight-channel punched paper tape for direct input to a data processing system. Operators can also produce punched tape off-line for later transmission. Thus tapes can be prepared in advance, checked for accuracy, accumulated, and transmitted automatically at a more rapid rate than would be possible with manual typing.

Since teletypewriter equipment pro-

Figure 18-7. Teletype Automatic Send-Receive set. (*Reproduced by permission of Teletype Corporation.*)

vides a fast means of written communication, the service is used extensively in transmitting prices, statistics, quotations, and similar data requiring written verification. Other applications include the transmission of invoices, payroll checks, personnel records, sales orders, freight bills, tracers, summaries of daily business activity, sales reports, production schedules, and other business data. For example, an associated group of gas companies set up a central service center to purchase and store supplies. Each member company uses a teletypewriter to transmit purchase requisitions to the center. The center fills requisitions from the forms received on their machine. Besides providing instant communications and a permanent record of each transaction, this procedure has en-

abled the group to reduce the cost of supplies by purchasing larger quantities.

Punched Tape Transmission Terminals. Punched tape transmission terminals consist of two units—a sender and a receiver. The sender includes a paper-tape reader and a signal generator. As the tape passes through the reader, the punched holes are sensed by pins connected to a signal generator. The signal generator sends signals representing the sensed holes to a data set for transmission over the communications channel.

The operation is reversed at the receiver which consists of a signal interpreter and a tape punch. As electrical signals are received, the pins in the tape punch are activated and holes are punched in tape.

Telespeed tape-to-tape equipment, also manufactured by the Teletype Corporation, will transmit messages and data at 105 characters a second using conventional telephone lines. However, Telespeed is strictly a tape transmission device and has no typewriter (Figure 18-8). Business data can be accumulated throughout the regular working day and transmitted at a rapid rate during nonworking hours or at intervals when the line is not in use. It is possible to alternate data transmission with voice communication on the same call.

Teledata (Figure 18-9) is another tape transmitter-receiver used at each end of communication circuits such as commercial telegraph lines, telephone circuits, or microwave systems. This device is able to transmit data in either direction by transmitting from tape and duplicating the tape at the receiving end. The paper tape may contain either five, six, seven, or eight channels.

Punched Card Transmission Terminals. Data can be transmitted from one location to another by means of punched card transmission systems. The IBM Data

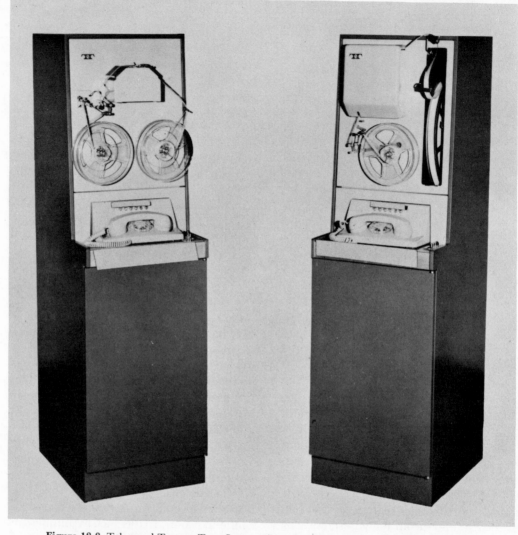

Figure 18-8. Telespeed Tape-to-Tape System. (*Reproduced by permission of Teletype Corporation.*)

Transmission System, for example, is composed of one or more sending terminals from which data is transmitted over dial or leased telephone channels. The transmission terminal contains a card reader as well as a ten-digit keyboard, functional keys, and an audio speaker (Figure 18-10). The audio speaker emits different sounds to indicate (1) that a connection is established between the sending and receiving terminals, (2) that the remotely located card punch is not ready to receive, (3) that a record was correctly transmitted, or (4) that a record was incorrectly transmitted.

After a connection is made by telephone between the sending and receiving

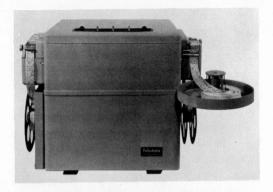

Figure 18-9. Teledata tape transmitter-receiver. (*Courtesy Friden, Inc.*)

stations, the operator lifts an exclusion switch located under the handset. This disconnects the telephone and connects the transmitting terminal to the line. Numerical data can be entered into the system manually through the keyboard or automatically by inserting a prepunched card. When the operator places a card in the reader, the data is converted to audio-range frequencies. These frequencies pass over telephone channels to a receiving location where they are reconverted. A data translator located on the left side of the receiving key punch converts the codes for punching.

Large quantities of punched card data can be transmitted by the system illustrated in Figure 18-11. The transmission terminal can also receive data from another terminal. In the sending mode, transmission speed is determined by the number of characters on each card, the type of circuit used, and the type of receiving unit used. For example, when a terminal reads cards containing 50 columns of data for transmission to a magnetic tape terminal, the average number of cards read each minute is 272. When the card transmission terminal is used as a receiving unit, speed is dependent on the number of characters punched in each output card. When 46 columns are punched, the rate of speed is 77 cards a minute.

Magnetic Tape Transmission Terminals. Magnetic tape transmission terminals provide direct transmission of magnetic tape data over dial or private communication circuits at the rate of 150 characters a second. Each terminal is designed to read tape for transmission or to write tape, depending on whether the toggle switch on the unit is set to send or receive. Because such terminals read or write tape with a high density of characters per inch, they are able to use tapes from or pre-

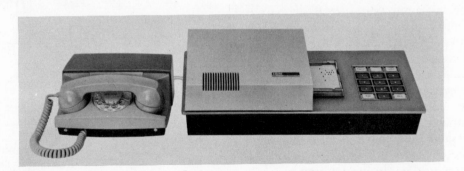

Figure 18-10. Data transmission system showing the combination telephone, transmitting subset, and transmission terminal. (*Courtesy International Business Machines Corporation.*)

Figure 18-11. Card transmission terminal used in transmitting or receiving punched card data at high speed. (*Courtesy International Business Machines Corporation.*)

pare tapes for the most commonly used tape devices. As a general rule there is no limitation in the length of each record transmitted, although most records are normally between 300 and 3,000 characters.

Computer Transmission Control Terminals. It is possible for data to be transmitted directly from one computer to another by connecting special data transmission control units to the computers (Figure 18-12). Transmitting units convert data from computer storage to the transmission language used by the common-carrier equipment. The data taken from main storage may have originated as input to the computer from cards or tape and may have been rearranged, edited, printed, or computed before being sent to the transmission unit.

As a receiver, the data transmission unit converts data from the transmission

language to binary coded decimal form and forwards the data to computer main storage. From this point various computer operations can be performed. These may include updating records in disk storage, rearranging and editing the data for printing, or recording the data in cards or magnetic tape.

These procedures are being used effectively in shifting large volumes of data from one computer center to another. This permits one center to back up another and allows the leveling of peak loads.

Figure 18-13 illustrates the use of a control terminal permitting a computer to communicate with a variety of remote terminals.

Handwriting   Transmission   Ter-

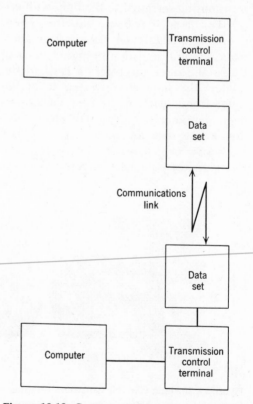

Figure 18-12. Computer-to-computer transmission.

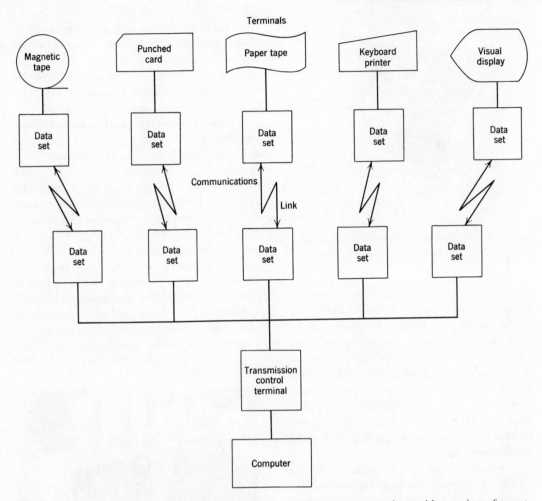

Figure 18-13. Transmission control terminal permitting computer to communicate with a variety of remote terminals.

minals. Handwriting transmission terminals are analog devices capable of direct transmission of handwritten messages, sketches, or other forms of graphic data over communication lines. Messages written at the transmitter are instantly reproduced on a roll of plain paper or on sprocket-fed printed forms in one or more remotely located receivers.

By connecting the handwriting transmission terminal to a data set, it is possible to alternately talk and write or receive any message, sketch, or graphic information (Figure 18-14).

This system is used by many banks, factories, hospitals, hotels, insurance companies, and the like, where there is a need for frequent and brief intercommunication.

Facsimile Terminals. Facsimile systems permit the two-way transmission of any type of document. Transmission in-

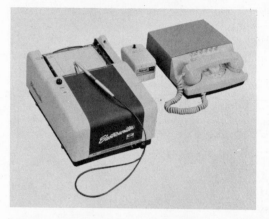

Figure 18-14. Handwriting transmission terminal. (*Courtesy Victor Comptometer Corporation.*)

volves the use of two machines that are basically duplicating devices. Each machine is connected to a common-carrier data set. When a document to be transmitted is placed in the sending terminal, a photoelectric device scans the document. The light and dark areas are then converted into corresponding impulses that are relayed to a receiving facsimile terminal where the original document is reproduced exactly.

Visual Display Terminals. Visual display terminals provide immediate visual access at a remote location to information stored within a computer system. The terminal consists of a keyboard, a signal generator-interpreter, a buffer, and a visual display screen (Figure 18-15).

An inquiry concerning an account, transaction, production schedule, or any such stored data can be quickly entered in the terminal keyboard. Coded signals are generated and transmitted by means of the data sets and communications channel to the computer system. The computer interprets the signals and searches its memory for the required information. The information is transmitted back to the visual display terminal in the form of coded signals. The signals are interpreted and displayed on the television-type screen. The displayed data can also be printed when models equipped with the optional printer feature are used.

Data Collection and Transmission Devices. For the most part, the terminals described above are used to transmit data previously collected, recorded, or stored in other devices. A somewhat different approach is represented by the integrated data collection and transmission system. The Friden Collectadata system is a good example of an integrated data collection and transmission system. This system is composed of four major units: a badge and punched card transmitter, badge transmitter, receiver, and central control. The system is designed for intraplant use within a two-mile range. Transmission

Figure 18-15. Display station. (*Courtesy International Business Machines Corporation.*)

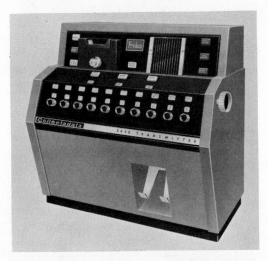

Figure 18-16. Collectadata transmitter incorporates punched card and badge reader for collection of manufacturing, inventory, and labor information at its source. (*Courtesy Friden, Inc.*)

beyond this distance requires the use of telephone lines and the addition of data converting units.

The transmitter (Figure 18-16) automatically reads and transmits job activity data from precoded 80-column punched cards and attendance data from coded employee badges. It also transmits variable data entered by means of ten automatic reset dials. To record time spent on a particular job, an employee inserts his coded identification badge with a punched card describing the job. To report attendance he inserts his identification badge only.

The badge transmitter (Figure 18-17) is a separate unit used for attendance recording only. This unit reads one ten-column laminated plastic identification badge.

The receiver (Figure 18-18) accepts data from transmitting units and punches eight-channel paper tape for use with computers or other tape-operated data processing machines, or for conversion to 80-column punched cards or magnetic tape.

Punching speed is 30 codes a second. Data is monitored with checks for parity and length of message.

The central control allots time to various transmitters in a programmed cable-sharing system, time dates every message, and monitors transactions for completeness.

COMMUNICATIONS FACILITIES

Broadly defined, a communications facility is a means by which data can be transmitted between two or more points. A complete range of facilities are available to suit any data communications requirement. Some of the common types of facilities and services as well as the communications companies that provide the services are presented in this section.

Common Carriers

Communications common carriers are companies authorized by the Federal

Figure 18-17. Collectadata badge transmitter used for attendance recording as part of source data collection system. (*Courtesy Friden, Inc.*)

Figure 18-18. Collectadata receiver receives and punches into eight-channel tape information transmitted from various points. (*Courtesy Friden, Inc.*)

Communications Commission or appropriate state agencies to furnish electrical communications services to the public. Services include communications facilities for voice, data, printed messages, and facsimile, as well as appropriate channels for television and telephoto.

The major common carriers providing interstate communications services are the American Telephone and Telegraph Company, which heads the Bell System, and the Western Union Telegraph Company. In addition, there are many independent telephone companies, the largest of which is General Telephone and Electronics Corporation. In general, the independent telephone companies offer the same types of services as the Bell System.

Communications Channels

The agreement between the communications common carrier and the user is basically an arrangement for the use of a certain type and grade of communications channel.

Types of Channels. The three basic channel types are called simplex, half-duplex, and duplex. A *simplex circuit* can transmit in one direction only. In most cases it is simplex because of the type of sending and receiving units. A *half-duplex circuit* transmits in both directions, but only in one direction at a time. A *full-duplex circuit* can transmit in both directions at the same time.

The possible volume of data communications and the flexibility of operations are greater with full-duplex circuits than for half-duplex or simplex circuits. However, the cost of the communications facilities and terminal equipment is also higher.

Grades of Channels. The grade of a channel indicates its capacity to transmit data. The capacity can be expressed in bits per second or a similar signal time rate.

The physical circuit or technique used may be a voice frequency circuit, a wire carrier channel, or a portion of a microwave band, depending on the facilities available in each geographical location. In any event, the user is primarily concerned with the fact that the available bandwidth is able to transmit the required volume of data.

The line speed of a channel, measured in bits per second, is directly related to the bandwidth of the channel. Thus, a high bit-per-second rate requires a wider channel or a greater number of cycles per second. The low-, medium-, and high-speed facilities are represented by three basic bandwidth classifications: narrow band, voice grade, and broadband.

Narrow-band channels generally have data communications capabilities in the range of 45 to 75 bits per second, although these are not specific limits. These channels are most commonly used with low-speed teletypewriter equipment.

Voice-grade channels have a line speed of approximately 2,400 bits per second. Voice-grade circuits do not transmit information in the form of digital pulses used in data processing equipment. Therefore, data sets are required to convert the pulses or "bits" generated by data processing equipment to signals suitable for transmission on the line. These signals are reconverted at their destination for delivery to the receiving equipment.

Broadband channels commonly use microwave transmission techniques to provide data communications at rates up to several million bits per second. The radio waves in this system tend to travel in a straight line, requiring relay stations with a dishlike antenna on high buildings or towers every 20 to 35 miles.

Communications Services

Communications services can be obtained on a public or leased (private) basis, depending on the needs of the user. Only those services related to the transmission of data are covered here.

DATA-PHONE Service. DATA-PHONE service provides for the transmission of data between a variety of business machines using regular local or long distance telephone networks. This is accomplished by connecting a DATA-PHONE data set to a business machine terminal (see Figure 18-5). The data set converts the signals from the transmitting device into tones suitable for transmission over the telephone network and provides the means for dialing the call.

The call is answered at the receiving DATA-PHONE data set either automatically or manually. When answered by an attendant, both the sending and receiving sets are in the normal "talk" mode. When the operators have confirmed that the business machine terminals are ready to send or receive data, they switch the connection from the "talk" mode to the "data" mode by simply depressing the "data" buttons on both sets. Thus, control of the line is transferred to the business machine terminals enabling them to transmit and receive data. At the completion of transmission, the operators disconnect the call by depressing the "talk" buttons and hanging up the telephones.

Data may also be transmitted to an unattended location by means of a DATA-PHONE data set that is arranged to answer calls automatically.

Rates for the transmission of data are the same as for ordinary telephone calls in addition to the monthly rate for the DATA-PHONE data set.

Wide Area Telephone Service. For those customers who must communicate frequently with widely scattered points, *Wide Area Telephone Service* (WATS) is offered. Monthly charges are based on the size of the service area in which calls are placed, not on the number or length of calls. Under the WATS plan, the United States is divided into six zones. The subscriber is billed a flat rate on a full-time or measured-time basis according to the zones to be called—the entire United States if desired. Under full-time service, the customer is provided an access line that he may use for twenty-four hours a day, seven days a week. In measured-time service, the access line is also continuously available, but the basic monthly rate covers only fifteen hours of service to telephones within the subscription area. WATS can be used alternately for voice communications and data transmission using DATA-PHONE service.

Teletypewriter Exchange Service. *Teletypewriter Exchange Service* (TWX) provides direct-dial point-to-point connections using input-output equipment such as keyboard printers, paper-tape readers, and paper-tape punches. TWX calls are established in the same manner as telephone calls by dialing from one station to another. Once the connection is established, operators may type two-way written messages, or messages or data may be sent automatically by means of paper tape.

Service is available throughout the continental United States, Canada, and Mexico. Messages may be transmitted overseas through connecting arrangements with international communications companies.

Western Union's counterpart of the Bell TWX service is called TELEX. This widely used service provides quick direct-dial two-way connections between subscribers in over 2,000 locations in continental United States, Hawaii, and 100 other countries. Direct connections to computers and other data processing equipment are possible.

The widespread availability of both the TWX and TELEX services facilitates the use of paper tape for transmitting data to a central office for further processing.

Broadband Exchange Service. Western Union's *Broadband Exchange Service* links two subscribers over transmission channels that they select as best suited to their communications needs. By means of a voice-data instrument containing ten push buttons, users can select the broadband width that will furnish optimum, economical data transmission (Figure 18-19). Type of transmission may include voice, facsimile, or digital data as contained in punched cards, punched tape, magnetic tape, and electronic storage devices. Thus, a firm desiring to have a problem solved could utilize the services of a computer at a remote location, possibly in a service center. Such services could be provided on a call-up basis through Broadband Exchange Service connections.

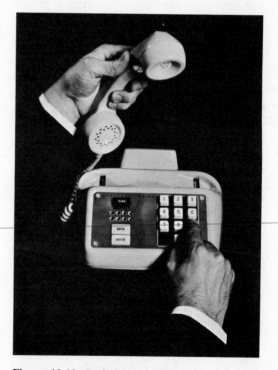

Figure 18-19. Push button voice-data instrument. (*Reproduced by permission of Western Union Telegraph Company.*)

Subscribers are furnished with voice-data instruments and Datasets. The Dataset converts digital pulses from data processing equipment to frequency tones for transmission over communications circuits. When a connection has been made, both sets are switched to the data mode, and transmission can begin. If during transmission either party wishes to return to voice mode, a signal can be given. Transmission is interrupted allowing both parties to pick up the handsets and begin conversation. Most long-distance transmission is over Western Union's microwave radio network.

Private Line Services. Both Western Union and the telephone companies provide services for the exclusive use of a single organization. Private-line voice services may be used alternately for voice communication and data transmission. Private-line teleprinter services are used with keyboard printers, paper-tape readers, and paper-tape punches. A private line can be set up on a two-point or multipoint basis.

TELPAK Service. TELPAK, the Bell System's broadband offering, is basically a private-line service with a bulk pricing arrangement intended for large users of communications. Users of this service have the benefit of various capacities, and the flexibility to arrange the facilities in any combination desired. For example, voice, teletypewriter, and data grade circuits may be combined within one TELPAK channel. The TELPAK capacity can also be used as a single large channel for high-speed data transmission such as facsimile, magnetic tape, and computer memory.

The rates for this service are lower than those for an equivalent number of single telephone lines.

Tariffs. For each common-carrier service provided, a tariff is published defining the service and the rate charged for

that service. Tariffs may include the rates for leasing lines, for lines and subsets, or for lines, subsets, and terminals. For the most part, the categories of service outlined in this section represent different methods of pricing rather than differences in basic facilities. To a great extent the wire services now used can be employed for the transmission of voice, data, or both alternately, through the use of DATA-PHONE data sets furnished by the telephone company. This may result in savings by combining telephone and data requirements.

Communications Switching

It is possible for connections between communications terminals to be permanently established, thus allowing continuous transmission. This is, however, a costly arrangement for large networks. A more economical and flexible method is to establish temporary connections between stations wishing to exchange information. The process of temporarily connecting two stations is called *switching*. The two basic methods of performing the switching function are message switching and line switching.

Message Switching. Message switching is used to transfer messages in a leased telegraph wire system. In message switching the sending and receiving lines are not directly connected. However, all of the lines are connected to the switching center. With this method the originating station sends its message directly to the switching center together with the destination address. After the entire message is recorded on punched tape at the switching center, it may be retransmitted promptly along the appropriate circuit, or it may be stored temporarily and sent out later. This is sometimes called "store and forward." Switching methods may be manual, semiautomatic, or fully automatic.

In *manual torn-tape switching* an operator at the switching center manually tears the incoming message off the punched tape receiving console and transfers it to a tape storage rack. A sending operator interprets the destination code, manually inserts the same tape in the appropriate outgoing transmitter, and the message is routed to its final destination.

Semiautomatic tape switching is a continuous rather than a torn-tape operation. In this case the operator in the switching aisle at the communications center reads the destination station recorded on the incoming perforated tape, depresses a push button corresponding to the specified station, and the message is forwarded.

In *automatic tape switching* the tape feeds automatically from the tape punch at the switching center and over the sensing pins of a tape reader. The reader interprets the codes representing the destination station, checks these codes against a directory, completes the proper circuit connection, and assigns the message to an outgoing line.

Line Switching. In line switching the communications center provides a direct connection between the two stations wishing to exchange information. The calling station first transmits to the switching center the code of the station to which information is to be sent. On the basis of the destination code, the switching center selects the line of the called station and electrically connects the calling and called lines. The actual switching may be done by an operator or automatically by the use of dial equipment. The dial telephone system is an example of line switching. Only after the switching process has been completed can the transmission of data take place. Type of transmission may vary. It may be voice alone, or it may be digital data as contained in punched cards, paper tape, magnetic tape, and electronic storage devices. During communication the two stations remain in direct contact.

Line switching is generally required for on-line real-time systems. However, message switching is likely to be more economical for most other types of data communications systems. Both line and message switching methods may be used to satisfy the data communications requirements of the larger information systems.

Review Questions

1. Briefly discuss the significance of data communications in today's society.
2. Define on-line data processing.
3. What is the significance of the U.S.A. Standard Code for Information Interchange?
4. What are the five stages of data transmission?
5. Describe the function of a data set or modem.
6. List at least five different types of data transmission terminals.
7. Describe the data transmission functions that can be performed by teletypewriters.
8. What is meant by the term "common carriers"?
9. Describe the three basic types of communications channels.
10. Low-, medium-, and high-speed data transmission facilities are represented by what three basic bandwidth classifications?
11. What is DATA-PHONE service? Explain how it is used.
12. Define communications switching.
13. What is the difference between message switching and line switching?

19

COMPUTERS AND AUTOMATION

The industrial use of computers encompasses a great variety of purposes ranging from routine administrative applications to the control of manufacturing operations and production systems. Modern industrial organizations use the computer for the full scope of their accounting activities — payrolls, billing, accounts payable, accounts receivable, financial planning, budgetary control, cost accounting, personnel accounting, management information systems, and so on. However, since business applications of this type are covered in other chapters, the discussion here will stress applications that are typical of industrial enterprises.

PRODUCTION PLANNING AND CONTROL

In manufacturing companies, the scheduling of production and control of inventory are of prime importance. Production scheduling computations are typically of such volume as to make them difficult to perform manually. Furthermore, since more than one satisfactory schedule may be possible, the computer is very useful in performing the complex calculations necessary to discover the best schedule for reducing costs and most effectively utilizing scarce production resources. Computer scheduling is also more dynamic since it facilitates quick responses to changes in the availability of or demand for materials and facilities after production has started.

In production planning it is necessary to ascertain in complete detail the number and skill of the workers needed, machine requirements, and all of the raw material and parts that will be required for the manufacture of every item. After the volume of production has been determined, a series of calculations of material requirements is carried out. Assemblies are broken down into subassemblies, subassemblies into parts, and so on, resulting in a complete list of every item required. This list is compared with existing inventories and, if raw materials, parts, or subassemblies must be procured, purchase requisitions and orders are issued.

Production control requires the careful coordination of men, machines, and materials. Computers are used to control overall production, and they also have the capacity to cater to each individual order. In the automobile industry, for example, many cars are built to fill specific orders from dealers or customers who may choose from among many thousands of combinations of colors, accessories, and optional equipment. In some plants customers' orders are recorded on punched cards and the data is fed into a computer. By using data collection devices, the computer controls the movement of the proper parts along feeder lines throughout the plant, thus assuring that the correct part gets to the right worker at precisely the right time.

INDUSTRIAL AUTOMATION

We have had the words *automatic* and *automaton* for a long time, but the word *automation* did not enter our language until about 1947. It soon captured the public imagination and is now familiar to nearly everyone—familiar but not always clearly understood. Perhaps this is because the word is relatively new. It is more likely, however, because the word has been subjected to various interpretations and has been associated with a number of controversial ideas, both technical and sociological.

Basically, automation involves the use of various technological devices and methods in performing manufacturing operations, or any other processes, without the direct intervention of the human hand. In a broader and more technical definition, automation has been described as "the substitution of mechanical, hydraulic,

pneumatic, electrical and electronic devices for human organs of observation, decision and effort, so as to increase productivity, control quality and reduce cost." *

When the term *automation* first came into existence it was usually associated with manufacturing operations. As applied to the industrial movement that started in the United States in the early 1950's, automation was defined as a production technique: the integration of machine tools into a fully automatic and, in some cases, self-regulating system. Today automation represents considerably more than the integration of a series of automatic machines. Automation is now being applied diversely in all levels of industry as well as in government and business. In fact, almost every activity is now affected to some extent by the use of automatically controlled devices and systems.

THE FOUNDATIONS OF INDUSTRIAL AUTOMATION

Historical developments in the mechanization and automation of data processing operations were outlined in Chapter 2. One of these developments, the electronic computer, has contributed most significantly to industrial automation. Here it has been combined effectively with other machines and processes that also have an interesting historical background, for present-day industrial automation did not develop spontaneously. Instead, it comprises elements of other stages of technological growth. It embodies the mech-

---

* Arnold, Pauline, and Percival White, *The Automation Age*, Holiday House, Pound Ridge, New York, 1963, p. 14.

anization of the Industrial Revolution, the mass production principles of the early twentieth century, and the automatic control principles that have developed since World War II. Before considering the role of the computer in industrial automation, let us briefly review the nature and origin of these other elements.

Mechanization

Since the beginning of history, human beings have sought ways of transferring to machines the burden of strenuous, repetitious, monotonous work. For centuries, man devised many ingenious and increasingly complex methods of utilizing his own muscular energy more effectively. What was needed eventually, though, was a new source of energy that could augment or supplant human energy, as well as the energy provided by harnessing water power and using domesticated draft animals. This was achieved by the important inventions and technological advancements of the Industrial Revolution, beginning around 1760, which enabled man to exploit in a major way the latent energy found in nature.

Industrial production was first mechanized by the steam engine; later the process of mechanization was extended much further by electric motors. The introduction of central-station power in 1881 made possible a multitude of inventions which, in turn, made modern mass production and automation possible.

Continuous Process

The early twentieth century witnessed a major technological advancement based on the principle of mass production. An essential element of mass production is the use of the continuous flow concept. This concept was known in the eighteenth century and was occasionally used in industry—flour mills, for example—but it was not widely used until this century.

A significant application of the mass-production principle occurred in the automobile industries of both Europe and the United States in the early 1900's. It was discovered that if workers moved from one car to another repeating the same task, this job specialization speeded production enormously. Soon it was recognized that it would be even better to have the workers stay put and have the jobs move by them. This assembly-line idea was adopted from the meat-packing industry which had used moving conveyors in Chicago since the 1870's. Thus, increased productivity, or output per man hour, was brought about by reorganizing the production process itself—an accomplishment that did not necessarily involve the introduction of new machines or new power sources.

During World War II the evolution of mass-production technology was completed by the development of automatic-transfer machines. A transfer-machine production line consists of a series of machines linked by mechanical handling equipment that moves parts automatically from station to station along the line. Under electronic control these machines can accept a piece of work, position it properly and fasten it in place, perform some operation on it, release it, transfer it to the next stage, and accept the next piece. All of this is accomplished without any direct human intervention. Consequently, transfer machines can perform in a single, integrated, automatically controlled process what was previously a series of individual job operations.

Automatic Control

The ability of machines to regulate themselves, which is a fundamental aspect of automation, is made possible by the technology of feedback. Feedback is accomplished by routing part of the output, or result, of a process back to the device that regulates the input of the process. Thus, if analysis of the feedback shows that the output is greater than it should be, the regulating device slows down the input; if the output is less than required, input will be increased.

Feedback principles have been known and applied for over a century. However, it was not until World War II that developments in the field of electronics permitted the manufacture of truly automatic control devices with wide applicability and highly efficient operation. These total automatic control systems are known as *servomechanisms.* A servomechanism is not a single instrument but a closely coordinated system of many instruments including sensing, measuring, transmitting, and control devices.

Among the sensing techniques employed are photoelectric cells, infrared cells, high-frequency devices, and X-ray components. The sensing unit, usually located near the output end of an automated system, observes the operations or finished products continuously. Information about what is being accomplished is transmitted to the measuring unit which compares the information it receives with the performance requirements stored in its memory. Any difference between the two, called an error, is determined and this information is relayed to the control unit. The control unit automatically activates forces that make the necessary adjustments to correct the error.

This cycle of continuous operations is called a "closed loop" because it is performed entirely by units built directly into the automated system. Thus, an automated system with a self-controlling closed-loop feedback has no need for a human operator to make corrections or adjustments in its performance. This contrasts with open-loop controls where an operator receives information about the results of a process, compares it with the desired performance, and makes adjustments in the input, if needed, to correct an error.

A good example of closed-loop feedback is the simple circuit used to control temperature in an electric oven. In this case the processing unit is the oven, the sensing device is the thermostat, and the control unit is the on-off oven heat switch. The control knob is set for a desired oven temperature which will then be held automatically as follows: when the thermostat senses that the oven temperature has risen above the level set by the position of the knob, the control device, or switch, corrects the error by switching off the electricity; similarly, when the thermostat senses that the temperature has fallen below the desired level, the control device switches the current on again.

This is an example of a simple form of what is called "on-off" control. Industrial applications normally require a more sophisticated type of control whereby the quantity being controlled is regulated automatically and continuously rather than by being switched on and off.

COMPUTERS AND AUTOMATIC CONTROL

Probably the most significant postwar technological development and the most important of all units employed in automation is the electronic computer. In addition to making a host of engineering and technical calculations never before feasible, the computer has become a significant factor in automatic control. Several of the outstanding roles of computers are described in the following sections.

Numerical Control of Machine Tools

One of the most important aspects of automation is *numerical control*, which is a means of automatically controlling the positioning and operation of machine tools. These tools are used to cut, drill, grind, press, turn, punch, mill, and otherwise alter the shape of metal pieces. In conventional methods this demands the constant attention of a skilled machine operator, especially if the part to be formed has an irregular contour. However, the metalworking industry is increasingly installing numerical control systems to produce metal parts automatically.

A numerical control system is one in which actions are controlled by the use of numerical data. The numerical control system reads numbers, translates them into instructions, directs the machine tool to perform the instructions, and compares machine performance with the instructions. Thus numerically controlled machinery is more than automatic machining; it is *automatic data handling*. "Data" comprises all of the numbers and mathematics used to describe a manufactured item.

The data used in controlling machine operations is generally recorded on a punched tape. In the early stages of numerical control, the preparation of control tapes was almost entirely a manual process. On all but the simplest parts, it was time-consuming and error-prone because

of the need for the part programmer to reduce all the necessary geometric equations to digital approximations and to perform the many thousands of calculations needed. The high level of mathematics required to define complex tool operations was quite prohibitive in terms of programming manpower when the only aid was a desk calculator.

The availability of electronic computers as calculating aids significantly reduced the time required to produce error-free control tapes. Further assistance was provided by the development of special problem-oriented numerical control programming languages which permit direct computer calculation and automatic control tape preparation. Two examples of the available English-like languages are APT (*A*utomatically *P*rogrammed *T*ools), and IBM's AUTOSPOT (*AUTO*matic System for *PO*sitioning *T*ools).

Figure 19-1 illustrates a computer-assisted numerical control operation using the APT system. As shown in the flow chart, the operation begins with a conventional engineering drawing of a part to be machined. From the drawing the part programmer writes a set of instructions that describe the operations necessary to produce the desired part. The program specifies the requirements of each machine-tool operation and includes statements defining the geometrical characteristics of the surfaces, required cutting operations, and machine-tool capabilities. These statements, written on coding sheets, form the source program. This program is punched into cards that are read into the computer. The processor program then converts the source statements into an intermediate format and calculates the detailed motions required for the accurate, proper positioning of the machine tool and for the necessary

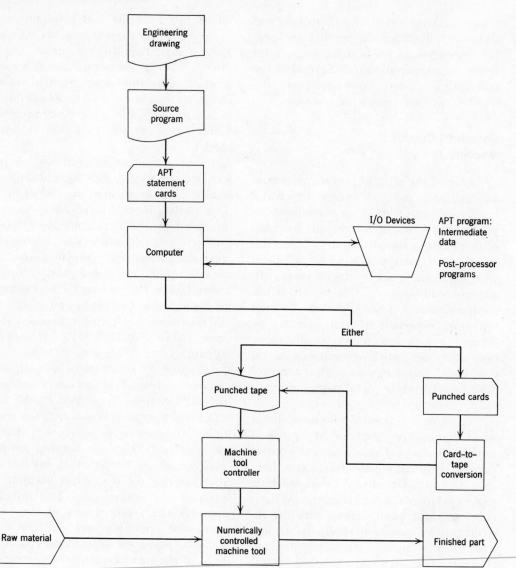

Figure 19-1. APT system flow chart.

cutting and drilling. Many thousands of calculations may be necessary to translate these statements into a sequence of error-free instructions meaningful to the machine-tool controller. By means of a user-written post-processor program, this in- termediate data is then converted to a se- ries of detailed instructions coded in nu- merical values, generally in the form of punched tape that can be read by the ma- chine-tool controller. The data is stored until needed and then fed into the machine-tool control unit that converts the data into actual machine motions. In some large installations, magnetic tape is used as the input medium for the machine-tool controller.

Under development are systems in which the computer is used as an integral, on-line element of the total numerical control system. In this case the computer actually controls and monitors machine-tool operations directly. Thus, through a feedback process the computer is able not only to regulate machine operations in response to variable conditions, but also to obtain information about production results. In this way, statistical data for production control and accounting purposes may be developed as a by-product of manufacturing operations.

Numerical control is not restricted to machining alone. The fundamentals of control by numbers are being applied increasingly to many other fields. For example, metal-forming equipment such as punch presses, tube or pipe benders, and metal fabricators have been equipped with controllers and are being operated under numerical control. Flame-cutting machines are used in the shipbuilding and steel industries to cut large steel plates under punched tape control, and numerically controlled inspection equipment has been built.

Process Control

In contrast with numerical control, which provides automation of discrete operations, *process control* provides automation of continuous operations. The process industries were the first to use computer control on a large scale. These are industries in which ingredients flow continuously through all stages of a process as they are converted from raw materials to an end product or group of products. Included in this category are petroleum refining, steel processing, electric power generation, and the manufacture of paper, chemicals, steel, cement, and food products.

Computer process control is being used increasingly in such industries to automate the manufacturing process and to control a large number of variables that are impossible for a man to control simultaneously. Factors occurring in production processes of this type, including variables such as time, weight, pressure, temperature, size, volume, and revolutions per minute, are monitored at critical places in the factory. By means of an analog to digital converter these continuous physical measurements are changed into discrete numbers. This data is instantly relayed to the computer for comparison with standards or planned results programmed into the computer beforehand. If there is a discrepancy between the two, the computer decides what adjustments are necessary and sends an appropriate command to the control mechanism in order to bring operations back to standard (Figure 19-2).

Since the computer continuously receives readings from process instruments, it may also print out relevant data at regular intervals. This data may include not only raw instrument readings but also computed yields and efficiencies for use by the process engineers or average and total flows for the accounting department. Thus, the control computer also serves as a data logger part of the time. For example, an IBM 1800 computer, installed at Mobil's Paulsboro, New Jersey, refinery, monitors instruments at 250 different data points, converts the data to digital formats, and prints out hourly reports

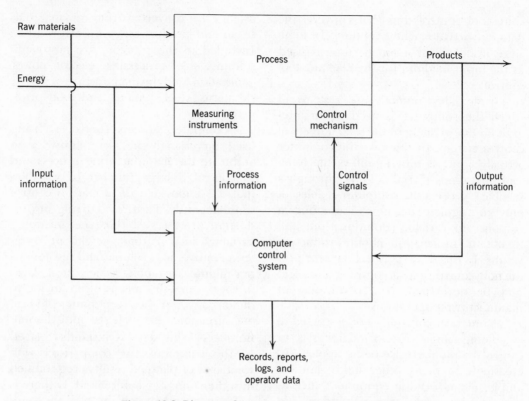

Figure 19-2. Diagram of a computer process control system.

that show the average value of all variables and overall material balance.* This computer is being used to control one of two thermal catalytic cracking units, which processes as much as 20,000 barrels of crude oil a day. Using a mathematical model of the process and pricing information, the IBM 1800 enables the unit to produce the most profitable mix of products — gasoline, liquid petroleum gas, and heating oil.

In many control systems today humans still read and compare measurements and make decisions about necessary corrections in the production proc-

ess. However, in many factories the processing of raw materials involves sequences of decisions for which all of the alternative possibilities are known. Thus, a computer can be programmed to aid in control of the entire factory through a closed loop system in which human intervention is required mainly to handle exceptional conditions that the computer indicates. The computer is highly reliable and capable of handling information of a very complex nature. Therefore, industrial engineers can now devise processes so intricate that they are feasible only with the aid of a computer.

Computers used to control industrial processes have certain characteristics that are worthy of note.

* "IBM Conducts Portable Process Press Conference," *Datamation*, July 1967, p. 83.

1. The central computer in such systems is generally a special-purpose computer that is smaller than would be required for problem-solving scientific systems or large-scale data processing systems.

2. There is generally provision for analog input and output because much of the information derived from sensing devices involves measurements. Such information is converted to digital form for processing.

3. Programming requirements are somewhat unique as compared to scientific or business data processing systems. Industrial program preparation demands specialists who are well trained in computer mathematics and in the nature of the process being controlled.

CYBERNATION

Within recent years the term *cybernation* has been coined to describe the application of a computer as a decision-making device in controlling an automatic process. The word is derived from *cybernetics,* a term used by the late Professor Norbert Weiner to mean the processes of communication and control in man and machines. He derived it from the Greek word meaning "steersman." The theory and practice of cybernetics, an interesting study in itself, underlies the systematic design and application of automation and computers.

It should be recognized that it is possible to construct complex control systems based on continuous monitoring and feedback loops without including computers. Not all automated industrial plants have computer systems and not all computerized plants are equally automatic. However, computers have given a new dimension to automatic control. By linking together machinery, sensing and measuring instruments, control devices, and electronic computers, systems can automatically start, stop, accelerate, decelerate, count, examine, store performance data, and measure and compare the dimensions of space, sound, time, temperature, and other physical characteristics.

Thus, it has become possible to develop integrated, self-regulating systems that can perform extremely complicated operations with little or no human assistance. Further, these cybernated systems perform with a precision and a rapidity that cannot be matched by humans. They also perform in ways that would be impossible or impractical for humans to duplicate.

In short, the advent of electronic control and computation has added one more stage of refinement in meeting the age-old objective of transferring burdensome and repetitious manual and mental tasks to machines.

INTEGRATION OF BUSINESS AND PROCESS CONTROL SYSTEMS

The purpose of a business information system is to collect information about the operations of an organization and to disseminate responses to this information. A process control system can be described similarly except that this system relates to a physical process rather than a business process.

These two functions are commonly regarded as essentially separate. Thus, the control computer in the process control system is independent both physically and functionally of the computer or computers used for the organization's information systems. This independence is attributable to several factors: the traditional separation of business and process control systems, the fact that the use of communications systems is a relatively recent development in data processing, and the past distinction between scientific and business computers.

In general there is a close interaction between the information required for control of the manufacturing process and that required for overall management of the business. For example, information about various factors of production, raw materials, process yields, and the status of work-in-process is of common significance. All of the data available to the process control system through measurement of the physical process can, of course, be made available to management by having a human operator record and report instrument readings periodically. Reports printed out by the control computer may also be transmitted for management use. However, as a result of technological advancements, it is now possible to capture data at its sources automatically and communicate it immediately rather than at some later time. First, it is now possible to obtain computers capable of both analyzing operating data for control of the physical process and reporting data for control of the business. Second, modern data communication techniques make it possible to transmit to a remote location the data required for management functions; and this can be accomplished at relatively little additional cost.

Although it is possible to collect management information automatically as a derivative of process control data, achievement to date in this area has been very limited. However, many companies are reported to have long-range plans for integrating their physical and business systems. In view of the potential economic benefits, it seems inevitable that process and manufacturing industries will exploit the opportunity to create integrated systems that will both control manufacturing processes and provide on-line information for use in carrying out engineering, financial, marketing, and other management functions.

Review Questions

1. What elements of other stages of technological growth are embodied in automation?
2. Explain the principle of feedback.
3. What is the difference between closed-loop controls and open-loop controls?
4. What is numerical control?
5. Describe the primary role of a computer in a numerical control system.
6. Briefly describe the manner in which a computer is used to control production processes.
7. Discuss the potential value of integrating physical and business systems.

20

SYSTEMS STUDY
AND DESIGN

In Chapter 1 some of the problems that created the need for more efficient data processing techniques were discussed. Subsequent chapters were devoted to the various methods that have been devised to solve these problems. Regardless of the methods employed, however, the benefits that are derived from a data processing system are primarily dependent on the effectiveness with which the system was designed. This chapter will introduce the techniques that are used in the study and design of a business system, which may be defined as a combination of personnel, equipment, and other facilities operating under a set of procedures designed to accomplish the objectives of an organization.

EVOLUTION OF BUSINESS SYSTEMS

Today's business systems are based upon principles that originated during the Industrial Revolution. Many of the operating concepts, such as assembly lines, were first perfected in the factory and have since been employed in the office. The industrial engineering work in factories that provided the basis for industrial automation was paralleled by the application of similar techniques leading to the automation of office activities.

Five stages of advancement are apparent in the development of business systems. The first stage consisted of the simplification of manual operations through the use of techniques known as work simplification. The second stage was that of mechanization which facilitated the combination of two or more functions in one operation. For example, the addition of tape mechanisms to adding machines and cash registers gave them the ability to record and summarize as well as to calculate.

Punched card equipment, which represented the third stage, introduced compatibility of machines that could perform a variety of functions through the use of standard punched cards.

In the fourth stage, integrated data processing extended the principle of compatibility to a wide range of equipment. Integrated data processing techniques made it possible for typewriters, accounting machines, addressing machines, and other equipment to be used with each other and with punched card equipment.

In the fifth stage of development, electronic computers enhanced the integrated data processing concept by providing the means of processing vast amounts of data at far greater speeds.

As these new and improved techniques developed, however, there was a tendency to apply them on a piecemeal basis as substitutes for the older methods of performing specific operations. Since the older methods were generally manual, the use of equipment was often restricted by systems concepts based on the capacity of humans. Thus, the greater versatility and capacity of the new equipment were not fully exploited.

The increased use of computers under the integrated data processing concept led to the realization that in some cases the new techniques were not being employed to the greatest advantage and that the decision-making ability of the computer could be put to far greater use. Out of this came the idea of regarding the entire business system as a unified entity which should be designed to take full advantage of equipment capabilities and new management science techniques as a better means of attaining business goals.

Under this approach the business system is viewed as a whole rather than as an organization composed of individual operations. This is the *total systems concept* which is the underlying principle of systems work today.

THE SYSTEMS ANALYST

As business systems requirements developed during the first half of the twentieth century the office manager, controller, or accountant was responsible for the design and installation of new systems and procedures. During the 1950's the use of analytic methods for solving operational problems was developed. These techniques, called *operations research*, originated in Great Britain during World War II. After the war, leaders in business, industry, and government modified and applied operations research methods to the solving of their problems.

The persons applying these techniques to the business systems became known as *methods engineers*. During the 1950's it was customary to have methods engineers design, or oversee the design of, new business systems. To do this competently the operations research departments had to employ data processing technicians and accountants as advisors. As a result it was common practice to form committees of several persons, each an expert in his field, and assign a project to this group for study. The ability of a committee to function efficiently in a creative endeavor such as this was often restricted. Many times the strongest rather than the ablest personality dominated the group, thereby making the measuring of performance and planning of a work program difficult.

The managers of data processing departments thought that they also should have a voice in the design of new systems, since they were responsible for making the systems work. Out of this developed a new profession originally titled *systems and procedures analyst*, and now more frequently called *systems analyst*. The systems analyst may be assigned to a separate department responsible to either the controller, methods engineer, or administrative manager. However, as experience has shown, when the systems analysts are under the control of a data processing manager reporting to the executive level, the systems installed usually meet more of the objectives of a good business system.

The systems analyst is ordinarily the key figure in the systems program. This does not mean that he carries out the program by himself. He is, however, a specialist who generally has the full-time responsibility for carrying out the continuing program of improvement. To succeed in this endeavor, he should enjoy working with people. He must be enthusiastic about his work and be recognized as an authority who can understand and improve the situation. He should have a basic curiosity, along with the innate ability to think beyond the immediate, to challenge precedent, and to create something new. He must be able to consider a problem without injecting personalities, emotions, or prejudices. He must be familiar with the organization and the philosophy of its management. He must be good in the communicative arts. That is, he must be capable of making clear and concise statements which cannot be misinterpreted. Finally, the systems analyst must have an understanding of human nature and the ability to deal with people on all levels, as the best designed system will never be a success without the understanding and cooperation of those concerned with its operation.

OBJECTIVES OF SYSTEMS STUDY AND DESIGN

The general objectives of systems study and design are met by developing new procedures or improving existing procedures so as to increase the effectiveness of operations and, if possible, to bring about greater economy.

Systems improvement can meet the objective of increased effectiveness in the following ways:

1. Improving service to customers.
2. Improving public relations.
3. Improving the quantity, quality, and form of information provided to management.
4. Eliminating conflicting or overlapping services.
5. Obtaining greater speed and accuracy in the processing of data and the preparation of reports.
6. Increasing executive efficiency.
7. Improving coordination of various operating units and personnel.
8. Obtaining greater operating efficiency by making possible quicker action on management decisions.

Greater economy would result from the following accomplishments:

1. Increasing clerical productivity.
2. Reducing operating and clerical costs.
3. Eliminating unnecessary functions and activities.
4. Reducing inventory and other working capital requirements.
5. Effecting maximum utilization of personnel and equipment.

PLANNING THE SYSTEMS STUDY

Before beginning the actual systems study, several preliminary steps should be taken. The first step is to define the objectives of the study. Has the development of new techniques or equipment made a change in the system necessary? Is the organization striving for a smoother operation, earlier reports, new reports, better reports, or improved economy of operation?

The next step is to outline the scope of the study. Is the study to include the entire system or be limited to a portion of the system? What people may be affected? Who has to be satisfied? After answering these questions, a time schedule, estimate of the facilities and funds required, and a plan of action can be prepared.

The study and design of a system require three major phases. First, it is necessary to acquire an understanding of the present system. Second, the results that are desired from the system must be determined. Finally, equipment must be selected and procedures devised to efficiently attain those results (Figure 20-1).

The success of systems work depends to a great extent on the thoroughness and skill with which these three phases are completed. Before considering the actual conduct of systems study and design, let us first outline the major tools and techniques that are used to assist in analyzing and interpreting existing conditions and new design proposals.

SYSTEMS STUDY AIDS

Organization Charts

The main value of the organization chart to the analyst is to show who is responsible to whom, and who has what personnel resources at his disposal. When a current organization chart is not available, the systems analyst should prepare one.

The formal organization chart should be pyramid-shaped and clearly show lines of responsibility. Solid lines on the chart indicate lines of authority and broken lines show advisory contact. Preferably, each box on the chart should have only one line entering it; otherwise the chart conveys more than one line of authority, which is a sign of poor management. Names may appear on the chart or be omitted, but if they are included the chart will require more frequent change than if only titles are used.

Several illustrations of organization charts may be seen in Chapter 3.

Flow Charts

To study and plan the use of data processing equipment it is necessary to employ some method of depicting the flow of data through a system and the sequence of operations performed. Flow charts provide a means of outlining the flow of data and operations so that they are easy to visualize and follow.

The *system flow chart*, which represents the broadest approach, is a very good tool for showing the total picture of a business system, and can be most helpful while studying the present system or designing a new one. The system flow chart illustrates in a general manner the flow of data and operations. The details are outlined on supplementary documents and are referenced by a numeric or alphabetic code. The system flow chart can be used to depict manual, mechanical, or computer operations or any mixture of these. However, emphasis is usually given to the flow of data throughout the system and the general sequence of operations rather than to how the operations are performed.

The flow chart in Figure 20-2 is typical of those used to graphically illustrate data flow in an existing system or in a system being designed. It stresses the flow of data with minimum regard for the details of the operations involved. The

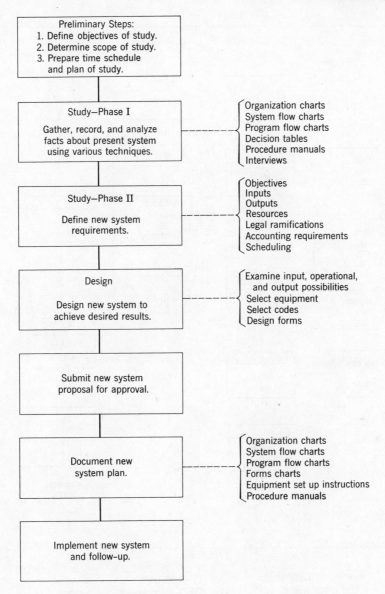

Figure 20-1. Steps in systems study and design.

flow chart in Figure 20-2 illustrates the following:

1. The chart can be drawn with three basic symbols, although it is not neces-sarily restricted to these symbols. The "flowerpot" is used to represent inputs, outputs, and files. The rectangular box is used to represent operations. The flow direction symbol, a line with or without

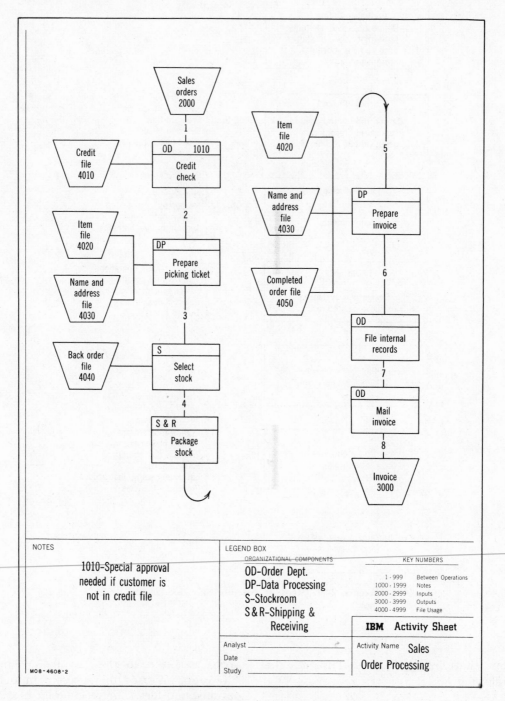

Figure 20-2. System flow chart.

arrows, represents the course of processing or data flow.

2. Numerals are placed between the symbols. They are generally in order with the sequence of operations.

3. Each operation box is related to the department that performs the function.

4. All special notes are related to their symbols by a key number.

5. Inputs, outputs, files, and operations often require more detailed notes than can be shown on the flow chart.

These details should be clearly stated on supplementary sheets and referenced to their symbols by number.

6. The flow chart clearly shows which files are used in each operation.

In addition to the three basic symbols illustrated in Figure 20-2, fourteen symbols are available to describe more specifically the equipment, machine operations, and manual operations that are involved in handling the flow of data. The symbols in Figure 20-3 are used by the majority of

 Processing. A major processing function.

Input-output. Any type of medium or data.

Punched card. All varieties of punched cards, including stubs.

Perforated tape. Paper or plastic, chad or chadless.

Document. Paper documents and reports of all varieties.

Transmittal tape. A proof or adding machine tape or similar batch-control information.

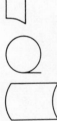 Magnetic tape.

Disk,
Drum,
Random access

Annotation. The addition of descriptive comments or explanatory notes as clarification. The broken line may be drawn on either the left or right, and connected to a flowline where applicable.

 Off-line storage. Either of paper, cards, magnetic or perforated tape.

Display. Information displayed by plotters or video devices.

On-line keyboard. Information supplied to or by a computer utilizing an online device.

 Sorting, collating. An operation on sorting or collating equipment.

Clerical operation. A manual offline operation not requiring mechanical aid.

Auxiliary operation. A machine operation supplementing the main processing function.

 Keying operation. An operation utilizing a key-driven device.

 Communication link. The automatic transmission of information from one location to another via communication lines.

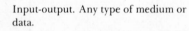

Figure 20-3. System flow chart symbols.

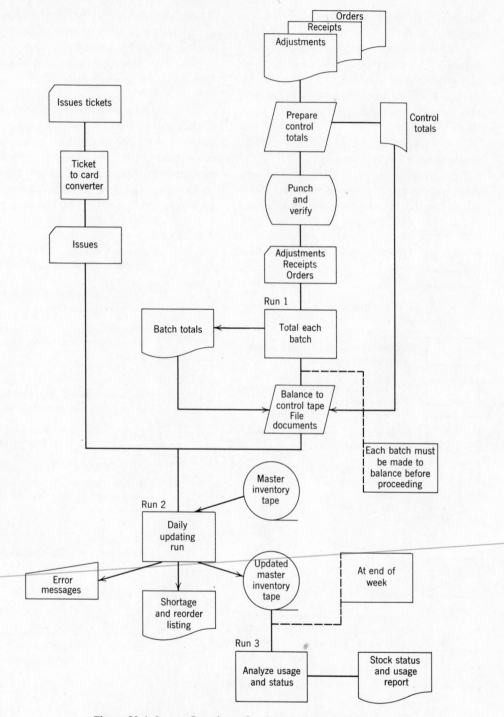

Figure 20-4. System flow chart of an inventory application.

systems analysts in the preparation of flow charts. These symbols are the ones recommended by IBM.

The United States of America Standards Institute (USASI), formerly the American Standards Association (ASA), adopted on June 8, 1966, a set of flow chart symbols (X3.5-1966). The USASI flow chart symbols are under consideration by the International Organization for Standardization (ISO) for world-wide usage. If and when ISO does adopt the USASI flow chart symbols, it is likely that IBM will revise their flow-charting symbols to be compatible. However, since the USASI symbols have not yet been universally adopted, the symbols recommended by IBM will be used here.

Figure 20-4 demonstrates the use of various symbols and flow-charting techniques in a more detailed type of system flow chart depicting an inventory application. It should be noted that the flow of the system is in the same general direction—top to bottom—and that arrow points are used only when needed to keep the flow clear.

A *program flow chart* emphasizes computer decisions and specific processing steps, thus showing individual problem solutions. In addition to the three basic symbols, six program flow chart symbols may be used (Figure 20-5), as well as the supplementary annotation symbol previously illustrated.

Since a program flow chart evolves from a system flow chart, a program flow chart includes a greater amount of detail such as the program logic used for coding and the specific processing sequences. For example, Figure 20-6 is a program flow chart depicting the details of the particular program shown as Run 2 on the system flow chart in Figure 20-4.

Flow-charting worksheets, such as the one used in preparing the flow chart shown in Figure 20-6, are helpful in producing good flow charts. They aid in squaring up flow lines, centering symbols in each position, and maintaining uniform spacing between symbols. In addition, the blocks with alphabetic and numeric coordinates prove helpful in documenting and cross-referencing.

Templates of the type shown in Figure 20-7 are used in drawing flow charts. The template illustrated contains all the symbols necessary for preparing both system and program flow charts.

After a program has been written and tested it may be used as input data for another program that can prepare *machine-generated program flow charts*. Computer prepared flow charts include such features as a standard format, automatic page numbering, automatic generation of page connectors, and automatic dating of charts. Several samples of machine-prepared flow chart symbols are shown in Figure 20-8. The major advantages of these flow

Decision. Points in the program where a branch to alternate paths is possible, based upon variable conditions.

Program modification. An instruction or group of instructions which changes the program.

Predefined process. A group of operations not detailed in the particular set of flow charts.

Terminal. The beginning, end, or a point of interruption in a program.

Connector. An entry from, or an exit to, another part of the program flow chart.

Off-page connector. Used instead of the connector symbol to designate entry to or exit from a page.

Figure 20-5. Program flow chart symbols.

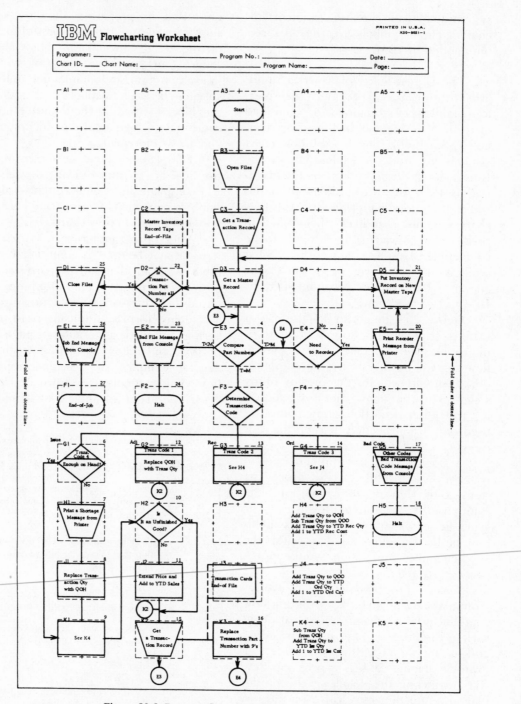

Figure 20-6. Program flow chart (related to Figure 20-4).

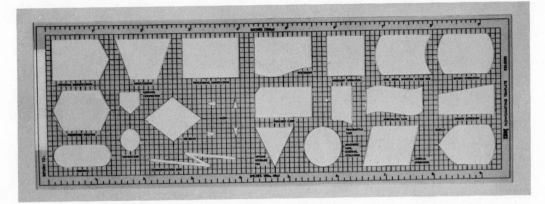

Figure 20-7. Flow-charting template.

charts are high quality output and ease of maintenance. It is evident from the manually prepared flow chart shown in Figure 20-6 that it would be almost impossible to insert one or two new symbols without redrawing the entire sheet. In view of this and other problems, program flow charts often become very messy and difficult to read, or the changes are not made at all because of the amount of time required to keep the flow chart current. These problems are overcome by the use of machine-generated flow charts. However, manually drawn flow charts should still be prepared before the program is written as they are a good pictorial representation of the data flow and logic of the program. Only after the program is written and tested should the machine-prepared flow chart be relied upon.

Process Charts

Underlying the search for more efficient data processing methods has been the principle of *work simplification*. This extremely important concept existed even before the advent of electronic computers and other labor-saving devices now in use.

Although work simplification is significant in any type of operation, it is especially valuable as a means of increasing the efficiency of manual data processing.

Work simplification may be defined as the analysis of routines so as to plan improvements that will make the work easier to perform, and thus will allow it to be done in less time and at less cost. A *routine* is a planned method of performing a specific piece of work. For example, the processing of sales transactions would include such routines as recording orders, preparing shipping documents, shipping the goods, accounting for payments received, processing claims or adjustments, and analyzing sales. The objectives and procedures of work simplification are comparable to processes called *methods analysis* and *procedure analysis*. Although certain distinctions could be made between these approaches, they are not considered sufficiently relevant to be included here. In effect, all three refer to the same objectives: greater effectiveness and more economy. Analysis of the flow of work through an organization and the methods of performing various operations is an important part of work simplification. Such an

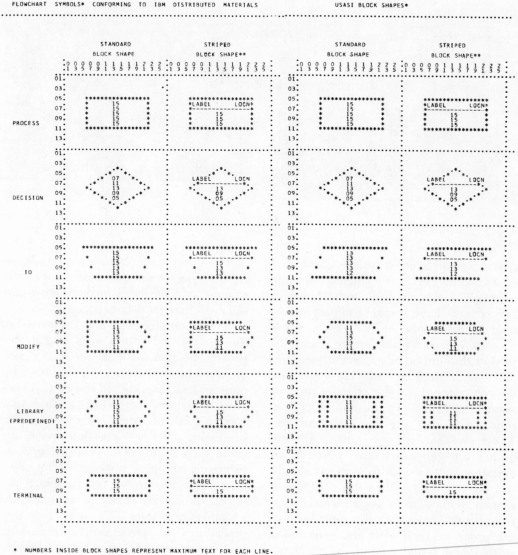

Figure 20-8. Machine-mode program flow chart symbols. (*Courtesy International Business Machines Corporation.*)

analysis is generally designed to (1) *eliminate* operations or steps that are not necessary; (2) *combine* operations that are closely related; (3) *change the sequence* of performing operations if this will result in improvement; and (4) *simplify* operations as they exist after eliminating, combining, and arranging have been completed.

Analysis may be accomplished by the use of such techniques as activity charts, office layout charts, work station analyses, and process charts. The last of these, the *process chart,* is one of the most effective techniques available for the analysis of manual operations. It is the oldest form of flow chart and was first used to depict clerical and mechanical office procedures. Accountants and methods engineers are the primary users of process charts.

The process chart is a means of depicting in symbol form the details of present and proposed steps of work in process. The illustrative symbols used in preparing the chart may represent documents, machines, or actions taken during the process. Emphasis is on where an action takes place, or who does it, rather than on how it is to be done. Charts also may include such details as distance in feet, whenever transportation is involved, and time required to perform each step.

A list of process chart symbols, along with the meaning of each, is shown in Figure 20-9. Some of the symbols illustrated are used in the *vertical process chart,* which is most frequently used to show:

1. The detailed steps in a relatively simple procedure.
2. A procedure involving only one document.
3. A procedure involving only one person.

All of the symbols may be used in the multicolumn or *horizontal process chart.* The horizontal chart is most frequently used to show:

1. A whole procedure.
2. A complex operation.
3. A procedure involving more than one document.
4. A procedure involving only one document but more than one operating group.

Figure 20-10 illustrates a simple horizontal process chart covering the first part

Origin of a record. This symbol is used to indicate the origin of a record, such as preparing a journal, typing a refund schedule, making a remittance register, or making a document register.

Handling operation. This symbol is used to indicate the performance of some other type of operation, such as slicing envelopes, sorting cards or records, adding a column of figures, or inserting bills.

Transportation. This symbol is placed at the intersection of the space and process flow lines, and is used to show that something is being moved from one place to another, such as from the mail room to the next work station.

Inspection. This symbol is used when something is verified or examined to determine the quality or correctness of the record or document, with acceptance or rejection implied.

This symbol is used to show a combined inspection and handling operation, such as verifying documents and drop sorting them by categories. It is frequently used without the intervening inverted triangles to indicate a "hand carry and wait for" operation. It is part of one continuous operation without "in and out" stops.

Temporary storage, delay or hold. This symbol identifies a point or time at which the record or document is inactive and waiting further action. This symbol is always used at the beginning and end of a series of operations by one operator.

This symbol is used to show that a series of operations are performed in some other organizational component, usually another branch or another division, when it is not necessary to detail the operations on the chart.

Storage. This symbol denotes final storage so far as the process in question is concerned, such as the closed ledger when the final account has been posted for the day's run.

Figure 20-9. Process chart symbols and conventions.

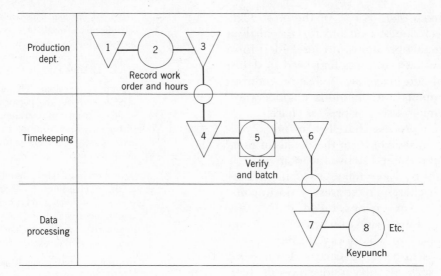

Figure 20-10. Process chart of time-reporting procedure.

of a time-reporting procedure. Several characteristics should be noted:

1. The flow can go from one operation or department to another. The small circle is used to indicate transportation.

2. A triangle is placed on each end of a group of operations performed by the same person.

3. Descriptive data may be entered under the symbol. When the data will not fit under the symbol, it may be entered elsewhere and referenced to the number in the symbol.

Decision Tables

Another aid in the study and design of systems is the *decision table*. The purpose of a decision table is to provide information concerning problems and solutions in a concise format that is easy to read and understand. This tabular approach is used to express complex decision logic in a manner that encourages the analyst to reduce a problem to its simplest form by arranging and presenting logical alternatives under various conditions. Decision tables can be used independently of, or to complement, flow charts.

A decision table defines all conditions (the prerequisites for an action) and separates them from all actions. Further, it relates given conditions to the appropriate actions. Alternative conditions that result in other actions constitute other rules which are written side by side. Figure 20-11 illustrates an airlines reservations decision table. The first rule in this table states: if the request is for first class (condition 1) and first-class space is available (condition 3), then issue a first-class ticket (action 1), and subtract 1 from the first-class seats available (action 3). In rule 2 the request is for first class, but no first-class seats are available. Tourist space is open and the passenger will accept tourist accommodations. The actions call for the issuance of a tourist ticket and the subtraction of 1 from the number of tourist seats available.

Two characteristics of decision tables are evident in the table shown in Figure 20-11. First, not only is the combination of entries for each rule different from that for all other rules, but also there is no combination of entries that satisfies the conditions of more than one rule. This is a decision table convention. Second, each detail of the decision-making process has been explicitly stated and every condition considered in a direct way. The decision table format clearly shows the relationships between problems and solutions.

Project Management Schedules

Management of the design, development, and implementation of complex projects is aided by such techniques as the Critical Path Method (CPM) and Program Evaluation and Review Technique (PERT), which is a refinement of the Critical Path Method. Basically, these are flow diagrams illustrating a series of activities that must be accomplished in order to complete a project, along with the time and resource requirements for each activity.

The activities are arranged in the form of a network which shows logical sequences of events, interdependencies, and interrelationships. Events are indicated as circles or blocks which are numbered for identification. An event does not represent the performance of work, but rather the point in time at which the event is accomplished, i.e., a milestone or checkpoint. Events are connected by arrows reflecting the activities required to complete the events (Figure 20-12).

CPM and PERT techniques aid in controlling projects, evaluating progress during their execution, and recognizing implications of project schedules. For example, analysis of a diagram may reveal that it will not be possible to complete a project as soon as desired, that some activities have been overlooked, or that the activities planned during some period of time require more resources than are available.

			Rules							
			1	2	3	4	5	6	7	8
Conditions	1	First class request	Y	Y	Y	Y				
	2	Tourist request					Y	Y	Y	Y
	3	First class open	Y	N	N	N		Y	N	
	4	Tourist open		Y	N		Y	N	N	N
	5	Alternate class acceptable		Y	Y	N		Y	Y	N
Actions	1	Issue first class ticket	X				X			
	2	Issue tourist ticket		X		X				
	3	Subtract one from first class avail	X					X		
	4	Subtract one from tourist avail		X			X			
	5	Place on tourist wait list			X				X	X
	6	Place on first class wait list			X	X		X		

Y = Yes   N = No

Figure 20-11. Decision table for handling airlines reservations.

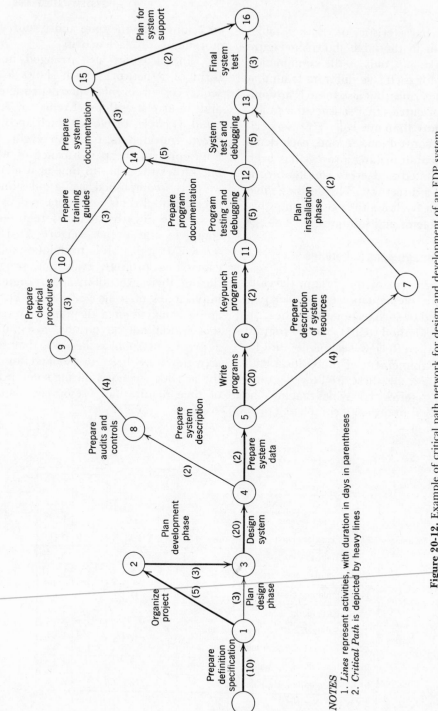

Figure 20-12. Example of critical path network for design and development of an EDP system.

NOTES
1. *Lines* represent activities, with duration in days in parentheses
2. *Critical Path* is depicted by heavy lines

Prepare
definition
specification
(10)

Organize
project
(5)

Plan
design
phase
(3)

Plan
development
phase
(3)

Design
system
(20)

Prepare
audits and
controls
(2)

Prepare
system
description
(2)

Prepare
system
data
(2)

Prepare
clerical
procedures
(4)

Prepare
training
guides
(3)

(3)

Prepare
system
documentation
(3)

Plan for
system support
(2)

Write
programs
(20)

Keypunch
programs
(2)

Prepare
description
of system
resources
(4)

Plan
installation
phase
(2)

Program
testing and
debugging
(5)

Prepare
program
documentation
(5)

System
test and
debugging
(5)

Final
system
test
(3)

Emphasis is generally on time scheduling as shown in the critical path network in Figure 20-12. However, advanced versions of PERT also include cost estimates. Thus, in addition to monitoring the progress of the project, the manager is able to compare continuously the actual cost expenditures with those estimated during the planning stage.

PERT and critical path scheduling have proved highly useful in scheduling and controlling major construction projects, research and development programs, and other large projects, as well as the design and development of systems projects.

Now that some of the tools used by the analyst to define an existing system or design a new system have been described, let us consider the actual systems study.

ANALYZING THE PRESENT SYSTEM

To acquire an understanding of the present system the analyst must first define the resources used in the system. The personnel, equipment, facilities, and finances must be noted in a manner that will clearly show their relation to the system. To gather this information the analyst will have to:

1. Analyze the organization charts and determine that they represent the actual lines of authority, and then identify the personnel operating the present system. If there is an informal organization that overlaps the formal structure, it also must be recognized.

2. Review operating procedures and verify that the procedure manuals represent the actual operations and identify the equipment and facilities used in the system. When up-to-date procedure manuals

do not exist, the analyst will have to spend more time with the managers operating the system in order to find out what resources are being used.

3. Prepare a system flow chart which reflects the resources used in the system. While developing the flow chart, the analyst may have to discuss certain operations with the people actually operating the system.

4. Interview personnel in order to obtain pertinent facts about various aspects of the system. Effective interviewing requires special skill. The interview procedure is facilitated if the analyst is recognized as an authority who can improve the situation. However, while gathering information from the operators, he should ask them for their ideas on how the system could be improved. This is important as it gives a feeling of participation that can make it easier to install the new system. It is also possible that a good idea may be brought to light. Either during the interview or following it the analyst should make concise notes about the interview and the subject discussed.

5. Record details of the present system. These details may include:

Inputs. The sources of data entering the system: how much, how often, and from where does it come?

Resources. Equipment, personnel, finances, facilities, and inventories used in the system.

Outputs. The reports produced: how often are they prepared, who uses them, and how are they used?

DEFINING SYSTEM REQUIREMENTS

Both while gathering information about the present system and afterwards the analyst must define the actual requirements of the system. A good analyst must be aware of management's general policies, attitudes, and objectives for the present and future. At this point in the survey the analyst should determine:

1. Where the particular system being studied fits into the total business system of making a product or performing a service.
2. What the system must do.
3. What inputs it must accept.
4. What outputs it must produce.
5. What resources it must use.

Next to management objectives, the knowledge of laws and regulations concerning the system under study is most important. Many of today's business systems were created primarily to satisfy one or more governmental requirements. The main legal responsibility of the systems analyst is to avoid any violation of laws or regulations in the business system being designed or changed.

While designing any business system the analyst must constantly be alert to the rules governing good bookkeeping and accounting practices: the rules on debit and credit entries, for example. Moreover, the analyst should have knowledge of the accounting doctrines, such as the doctrine of consistency. Simply stated, the accountant starts with source data and builds toward final results, whereas the auditor starts with the final results and tracks back to the source. Therefore, a trail must always be left for the auditor to travel; otherwise, he may have to exert a great amount of effort to do his job.

A good system also provides for balancing to control figures at the proper places in the procedure, and provides instructions for correcting out-of-balance conditions. Avoiding errors often requires a great amount of special effort, and detecting errors often requires duplication

of manual effort. It must be determined whether the degree of accuracy is sufficiently critical to justify the cost of avoiding and detecting errors.

Another requirement of a good system is that it be straightforward and easily followed by operating personnel. The more exceptions there are in a procedure, the more opportunity there is for operator error. As work progresses, certain interruptions arise for checking, questioning, making minor adjustments, and receiving instructions. These are variable factors which are present, to some degree, in all operations. However, the fewer of these interruptions and questions there are in a system, the more efficient the operation will be.

Finally, a good system requires the effective scheduling of operations. The effectiveness of data processing operations is determined by the coordination of machines, personnel, and work. While scheduling may take many forms, the broad objective as it applies to data processing is to produce the desired reports on time, with a minimum number of machines and personnel. The more difficult it is to schedule the jobs, the more important it is to do so.

DESIGNING THE NEW SYSTEM

Determining Input, Operational, and Output Methods

The first step in designing the new system is to examine the various ways in which source data can be entered into a system, operated on, and reported or recorded. Source data can first be punched into cards or paper tape, recorded by mark-sensed notation or magnetic ink, or read by an optical character recognition device. Output alternatives available are printed reports, punched cards, paper tape, or data transmission. File possibilities include magnetic tapes, disks, drums, or cards. The operations (the process between input and output) can be performed in a number of ways which have been discussed in detail in preceding chapters. The analyst also must examine the possibility of combining minor operations or splitting oversized operations. He must decide what audit and control requirements should be imposed and with what frequency the operations need to be performed.

Selecting Equipment

The selection of equipment is a complex and challenging task. Sound decisions require careful consideration of such factors as general requirements of the system, volumes of data, anticipated future expansion, available financial resources, and relative cost of various methods.

Equipment selection is generally based on the following principles:

1. Lack of repetition in an application dictates that the operation be done manually with mechanical assistance where helpful.

2. If the operation is repetitive but does not require random processing or maintenance of current balances, it is generally most economical to use punched card equipment. This is especially true when processing data that can be batched or grouped, as in payroll preparation.

3. If the operation is highly repetitive or requires considerable calculating within each repetitive cycle, it will probably be most practical to use a computer.

These principles make it apparent that not all applications belong on a computer; some do not even justify using punched card equipment. For example, the criterion of repetition which is necessary for selection of a computer or punched card equipment could not be met by an organization that processes ten invoices a day. This is not sufficient repetition to justify a method other than manual or mechanical. However, the processing of 100 invoices a day could justify the use of punched card equipment, and if there were numerous calculations to be performed on each invoice, this might justify a computer. Furthermore, if current stock inventory balances were a requirement, then a computer with large random access storage might be justified. It should also be pointed out that if a type of equipment is installed with a capacity in excess of the basic requirements, the available time may be used for additional applications that are desirable but that would not otherwise have been considered.

Another consideration in the selection of equipment is the decision of whether to rent or purchase the equipment proposed. Occasionally the equipment will be rented for several years and then when it and the system have proved satisfactory it may be purchased. Some of the rent versus purchase factors are:

1. Rented equipment can readily be replaced by newer equipment as it is developed.

2. Equipment rental rates generally include maintenance provisions.

3. Purchase contracts usually do not provide for maintenance beyond a short warranty period.

4. The purchase cost of equipment can usually be recovered in from five to

seven years, provided the equipment has not been made obsolete by technological advancements.

5. Cash or credit conditions of the company may be a major factor.

6. Income tax and property tax considerations can also be an important factor.

These considerations make it apparent that the decision of whether to rent or purchase equipment is most frequently made at the executive or corporate levels of management.

Selecting Codes

One of the most important considerations in designing a new system is the selection of coding methods. The use of a wrong or inadequate code can contribute to the ineffectiveness of a system.

Events or transactions must be classified in many ways so that the data may be used for as many management purposes as required. Therefore, in constructing codes full consideration must be given to the purpose such codes will serve. The selection of the proper code for a specific application not only assists in identifying data, but also facilitates the machine processing that is required before and during the preparation of a desired report.

To be effective a code should include the following characteristics:

1. Flexibility—It should be possible to make additional entries of coded data in proper sequence.

2. Scope—It should be possible to expand the code to include additional categories.

3. Operation—The code should be adequate to cover all of the necessary segregations within the established categories.

4. Convenience—The code should be easy to apply.

5. Construction—The code should meet all applications requirements with the least possible number of digits.

6. Identification—If possible, the code should provide for visual identification.

Designing Forms

Another important consideration in the design of a new system is forms design. Many factors affect the design of both input and output forms. When considering a new form the first questions should always be:

1. Is this form really necessary?

2. What form(s), if any, will it replace?

3. Can existing forms be revised to include the required information?

4. How was this information previously supplied?

After gathering satisfactory answers to these questions the analyst can proceed with the design of the new form.

The most important principle of form design is to plan the form with the user(s) in mind. Other considerations are:

1. How many copies are to be prepared?

2. Will the form be permanent?

3. Is it for internal or external use?

4. What quality of paper and size of form should be used?

5. Is the form simple and easy to understand?

6. Is the make-up of the form straightforward and in accordance with accepted accounting practice?

The following principles contribute to good form design:

1. Bold type should be used to emphasize important information.
2. In columns for money, sufficient space for the largest amount must be provided.
3. If writing is near the binding edge, it should be visible.
4. Filing information should be near the top of the form.
5. Every form should have a title.
6. Headings should be as small as possible, leaving sufficient space for written data.
7. A good printing style should be selected to make the form attractive in appearance.
8. The form should include only essential information.
9. The form should be designed so that a minimum of recording and recopying is required.
10. If the form precedes another form, or is dependent on another form, the same general sequence and arrangement should be followed so that recopying and recording can easily be accomplished.

After the form is designed, it should be analyzed to determine whether it is sufficiently clear and all necessary instructions are printed on the form. Final analysis should take into consideration all principles of good form design.

If the form is designed for completion by other than manual means, one of the ways of assuring that the printed information will be aligned within the form is to lay out the data to be printed on a spacing chart. Spacing charts are usually furnished by the forms manufacturer or the manufacturer of the printing device, e.g., typewriter, accounting machine, or computer printer.

NEW SYSTEM PROPOSAL

After all alternatives have been considered, the analyst must then put the ideal segments together to form a sensible systems approach which will accomplish the objectives of the organization. One reason for examining all of the alternatives is to ensure that the new system will not be restricted by the limitations of the past.

When a general plan of the new system has been prepared, a final review of the system should be made to determine its feasibility. The review should include consideration of the following questions:

1. Will the plan work in actual practice?
2. Can the company afford the approach?
3. Will management go along with the changes required?
4. Will the supervisors and workers recognize it as a better way of doing the work?
5. Does it conform to all legal requirements?
6. Will the new system be simple and easy to understand?
7. Will it do the job completely?

After finding and testing the best concept for the new system, and prior to the final drafts of procedures, forms, formats, resource requirements, and so on, a report should be prepared. This report should describe the purpose of the particular system being studied and its relation to other systems in the application area. The new system should be outlined briefly with estimated volumes of work and proposed schedules. Resources that will be required by the system must be described and estimates of the cost of implementation must be made. This report, sometimes called an intent agreement, management abstract, or system proposal should be agreed to by all responsible parties concerned. Often these people are noncommital during the survey, then when asked to endorse the final report they become wary and have a few final thoughts that could cause a change in the approach. It is much better to find out about necessary changes before many hours have been spent documenting the system.

NEW SYSTEM PLAN

The techniques for describing the new system in detail vary in degree and complexity. No other facet of data processing has as little uniformity or lack of standards. There is, however, a certain sequence to the methods for documenting a system that will prove most practical. They are as follows:

1. Construct a flow chart of the system. Prepare a narrative statement for each complex step shown in the flow chart.

2. Prepare formats of, and specifications for, the forms required. Input and output forms can best be laid out on a form design space chart.

3. Prepare charts showing organizational changes. Support the charts with detailed duties statements for each new type of position.

4. Describe other resources such as facilities and equipment required by the new system. Lay out floor plans or forms flow charts if necessary.

At this point some concerns have the systems analyst turn the job over to a programmer or data processing analyst for completion. In other concerns the systems analyst will complete the documentation and installation plans. There are advantages to either way. However, the latter is probably the better approach as the analyst can better realize a sense of accomplishment. Also, he can remain knowledgeable about all facets of data processing and thereby be more versatile and valuable to the company.

The final steps for completing the new system are:

1. Write procedure manuals. These procedures can be in narrative form, flow chart form, or a combination of the two. Better yet, individual job instruction sheets may be used. The techniques for preparing manuals are a matter of management choice.

2. Prepare punched card machine wiring-panel planning charts or computer program flow charts.

3. Wire and test panels, or write and test computer programs. A good aid in developing a test for a panel or program is to make notes of requirements and conditions to be met as the system is being designed and documented.

4. Produce setup instructions for each panel or program. Identify every halt condition and explain how to proceed.

NEW SYSTEM IN OPERATION

The first part of the plan for installing the new system is to determine whether the system may be installed in part or all at once, and then set the installation schedule. The next steps are to order equipment and schedule the preparation of the facilities; plan for the training or recruiting of personnel; and order forms, cards, and supplies. The best plan will bring together resources, personnel, and supplies at approximately the same time, just before the planned system's starting date.

At the start of any new system the analyst should be available to the operating personnel, as there will be certain minor adjustments to be made in the procedures. Some planned work loads may be too heavy or too light, certain operations may require reappraisal, and schedules may require adjustment. The analyst should remain in close contact with the new system until all problems appear to be resolved.

In looking back, it can be seen that the systems analyst is engrossed in the new system from its design through its successful installation. No detail may be ignored without creating a problem at some stage of the installation process. The ease with which a new system is installed is an indication of the analyst's ability.

The job of the systems analyst does not end with the installation of the new system, however. His work is not complete until there has been a follow-up to verify the adequacy of the system. During the follow-up the analyst must:

1. Determine that all parts of the new system are operating efficiently.

2. Make any modifications or refinements in the system or in written procedures that may be required by operating experience.

3. Determine that the objectives of the system are being met.

If final evaluation reveals that anticipated savings are being realized, that output of the system is on schedule, and that the quantity and quality of information are fulfilling management requirements, then it can be assumed that the system was well planned and implemented.

Review Questions

1. What were the five stages of advancement in the development of business systems?
2. Define the total systems concept.
3. What is the primary responsibility of the systems analyst?
4. What are the general objectives of systems study and design?
5. What are the three major phases of systems study and design?
6. List the systems study aids that may be used to assist in analyzing and interpreting existing conditions and new design proposals.
7. How is the system flow chart helpful in the study of an existing system?
8. Describe the three basic symbols used in a system flow chart.
9. Explain the difference between a system flow chart and a program flow chart.
10. What is the primary purpose of a decision table?
11. Briefly describe the five steps in analyzing the present system.
12. What is the first step in designing a new system?
13. Equipment selection is generally based on what three principles?
14. What are the characteristics of a good code?
15. What is the most important principle of form design?
16. Explain the four methods that may be used in documenting a new system plan.
17. What are the final steps in completing a new system?

Absolute address. An address assigned by the machine designer to a particular storage location. A pattern of characters that identifies a unique storage location without additional modification.

Access time. The time interval between the instant at which data is called for from a storage device and the instant delivery is completed, that is, the read time. Also the time interval between the instant at which data is requested to be stored and the instant at which storage is completed, that is, the write time.

Accumulator. A storage device in the arithmetic unit in which the results of arithmetic and logical operations are formed.

Adder. A device whose output represents the sum of the quantities represented by its inputs.

Address. A label, name, or number identifying a register, a storage location, or a device from which information is received or to which it is transmitted. Any part of an instruction that specifies the location of an operand for the instruction.

Address modification. The process of changing the address part of a machine instruction by means of coded instructions.

Address register. A register in which an address is stored.

ADP. Automatic data processing. A system that uses a minimum of manual operations in processing data.

ALGOL. An abbreviation for algorithmic oriented language. An international procedure oriented language.

Alphanumerical code. A system in which characters may be either letters of the alphabet, numerals, or special symbols.

Analog computer. A calculating device that operates on numbers represented by measurable physical quantities such as the rotation of a shaft, the amount of voltage, temperature, etc.

Arithmetic unit. The part of the computer processing section that does the adding, subtracting, multiplying, dividing, and comparing.

Array. A series of items arranged in a meaningful manner.

Assembly program. A computer program that takes sequential instructions written by the programmer in a nonmachine language and changes them to codes or language used by the machine on which the program is to be run.

Automatic programming. The process of using a computer to perform some stages of the work involved in preparing a program.

Automation. The implementation of processes by automatic means. The investigation, design, development, and application of methods of making processes or machines self-moving or self-controlling.

Auxiliary operation. An operation performed by equipment not under continuous control of the central processing unit.

Auxiliary storage. A storage that supplements another storage.

Bandwidth. The difference, expressed in the number of cycles per second, between the two limiting frequencies of a band.

Batch processing. A method by which a number of similar transactions or problems are grouped for processing in sequence during a single continuous machine run.

Baudot code. A system of coding for transmission of data in which five bits represent one character.

Binary coded decimal (BCD). A decimal notation in which the individual decimal digits are represented by a pattern of ones and zeros; e.g., in the 8-4-2-1 binary coded decimal notation, the number twelve is represented as 0001 0010 for 1 and 2, respectively, whereas in pure binary notation it is represented as 1100.

Binary number system. A number system using the base two, as opposed to the decimal number system which uses the base ten.

Bit. The smallest unit of information in the binary number system. An abbreviation of "binary digit." Normally, a bit refers to one ("on"), while a no bit means zero ("off").

Block. A group of machine words considered or transported as a unit. In flow charts, each block represents a logical unit of programming.

Block diagram. A diagram of a system, instrument, computer, or program in which selected portions are represented by annotated boxes and interconnecting lines.

Block sort. A sort of one or more of the most significant characters of a key to serve as a means of making groups of workable size from a large volume of records to be sorted.

Boolean algebra. A process of reasoning or a deductive system of theorems using a symbolic logic, and dealing with classes, propositions, or on-off circuit elements. It employs symbols to represent operators, such as AND, OR, NOT, EXCEPT, IF, THEN, etc., to permit mathematical calculation.

Bootstrap. A technique for loading the first few instructions of a routine into storage, then using these instructions to bring the rest of the routine into the computer from an input device. This usually involves either the entering of a few instructions manually or the use of a special key on the console.

Branching. A computer programming term indicating that a sequence of steps has been completed or is to be broken and that the sequence is to be repeated or changed to a new one.

Broadband. Data transmission facilities capable of handling frequencies greater than those required for high-grade voice communications, i.e., greater than 300 characters per second.

Brush. An electrical conductor for reading data from a punched card. Normally each brush has a corresponding hub on the control panel.

Buffer. A temporary or intermediate storage unit used to hold data being transmitted between internal and external storage units or between input-output devices and internal storage.

Bus. A circuit used to transmit signals or power.

Byte. A sequence of adjacent binary digits operated upon as a unit.

Card code. The combination of punches used to represent alphabetic and numerical data on a punched card.

Card column. One of the vertical areas on a punched card in which a digit, letter, or symbol may be recorded.

Card feed. A mechanism that moves cards serially into a machine.

Card gauge. A metal plate, precisely inscribed with all punches of an 80-column card, used to check the accuracy of punching registration.

Card hopper. A device that holds cards and makes them available to a card feed mechanism. Synonymous with input magazine.

Card jam. A pile-up of cards in a machine.

Card punch. A device or machine that punches holes in cards in specific locations to store data that can be conveyed to other machines or devices by reading or sensing the holes.

Card stacker. An output device that accumulates punched cards in a deck.

Card system. A system that utilizes only punched cards as the medium for bearing data.

Cathode ray tube. An electronic vacuum tube containing a screen on which output data may be displayed in graphic form or by character representation.

Central processing unit (CPU). The unit of a computing system that contains the arithmetic, logical, and control circuits necessary for the interpretation and execution of instructions.

Chad. A portion of tape or card that is removed when a code is punched.

Chadded. The method of punching tape in which chad results.

Chadless. A type of punching of tape in which each chad is left fastened by about a quarter of the circumference of the hole at the leading edge.

Channel. A path over which information is transmitted, generally from some input-output device to storage. With reference to magnetic or punched tape, a channel is one of the parallel tracks in which data is recorded.

Character. A decimal digit, alphabetic letter, or a special symbol.

Character recognition. The identification of characters by automatic means.

Check digit. One or more redundant digits in a character or word which depend on the remaining digits in such a fashion that if a change of digits occurs in data transfer operations, the malfunction of equipment can be detected.

Checkpoint. A reference point to which error-free operation of the program has been verified and to which the program may return for restart in the event of subsequent failure.

Circuit. A system of conductors and related electrical elements through which electrical current flows. A communications link between two or more points.

Clear. To remove all information from a storage device of a machine and restore it to a prescribed state, usually that denoting zero or blank.

COBOL. Common business oriented language. A coding language by which business data processing procedures may be precisely described in a standard form.

Code. A set of rules that is used to convert data from one representation to another.

Collate. To take two or more sets of related information already arranged according to the same sequence and to merge them in sequence into a single set.

Collator. A device to collate or merge sets of cards or other documents into a sequence.

Column binary. Pertaining to the binary representation of data on punched cards in which adjacent positions in a column correspond to adjacent bits of data, e.g., each column in a 12-row card may be used to represent 12 consecutive bits of a 36-bit word.

Command. A group of signals or pulses initiating one step in the execution of a computer program. Also called instruction.

Common language. A coded structure that is compatible with two or more data processing machines or families of machines, thus allowing them to communicate directly to one another.

Compare. To examine the representation of a quantity for the purpose of discovering its relationship to zero, or of two quantities for the purpose of discovering relative magnitude or identity.

Compiler. A programming system that produces a program from a series of source statements. It is capable of replacing single entries with a series of instructions or a subroutine. The compiler produces an expanded and translated version of the original or source program.

Computer word. A sequence of bits or characters treated as a unit and capable of being stored in one computer location.

Console. The component of a data processing system that provides facilities for manual control and observation of the system's operation.

Constant. Data with a fixed value or meaning that is available for use throughout a program.

Continuous form. Paper or card forms attached for continuous feeding in an accounting machine or computer output device carriage.

Control panel. The demountable panel containing the external wiring to govern machine operations.

Control unit. The part of a computer system that effects the retrieval of instructions in proper sequence, the interpretation of each instruction, and the application of the proper signals to the arithmetic unit and other parts of the system in accordance with this interpretation.

Converter. A unit that changes the representation of data from one form to another so as to make it available or acceptable to another machine, e.g., from punched cards to magnetic tape.

Corner cut. A diagonal cut at the corner of a card to facilitate identification by sight or by a special rail brush.

Counter. A device, register, or storage location for storing integers, permitting these integers to be increased or decreased. A device used to represent the number of occurrences of an event.

CPU. An abbreviation of central processing unit.

Cybernetics. The comparative study of the control and communication of information-handling machines and the nervous system of man in order to understand and improve communication.

Cycle. An interval during which one set of events or phenomena is completed. A set of operations that is repeated regularly in the same sequence.

Data. A general term used to denote any facts, numbers, letters, and symbols, or facts that refer to or describe an object, idea, condition, situation, or other factors.

Data communications. The transmission of data between two or more points.

Data processing. Any operation or combination of operations on data to achieve a desired result.

Data reduction. The transformation of raw data into more useful form.

Debug. To detect, locate, and remove all malfunctions from a computer or all mistakes from a routine.

Decision table. A table that combines contingencies to be considered in the description of a problem, along with the actions to be taken. Decision tables are sometimes used instead of flow charts to describe and document problems.

Deck. A collection of punched cards, commonly a complete set of cards which have been punched for a specific purpose.

Decode. To apply a code so as to reverse some previous encoding.

Decoder. A device that decodes. A matrix of switching elements that selects one or more output channels according to the combination of input signals present.

Detail printing. Printing information from each punched card passing through the machine.

Diagnostic check. A specific routine designed to locate a malfunction in the computer or a mistake in coding.

Digital computer. A calculating device utilizing numbers to express all the variables and quantities of a problem.

Direct access. An addressing scheme or random-access storage medium which permits direct addressing of data locations.

Direct address. An address that specifies the location of an operand.

Display station. A device which provides a visual representation of data on the face of a cathode ray tube.

Dump. A copying or print out of all or part of the contents of a particular storage device. Synonymous with memory dump.

Duplicating. The automatic punching of information from a card or tape into succeeding cards or tape.

EAM. Electrical accounting machine. Generally refers to punched card equipment.

EBCDIC. An abbreviation of Extended Binary Coded Decimal Interchange Code.

Edge-notched card. A card in which holes have been punched around the edges. Notches made in the holes are used in coding information for a simple mechanical-search technique.

Edge-punched card. A card of fixed size into which information may be recorded or stored by punching holes along one edge in a pattern similar to that used for punched tape.

Edit. To rearrange information. Editing may involve the deletion of unwanted data, the selection of pertinent data, and the insertion of symbols.

EDP. Electronic data processing.

Electronic data processing system. The general term used to define a system for data processing by means of machines utilizing electronic circuitry at electronic speed, as opposed to electromechanical equipment.

Emitting. Originating digits, letters, and special characters electrically within the machine rather than from the punched card.

Erase. To replace all the binary digits in a storage device by binary zeros. To remove data from a magnetic surface or other memory unit.

External storage. The storage of data on a device such as magnetic tape which is not an integral part of a computer, but is in a form prescribed for use by a computer.

Feedback. The process of returning portions of the output of a machine, process, or system for use as input in a further operation.

Ferromagnetics. In computer technology, the science that deals with the storage of information and the logical control of pulse sequences through the utilization of the magnetic polarization properties of materials.

Field. A group of related characters treated as a unit in computer operations. A set of one or more columns of a punched card consistently used to record similar information.

File. A collection of related records treated as a unit.

Fixed point. An arithmetic system in which all numerical quantities are expressed in a specified number of places with the radix point implicitly located at some predetermined position.

Fixed word length. Pertaining to a storage device in which the capacity for digits or characters in each unit of data is a fixed length as opposed to a variable length.

Flip-flop. A circuit or device containing active elements capable of assuming either one of two stable states at a given time.

Floating point. A system of representing numerical quantities with a variable number of places in which the location of the point does not remain fixed.

Flow chart. A graphical representation of the definition, analysis, or solution of a problem using symbols to represent operations, data flow, and equipment.

Format. The arrangement of data on a form or in storage.

FORTRAN. Formula translator. A programming language designed for problems which can be expressed in algebraic notation, allowing for exponentiation and up to three subscripts. The FORTRAN compiler is a routine for a given machine which accepts a program written in FORTRAN source language and produces a machine language object program.

Gangpunching. The automatic punching of data read from a master card into the following detail cards.

General purpose computer. A computer that may be used to solve a wide variety of problems.

Generator. A program for a computer that generates the coding of a problem.

Group indication. Printed information identifying a group of data.

Group printing. Printing group totals and group indication as cards pass through an accounting machine.

Hardware. A colloquialism applied to the mechanical, electrical, and electronic features of a data processing system.

Hash total. A sum of numbers in a specified field of a record or batch of records used for checking or control purposes. The total may be insignificant except for audit purposes, as in the case of part numbers or customer numbers.

Head. A device that reads, records, or erases data on a storage medium, e.g., an electromagnet used to read, write, or erase data on a magnetic drum or tape, or the set of perforating, reading, or marking devices used to punch, read, or print on paper tape.

Header card. A prepunched record of the basic information pertaining to a specific individual or firm which is used to automatically create the upper portion of a document.

Heuristic. Exploratory method of problem solving in which solutions are discovered by evaluation of the progress made toward the final result.

Hexadecimal numbering system. A numbering system using the equivalent of the decimal number sixteen as a base.

High-order position. The leftmost position of a number or word.

Hollerith code. A standard 12-channel punched card code in which each decimal digit, letter, or special character is represented by one or more rectangular holes punched in a vertical column.

Housekeeping routine. That part of a program usually performed only at the beginning of machine operations which establishes the initial conditions for instruction addresses, accumulator setting, switch settings, etc.

Hybrid computer. A computer system that combines analog and digital capabilities.

IDP. Integrated data processing.

Index word. A storage position or register, the contents of which may be used to modify automatically the effective address of any given instruction.

Indexing. A method of address modification which is performed automatically by the data processing system.

Indirect address. An address that specifies a storage location containing either a direct address or another indirect address.

Information retrieval. The methods and procedures for recovering specific information from stored data.

Initialize. To set program variables, such as addresses, counters, program switches, etc., to zero or other starting values at the beginning of, or at prescribed points in, a computer routine.

In-line processing. The processing of data in random order without preliminary editing or sorting.

Input. Information transferred into the internal storage of a data processing system, including data to be processed or information to help control the process.

Instruction. A set of characters which, when interpreted by the control unit, causes a data processing system to perform one of its operations.

Instruction register. The register that stores the current instruction governing a computer operation.

Integrated data processing. A system that treats all data processing requirements as a whole to reduce or eliminate duplicate recording or processing while accomplishing a sequence of data processing steps or a number of related data processing sequences.

Interface. A common boundary between two systems or devices.

Internal storage. Storage facilities integrated as a physical part of the computer and directly controlled by the computer.

Interpret. To translate into or restate in human language. To print at the top of a punched card the information punched in it, using a machine called an interpreter.

Interrupt. A break in the normal flow of a system or routine. Usually the normal operation can be resumed from that point at a later time. An interrupt is usually caused by a signal from an external source.

Joggle. To align a deck of cards by jostling them against a plane surface.

Key punch. A keyboard-operated device that punches holes in a card to represent data.

Label. One or more characters used to identify or describe an item of data, record, message, or file. Occasionally it may be the same as the address in storage.

Lacing. Extra multiple punching in a card column to signify the end of a specific card run. The term is derived from the lacework appearance of the card.

Language translator. A general term for any assembler, compiler, or other routine that accepts statements in one language and produces equivalent machine language instructions.

Library. A collection of standard proven computer routines, usually kept on a library tape or random access file, by which problems or portions of problems may be solved.

Line printing. The printing of an entire line of characters as a unit.

Literal. A symbol that names and defines itself.

Load. To put data into a register or into internal storage. To put a magnetic tape onto a tape drive, or to put cards into a card reader.

Load-and-go. An operating technique in which there are no stops between the loading and execution phases of a program, and which may include assembling or compiling.

Logarithm. The exponent of a number, indicating how many times the number must be multiplied by itself to produce another given number.

Logical operations. Nonarithmetical operations such as selecting, sorting, matching, comparing, etc.

Logical record. A record whose scope, direction, or length is governed by the specific nature of the information or data that it contains rather than by some feature or limitation of the storage device that holds it. Such records differ in size from the physical records in which they are contained.

Loop. The repetition of a group of instructions in a routine until certain conditions are reached.

Low-order position. The rightmost position of a number or word.

Machine language. The instructions written in a form that is intelligible to the internal circuitry of the computer; not ordinarily comprehensible to persons without special training. Sometimes called "actual" or "absolute."

Machine-sensible. Term denoting information in a form that can be read by one or more machines.

Macro instruction. A symbolic instruction in a source language that produces a number of machine language instructions. It is made available for use by the programmer through an automatic programming system.

Magnetic card. A card with a magnetic surface on which data can be stored by selective magnetization of portions of the flat surface.

Magnetic core. A small doughnut-shaped piece of ferromagnetic material, about the size of a pin head, capable of storing one binary digit represented by the polarity of its magnetic field. Thousands of these cores strung on wire grids form an internal memory device. Cores can be individually charged to hold data and sensed to issue data.

Magnetic disk. A storage device by which information is recorded on the magnetizable surface of a rotating disk. A magnetic disk storage system is an array of such devices, with associated reading and writing heads mounted on movable arms.

Magnetic drum. A rotating cylinder, the surface of which is coated with a material on which information may be recorded as small magnetic spots representing binary information.

Magnetic ink. An ink that contains particles of a magnetic substance whose presence can be detected by magnetic sensors.

Magnetic ink character reader. A device capable of interpreting data typed, written, or printed in magnetic ink.

Magnetic tape. A tape or ribbon of material impregnated or coated with magnetic material on which information may be placed in the form of magnetically polarized spots.

Magnetic thin-film. A layer of magnetic material, usually less than one micron thick, often used for logic or storage elements.

Management information system. Usually regarded as an on-line computer and communication system designed to furnish management personnel with data for decision making. Generally, the data provided is in response to on-line interrogation.

Mark sensing. A technique for reading special electrographic pencil marks on a card and automatically punching the data represented by the marks into the card.

Mass storage. An auxiliary storage medium whereby data is magnetically recorded in tracks or channels on the surface of cards or strips stored in demountable cells or cartridges.

Master card. The first card of a group containing fixed or indicative information for that group.

Master file. A file of records containing a cumulative history or the results of accumulation; updated in each file-processing cycle, and carried forward to the next cycle.

Matching. Checking two files to see that there is a corresponding card or group of cards in each file.

Mathematical model. A mathematical representation of the behavior of a process, device, or concept.

Matrix. In mathematics, a two-dimensional rectangular array of quantities. Matrices are manipulated in accordance with the rules of matrix algebra. In computers, a logic network in the form of an array of input leads and output leads with logic elements connected at some of their intersections.

Memory. The part of a computer that stores the program, holds intermediate results and various constant data. Same as storage.

Memory dump. To copy the contents of all or part of a storage, usually from an internal storage into an external storage.

Merge. To combine items from two or more similarly sequenced files into one sequenced file without changing the order of the items.

Message switching. The technique of receiving complete messages and forwarding the messages at a switching center.

MICR. Magnetic ink character recognition. Machine recognition of characters printed with magnetic ink.

Microsecond. One-millionth of a second.

Microwave. Very short electromagnetic waves used in high-capacity communication networks for transmitting voice or data messages at ultra-high speeds.

Millisecond. One-thousandth of a second.

Mnemonic. Assisting, or intended to assist, memory.

Modem. A contraction of MOdulator DEModulator. Its function is to interface with data processing devices and convert data to a form compatible for sending and receiving on transmission facilities.

Modifier. A quantity used to alter the address of an operand.

Modify. To alter in an instruction the address of the operand; to alter a subroutine according to a defined parameter.

Multiprocessing. A computer configuration consisting of multiple arithmetic and logical units for simultaneous use.

Multiprogramming. A technique whereby more than one program may reside in primary storage at the same time and be executed concurrently by means of an interweaving process.

Nanosecond. One-billionth of a second.

Needle checking. Verifying that all cards in a deck contain the same punch in a given column. The prod or needle, pushed through the punched hole, stops at a card containing a different punch.

Nondestructive read. A read process that does not erase the data in the source.

Normalize. In programming, to adjust the exponent and fraction of a floating-point quantity so that the fraction lies in the prescribed normal standard range.

Numerical analysis. The study of methods of obtaining useful quantitative solutions to problems that have been stated mathematically, and the study of the errors and bounds on errors in obtaining such solutions.

Numerical control. Pertaining to the automatic control of processes by the proper interpretation of numerical data.

Object program. A program in machine language; generally, one that has been converted from a program written in symbolic language.

OCR. Optical character recognition. The machine recognition of printed characters.

Octal. Pertaining to the number base of eight. In octal notation, octal 214 is 2 times 64, plus 1 times 8, plus 4 times 1, and equals decimal 140.

Off-line. Equipment or devices not under the direct control of the central processing unit.

Off-line storage. A storage device not under control of the central processing unit.

Off-punching. Punching not properly positioned in a card.

On-line. Peripheral equipment or devices in direct communication with the central processing unit, and from which information reflecting current activity is introduced into the data processing system as soon as it occurs.

On-line storage. A storage device under direct control of the central processing unit.

Operand. That which is operated on. An operand is usually identified by an address part of an instruction.

Operating system. An organized collection of techniques and procedures for operating a computer.

Operation. A defined action; one step in a procedure. The action specified by a single computer instruction. That which occurs when something is created, changed, or added to, such as writing, calculating, posting, or computing.

Operation code. The part of the command code of an instruction which designates the operation to be performed.

Operations research. The use of analytic methods adopted from mathematics for solving operational problems. The objective is to provide management with a more logical basis for making sound predictions and decisions.

Optical scanner. A device that optically scans printed or written data and generates its digital representations.

Output. Information transferred from the internal storage of a data processing system to any device external to the system. Also, the results of operations performed on the data in data processing.

Overflow. In an arithmetic operation, the generation of a quantity beyond the capacity of the register or location which is to receive the result.

Over punches. To add punches, usually control punches, to a card column that already contains one or more holes.

Parallel. To handle simultaneously in separate facilities. To operate on two or more parts of a word or item simultaneously.

Parameter. A quantity to which arbitrary values may be assigned but which remain fixed for each program. In a program generator, parameters are used to specify certain machine hardware and data limits to be observed in the program being generated.

Parity bit. A binary digit appended to an array of

bits as required to make the sum of all the bits always odd or always even.

Parity check. A check that tests whether the number of ones (or zeros) in an array of binary digits meets the established odd or even standard.

Patch. A section of coding inserted in a program in order to rectify an error in the original coding or to change the sequence of operation.

Peripheral equipment. Units that work in conjunction with the computer but are not part of the computer itself, e.g., tape reader, card reader, magnetic tape feed, high-speed printer, typewriter, etc.

Plugboard. A removable panel containing an array of terminals that can be interconnected by short electrical leads in prescribed patterns to control various machine operations. Synonymous with control panel.

Powers code. A system of representing data by round holes punched in a 90-column card, invented by James Powers and now used with equipment produced by the UNIVAC Division of Sperry Rand Corporation.

Procedure. A precise step-by-step method for effecting a solution to a problem.

Process control. A system in which computers, usually analog computers, are used for automatic regulation of operations or processes.

Processor. A machine-language program that accepts a source program written in a symbolic form and translates it into an object program acceptable to the machine for which the source program was written.

Program. The complete plan for the solution of a problem; more specifically, the complete sequence of machine instructions and routines necessary to solve a problem.

Program card. A punched card, punched with specific coding, placed around a program drum to control automatic operations in a card punch and verifier.

Programmer. A person who prepares the planned sequence of events the computer must follow to solve a problem.

Punched card. A heavy stiff paper of uniform size and shape suitable for being punched with a pattern of holes to represent data and for being handled mechanically.

Punched tape. A tape, usually paper, on which a pattern of holes or cuts is used to represent data.

Radix. The fundamental number in a number system, e.g., 10 in the decimal system, 8 in the octal system, and 2 in the binary system. Synonymous with base.

Random access storage. A storage device, such as magnetic core, magnetic disk, and magnetic drum, in which each record has a specific, predetermined address which may be reached directly. Access time in this type of storage is effectively independent of the location of the data.

Raw data. Data which has not been processed. Such data may or may not be in a form acceptable by machines.

Read in. To sense information contained in some source and to transfer this information by means of an input device to internal storage.

Read out. To transfer data from internal storage to an external storage device, or to display processed data by means of a printer, automatic typewriter, etc.

Real time. The processing of data derived from a particular operation in a sufficiently rapid manner that the results of the processing are available in time to influence the continuing operation.

Record. A collection of related items of data treated as a unit.

Register. A device capable of temporarily storing a specified amount of data, usually one word, while or until it is used in an operation.

Registration. The accuracy of the positioning of punched holes in a card.

Remote processing. A method of using a computer system from remote locations. This direct access connection can be accomplished using conventional voice grade telephone lines to exhange information between the computer and terminals.

Report generator. A programming system for producing a complete report given only a description of the desired content and format of the output reports, and certain information about the input file and hardware available.

Reproducing (Punched Card). Copying punched information from one deck of cards into another.

Routine. A set of coded instructions arranged in a logical sequence and used to direct a computer to perform a desired operation or series of operations.

Row binary. A method of representing binary numbers on a card where successive bits are represented by the presence or absence of punches in a successive position in a row as opposed to a series of columns. Row binary is especially convenient in 40-bit word, or less, computers wherein the card frequently is used to store 12 binary words on each half of an 80-column card.

Run. A single, continuous performance of a computer routine.

Selecting. Removing cards from a file, or processing cards according to predetermined conditions.

Sequence checking. Checking items in a file to assure that they are all in ascending (or descending) order.

Sequential processing. The procedure of processing data records in the same order that they occur.

Serial. The handling of data in a sequential fashion, such as to transfer or store data in a digit-by-digit time sequence, or to process a sequence of instructions one at a time.

Serial operation. The flow of information through a computer in time sequence, using one digit, word, line, or channel at a time, as opposed to parallel operation.

Servomechanism. A device to monitor an operation as it proceeds, and make necessary adjustments to keep the operation under control.

Shift. To move the characters of a unit of data to the right or left.

Short card. A punched card of less than 80 columns.

Sight checking. Examining a group of cards for identical punching by viewing a light source through the punched holes.

Software. The programs and routines used to extend the capabilities of computers, such as compilers, assemblers, routines, and subroutines. Also, all documents associated with a computer, e.g., manuals, circuit diagrams. Cf. hardware.

Solid state. Refers to electronic components that convey or control electron flow within solid materials such as transistors, crystal diodes, and ferrite cores.

Sort. To arrange items of information according to rules dependent on a key or field contained in the items, e.g., the arranging of items according to date, code number, etc.

Source document. The original paper on which are recorded the details of a transaction.

Source program. A program usually written in some form of symbolic language and intended for translation into a machine-language program.

Special character. A character that is neither a numeral nor a letter, for example, $ / & #.

Special purpose computer. A computer designed principally to solve a restricted class of problems.

Storage. A device into which data can be entered, in which it can be held, and from which it can be retrieved at a later time.

Stored program computer. A computer that has the ability to store, to refer to, and to modify instructions to direct its step-by-step operations.

String. A set of records in ascending or descending sequence according to a key contained in the records.

Subroutine. A subset of a routine, usually a short sequence of instructions designed to solve a specified part of a problem.

Summary punch. A card-handling machine which may be connected to another machine such as an accounting machine and which will punch out on a card the information produced, calculated, or summarized by the other machine.

Supervisor. The general reference to the programs of a system that are responsible for scheduling, allocating, and controlling the system resources and application programs.

Switch. A point in a programming routine at which two courses of action are possible, the correct one being determined by conditions specified by the programmer; a branch point.

Symbolic address. An address expressed in symbols that are convenient to the programmer.

Symbolic program. A program written in a language that makes use of mnemonic codes and in which names, characteristics of instructions, or other symbols convenient to the programmer are used instead of the numeric codes of the machine.

Systems analysis. The study of an activity, procedure, method, technique, or a business to determine what must be accomplished and how the necessary operations may best be accomplished.

Table look up. To obtain a function value corresponding to an argument, stated or implied, from a table of function values stored in the computer. Also, the operation of obtaining a value from a table.

Tabulating system. Another term sometimes used to describe a punched card data processing system.

Telecommunication. Any transmission or reception of signals, writing, sounds, or intelligence of any nature by wire, radio, visual, or any other electromagnetic means.

Test deck. A set of cards representative of all operations performed in a particular application. Used to test control panel wiring and machine operations.

Test routine. A procedure that shows whether or not a computer is functioning properly.

Time sharing. A computing system that permits many users to operate or use the system simultaneously or apparently simultaneously in such a way that each is unaware of the fact that the system is being used by others.

Total systems concept. The complete integration of all major operating systems within a business organization into one functional organized system operating under the discipline of a data processing facility.

Transistor. A tiny solid electronic device that performs the same function as a vacuum tube. In a vacuum tube, current flows through the gas and space within the tube. In a transistor, the current travels through solid materials only, which explains the familiar term "solid state."

Unit record. A record in which all data concerning each item in a transaction is punched into one card.

Update. To put into a master file changes required by current information or transactions.

Utility program. Standard programs prepared and generally used to assist in the operation of a data processing system.

Verify. To determine whether a transcription of data or other operation has been accomplished accurately. To check the results of keypunching.

Word. A set of characters which occupies one storage location and is treated by the computer circuits as a unit and transported as such.

X-punch. A punch in the second row, one row above the zero row, on a Hollerith punched card.

Y-punch. A punch in the top row, two rows above the zero row, on a Hollerith punched card.

Zero suppression. The elimination of nonsignificant zeros to the left of the integral part of a quantity before printing operations are initiated.

Zone punches. Punches in the Y, X, and O position on a Hollerith punched card used in combination with digit punches 1 to 9 to code alphabetic and special characters.

INDEX